THE **TALIBAN** AND THE **CRISIS** OF **AFGHANISTAN**

THE **TALIBAN** AND THE **CRISIS** OF **AFGHANISTAN**

Edited by Robert D. Crews and Amin Tarzi

Harvard University Press
Cambridge, Massachusetts • London, England

First Harvard University Press paperback edition, 2009.

Library of Congress Cataloging-in-Publication Data
The Taliban and the crisis of Afghanistan : / edited by
Robert D. Crews and Amin Tarzi.
p.   cm.
Includes bibliographical references and index.
ISBN 978-0-674-02690-2 (cloth : alk. paper)
ISBN 978-0-674-03224-8 (pbk.)
1. Taliban.   2. Afghanistan—History—1989–2001.   3. Afghanistan—
History—2001–   I. Crews, Robert D., 1970–   II. Tarzi, Amin.
DS371.3.T354 2008
958.104′6—dc22   2007031807

CONTENTS

Maps   vii

Note on Transliteration   ix

Introduction   1
Robert D. Crews and Amin Tarzi

1. Explaining the Taliban's Ability to Mobilize the Pashtuns   59
   Abdulkader Sinno

2. The Rise and Fall of the Taliban   90
   Neamatollah Nojumi

3. The Taliban, Women, and the Hegelian Private Sphere   118
   Juan R. I. Cole

4. Taliban and Talibanism in Historical Perspective   155
   M. Nazif Shahrani

5. Remembering the Taliban   182
   Lutz Rzehak

6. Fraternity, Power, and Time in Central Asia   212
   Robert L. Canfield

7. Moderate Taliban?   238
   Robert D. Crews

8. The Neo-Taliban   274
   Amin Tarzi

   Epilogue: Afghanistan and the Pax Americana   311
   Atiq Sarwari and Robert D. Crews

   Notes   359
   Contributors   419
   Acknowledgments   421
   Index   423

MAPS

1 The Provinces of Afghanistan   x

2 Taliban Expansion   xi

3 Physical Geography   14

4 The Major Ethnic Groups of Afghanistan   16

NOTE ON TRANSLITERATION

The editors have attempted to simplify transliteration of non-Latin terms and names for a general audience of nonspecialists. We have avoided diacritical marks, except in a few proper names, and adopted spellings commonly used in English—for example, "Abbas" instead of "ʿAbbas," "Masud" in place of Masʿud," and "mullah" rather than "mulla." Names in common usage have not been transliterated and are presented in a form familiar to readers of English, such as "Hamid Karzai." When terms of Arabic origin are used in reference to Afghanistan, the Persian/Dari transliteration has been adopted, such as "mujahedin," not "mujahidin" (and in cases where Iranian Persian and Dari differ in pronunciation, the Dari has been used). Given the wide variation in the spellings of Pakistani parties and organizations, the editors have followed Muhammad Amir Rana's *A to Z of Jehadi Organizations in Pakistan*.

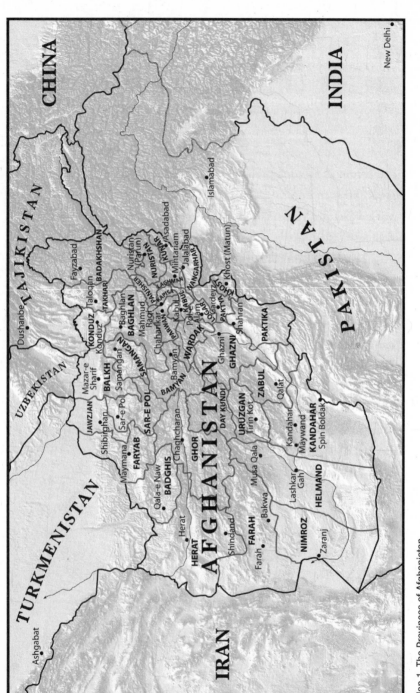

Map 1. The Provinces of Afghanistan

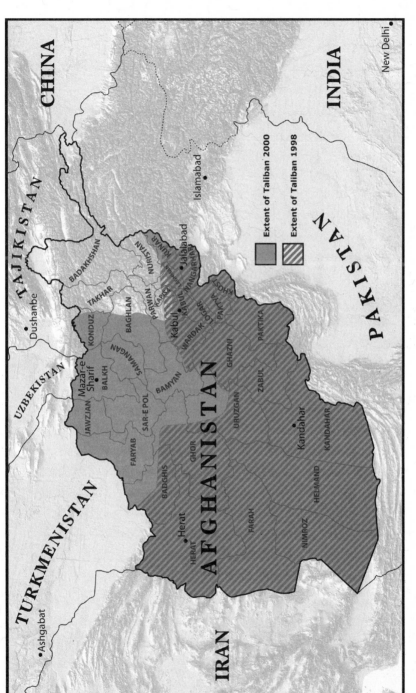

Map 2. Taliban Expansion

Introduction

Robert D. Crews and Amin Tarzi

On February 2, 2007, the residents of the southern Afghan town of Musa Qala awoke to see the white banner of the Taliban flying above the town center where the black, red, and green flag of the national government had been the day before. Several hundred armed Taliban fighters had seized this district center in the north of Helmand Province and expelled the local authorities without a fight. On April 1 they hanged three "spies," leaving their bodies in strategic locations, in the center and at the northern and southern entrances to the town, to dramatize the restoration of Taliban rule. A number of residents fled, fearing NATO air strikes; others remained in Musa Qala. As brilliant red poppy flowers bloomed across the fertile Helmand River Valley, the heart of global opium cultivation, many farmers in the district supported the change of regime. "The Taliban tell us 'as long as we are here, no one can destroy your poppy,'" a local harvester explained, adding, "The government cannot come here now, because there is another power here. It is the government of the Taliban."[1]

Accompanied by a campaign of suicide bombings, kidnappings,

1

and assassinations in 2006 and 2007, the fall of Musa Qala and other locales across southern, central, and eastern Afghanistan to Taliban forces—as well as increased Taliban activity in the neighboring provinces of Pakistan—signaled a turning point in a war nearly forgotten by most outsiders. On October 7, 2001, the United States had launched a campaign to destroy the Taliban in retaliation for the terrorist attacks of September 11. An extensive bombing operation supported local anti-Taliban militias, Central Intelligence Agency operatives, and U.S. Special Forces in driving the Taliban from the 90 percent of the country that they ruled. By November 12, Afghan militias allied with the United States had seized the capital, Kabul. A month later, the story of the Taliban came full circle when Taliban fighters abandoned their last stronghold, Kandahar, Afghanistan's second city and the birthplace of the movement.[2]

By the end of the year, the Taliban presence had faded from the country. Their fighters melted back into village communities and disappeared into rugged mountain enclaves. Many found refuge in Pakistan. The foreign fighters and radicals around Osama bin Laden also vanished. The movement of Muslim clerics and madrasa students that had emerged suddenly in 1994 in the south of the country and had swept across all but a narrow strip of northern Afghanistan seemed to evaporate just as abruptly as it had appeared. With the establishment of a new government, the United States and other international sponsors announced the birth of a "post-Taliban" order and the restoration of security and stability to Afghanistan and the wider region. The Taliban moment in Afghan history had passed.

The flight of the Taliban seemed to usher in a new era—or, by some accounts, mark a return to a more authentic Afghan past. As women returned to public life and music reappeared, Afghanistan acquired the appearance of a land liberated from occupation by an alien power. Towns were now free of the madrasa students who had brutally herded men into mosques and confined women to domestic spaces. Pledging billions of dollars in aid, international donors promised to reconstruct the torn fabric of Afghan life. They offered schools, hospitals, and roads. With foreign assistance, the new government promised to rid the country of armed men and poppy fields and revitalize the country through development.

Yet six years after the dispersal of the Taliban, the historical break announced by the new government and its international backers now appears less convincing. Though no longer in formal control of the Afghan state, the Taliban exhibited signs of recovery beginning in 2003. Some of their members and sympathizers adapted to the new political order. Figures such as Mullah Abdul Salam "Roketi," whose skill with the firing of rockets gave him his *nom de guerre*, had won a seat in parliament. But many more committed themselves to undermining the post-Taliban government. Groups claiming to represent the Taliban destabilized areas in the central, eastern, and southern provinces; they also hindered reconstruction in the north and west, murdering aid workers, burning schools, and attacking Afghan and coalition forces in suicide bombings.[3] With the government of Hamid Karzai still confined to Kabul, the illicit production and smuggling of opium came to dominate the national economy and fund provincial militias. By 2006 these militias included fighters who, under the white banner of a seemingly resurgent Taliban, waged increasingly lengthy and bloody battles against the Afghan government and its foreign backers throughout the country. In the fall of 2006, Mullah Sabir, who claimed to be the Taliban "governor" of Ghazni Province southwest of Kabul and the commander of nine hundred fighters, boasted in an interview that "half of Afghanistan is under our control again. We have advanced to the gates of Kabul. President Hamid Karzai is captive in his palace." Following Taliban threats of a spring offensive dubbed "Ambush" and a wider campaign of suicide bombing, Mullah Mansur Dadullah, a commander in Helmand Province, touted an even more forceful return of the Taliban. In June 2007 he maintained that, in addition to controlling eight districts in Helmand, the Taliban "rule Kandahar, Uruzgan, Ghazni, Qalat, Jalalabad, and Kunar." "The authority of government troops is almost completely limited to the cities," he declared, "[and] the country is under our control." Though hyperbolic and difficult to verify given the deteriorating security situation, such claims received backing from Afghans who increasingly expressed nostalgia for the security of the Taliban era and from the assessment of scholars such as Gilles Dorronsoro, who warned that the Taliban held sway in "more than one third of the country."[4]

The Taliban movement remains one of the most elusive forces in modern history. At the center of international politics since 2001, the Taliban have nonetheless continued to mystify analysts and opponents alike. In 1994 a ragtag group of armed young men announced their intent to restore moral order and justice to Afghanistan, punishing robbers, adulterers, and rapists as they spread their rule. Their leader, Mullah Muhammad Omar—who adopted the honorific *Mujahed* (soldier of holy war) during the anti-Soviet jihad—later spoke of a vision that had come to him in a dream, inspiring him to forge a "true Islamic order."[5] Self-proclaimed students and clerics—*taliban* is the Persian plural form of "madrasa student" or "seeker of knowledge" *(talib)*—they promised salvation for a country suffering predation at the hands of rival factions of *mujahedin* fighters. Following a coup d'état by Afghan communists in April 1978 and a Soviet invasion to bolster the cause of socialist revolution in December 1979, the mujahedin had managed to resist and eventually repel the Red Army. Abandoned by their American Cold-War sponsor, however, they proved unable to govern the country when the Afghan communist government finally collapsed in 1992.

Between 1994 and 1996, the Taliban achieved a succession of re-markable strategic victories against their mujahedin rivals. In September 1995 they captured the western town of Herat, and in September 1996 they took the eastern town of Jalalabad. Within only two years, they had gained control of most of the country. They organized air, armor, and infantry assaults in some locales. They negotiated their way into others, becoming the masters of many towns and villages without firing a shot. They gained the support of the Pashtuns, the group commonly identified as the largest ethnic group in Afghanistan, and won the patronage of Pakistan, Saudi Arabia, and the United Arab Emirates. In its first two years, the movement also attracted the interest of the United States. Washington championed the American oil company Unocal, which sought an Afghan intermediary to facilitate the transport of newly accessible Central Asian oil and natural gas to world markets, all while bypassing key rivals, Russia and Iran. To the frustration of these prospective partners, the Taliban regime soon showed ambitions beyond the securing of pipeline routes for foreign sponsors.

In September 1996 the Taliban captured Kabul. While their leaders sought recognition as the winners of the Afghan civil war—and the United States and a few other countries appeared poised to offer it—the Taliban simultaneously launched a theatrical and bloody campaign to impose their vision of Islamic discipline on Kabul's residents. The foot soldiers of the Taliban, including many who were raised in orphanages and refugee camps in Pakistan (and had even adopted Urdu as their primary language) saw in the capital a modern-day Sodom and Gomorrah. For the first time in many of their lives, they met unveiled women and clean-shaven men. They heard music coming from the cassette sellers' stalls at the market, saw Bollywood videos, and encountered children's pet birds and the kites brilliantly immortalized by Khaled Hosseini's *The Kite Runner.*

The brutalities that these fighters visited upon the women and girls of urban Afghanistan were largely responsible for reversing the early cooperation between the Taliban and the American oil interests. Under pressure from human rights and feminist activists, the administration of President Bill Clinton publicly distanced itself from the Taliban, whose refusal to extradite bin Laden following his flight to Afghanistan in May 1996 further undermined the search for common cause. And while human rights and aid groups drew attention to their repressive gender policies, the Taliban campaign in the central and northern regions continued mostly out of wider public view. There the students and clerics confronted recalcitrant non-Pashtun populations, including one of the principal enemies of their seminary learning, the Shiites. Hazara communities, in particular, became the object of murderous sectarian campaigns. Their devotion to Shiism and their outsider status, exemplified by the character Hassan in *The Kite Runner,* made them the targets of a systematic campaign of mass murder.

Though such actions nearly prompted war with Iran, the international community remained divided in response to a regime whose behavior seemed so unpredictable. In 2000, as drought spread throughout Afghanistan and further imperiled one of the poorest countries on earth, the Taliban called for humanitarian aid; in March 2001 they outraged international opinion by shelling the ancient Buddhist statues of Bamyan as part of their war to rid Afghanistan of "idolatry." But even this assault produced contradictory responses. The U.S. Drug Enforcement Agency continued to pursue cooperation with Taliban leaders who promised to target Afghanistan's burgeoning opium economy. As late as summer 2001, Washington relied on the Taliban to aid in its "war on drugs."

Traveling by Toyota trucks and wielding guns and whips made of radio antennas, the Taliban strung television sets as well as audio and videotapes, along with the bodies of their political opponents, on lampposts and trees in a spectacular assault on the modern world. Their reclusive leader Mullah Omar rarely appeared in person and avoided being photographed. Yet their dramatic style of rule demanded spectators: they turned soccer stadiums into killing fields, stoned women, turned their artillery on statues, and ultimately sacrificed their regime rather than surrender Osama bin Laden to the Americans.

In the 1990s, journalists, scholars, and policymakers struggled to interpret the violent rule of the Taliban. They had appeared at a moment when the numerous conflicts that dotted Africa, the Balkans, the former Soviet Union, and elsewhere seemed to reflect the resurgence of essential cultural, ethnic, tribal, and religious identities. Scholars and journalists warned that the relative stability of the Cold War world had given way to "the coming anarchy" and to new kinds of conflicts defined by "the clash of civilizations." Defying the ideological affiliations of the Cold War, the seemingly senseless and irrational violence of groups in Somalia, Rwanda, Chechnya, Bosnia, and elsewhere threatened the civilized world, a number of commentators argued, by unleashing a primitive anarchy, a "new barbarism."[6]

In the wake of the Soviet withdrawal of 1989 and the collapse of the Soviet-led communist bloc in 1991, the fighting between the Afghan communist government and the mujahedin, on the one hand, and among the mujahedin factions, on the other, appeared to amount to little more than a brutish struggle for power. To some observers, ethnicity now fueled the Afghan civil war, as each resistance party took on the guise of groups expressing ethnic solidarity against all others. Beginning in 1994, journalists and diplomats watching Afghanistan marveled at the Taliban's seeming ability to bring order to the rapidly expanding territory under their control. Afghans themselves spoke of a desire for security—a demand that the Taliban claimed to fulfill. When describing themselves, the Taliban would frequently tell the story of their spontaneous organization to punish local commanders who had raped young girls (or, according to some accounts, young boys) in Kandahar province. From 1996, international media focused on the religious ideology of the Taliban, and specifically on their gender policies.

Yet outsiders never had a unified view of the movement. Pointing to the Pashtuns' purported majority status as well as to their dominant historical role in Afghan politics, some saw the Taliban as the legitimate incarnation of traditional Afghan values. While some of these commentators recoiled at the brutality of Taliban fighters, they tended to see such behavior as essentially consistent with a rural society marked by "tribalism" and "religious fundamentalism." Many highlighted the religious ideology of the Taliban and maintained that the movement reflected the aspirations of Muslim militants everywhere. The Taliban obsession with the veiling and isolation of women and the disciplining of interactions between the sexes, together with their draconian punishments, appeared to signal a return to a medieval world of fanatical theocracy. Later, most observers tended to see their intransigence in the face of calls to surrender bin Laden following the attacks of September 11 as final confirmation that the Islamic utopia envisioned by Mullah Omar was nothing more than a backward-looking and apocalyptic fantasy that would quickly collapse under American bombs.

Other analysts saw more complexity in the movement. They argued that the Taliban were about much more than a return to an idealized Islamic past, and that they had complicated origins and goals. Highlighting the intersection of security and energy interests, the journalist Ahmed Rashid brilliantly uncovered how Pakistani authorities had helped launch the movement and how energy companies with connections in Washington hoped to use the Taliban to secure pipelines from Central Asia to the Indian Ocean. Once in power, the Taliban seemed to stray from their Pakistani and American sponsors and link their fate with bin Laden instead. When American-led pressure severed the international ties that sustained the regime, the rapid fall of the Taliban appeared to support this image of the Taliban as a creature of foreign interests ranging from Pakistani intelligence and Western oil companies to Arab governments and terrorist networks. After 2001, most journalists continued to underscore the central role of Pakistan and al-Qaeda in fomenting instability and backing a resurgence of the Taliban.[7]

At the same time, the collapse of the regime confirmed the views of those who saw it primarily as an indigenous movement devoted to reestablishing order by imposing the religious and cultural values of rural Pashtun tribesmen. To many journalists, politicians, and human rights activists, Taliban misrule accounted almost exclusively for the poverty, violence, and gender discrimination visible in Afghanistan in the 1990s.[8] Their commitment to an Islamic order built upon Pashtun tribal norms, together with the conventions of hospitality and honor that sustained their alliance with bin Laden, provoked widespread opposition among non-Pashtuns and undermined their capacity to govern the country. Fatalistic and incompetent, the Taliban seemed capable only of destruction and doomed to failure as an anachronistic band of religious zealots in a modern, secular era.

Such representations of the movement proved illusory, however. The Taliban were far from an ephemeral expression of a quixotic attempt to revive a medieval theocracy. In 2001 they suffered a peculiar defeat. But the Taliban phenomenon nonetheless persisted. They reemerged and continued to shape the politics of Afghanistan, its neighbors, and the world beyond. That a variety of militant groups fighting under the Taliban banner would within three years form not one insurgency, but multiple and distinct insurgencies, with considerable popular support and capable of challenging Afghan, NATO, and American-led coalition forces in pitched battles—and even, however briefly, hold government outposts and entire districts in 2006 and 2007—only deepened the mystery enshrouding the Taliban phenomenon.

This book revisits the paradoxes at the heart of the Taliban movement—and a civil war that has raged in Afghanistan for nearly thirty years. It brings together scholars of Afghan history, politics, society, and culture to offer interdisciplinary perspectives, grounded in an understanding of the country's past, on the Taliban. These essays are the first to analyze the Taliban movement from its inception in 1994 to its splintering and transformation into a fractious, but lethal, constellation of guerilla fighters in the present. They share a common focus on Afghanistan's internal political dynamics, while analyzing how Afghan actors have engaged the outside world.

Previous portrayals have largely focused on the origins of the movement. In underscoring the Taliban's connections to Pakistani security services, mafia elites, energy companies, Islamic radicals, and al-Qaeda, journalists and scholars have captured key aspects of the movement.[9] But a stress on the foreign and conspiratorial origins of the movement reveals only a partial picture. It tells us less about how the Taliban succeeded in capturing most of the country, how they held this territory for so long, and why the movement collapsed suddenly in late 2001. Nor does this approach explain how, since 2002, various actors—best understood as the "neo-Taliban"—have reinvented the movement, reassembling assorted fragments and returning to the Afghan political arena to survive the group's ten-year anniversary and reemerge as the most serious oppositional force in the country, with de facto control over large swaths of territory within Afghanistan and along the Afghan-Pakistan frontier.

Contemporary Afghanistan shares many of the features that social scientists have identified as favoring insurgencies the world over—rough, mountainous terrain, poverty, popular mistrust of the state, large family size (allowing sons to risk becoming militants), foreign support and cross-border sanctuaries, as well as an easily transportable commodity (in this case, opium) for financing. The case of Afghanistan is nonetheless unique. One of the central premises of this book is that the tenacity of the Taliban—their refusal to exit the stage of Afghan politics—can be understood only by situating them within the history of Afghanistan and its heterogeneous regions and peoples. Shifting from a focus on origins, this book investigates broader questions relating to the character of the movement, its evolution over time, and its capacity to affect the future of Afghanistan and the region. It does not, however, present a unitary view of the phenomenon. Readers will encounter different points of view and different emphases.[10]

While presenting a range of interpretations and approaches, the authors focus on three overlapping themes. One primary concern is to elucidate the underlying historical patterns that gave rise to the Taliban and placed limits on the possibilities of Taliban rule. Did the Taliban represent the ascendance of "traditional" Afghan political forces, or were they a wholly novel entity that broke completely with the Afghan past? Did their government falter because of its ideology or because it faced the same obstacles—scarce resources, poor infrastructure, and independent-minded communities—that have bedeviled other would-be rulers of Afghanistan? These debates highlight what was distinctively "Afghan" about the Taliban phenomenon and what it owed to transnational Islamist and other networks. At the same time, they reveal key structural features of Afghan politics and show how the Taliban have a deep-running ideological and social base, likely guaranteeing them a central position in future political struggles.

A closely related area of emphasis centers on the crisis of state power in Afghanistan. The civil war sparked by the communist assault on rural Afghan society nearly three decades ago has been as much a cause as a product of Kabul's inability to rule the country. Already weak before 1978, the Afghan state apparatus collapsed when urban and secular-minded revolutionary elites used it to unleash violence on a resistant population that the communists had pledged to remake by empowering women, minorities, and the rural poor. It has never recovered.

This book examines Taliban efforts to reconstruct these governing institutions, a critical feature of the Taliban project neglected in other accounts. The Taliban largely failed in their efforts, but this was not due to their ideology alone. Attention to what they tried to achieve reveals much about the movement and highlights similarities to non-Islamic states committed to radical social transformations. Like such revolutionary regimes, they inherited the structural constraints that dogged their predecessors. The formidable challenges of ruling Afghanistan fractured the movement and radicalized many of its already highly ideologized factions. These same difficulties have fueled opposition to the Karzai government, forcing its officials, like the Taliban before them, to search for strategies to integrate domestic foes and to secure the all-important foreign patrons on whose largesse the survival of the central government depends.

A third line of inquiry explores how diverse Afghan communities have contended with state power. Under the Taliban, regional, ethnic, sectarian, and other differences played an essential role in Afghan politics, even if foreign observers have strained to grasp their importance. Many of the essays in this book analyze how Afghans experienced Taliban rule, showing how historical memories as well as ethnic, regional, and other identities colored these perspectives. Relations among the country's diverse groups and regions are central to understanding how a collection of clerics and religious students seized control of the country, how they struggled to rule, and how they have adapted to new political circumstances since 2001. Many of the interpretations offered here are based on previously overlooked or newly available sources, including those collected during field-work in Afghanistan. As a work of contemporary history, the book does not present explicit policy recommendations. Afghanistan's recent past has been all too often scarred by political prescriptions that have sought to impose rigid schemes of transformation adapted from modernization and other universalizing theories. Attentive to what is distinctive about the politics, identities, and institutions of Afghanistan, this book aims instead to offer a historical perspective that suggests ways to learn from a very complicated past. It seeks to add complexity and nuance to contemporary debates about international policy while highlighting, where possible, many of the concerns of Afghans.

A deeper investigation of the Taliban must start with an appreciation of the varied human and physical geography of the region. Of the underlying structural features that have set limits on Afghan politics, the political geography of Afghanistan stands out as perhaps the most important. Its most striking feature is the Hindu Kush, a mountain range that cuts a diagonal across the country from the northeast toward the southwest (see Map 3). Geographers have identified at least eight climatic zones and up to a dozen distinct geographic areas, ranging from a monsoon region in eastern Afghanistan to the snow- and frost-covered central highlands and the sandy deserts of the southwestern province of Nimroz, "the land of the noontime sun."[11]

This variegated terrain has yielded, in turn, an extraordinarily complex landscape of human diversity. Scholars do not agree about the precise number of communities to be classified, or if such classi-

Map 3. Physical Geography

fications have even focused on groups that lend themselves to comparison with one another. Lacking a comprehensive modern census and a consensus about how groups are to be enumerated, scholars estimate that Afghanistan contains anywhere from fifty to two hundred ethnic groups. As anthropologists have learned, however, many Afghans do not necessarily identify with such categories of classification. How Afghans have viewed such labels depends upon specific political and social contexts and has proved highly variable over time.[12]

In the late nineteenth century, Afghanistan took shape as a buffer state between the Russian and British empires. Imperial competition gave form to this territory. European powers not only defined its borders; they sought to define its politics as well. The result was the creation of a monarchy charged with managing the population inhabiting a space in between rival empires. London and St. Petersburg agreed that the Amu (Oxus) River would mark the northernmost border of this new country.

Determining the remaining borders proved considerably more complicated. The western border emerged as a product of negotiations among the Afghan monarch, Britain, Russia, and Iran. It cut through a highland plain long claimed by Iran, severing the oasis town of Herat politically, but not culturally, from Tehran. In 1893 the British imposed a border on Afghanistan's southern and eastern frontiers. Known as the "Durand Line," it ran through a vast area inhabited primarily by Pashtun tribes in the northwestern borderlands of British India and, after 1947, Pakistan.

This Afghan-Pakistan border remained contested, however. The Kabul government opposed it, and some Pashtun intellectuals on both sides rejected it as an impediment to dreams of a "Pashtunistan," a state that would bring together Pashtuns divided by this 2,430-kilometer border. Even the Taliban regime refused to recog-

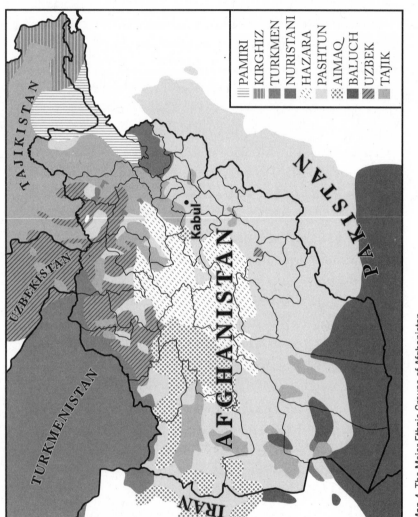

PAMIRI
KIRGHIZ
TURKMEN
NURISTANI
HAZARA
PASHTUN
AIMAQ
BALUCH
UZBEK
TAJIK

TAJIKISTAN

UZBEKISTAN

TURKMENISTAN

PAKISTAN

Kabul

AFGHANISTAN

IRAN

Map 4. The Major Ethnic Groups of Afghanistan

nize it.[13] Many Pakistani elites have been ambivalent about this border as well. Established as a homeland for a "Muslim nation," Pakistan has inspired religious solidarities that have called into question its boundaries with Afghanistan, India, and the disputed territory of Kashmir. On the ground, local populations have largely disregarded the Afghan-Pakistan border, crossing back and forth without state control from Afghan territory to the North West Frontier Province, Baluchistan, and the Federally Administered Tribal Areas, which include the restive agencies of North and South Waziristan. Militants and smugglers are not the only ones to pass freely across this frontier. Hundreds of thousands of nomadic tribesmen, merchants, laborers, students, refugees, travelers, and others move across it annually in search of land, trade, work, education, marriage, and family.

Nowhere did these borders enclose a homogeneous ethnic or religious group. The country became known as "Afghanistan," or the "land of the Afghans," following the "Afghan," or Pashtun, ruling dynasty. Yet the country was not home to all Pashtuns. Millions of Pashtuns, perhaps two or three times the number of those in Afghanistan, remained under British (later, Pakistani) rule. Similarly, as Map 4 illustrates, non-Pashtun communities, including those whom ethnographers would subsequently label Baluch, Uzbeks, Turkmen, Kirghiz, Tajiks, and others, lived on both sides of the state's boundaries.

The area enclosed by these borders presented its rulers with formidable challenges. It lacked access to ports and had only one navigable river, the Amu, which formed its northern border. The greater part of the country was desert. The rest was made up of steppe, with relatively small clusters of forested zones. Human habitation has been largely limited to mountain valleys, river corridors, and other irrigable pockets. The population is most dense in the northeast, around Kabul and the valleys to the east. Whereas some of these valleys are overpopulated, large swaths of the southern and western deserts support only small-scale communities or are uninhabited entirely. No Afghan government has even succeeded in counting this population. On the eve of the civil war, a partial census revealed a population of roughly fourteen million; this figure included one million nomads, though perhaps a million more Afghans practiced some form of seasonal migration. The next decade of fighting may have claimed the lives of roughly 9 percent of this population, made 11 percent internal refugees, and forced 33 percent to flee the country.[14]

This population pattern, the country's rugged topography, and its varied climates have constrained transportation and communication infrastructure and have thus made the task of ruling Afghanistan's diverse regions a daunting enterprise. King Habibullah introduced the automobile in 1907, but caravans of camels and donkeys remained the primary means of connecting the disparate parts of the country. This began to change only in the early 1930s, when a new road linked Kabul through mountain passes to the north and a wider network of roads traced a ring around the country from the capital to Gardez, Kandahar, Herat, the northern towns of Shibirghan and Mazar-e Sharif, and back to Kabul.[15] The expansion of telegraph lines and air travel only gradually facilitated the projection of state authority beyond Kabul.

The structure of Afghan society further curbed the state-building efforts of elites. Afghanistan has long been a sea of small, heterogeneous villages—a landscape colorfully sketched by Rory Stewart in *The Places in Between*. Before the Soviet invasion, some 85 percent of Afghans lived in the countryside. Most villages had fewer than 500 inhabitants. Only a dozen or so had more than 5,000 residents. Nearly a million Afghans lived in Kabul, which dwarfed the other major cities, Kandahar, Herat, and Mazar-e Sharif, with populations between 100,000 and 200,000. The dislocations of the civil war transformed the major cities; the arrival of refugees fleeing fighting and starvation more than doubled the size of these urban populations. By the late 1980s, between one-quarter and one-third of all Afghans were to be found in the largest cities.[16]

A geographic perspective on Afghanistan's crisis sheds light on another constant of modern Afghan politics: the strained relationship between the capital and the heterogeneous regions that make up the country. Between the 1930s and the 1970s, the pre-revolutionary government's development projects—such as the American-sponsored project to irrigate the Helmand River Valley through massive dam construction—had the effect of further differentiating among the country's regions.[17] Despite wartime urbanization, Afghanistan has remained a country marked by distinctive regional differences. Successive Afghan governments, whether dominated by a monarch, Mullah Omar, or Hamid Karzai, have had to contend with the challenge of projecting authority from Kabul into far-flung locales with only rudimentary means of transport and communication.

The challenge has not simply been one of geography and space. When the centralized authority of the revolutionary Afghan state broke down in 1978 and 1979, power largely devolved upon local elites. The anti-Soviet jihad proved so successful in part because it grew out of highly localized resistance movements. Though Afghan political parties in Pakistan and Iran would later seek to dominate these centers of military activity, or "fronts," by controlling their access to weapons and money, militia leaders carved out broad political autonomy for themselves and their clients. Known in the international press as "warlords," they have since struggled to maintain this form of self-rule, despite the centralizing efforts of the Taliban and, later, the Karzai government. In numerous locales, the mujahedin who came to power in their struggle against the Soviets have retained control of these regions to the present, interrupted only by a relatively brief period of Taliban rule.[18]

The localism that has structured Afghan politics since the late 1970s has been reinforced by mobilization inspired partly by a language of ethnic solidarity. The role of ethnicity in the Afghan civil war remains one of the most controversial themes of scholarly debate about Afghanistan. Following the Soviet invasion, foreign journalists tended to see Afghans as a more or less homogeneous population of armed tribesmen.[19] This view has persisted even though numerous Western scholars have since the 1950s presented more complex portraits of Afghan society. Indeed, anthropologists pioneered the field of Afghan studies in Europe and the United States. They elaborated theories about the phenomenon of ethnicity whose influence reached far beyond the Afghan context. In the 1990s, a wider public seized upon this attention to Afghanistan's heterogeneous ethnic groups. In a period that included the breakup of the Soviet Union, the bloody dissolution of Yugoslavia, and the proliferation of civil wars in Africa, observers increasingly viewed the intra-Afghan factional fighting through the lens of ethnic conflict.[20]

Within Afghanistan itself, the politics of ethnicity have proved more complicated. Under the guidance of Soviet nationality policies, the Afghan communists focused on ethnic labels as means to categorize minority groups whom they targeted for liberation. In a challenge to the late monarchy's efforts to equate Afghan culture with arts and literature in Pashto (the primary language of the Pashtuns), the Soviet-inspired communists elevated Uzbek, Baluchi, Pashai, Turkmen, and a Nuristani dialect to the status of "national languages" enjoying official patronage in radio, television, and the press.[21] The communist regime also elevated the status of non-Pashtuns in the traditionally Pashtun-dominated military. Soviet advisers preferred

Tajik and Uzbek interpreters. By the mid to late 1980s, the percentage of Tajiks in the army surpassed their percentage in society at large.[22]

Whereas the communist regime promoted ethnic identification, the mujahedin formally ignored it. Ethnic categories nonetheless entered public consciousness in a variety of ways in the 1980s. Interaction with relief workers, scholars, intelligence officials, and journalists in particular prompted such identification, if only for specific foreign audiences. Intellectuals from the urban-based and émigré political parties also cultivated the use of ethnic categories.[23]

Yet ethnicity is not a clear marker of political affiliation in Afghanistan. Problems of classification and interpretation become magnified when categories such as "Pashtun" or "Tajik" are examined in particular contexts and their capacity to affect political dispositions are investigated more closely. Alongside the Kurds, the Pashtuns form one of the largest communities claiming descent from a common ancestor. This shared genealogy nonetheless encompasses diverse lines of succession. Pashtun communities have historically acted independently from, or in conflict with, one another. Moments of cooperation have tended to be ephemeral. Within the Pashtun subtribes that stretch across two states and a space of some 100,000 square miles, neither social nor cultural solidarity can be taken for granted.[24] Indeed, the boundary separating Pashtuns from others has been fluid in a variety of contexts. Some self-identified Pashtuns speak only Dari (the dialect of Persian spoken in Afghanistan), while some Tajiks speak only Pashto, though they are not regarded by surrounding Pashtuns as members of their community because they do not own land or belong to the Pashtun tribal structure. In political terms, today's Pashtun tribes of Kandahar Province, for example, are dominated by perhaps a half dozen notable families, which include the Karzais. These elites utilize patron-client relationships in local administrative and security organs, as well as the backing of their own militias (which are partially integrated into the Afghan National Army) and the profits from drug trafficking, to control the province and exercise considerable autonomy from Kabul. In Paktya, by contrast, tribes practice a more egalitarian form of politics based on consensus building and tribal norms, though they guard their independence from the central government even more fiercely.[25]

The label *Tajik* is no less problematic. Afghans have long applied the term to Dari-speaking town-dwellers who do not have tribal affiliations. The disputed identity of the leaders of the anti-Taliban Northern Alliance serves as an instructive case. These commanders from the Panjsher Valley just north of Kabul emerged in the wake of the Taliban collapse as the most powerful "Tajiks."[26] Having taken the capital in November 2001 (apparently in violation of American orders), they seized key ministries as the Karzai government took shape. Despite their characterization in the international press as a Tajik force, many Afghans regard them as nothing more than "Panjsheris" who represent their home region but who do not speak for the interests of all Tajiks in the country. The self-identification of another veteran of the jihad and the anti-Taliban struggle is even more illuminating. Ismail Khan, a former army officer and commander who governed the key western city of Herat and its environs from roughly 1989 to 1995 and from 2001 to 2004, is also commonly associated with the Tajik-led Northern Alliance. Yet, as the German anthropologist Bernt Glatzer notes, he has consistently avoided identification with any macro-ethnic label such as *Tajik*. In Herat, Ismail Khan is known instead as a "Shindandi" (reflecting his place of origin, Shindand) or simply as "Khwaja," a follower of the eleventh-century Muslim mystic Khwaja Abdullah Ansari.[27]

Such localized identities continue to predominate in many parts of the country; and where ethnic boundaries are acknowledged by Afghans, they do not necessarily define all social relations. The drug trade, for example, transcends ethnic frontiers. In southwestern Afghanistan, as Lutz Rzehak points out in this book, drugs bring together Pashtuns and the Baluch, who inhabit both sides of the porous Afghan-Iranian border. Intermarriage between Baluch brides and Pashtun grooms solidifies bonds between merchant families. Trafficking in weapons and other contraband follows the same networks and crosses ethnic, regional, and national lines. Figures such as the anti-Soviet and anti-Taliban commander Ahmad Shah Masud, Rzehak's essay shows, also enjoyed status as a national martyr among diverse ethnic groups, though perhaps not among all Pashtuns.

Afghan understandings of community boundaries have shifted repeatedly since the communist coup and civil war. Militia commanders and politicians have sought to use linguistic and ethnic labels to mobilize followings, and larger coalitions based on language and ethnicity have emerged, if only in situational—and often temporary— political contexts in the last two decades. The anti-Soviet jihad did not immediately smooth over tensions within the largest ethnic or linguistic communities or forge solidarity among all Pashtuns or all Tajiks. Communists and anticommunists could be found in the same community. During the 1980s, for example, Hazara political factions inspired by a wide variety of concerns waged deadly conflicts against one another in central Afghanistan.

Launched during the communist period, the political mobilization of non-Pashtuns intensified when central authority nearly collapsed entirely in the early 1990s. Elites speaking on behalf of the once fractious Hazaras began to assert a national consciousness, as Robert L. Canfield has shown.[28] Organized principally around one of the main resistance parties, Hizb-e Wahdat-e Islami-ye Afghanistan (Party of Islamic Unity of Afghanistan), Hazaras challenged their subordination to other groups and claimed a stake in national politics. In western Afghanistan, inhabitants of the town of Herat have long identified themselves as "Heratis." More recently, however, younger Heratis who left the town seeking work or safety have begun to associate themselves with "Tajiks." As the anthropologist Glatzer observes, this identification reflects a political perspective, "namely a rejection of the possible Pashtun dominance of the country."[29]

This linkage between political power and Pashtun identity has been a central point of dispute in Afghan communities' estimation of the legitimacy of successive governments. Pashtun elites have historically viewed themselves as the natural masters of the country, a claim endorsed by key foreign sponsors. One of the most fundamental— and controversial—arguments offered in support of Pashtun primacy in Afghan political affairs cites their supposed demographic weight. Claims about majority status are, of course, political. In fact, in the absence of a systematic census, estimates of the Pashtun population vary widely. According to United Nations figures, Pashtuns account for about 38 percent of the population, while the Central Intelligence Agency's calculations have fluctuated. The 2006 CIA *World Factbook* puts their number at 42 percent.[30] Though most scholars, too, have presumed that the Pashtuns form the largest group, Conrad Schetter points out that these researchers have arrived at significant variations, calculating that Pashtuns compose anywhere from 35 percent to 70 percent of the total population of Afghanistan.[31]

For many Pashtuns, this presumed numeric superiority has reinforced the political supremacy of the Pashtuns, the people who had historically formed the state and, as the true *Afghans* (as they are known in Persian), had given the country its name. Many Pashtuns have entertained the idea that Afghanistan is their land, where non-Pashtuns may live but do not fully belong. From the outset of the evolutionary process that began in 1747 and led to the gradual formation of a distinct political nation-state, later known as Afghanistan, Pashtuns have been at the helm.

There have only been two episodes in Afghanistan's history when a Pashtun did not rule. For a brief period in 1929, Habibullah Kalakani, an ethnic Tajik, became the ruler of Afghanistan. He has, however, been regarded in the official Afghan chronicles as an aberration caused by internal mistakes and foreign interference. The fact that Kalakani's surge to power was caused mainly by a Pashtun-led rebellion against King Amanullah, himself a Pashtun, is often overlooked. The second period of non-Pashtun rule, again by a Tajik, occurred from 1992 to 1996, when Burhanuddin Rabbani, leader of the Jamiat-e Islami-ye Afghanistan (Islamic Society of Afghanistan), served as president. The Pashtuns viewed this period as one of turmoil and conflict. Rabbani never fully exercised authority over Afghanistan, nor did he have a foreign sponsor strong enough to sustain him in the face of internal power struggles.

In 1996 the Taliban ousted Rabbani's fragile regime from Kabul, and the Pashtuns once again rose to power. Despite the Taliban regime's draconian policies and their increasingly negative image around the world, the regime maintained a genuine level of support among the Pashtun population. Surprisingly perhaps, the regime also appealed to numerous technocratic and well-educated Pashtuns who lived in Western countries, where groups such as the "Taliban Support Council" in London often became apologists for the Taliban.[32] The allure of the Taliban for Pashtuns has roots in both the epoch of Afghan monarchical dynasties of the twentieth century as well as in recent Afghan history. Under the monarchy, Pashtun rulers began distancing themselves from Pashtun ethnic and social customs. They conducted government affairs in the Persian language instead of Pashto and, critics argued, were abandoning the customs of their ancestors. The Pashtuns saw in the Pashto-speaking Taliban an opportunity to return to their glory days.

The communist and postcommunist periods of Afghan history had further stripped the Pashtuns of any vestiges of absolute authority. The Pashtuns felt their exclusive mastery of Afghanistan slip away in the ideological equality propagated by the revolutionary rhetoric of the communist People's Democratic Party of Afghanistan (PDPA). The resistance to the PDPA governments and their Soviet backers further diluted the Afghan political landscape. Six out of the seven main resistance parties, which referred to themselves as mujahedin and were based in Peshawar, Pakistan, were headed by a Pashtun and relied on Pashtuns for their support. Rabbani led the seventh party, the Jamiat-e Islami. A Tajik-dominated group, it not only was one of the strongest resistance groups but also had among its members Ahmad Shah Masud, the celebrated resistance leader.[33] The Iranian-based Shiite parties also formed part of the resistance. Operating independently of the Pashtun-dominated groups, they were antagonistic toward the Pashtuns and rejected the notion that Afghanistan was the Pashtuns' home and that ethnic groups such as the Hazaras were merely permanent guests, or in the case of the Turkic peoples north of the Hindu Kush, conquered subjects.

The Shiites and other groups challenged Pashtun power by espousing a reorganization of the country along federal lines. To the Pashtuns, this was tantamount to the partition of Afghanistan. The main Shiite party based in Iran proposed, for example, a draft "Constitution of the Federal Islamic Republic of Afghanistan." This not only divided Afghanistan into six states *(aiyalat)* with separate constitutions and laws, but also introduced the Shiite Jafari school of jurisprudence into the system. The Pashtuns, adherents of the Sunni Hanafi school of jurisprudence, rejected the notion that these schools were equally valid.[34] General Abdul Rashid Dostum, the Uzbek militia leader who ruled most of northern Afghanistan independently from 1992 until the advent of the Taliban, also proposed a federal state structure.[35]

With the fall of the PDPA's last government in 1992, the Pashtun-dominated parties hoped to gain control of Afghan politics. However, the Tajik-supported Rabbani was appointed as interim president of the newly established Islamic State of Afghanistan and refused to leave office at the end of his term. This plunged the country into further fighting and gave rise to anxieties among Pashtuns about a government in Kabul that was not dominated by them. Thus, many of the supporters of the Taliban—as well as their opponents—interpreted their capture of Kabul in 1996 as an effort to restore Pashtun supremacy.

Were the Taliban then essentially an ethnic movement that deployed religious language and symbols to mobilize and unify Pashtun communities to recapture the state? A look at the prehistory of the movement is revealing. In the 1980s and early 1990s, more than half of the figures who later would rise to the highest ranks of the Taliban belonged to one of the traditionalist resistance parties, the Harakat-e Inqelab-e Islami-ye Afghanistan (Islamic Revolution Movement of Afghanistan). Headed by a cleric, Mawlawi Muhammad Nabi Muhammadi, it had emerged in the early 1980s as one of the most important parties and had attracted significant numbers of Uzbeks and other non-Pashtuns. With time, however, the party's pro-Pashtun orientation appealed only to Pashtun communities. Its leader increasingly drew on a base of power around a madrasa in Logar Province south of Kabul. The party consisted of clerics who sympathized with the leader's view that Islamic law should be the law of the land, that the customary law of the Pashtuns (Pashtunwali) was fully in accord with the sharia, and that Afghanistan would benefit from a strong, centralized state unburdened by the competing claims of minority ethnic and religious communities. Moreover, it was one of two resistance parties to publish its views chiefly in Pashto.[36] Already during the jihad period, it had organized a fighting structure around local madrasas in which students, either orphans or the sons of the poorest families, were subordinated to their instructors both in the school and in the field. Mullah Omar was said to be one such commander attached to this party.[37]

For many Afghans, the defining characteristic of the movement was its Pashtun character. Originating in the heavily Pashtun areas of western Pakistan and southeastern Afghanistan, the movement recruited from Pashtun communities throughout the country as it grew. Though predominantly Pashtun and chiefly composed of religious students and clerics, the movement was nonetheless internally diverse. Indeed, the anthropologist Glatzer has likened it to a "caravan," which assembled heterogeneous followers as it traversed the country and gathered momentum.[38] As Robert L. Canfield suggests in his essay in this book, the Taliban can also be understood as a dynamic "cultural body" that evolved as new groups joined the movement and introduced their own distinctive outlooks, resources, and influences.

Thomas Ruttig, a German journalist and diplomat, has discerned six distinct groups—all essentially Pashtun—within the movement. In addition to the mujahedin commanders, such as Mullah Omar, who formed the top leadership councils *(shuras)* and the madrasa students and orphans who served as foot soldiers, the Taliban caravan attracted young mujahedin fighters from other locales. When the Taliban expanded their reach beyond their core area in Kandahar, these young fighters, frequently defectors from the commander Gulbuddin Hekmatyar, reached agreements with Taliban leaders that allowed them to retain local control under the Taliban umbrella. At the same time, Pashtun officers who had served for the communist regime and belonged to the Khalq wing of the PDPA defected, bringing with them critical expertise in the use of aircraft and tanks, to a movement that they viewed as a vehicle for restoring Pashtun power.

Pakistanis make up the last of Ruttig's two Taliban constituencies. The Pakistani government and religious parties recruited a separate body of foot soldiers from madrasas in Pakistan. According to Ruttig, the aims of the Pakistani Taliban often differed from those of the Afghan Taliban, and conflicts between the groups exploded into shoot-outs on numerous occasions. (In 2000, for example, Taliban leaders had to intercede to break up fighting between factions of the Lashkare Jhangvi, a group that trained in Afghanistan and launched terrorist attacks against Shiites and government officials in Pakistan.) For some of these fighters, the Afghan battlefield was mere preparation for more important struggles that they hoped to launch in the future in Kashmir and India, or within Pakistan itself. Their most famous recruits were the American John Walker Lindh and the Australian David Hicks, who were drawn to Afghanistan by Pakistani groups affiliated with the Taliban and al-Qaeda, such as Harkatul Mujahideen and Lashkare Taiba.[39] Finally, Pakistani military and technical advisers played a critical role in transforming this caravan into a standing army, organized into brigades and divisions with rapid mobility and modern communications. They were responsible for the basic infrastructure of Taliban rule, an achievement visibly demonstrated by the fact that Afghan cities under the Taliban could be reached by dialing Pakistani telephone prefixes.[40]

In areas with mixed populations outside of the Pashtun belt, joining the caravan became a way for Pashtun minorities to offset disadvantages vis-à-vis their non-Pashtun neighbors. When the Taliban seized the ethnically diverse northern province of Konduz in June 1997, local Pashtuns embraced the Taliban soldiers as their saviors from the rapacious rule of the Uzbek general Dostum. Young Pashtun men joined the movement with enthusiasm, even though they had not been trained in Pakistani madrasas. Expecting the "peace and security" supposedly introduced elsewhere by the Taliban, Pashtuns like Gulbuddin (who uses one name) greeted the Taliban "with open arms" because "the Taliban seemed to represent a way for us Pashtuns to end the discrimination that we had suffered under the ethnic Uzbek and Tajik mujahedin commanders."[41]

Young villagers such as Gulbuddin were drawn to more than the fellowship of Pashtuns or the prospect of Pashtun power. They were simultaneously attracted to the religious message of the Taliban. Gulbuddin donned a "white headband like my colleagues" and traveled "from village to village enforcing what I believed to be the sharia laws enshrined in the Koran." "We had been told that they believed passionately in Islam" he recalled, "and we thought that they would help cleanse our area of infidels."[42]

Non-Pashtuns, such Taliban maintained, could not be good Muslims. Even in the predominantly Sunni province of Nimroz, bordering Iran in southwestern Afghanistan, they targeted the Baluch population as unbelievers to be "illuminated with the light of Islam." Abdul Rahman Pahwal, a Baluch intellectual who left a memoir-like description of the province under the Taliban, claimed that Mullah Omar had issued a fatwa declaring, "The people of Nimroz have given up Islam and have given themselves over to Shiism." Pahwal's polemical account of the Taliban highlights the anti-Shiite and anti-Baluch antipathies that they directed against locals. Omar authorized his commanders, Pahwal charged, "to kill all people in Nimroz, whether man or woman, and to monopolize their property, and subsequently to wed their daughters by force and thereby in this way to cleanse this region of the enemies of Islam and those pagans who fight against us with the official support from the other side of the border."[43] Pashtuns, too, could be suspect if they did not conform to Taliban practices. The very small number of Pashtuns who belonged to the minority Ismaili community reportedly fled the Taliban for Pakistan.[44]

The Taliban commitment to purifying the land of the ungodly set them at odds with various ethnic groups who did not share their religious interpretations, but Shiites especially became the target of mass killings. The context of civil war and reprisal killings, in particular, sharpened these antagonisms and seems to have legitimized new forms of mass violence. When the Taliban failed to take the ethnically mixed town of Mazar-e Sharif in the north in May 1997, local commanders murdered some two thousand Taliban prisoners of war. In August 1998 the city finally fell to the Taliban, who now sought revenge against the enemies of their sectarian ideology. They disarmed Uzbeks and Tajiks but systematically targeted Hazaras for murder. At a tomb said to be the burial place of the caliph Ali, the Taliban reportedly killed several dozen men in a ritualized fashion according to Islamic prescriptions for the slaughter of animals.[45] Within a few days, they murdered some four thousand Shiite Hazaras and nine members of the Iranian consulate there. Similarly, between September 1998 and May 1999, the Taliban and Hazara militias fought brutal battles for control of the central region of the Hazarajat.

In search of wider legitimacy, the Taliban nonetheless refuted claims that they represented Pashtuns alone. In interviews with foreigners, they highlighted the presence in their ranks of a few non-Pashtuns, who had joined the movement in its earliest stages. Some Ismailis from Badakhshan, for example, may have initially thrown their support behind the Taliban to settle old scores against Rabbani's regime. Even after the collapse of the regime in 2001 and intensive Taliban recruitment in Pashtun communities between 2005 and 2007, Mullah Omar continued to deny that the movement was, at root, a Pashtun phenomenon. In early 2007 he insisted that "without doubt the people of the region are behind us, not on a tribal or ethnic basis but in a national and Islamic spirit."[46]

Despite the predominance of Pashtuns, the Taliban have never been a monolith. Moreover, it was not their Pashtun identity alone, but the way they ruled, that dictated how many communities have responded to them. Some Taliban officials displayed pragmatism in non-Pashtun locales. In Nimroz, as in other areas, locals recalled an initial period of security as the Taliban punished thieves and corrupt petty officials.[47] Even Mullah Omar may have on occasion disciplined subordinates who treated local populations with extreme severity; for example, he apparently disarmed one of his top commanders, the one-legged Mullah Dadullah, after his brutal murder of Hazaras in Bamyan in 2000.[48]

As in Pashtun communities, non-Pashtun elites frequently took the initiative in opening up talks in hopes of softening Taliban rule. Negotiated submission could secure benefits that defeat on the battlefield could not. Even a few Hazara communities appear to have succeeded in placing limits on Taliban control. In the Jaghori district of the Hazarajat, elders elected to send delegations to Kabul, Kandahar, and Ghazni (the provincial capital) to bargain with various factions of the movement. In exchange for their acquiescence, the Hazaras argued, within a religious framework, for toleration of their Shiite faith and, significantly, for permission to continue to educate girls. Although the Taliban ultimately engaged in some violence against the residents of Jaghori, informants later told a group of researchers that they managed to persuade lower-level Taliban officials to permit some access to schooling and work for girls and women. These relatively permissive practices were then curtailed only when visiting delegations of senior Taliban officials arrived. These local communities' concern with maintaining good relations with neighboring Pashtuns in the province played an important role during the period of Taliban rule; and it proved decisive when locals helped Taliban flee from the region when they came under attack in 2001.[49]

Similarly, in Nimroz, where few Pashtuns were to be found, the Taliban initially appointed as governor a descendant of a local Baluch tribe. He earned a reputation for largely respecting local customs, even though he had grown up in Pakistan, made Urdu the official language of provincial administration, and favored Pashto speakers over those who spoke Baluchi or Persian. But following a rebellion led by Baluch mujahedin, the Taliban sent another governor from Pakistan. He spoke Pashto, burned a local library, and charged that the Baluch had been corrupted by their Iranian neighbors and had become "Shiites."[50] In Nimroz and elsewhere, life under the Taliban ultimately discredited the movement among non-Pashtuns. The Taliban thus sharpened the divide between Pashtuns and non-Pashtuns and contributed to the further ethnicization of Afghan politics. The experience of Taliban rule broadened this process of affiliation with the larger non-Pashtun ethnic groups among populations that were previously less exposed to such categories of identification.

Yet the Taliban were more than an ethnic militia. As Abulkader Sinno shows in this book, the Taliban were only one of several Pashtun groups who, with the assistance of generous Pakistani aid, had attempted to bring other Pashtuns under their control. The Taliban did not succeed merely because they were Pashtuns. And as Juan R. I. Cole points out in his essay, the Taliban did more than simply impose Pashtun customs. Indeed, viewing themselves as reformers, Mullah Omar and the movement's leaders set out to purify the religion of all Afghans—a policy that put them at odds with Pashtuns, especially in the eastern provinces of Paktya, Khost, and Paktika, who resisted the alteration of Pashtun customary legal practices, or Pashtunwali. Historically, Pashtunwali had been a repertoire of legal norms and conceptions of honor and hospitality that marked many Pashtuns' autonomy from the state—and from the entire corpus of sharia law. The Taliban broke from the Afghan past when they made their conception of Pashtunwali, traditionally an alternative to the juridical authority of the state for many Pashtun tribes, the legal linchpin of a self-proclaimed Islamic state.[51]

If the Taliban were committed to an Islamizing project and not just ethnic predominance, what kind of "Islamic" regime did they establish? And should their movement regain power, what might they envision for the future? Despite observers' frequent resort to the label *medieval* to characterize the religious politics of the Taliban, the movement should be seen rather as a product of very modern political struggles rooted in both regional and global developments. From the outset, the Taliban elite have conceived of themselves in a hybrid political vocabulary. Though they ultimately would call their polity an "Islamic emirate," they also employed language adopted by political actors everywhere in the modern era. The original Taliban regarded themselves as constituting a "movement," a term that implied broad political legitimacy and the capacity to mobilize a fractured and war-torn society. Their decision to identify themselves as "Afghanistan's Taliban Islamic Movement" (in Pashto, *Da Afghanistan da Talibano Islami Tahrik*) was a gesture that established not just a religious, but a modern—and national—framework for their politics.

The regional context was critical. The Islamization of Pakistani politics from the 1970s gave Afghan Islamists an important base for their activities. During the Cold War, American patronage for Afghan Islamists further amplified their power along the Afghan-Pakistan frontier. The 1979 revolution in Iran, as Vali Nasr has argued, not only inspired Islamists throughout South Asia but, more importantly, politicized the sectarian divide between Sunnis and Shiites along this frontier.[52]

The Afghan religious landscape that such changes began to re-work had been marked by extraordinary diversity. Contrary to stereo-types dating to the British colonial era about the "mad mullahs" and millenarian jihadist movements that supposedly defined religion among the frontier peoples, and among Pashtuns in particular, reli-gious practices and ideas among these Afghan and Pakistani commu-nities were varied and complex, differing by locale and social group. They ranged from pacifist, nonsectarian political mobilization to de-votional rites and festivals livened by song.[53] The Taliban defined themselves against many of these local traditions in the name of an ostensibly more authentic and universal understanding of the faith, but they, too, ultimately retained a localistic cast. They were shaped by the distinctive political milieu of the Pashtun belt extending across the Afghan-Pakistan border. In their traditionalist religious ideology and social composition, they diverged markedly from Islamist move-ments in Egypt, Indonesia, Turkey, Iran, and even Pakistan, which have been led by engineers, professors, doctors, and others educated outside of clerical institutions, and many of which have adapted to political democratization and pluralism in recent years.[54]

The Taliban radically proclaimed the return of "tradition," but clerical rule of this kind was new to Afghanistan and indeed to other Muslim societies. The French scholar Gilles Dorronsoro has aptly called this phenomenon a "clerical revolution" that produced "a re-gime unique in the history of the Muslim world."[55] Indeed, Taliban spokesmen themselves referred to their rise as a "revolution."[56] To be sure, mullahs had mobilized opposition to the government in Kabul in the past. In the 1920s they spearheaded resistance against King Amanullah's attempts to strengthen the power of the central government through laws limiting clerical authority, imposing new taxes, enforcing conscription, compelling the adoption of Western-style hats and suits, and introducing legal changes relating to the family, marriage, and the unveiling of women. During the same period many also opposed the education of girls and the appearance of women outside the home.[57]

Afghan religious authorities never formed a homogeneous group, however. Families tied to the mystical Sufi orders of the Naqshbandis or Qaderis or who traced their lineage to the family of the Prophet enjoyed particular prestige.[58] Others had very little formal training in Islamic learning and enjoyed a more modest reputation as the prayer leaders, teachers, and spiritual guides of local communities. Standing outside the tribal system, mullahs often mediated among feuding factions and succeeded in unifying local communities in times of war or revolt. From the late nineteenth century, state-building monarchs in Kabul co-opted many of them, while seeking to order and regulate the rest under an administrative hierarchy. Clerics conferred authority upon Afghan rulers at coronations and other ceremonies and, equally important, acted on their calls to lead the Pashtun tribes of the eastern frontier in jihad against the British. Between the revolt of 1929 and the communist coup of 1978, however, the Afghan state did not face a serious challenge from the men of religious learning and piety *(ulama)*.[59]

Paradoxically, the more dangerous threat to the Afghan monarchy came from the left, and it was the Afghan Marxists who, in turn, triggered the emergence of a powerful clerical opposition. The Marxists' resort to violence in 1978 following their seizure of power in April provoked a resistance led by Muslim leaders. From 1978 they challenged the policies of the communists, who, like the Afghan modernist reformers of the 1920s, had made the transformation of the status of women a central part of their program of state intervention in

Afghan society. Clerics defended traditional marriage practices targeted by the regime (such as the payment of a compensation to the bride's family) and resisted the regime's frequently violent campaign against illiteracy, which also focused on women. For their part, women in Kabul and elsewhere joined the resistance; in places like Kabul many adopted the veil as a symbol of their opposition to the new government.[60]

Viewed within the wider context of Afghan politics, the Taliban were not the first political organization committed to Islamizing Afghan society. In the late nineteenth century, Amir Abdul Rahman (r. 1880–1901) had utilized Islamic law courts to expand the reach of the state and had attempted to ground his monarchical rule in religious precepts.[61] Aimed at expanding royal authority and limiting the power of clerics in some spheres of public life, the codification of Afghan laws in the 1920s synthesized some elements of Pashtunwali and the sharia. It formalized many of the provisions later associated with the Taliban: adulterers were to be lashed or stoned to death, and non-Muslims such as Hindus were to wear distinctive badges.[62]

Decades later, the mujahedin pursued a more ambitious project of Islamization. Between 1992 and 1996, Rabbani's government imposed severe restrictions on women and sought to exclude them from public life. Gulbuddin Hekmatyar, a mujahedin commander and chief beneficiary of American, Saudi, and Pakistani support against the Soviets, distinguished himself as a proponent of the disciplining of Afghan women in refugee camps in Pakistan; and his followers were credited with acid attacks on unveiled women there. As Neamatollah Nojumi notes in his essay in this book, Hekmatyar's fighters claimed religious legitimation for the rocket attacks on Kabul in the early 1990s that claimed the lives of thousands of male and female civilians.[63]

While notable Taliban figures—including Mullah Omar—joined

in the jihad against the communists, the mujahedin parties must be distinguished from the movement that would become the Taliban. Islamist intellectuals such as Rabbani and Hekmatyar led these parties in exile. From Pakistan and Iran, they operated patronage networks stretching from the Afghan refugee camps and madrasas to the headquarters of guerrilla fighters in Afghanistan. Based in urban centers and led primarily by university professors and engineers inspired by foreign Islamist thinkers, these parties offered Afghans models of religious authority that were far removed from the everyday and locally oriented piety of diverse Afghan communities. They controlled access to weapons, food, and other resources that they received from the United States and Saudi Arabia, but they never dominated the minds of the fighters on the ground. Members of local communities frequently affiliated with more than one party or personality in order to receive patronage, but they largely kept party ideologies at a distance.

When Arab countries began funneling oil money in support of the jihad in the early 1980s, disputes emerged among Afghan resistance leaders about the extent to which these Arab donors' notions of proper religious practice would be imposed on Afghans. As David Edwards has noted, the head of the party that received the most Arab support provoked controversy when he changed his name from "servant of the Prophet" (Abdul Rasul) to "servant of God of the Prophet" (Abdul Rabb al-Rasul) and grew a lengthy beard; his critics charged that, in giving up a name that some Arabs judged polytheistic, he "was even willing to change his name and his appearance" to curry favor with his Wahhabi patrons.[64] Such leaders succeeded in eliminating secular and liberal alternatives to their predominance, as Nojumi's essay shows, but they were unable to unify the resistance commanders scattered throughout Afghanistan, or, after the fall of the communist regime, to construct a viable postcommunist state.

At the same time, the Islamizing project of the Taliban was a direct outgrowth of the Cold War. The United States committed some $3 billion dollars in covert aid to the anti-Soviet jihad. The Saudis matched this funding. To guarantee Pakistani cooperation, Washington offered $1.5 billion in military aid and overlooked the development of Islamabad's nuclear bomb program.[65] Together the Soviets and Americans transferred nearly $11 billion in weapons to the warring parties in Afghanistan.[66] Heroin and opium smuggling also fueled the anticommunist struggle. The conflict laid the foundations of a vast network of guerilla fighters—including future members of al-Qaeda—who reemerged in conflict zones throughout the globe in subsequent years.

The American anticommunists' preference for Muslim radicals was of crucial importance for future developments. Looking back to the American experience in Vietnam, American politicians saw an opportunity to "bleed the Russians." They publicly called the mujahedin "freedom fighters" and dismissed those who pointed to the danger of supporting "fundamentalists" or who advocated identifying secular-minded Afghan elites. William Casey, director of the Central Intelligence Agency, apparently saw an affinity between Catholicism and Islam as threats to the Soviet Union. If Catholicism could serve as an oppositional force in Poland, Casey reasoned, Islam could do the same in Central Asia. He even proposed sending translations of the Quran in local languages with the hope of stirring unrest among Muslims in the neighboring Soviet republics. While Washington may have tried to provoke the Soviet invasion by supplying anticommunists in Afghanistan in July 1979, it certainly tried to prolong the war after the Soviets began plans for withdrawal. In the end, the United States insisted on a government of Islamists that excluded communist representation. Joined by the Kuwaitis and Iraqis, the Saudis and Americans continued to fund the mujahedin after the Soviet withdrawal.[67]

Unleashed by the United States and Pakistan, the mujahedin—together with the weapons and drugs networks that sustained them—proved difficult to control. Despite their increasing resort to ethnic categories in search of clients, the resistance leaders failed to hold the loyalties of their fighters or reach sustained agreements with their rivals. As the target of their internecine struggles, the population of Kabul suffered. Rockets rained down on the residents of the capital, who in turn relied on international aid to survive. Even as the United States turned its attention away from the conflict, the mujahedin commanders continued to look to Afghanistan's neighbors—Pakistan, India, Russia, Iran, and the Central Asian republics—for leverage against their foes. Amid the humanitarian catastrophe, many remained committed to Islamizing Afghanistan while they fought one another for control of Kabul.

The Taliban emerged in southern Afghanistan, as one of their diplomats in New York later explained, "to free Afghanistan from the vicious circle of anarchy, chaos, and corruption" caused by the mujahedin—and to combat moral disarray and irreligion.[68] The reputation of the student movement for simple piety aided their rise in Pashtun areas where mujahedin commanders had abused local populations, betraying their religious commitments and undermining their authority. The Taliban leaders included veterans of the jihad, and spokesmen such as Abdul Hakim Mujahed would later claim that, as "Islamic students," they fought valiantly as in times past "whenever a foreign power invaded Afghanistan and threatened [the] freedom and independence of the Afghans." Thus, the Taliban would assert that they "played a paramount role in mobilizing, planning, and directing the holy Jihad."[69]

Despite such attempts to position themselves at the vanguard of the anticommunist struggle as the most authentic and pure saviors of a traditionalist Afghanistan, the movement brought something novel and unique to the Afghan political scene. The group was headed by mullahs, a social group who enjoyed only modest prestige before the jihad. The Taliban highlighted the fact that they represented a challenge to the generation of Islamist party leaders and commanders who had squandered their time in power. While constantly invoking tradition, they presented themselves as a new force in Afghan politics and, at times, as hostile critics of an alien Afghan culture.

In key respects, then, this was more than a clerical movement, because it also drew on the power of youth. It took on the name of the madrasa students, not their teachers. Its authority derived less from power in secular matters, like that exercised by khans or other elders and men of influence, than from religious authority and military prowess. Here, too, youth challenged the age hierarchies of Afghan society. Socialized in an all-male environment in the boarding schools and orphanages that made up the madrasa network along the Afghan-Pakistan border, the young soldiers of the movement had only the faintest, if any, memories of pre-revolutionary Afghanistan. Many were under fourteen years of age. "It is not the values of the village," William Maley has argued, "but the values of the village *as interpreted by refugee camp dwellers or madrasa students most of whom have never known ordinary village life* that the Taliban seek to impose on places like Kabul."[70]

In a country in which some 30 percent of Afghan children had engaged in some kind of fighting, the Taliban—like their opponents—called on children to fight. Truckloads of child soldiers arrived from the Pakistani madrasas in advance of major Taliban offenses. In fact, in January 2002 the first American fatality in Afghanistan may have come at the hands of a fourteen-year-old sniper in Paktya Province. American forces identified several other young fighters as Taliban or al-Qaeda and eventually imprisoned several of them at their detention facility at Guantanamo Bay.[71] After 2001 the intergenerational tensions at the heart of the movement continued to animate Taliban radicalism. In the first half of 2005, the Taliban claimed credit for a series of very uncommon occurrences in Afghanistan: the murder of roughly a dozen mullahs. They had punished their superiors, a spokesman explained, because the mullahs had supported "the presence of Jews and Christians in Afghanistan." In April 2007 a pro-Taliban group released a propaganda video showing a young Afghan boy beheading a Taliban fighter who had supposedly betrayed the movement by becoming a spy.[72]

The Taliban differed from their mujahedin predecessors, too, in their conception of the "Islamic state." In 1992 the mujahedin had announced the formation of this mode of government, but the Taliban would devise a very different model for their "emirate." Their peculiar understanding of this form of rule was shaped less by distant foreign models than by the history of Afghanistan and its shared frontier with Pakistan. Viewed within a broader time frame, the Taliban movement can be traced to the emergence of sectarian groups under British colonial rule in India. In 1867, Sunni Muslim scholars committed to "reform" of the faith founded the madrasa of Deoband in northern India. They targeted the visitation of shrines and reverence for charismatic holy men and other forms of devotion favored by the common folk; and they reserved special enmity for Shiites.[73] From the nineteenth century, Afghans looked to Deoband for religious instruction, and despite repeated bans issued by Kabul to discourage young Afghans from studying with the Deobandis, the teachings of this institution spread widely within communities in Afghanistan.[74]

In the postcolonial period, a network of madrasas affiliated with Deoband spread throughout India and, especially, Pakistan. The Deobandis represented a major force in Pakistani politics, particularly since the reign of Prime Minister Zulfiqar Ali Bhutto (1971–1977), who tried to broaden popular support for his regime by selectively accommodating the demands of Islamists and the ulama. Under pressure exerted by the political arm of the Deobandi ulama, the Jamiat Ulema-e-Islam, and similar groups, Pakistan's military dictatorship Islamized the country's legal codes and expanded madrasa construction. The Soviet invasion of Afghanistan in 1979 triggered an exodus of more than three million refugees to Pakistan. The Jamiat Ulema-e-Islam's network of madrasas then extended into the refugee camps established in the North West Frontier and Baluchistan provinces bordering Afghanistan. This and similar groups provided the Afghan refugees with social services. Offering free room and board, their schools took in orphaned and impoverished Afghan children.

Beginning in the early 1980s, Pakistani Deobandis led campaigns against Shiites (who made up some 15 to 25 percent of the Pakistani population). Here, too, the Cold War context contributed to radicalization and sectarian violence that persists to the present: Muhammad Qasim Zaman notes that "this sectarian militancy has been led by lower-ranking ulama, who have tended to combine a humble socio-economic background and madrasa training with, often, military training in Afghanistan in the course of the Afghan struggle against Soviet occupation or during the subsequent civil war."[75] Paradoxically, it was during Benazir Bhutto's second term as prime minister (1993–1996) that the Harvard- and Oxford-educated female head of state struck an alliance with the Jamiat Ulema-e-Islam to advance Pakistan's interests in Afghanistan through the Taliban. Their anti-Shiite creed was thus very much molded by the sectarian environment of Pakistan, where the Deobandi madrasas and their political affiliates had made violent anti-Shiism a central platform of their strategy to mobilize Islamist sentiment.

While the Taliban shared ideological affinities with the Pakistani religious parties who had assisted their rise to power, their leadership introduced a highly distinctive form of rule. The Taliban leadership valued secrecy and attempted to shield its inner workings from outside view.[76] Even before the Taliban became concerned that their dealings with bin Laden had attracted the unfriendly attention of foreign security services, its clerical elite cultivated confidentiality. Eager to project an image of humble piety and disinterested justice, they fostered an aura of anonymity. Mullah Omar avoided being photographed and scarcely appeared in public. Omar had not distinguished himself during the anti-Soviet jihad; indeed, accounts of his activities and affiliations with various Islamist parties during the war are sketchy and contradictory.[77] Of common birth and only intermediate clerical education, Omar seems to have limited others' access to him in order to forge the image of a charismatic persona. Like the movement's foot soldiers, he scorned the capital. He did not move there from Kandahar, even when the Taliban seized Kabul in September 1996. Remaining in the heart of the Pashtun belt, Omar eschewed the cosmopolitanism—and factionalism—of the multiethnic and polyglot capital.

His only appearance in front of a large crowd was a pivotal moment in the history of the movement: in April 1996 he spoke before a crowd of some fifteen hundred clerics in Kandahar. At this gathering, Omar, then in his mid-thirties, improvised a novel political ritual, once again breaking with Afghan rulers before him: at this gathering, he staged an exceptionally rare public viewing of a cloak said to belong to Muhammad, and said to have miraculous qualities, in order to claim for himself the legacy of the Prophet and to assert that the Taliban ruled in continuity with the first embattled community of Islam. After raising the sacred garment before the clerics gathered below the mausoleum that housed the object, Omar received their blessing, along with the title Commander of the Faithful *(Amir al-Muminin)*, which only one nineteenth-century Afghan ruler had held before him.[78] While he continued to bear the name *Mujahed* in his pronouncements, the title implied an assertion of authority over Muslims throughout the world.

Similarly, the Taliban held up the "first Islamic government, created in Medina by the Prophet Mohammad" as the model for their state. Upon seizing Kabul, however, the Taliban would demarcate the national boundaries of their territory by calling their government the "Islamic Emirate of Afghanistan."[79] This disjuncture reflected contradictions—and political contestation—at the core of the movement.

Like other revolutionary regimes, the Taliban state had utopian visions but remained captive to the society and international context in which it functioned; more important, would-be state builders had to contend with the legacy of the Afghan state tradition and its historic dependency on outside powers for support. Even the most revolutionary Taliban practice—the administration of justice—was ultimately contained, like other Islamic legal systems in the modern era, within a hierarchical appellate structure culminating in a "Supreme Court." In practice, the Taliban government consisted of two parts: a six-man "council" headed by Omar that remained in Kandahar and a "council of ministers" composed of twenty-three ministries inherited from previous regimes. The Taliban adapted the traditional ministerial government of Afghanistan to its purposes by placing the ministries under the control of the Kandahari council. But unlike previous governments in Kabul, a cleric appointed from Kandahar now headed each ministry. "We must pray to the Almighty," announced an organ of the Taliban leadership in July 1997, "that under the leadership of the clergy we should always have peace, security, and stability in our country."[80]

And like other revolutionary states, despite the strategic secrecy of Mullah Omar, the Taliban could not stop talking about themselves and performing public rites to dramatize their Islamizing agenda. But this was propaganda of the word and the theater, rather than that of the image. Radio has been their principal medium for communicating their message to a population marked by multilingualism but low rates of literacy. The street was their theater. Yet they also developed various print resources, including an Internet site and newspapers in a variety of languages in Afghanistan and, through their sympathizers in the religious parties, in Pakistan. Increasingly after 2001, Taliban spokesmen turned to "night letters"—leaflets distributed to the doors of homes at night in villages and towns—as well as to satellite television and Internet outlets to distribute their messages.

However, the iconoclasm and indeed the iconophobia of the Taliban further distinguished them from the mujahedin. In the struggle against the Soviets, Afghan fighters, like the Ayatollah Khomeini's revolutionaries before them, distributed images of fallen "martyrs" widely, though unlike previous Afghan rulers—and even their revolutionary neighbors in Iran—they excluded women from the ranks of heroes whose lives were to be celebrated as models for others. When the Taliban came to power, death became more anonymous. They banned photographs and the commemoration of martyrs, practices that had been central to the resistance parties' propaganda on behalf of the jihad.[81]

While the mujahedin had harassed and brutalized women and ethnic rivals, and the Rabbani government had created a Department for the Promotion of Virtue and the Prevention of Vice, the Taliban break from their rivals was striking in this respect as well. Alongside a new ministry for refugees and victims of the war, the chief Taliban innovation in reworking the Afghan state-building legacy was the creation of an aggressive Ministry for the Promotion of Virtue and the Prevention of Vice. Drawing perhaps on Rabbani's department, this new institution was apparently also inspired by similar institutions in the Persian Gulf states with whom the Taliban leadership had extensive contacts.[82] Omar's public decrees regarding the responsibilities of the ministry identified one of its duties as the enforcement of Hanafi legal principles, though critics charged that, in practice, the Taliban confused Pashtunwali with the sharia.[83] Mullah Omar's decrees are revealing in so far as they concentrate on aspects of the sharia that the Taliban leadership identified as most significant: they detail rules about the dress and comportment of women, men's beards and hair, the wearing of turbans, and other symbols of Muslim piety that were the focus of the Taliban's campaign to Islamize an ostensibly sinful land.[84]

For the residents of Kabul, Herat, and Mazar-e Sharif, the zealous personnel of this ministry represented the face of the Taliban order. They patrolled the streets armed with whips, radio antennas, and Kalashnikovs searching for violators of Taliban rules regarding mosque attendance, dress, music, and other matters of public decorum over which they asserted clerical authority. Young people were drawn to this form of power. But like other police forces the world over, they also received assistance from community members who may have either sympathized with their vision of Islam or who hoped to use them against personal enemies. In Konduz, for example, the Pashtun youth Gulbuddin and his fellow Taliban enforcers got help from locals who offered "tips" about neighbors who violated Taliban bans on music and television. Among their local supporters,

Gulbuddin identified barbers as "the biggest Taliban supporters because we always provided them with steady work."[85]

In policing the urban population, the young clerical students and fighters attached to the ministry injected new forms of violence into Afghan cities. To be sure, tens of thousands of Kabulis and Heratis had suffered during the Soviet onslaught; and the mujahedin militias recklessly bombed whole city blocks in their struggle for power following the flight of the communists. Many of the mujahedin parties held Taliban-like views of women, and Hekmatyar, the favorite of the Pakistanis and Americans, led forces that committed numerous atrocities against women and other civilians. Commanders like Hekmatyar faulted their victims, accusing them of being "unbelievers." Yet the Taliban resort to brutality had more than strategic aims, like seizing particular neighborhoods in the capital; it was about creating a new world. It was both more commonplace as a strategy of rule in everyday life and more oriented toward spectacle and the punishment of the godless: the Taliban conducted public executions of alleged adulterers, homosexuals, and others by stoning, crushing by tank, hanging, and machine gun. Taliban violence was more systematic than that of their predecessors of the civil war period; the mujahedin robbed, raped, and rocketed civilian populations in search of profits and power, but the Taliban had more utopian aspirations, though they, too, sought to control territory and accumulate resources. The Taliban approach was more intimate, and their choice of targets, including elders, women, and, more recently, mullahs, broke with traditional taboos.

The Taliban forcibly introduced new religious practices to many communities. The movement drew strength from villages and their antipathy for the city, but it was also committed to the reform of religious life everywhere.[86] The Taliban did not simply impose the mores of the imaginary pre-war village on the city. Indeed, they assaulted religious practices shared in common by urban and rural Afghans.

For the first time in Afghan history, celebration of Nowruz, the first day of the year according to the solar calendar, was prohibited. The Taliban Radio Voice of Sharia declared the holiday "un-Islamic," and police banned Afghans from visiting ancestors' graves, as Afghan men and women had done for centuries past. The Taliban tried to do away with the solar calendar altogether, replacing it with the lunar calendar followed in Arab lands.[87]

At the same time, the Taliban were not the passive transmitters of the religious ideology of al-Qaeda or other Arab missionaries, as many post–September 11 accounts have claimed. Of course, they remained dependent upon the madrasas and financial resources of the Afghan-Pakistan frontier. In that sense they were by definition a cross-national phenomenon—like the Pashtun communities from which they drew their ranks. At the same time, the Taliban raised their own domestic revenues from taxing opium and heroin, the lucrative transit trade between Iran and Pakistan, and the export of lumber and other commodities. Their opponents frequently accused them of expropriating property as well. Omar may have grown closer to bin Laden toward the end of his rule, but the extent to which this affected Taliban policies remains unclear. Bin Laden praised (and perhaps encouraged) the destruction of the Buddhas of Bamyan, but this spectacle did not prevent the Taliban Foreign Ministry from seeking international recognition—and the critical financial resources upon which all Afghan states have depended—from abroad. The Taliban ban on the cultivation of hashish in 1999 and of opium in 2000 were measures intended, in part, to improve the image of the regime in the international community. If one constant of Taliban rule was the activity of the Ministry for the Promotion of Virtue and Prevention of Vice, the other was the Taliban desire for Afghanistan's seat at the United Nations (a post initially reserved for the once pro-Taliban Karzai).

In a statement of April 9, 2001, the head of al-Qaeda praised

Omar for "great Islamic decisions, the most recent of which include the destruction of the idols, the prohibition of growing opium, and the proud stance against the campaign of global unbelief."[88] Yet Omar appears to have been somewhat less interested in the problem of "global unbelief." As Robert D. Crews notes in his essay, the visit by a Chechen delegation did not bring about grand expressions of solidarity between the Taliban and the Chechen rebels, as is frequently imagined in newsrooms and spy agencies, but instead yielded bitter arguments, mutual incomprehension, and, on the Chechen side, a bewildered rejection of the Islamic legal prescriptions of their Taliban hosts. For his part, bin Laden seems to have operated autonomously of Omar: Khost, the site of al-Qaeda bases that the Clinton administration bombed in August 1998, was never a Taliban stronghold. Though inhabited by Pashtuns, Khost was a center of unrest and sought to maintain distance from the Kandahar-centered regime. The limits of the Taliban's internationalist commitments became apparent again in 2001 when, despite having lashed out at the international community with the Bamyan events, the regime nonetheless accepted payment from Washington for its anti-drugs campaign. In 2001, commentators concluded that Afghanistan was the critical nexus of al-Qaeda activities. But this may have been only partly true. If such networks can be identified with fixed locales—a dubious proposition—then Hamburg may have been a more likely candidate. Alternatively, the Indian Ocean and, since 2003, Iraq and the tribal areas of Pakistan are spaces that have allowed for the circulation of radicals, with or without a Taliban regime in power.[89]

Numerous observers—critics and defenders alike—have still taken at face value the traditionalist rhetoric of the movement. Wahid Muzhda, an official who worked in the Taliban Ministry of Foreign Affairs and who, since 2001, has remade himself as an authority on the movement, has depicted it primarily as a phenomenon reflecting the worldview of rural and uneducated Afghans.[90] Outside of Afghanistan, expatriate figures such as Hamid Karzai spoke on behalf of many Pashtuns in defending the Taliban as representatives of the popular will. Similarly, in an essay in the *Washington Post* in early October 1996, Zalmay Khalilzad, the future Bush administration ambassador to Afghanistan and, later, Iraq and the United Nations, vouched for their ostensibly traditionalist credentials. Simultaneously lobbying on behalf of the oil company Unocal, Khalilzad likened their religiosity to that of America's geopolitical allies in Saudi Arabia, arguing, "The Taliban does not practice the anti-U.S. style of fundamentalism practiced by Iran—it is closer to the Saudi model." In this view, the Islam of the Taliban was a legitimate form of local culture, little more than "a mix of traditional Pashtun values and an orthodox interpretation of Islam." Indeed, he saw nothing serious to object to in Taliban ideology. He cited rumors of bin Laden's departure from Afghanistan as further evidence of "some common interest between the United States and the Taliban."[91]

For their part, opponents of the Taliban, who frequently linked them to supposedly analogous Islamist movements and parties in the Middle East, the Caucasus, Central Asia, Africa, and South Asia, tended to forget the role of Moscow and Washington and their proxy warriors in laying the path for the rise of the Taliban. Many of them also neglected the human rights abuses of the mujahedin, including those that formed the Northern Alliance that aligned with U.S. forces against the Taliban, and seemed to imagine that the misogyny of the Taliban was somehow representative of Muslim societies everywhere. Although the wearing of the burqa preceded the Taliban, and has persisted after 2001, it became synonymous with Taliban rule and of the dangers of Islamic law.[92]

The revival of the Taliban—or, as Amin Tarzi shows in his essay, the "reinvention" of the movement—since 2001 confirms that the Taliban play a more complicated role in Afghanistan and the wider region than a narrow focus on veiling will reveal. Afghans may have begun to defect from the regime on the eve of its fall in 2001, in part because it failed to alleviate suffering caused by a severe drought.[93] Out of power, however, proponents of the movement have retained, or regained, a certain appeal, especially given the many failures of the post-Taliban government to improve the lives of Afghans in many regions of the country.[94] Six years later, the Taliban clearly have not lost sight of their vision for Afghanistan, nor have many Afghans fully abandoned their support for the movement.

Despite parliamentary and presidential elections and internationally supported reconstruction efforts, the Taliban have transformed themselves into a guerilla movement fighting against the Karzai government as well as American- and NATO-led forces and have become the most deadly opposition force in the country. With Afghanistan leading the world in opium production, revenues from this trade dominating the Afghan economy, insurgent military expertise arriving in the country from the front lines of the Iraq war, and NATO increasingly becoming divided on the mandate of its Afghan mission, the Taliban appear poised to offer even more serious challenges to their opponents.

Our inquiry into the problem of the Taliban begins with a basic historical question. Are the Taliban, a militantly traditionalist movement, in fact a new phenomenon in Afghan history, and a modern one at that? Most observers have come to see the Taliban essentially as a foreign creation, an instrument of Pakistan's geopolitical interests in the post–Cold War world. At the same time, many have pointed to the movement's utopian theology harkening back to an imagined period of early Islamic purity to characterize the movement as essentially "medieval" and "antimodern." What is missing from this view, as many contributors demonstrate in their essays, is a consideration of the many continuities and ruptures in Afghan history.

Chapter 1 tackles one of the most disputed themes in the study of Afghan politics by focusing on the Pashtun community as the historic key to ruling Afghanistan. Challenging the primary role commonly attributed to Pakistan, Abdulkader Sinno shows that other Pashtun groups received far greater resources from abroad, but that only the Taliban have managed to integrate, or otherwise marginalize, Pashtun elites in their rise to power. The Taliban received broad support from war-weary Pashtun communities not simply because they were fellow Pashtuns and zealous Muslims or because they wielded money and strategic support from al-Qaeda and Pakistan. Rather, the Taliban managed to accomplish their goals because they were skillful at engaging in local, intra-Pashtun politics. Far from stepping into a power vacuum, as many have claimed, the Taliban gained the backing of Pashtun notables and their clients by co-opting or bypassing tribal elites, presenting themselves as neutral actors, and insisting that they were unlike recent rulers.

If Taliban success among Pashtuns hinged on their mastery of the tribal milieu, the groundwork for their ascendance was laid in the religious sphere in the 1980s and early 1990s by the interplay of the domestic and international factors that first set the stage for the rise of Islamism in Afghanistan. In Chapter 2, Neamatollah Nojumi concentrates on the critical linkages forged during the civil war between the Afghan political parties based in Pakistan and Iran and the localized centers of the anti-Soviet resistance within Afghanistan. In reconstructing these networks, Nojumi argues that the institutionalization of Islamism in Afghanistan was far from a natural outgrowth of indigenous Afghan politics. The marginalization of alternative resistance leaders and the rise of clerical rule grew instead out of the patronage networks established in Islamabad and Tehran, which linked the Islamist agendas of Afghanistan's neighbors to support for a small number of Afghan Islamists, who waged war against other kinds of political leaders. Pakistan, in particular, came to wield influence not only over elites but over the more than three-million-strong Afghan refugee population within its borders. The Taliban that emerged from these camps and their madrasas grew out of an alliance of regional powers and a handful of radical Afghan and Pakistani Islamists.

Born in the Cold War and endowed with an extraordinary capacity to survive, the Taliban phenomenon has been anything but a throwback to medieval times. Chapter 3 presents an exhaustive analysis of the repressive gender policies of the Taliban in power. Arguing that the Taliban presented themselves as an alternative modernity—an "Islamic countermodernity"—Juan R. I. Cole shows how the Taliban utilized modern techniques of rule, from mass spectacle to surveillance, tanks, and radio, both to challenge tribal custom and to redraw the boundaries between public and private. The regulation of gender roles was crucial to the Taliban project, just as it has been central to other modern orders. What fundamentally distinguished the Taliban from contemporary societies elsewhere was their brutal insistence on projecting power in novel ways: by dramatically privatizing women and making religion public.

Whereas Cole highlights that which was new about Taliban rule, M. Nazif Shahrani explores, from the perspective of state building, how the Taliban movement conforms to structural features of Afghan politics in earlier periods. In Chapter 4, Shahrani shows how ruling elites drawn from the Pashtun tribes have repeatedly tried to forge a state dominated by Pashtuns. Beginning in 1880, Shahrani argues, Pashtun elites have embarked on a project of "internal colonialism," subjugating non-Pashtuns in a series of violent campaigns. Even Taliban attitudes toward women, Shahrani notes, had historical precedents. Cleavages between Pashtuns and non-Pashtuns proved to be particularly explosive during the Taliban era because non-Pashtuns had, since the civil war and the collapse of centralized authority, grown more assertive in expressing their group identities and in demanding political rights, both for administrative and cultural autonomy and for a stake in Afghan politics at the national level. "Talibanism" is hardly a novelty, Shahrani contends, and this ideology, fed by the conflicting political ambitions of Pashtuns and non-Pashtuns, appears likely to persist.

Like Shahrani, Lutz Rzehak examines how non-Pashtuns have perceived the Pashtun-dominated Taliban. Drawing on fieldwork in the southwestern province of Nimroz, in Chapter 5 Rzehak recounts how Baluch communities maintained complex relations with local Pashtuns, and how this changed after the arrival of not one, but two, very different Taliban governments. Rzehak's attention to the centrality of oral communication in Afghanistan reveals the complex ways in which the Baluch have remembered the period of Taliban rule and how these rearticulate boundaries among Afghanistan's diverse communities. These stories, songs, prayers, and poems shed light on how Afghans have viewed the world around them and how, in the face of shifting international politics and access to radio, television, and other mass media, these modes of understanding continuously change.

In Chapter 6, Robert L. Canfield also explores the emergence of new identities among Muslims of Afghanistan and the surrounding region. Canfield reconstructs how the varied groups that would ultimately constitute the Taliban became linked to international Islamist networks, which insisted on the globalization of formerly localized grievances. According to Canfield, Afghan Islamists have for the first time begun to link their fate to that of like-minded thinkers in Palestine, Iraq, and elsewhere. They also share, he argues, a cosmology and eschatology that posits the necessity of consigning power to religious authorities because the end of days draws near.

Despite the attraction of such ideas for many constituencies within the movement, the Taliban nonetheless remained internally heterogeneous. Several essays approach the movement as a dynamic and variegated composite of different actors whose alliances shifted as a result of internal contests for power and external challenges. The seemingly invincible orphans and madrasa students that sped from victory to victory in fleets of Toyota trucks in the mid-1990s experienced a difficult time when they turned to constructing a state to claim legitimacy and guarantee survival in the international system. Like previous Afghan regimes, the Taliban confronted the task of ruling a country with a diverse population, rugged geography, weak infrastructure, and interfering neighbors.

The trials of ruling Afghanistan proved more difficult for the Taliban than has been previously understood. Important internal differences emerged within the movement. When the Taliban began to seek international recognition as a legitimate Afghan government, self-identified "moderates" presented the world with a different face. In Chapter 7, Robert D. Crews argues that the challenges of state building and the continued need for international support compelled factions within the regime to construct an alternative means of engaging foreign states and organizations and interacting with Afghan populations where the reach of the state was limited. For the benefit of a foreign audience, Taliban interlocutors helped create the category of "moderate Taliban," and domestically they adopted nationalist rhetoric. Thus the conflicts among competing currents within the movement depended upon the success of Taliban strategies of rule and how local communities responded to them.

This internal differentiation and ideological dexterity allowed parts of the movement to return to politics—and ultimately mount several distinct insurgencies—following their dispersal in 2001. In Chapter 8, Amin Tarzi shows how the movement fragmented as it collapsed. While some Taliban elites benefited from amnesties offered by the new U.S.-backed Afghan leadership and others were the target of official campaigns to integrate moderate Taliban, Mullah Omar and many of his closest followers scattered. Tarzi argues that a variety of groups, each with distinct goals and strategies, have reemerged to claim the Taliban name. Although these groups may not reflect any unified structure, or even real continuity in personnel, these "neo-Taliban," as Tarzi calls them, form the central nodes around which a patchwork of groups has begun to coalesce in opposition to the government of Hamid Karzai and his foreign sponsors. Backed by international militant networks, and in part by local Pashtun populations who are alienated from Kabul and oppose the presence of the United States and other NATO member states, these disparate groups fighting under the Taliban banner have demonstrated that this symbol retains its power among many Afghans. Disappointed by unfulfilled promises of security and reconstruction, and distrustful of foreign soldiers, the poppy farmers of Helmand have joined numerous Afghans in other provinces in looking again to the Taliban for salvation.

As Atiq Sarwari and Crews show in the epilogue, the post-Taliban Afghan government, handicapped by a deep historical legacy and a neocolonial foreign presence, has failed to create alternatives to the vision of order offered by the Taliban. Indeed, the politics of the post-Taliban state spawned heterogeneous insurgencies whose popular support base grew steadily in 2006 and 2007 and which threatened to pose an even greater challenge to the government in Kabul and regional stability in 2008. Drawing together these strands of inquiry, this closing chapter traces structural continuities in the nature of Afghanistan's crisis from the Taliban collapse through the present period marked by American-backed reconstruction and Taliban-led insurgencies.

CHAPTER ONE

Explaining the Taliban's Ability to Mobilize the Pashtuns

Abdulkader Sinno

If history is any guide, whoever mobilizes the Pashtuns rules Afghanistan, and Afghanistan cannot be ruled without their consent. Two rulers with little support among the Pashtuns—the Tajiks Habibullah Kalakani and the savvy Ahmad Shah Masud—tried and failed. Great powers, including the British and the Soviets, and their client regimes also faltered in similar ways. The United States has so far postponed a wider insurgency only by avoiding the disarmament of local leaders and the disruption of poppy production. Neither the United States nor its client Hamid Karzai rule Afghanistan, and they are far from having a monopoly on the use of violence within its borders. Since 1978 only the Taliban have managed to mobilize the Pashtuns. Moreover, they have done so with fewer resources, less expertise in institution building, and in a shorter period of time than others who tried and failed. Why did the Taliban then enjoy this unique success in mobilizing Pashtuns?

The Taliban grew from a small group of idealistic students with little military training into a sprawling organization that dominated some 90 percent of Afghanistan in less than five years. They swept away all the warlords who partitioned and terrorized the country—petty and mighty alike—with the single exception of Masud's organization, to impose a nearly unified political order for the first time since 1979.

The rise of the Taliban represents one of those events that social scientists have accepted rather more than analyzed. Most existing interpretations of the rise of the Taliban are either politically or ideologically motivated, or they simply lack rigor. These explanations point to causes (for example, why the Taliban grew) but fail to explain the processes that led to their emergence and nearly successful unification of Afghanistan when all other attempts had failed. Compelling interpretations are scarce because of a shortage of reliable information about what really happened during the first critical months of the Taliban's quest. Afghanistan was ignored because of its insignificance and seeming irrelevance to the West, and because feuding local leaders made it one of the least hospitable places in the world for academics and journalists alike.

Yet the rise of the Taliban constitutes an important social scientific puzzle that warrants more attention. Any successful analysis must explain how they mobilized the Pashtuns, and must meet a crucial test: It must account for the failure of other Pashtuns—including the Afghan communists, Gulbuddin Hekmatyar, and even Hamid Karzai—to do the same.

Existing explanations remain inadequate. Many highlight foreign factors, particularly Pakistani military support and Saudi financing. Others focus on developments within Afghanistan, pointing especially to a political "vacuum," ethnic strife, and the general state of exhaustion of a war-torn Afghan society.

The answer lies instead in the fact that the Taliban were able to assimilate or sideline many entrenched and hardened local Pashtun leaders by (1) undercutting the leaders' support and directly appealing to their supporters, (2) capitalizing on their own momentum to increase their appeal to local leaders and their followers alike, and (3) making effective use of expert knowledge of the Pashtun power tapestry and devising sophisticated strategies that sidelined opposition at little cost. Solving the puzzle of the rise of the Taliban highlights the tribulations of the American-backed state-building project and helps us assess the odds of a further reemergence of the Taliban. At the same time, it sheds light on the underlying processes involved in the production of prior social upheavals—such as the tribal revolts in Afghanistan and elsewhere, the Mongol conquests, and perhaps even the early stages of the great venture of Islam—that have channeled, focused, and amplified energies in similar societies.

In 1979 the brutal Soviet invasion produced a loosely structured Afghan resistance that was mostly brought together by the flow of money from sponsors and the clarity of the mujahedin's cause. In 1989 the Soviets left a devastated and disordered Afghanistan. The withdrawal of the Soviets generated euphoria among the mujahedin and their supporters. Virtually all observers and participants predicted that the regime of Najibullah, the communist leader left in place by the Soviets, would collapse within a year. The United States and Pakistan attempted to give the mujahedin the trappings of an alternative government by encouraging them to form the Afghan Interim Government and by supplying them with better weapons. This government was a facade, however, and the Pakistanis increased their support for their traditional favorite among the mujahedin, Gulbuddin Hekmatyar, and his faction, the Hizb-e Islami (Islamic Party), in hopes of imposing a unified organizational structure under the influence of Islamabad.

In 1992 the Soviet-crafted regime in Kabul collapsed when its constituent factions realized that the flow of resources from Moscow was about to dry up. As the government fell apart, Pashtun officials went over to Hekmatyar. Shia figures sided with the main Shia resistance party, the Hizb-e Wahdat-e Islami-ye Afghanistan (Party of Islamic Unity of Afghanistan); and a faction of the Afghan communist party, the Parchamis, joined Ahmad Shah Masud's resistance group, the well-organized Supervisory Council (Shura-ye Nazar). The communist regime's strongest militia under Abdul Rashid Dostum defected and entered the conflict as the National Islamic Movement of Afghanistan (Junbesh-e Melli-ye Islami-ye Afghanistan).

Aided by foreign sponsors such as Russia, India, Pakistan, Iran, and the Central Asian republics, as well as various Arab states and militants, these competing factions battled for Kabul and other regions, prolonging the damage and suffering caused by the Soviet occupation. In western Afghanistan, the mujahedin commander Ismail Khan consolidated his control over the area around Herat but did not attempt to project his power on a national level. This state of anarchy and shifting alliances persisted until the rise of the Taliban, who forced these rivals into a discordant alliance.

The major factions led by Dostum, Hekmatyar, Masud, Ismail Khan, and Abdul Ali Mazari generally recruited members of specific ethnic groups. But in the fragmented Afghanistan of 1994, they were not alone. They competed with smaller clans and loosely structured councils, with whom they shared their ethnic territories. Once held together by ties of patronage, many of the mujahedin parties splintered when foreign aid ceased to reach their leadership in Peshawar, Pakistan. The more centralized Hizb-e Islami and Jamiat-e Islami-ye Afghanistan, led by Burhanuddin Rabbani, managed to keep the loyalty of some clients intact by maintaining access to foreign aid, which they disbursed among followers as well as centralized fighting units. In lieu of the resources once distributed by the now-defunct Peshawar parties, their former clients sought out new local sources of income, including taxation, road tolls, poppy cultivation, and banditry. Of the large ethnic organizations, Hekmatyar's Hizb-e Islami was the least able to dominate its ethnic space—the Pashtun belt.

The Taliban made their first significant appearance on the Afghan scene when the larger organizations were occupied with fighting each other for control of Kabul.[1] In a well-organized assault in September 1994, the Taliban took control of Spin Boldak, a run-down town that functioned as a border-crossing point for smugglers and that contained an enormous weapons and ammunition depot under the control of Hekmatyar's Hizb-e Islami.[2] A shocked Hekmatyar attributed the success of the Taliban assault on Spin Boldak and their seizure of his weapons cache to support from Pakistani artillery. Indeed, it was with such aid that he himself had been able to take control of the town six years earlier. But where had the Taliban come from?

As students in the religious schools (madrasas) that dot the Afghanistan-Pakistan frontier, talibs frequently participated in the anti-Soviet and anti-Najibullah jihads as members of the mujahedin parties based in Peshawar. Once the jihad ended and the surviving organizations turned their guns against each other, many disgruntled former mujahedin crossed the border to take advantage of the free religious education and room and board provided by the madrasas. Most madrasas belonged to sprawling networks set up and managed by two Pakistani religious parties, the Jamiat Ulema-e-Islam (Association of the Ulama of Islam) led by Mawlana Fazlur Rehman and the Islamist Jama'at-e-Islami (Islamic Party). Because these talibs could no longer look to the Peshawar parties, and because they did not share the modernist anti-tribal Islamism of Hekmatyar, they did not have an organization to push their agenda throughout Afghanistan. The original members of the Taliban came from this pool of talibs that studied in the Jamiat Ulema-e-Islam schools.

One of the Taliban's chief supporters was Nasirullah Khan Babar,

Benazir Bhutto's interior minister and advisor on Afghan affairs. Babar is said to have been the chief advocate of shifting support from Hekmatyar to the Taliban after Hekmatyar failed to break the stalemate around Kabul and the Taliban proved their worth by freeing a Pakistani convoy held captive by militiamen in Kandahar. The liberation of the convoy was particularly significant because Bhutto and Babar were personally involved in making the preparations for the symbolic trip, which they hoped would herald a historic resumption of trade with newly independent Central Asia.

After freeing the Pakistani convoy in November 1994, the Taliban swept through Kandahar, occupied its strategic points, and dismantled its most vicious criminal bands of former government militiamen.[3] They earned much popular approval by disarming all other groups and imposing strict discipline in what had become an extremely lawless and hazardous area. They tore down the numerous checkpoints that extorted money from traders and travelers and imposed a traditional tribal code of social behavior that provided reassurance to a society traumatized by nearly fifteen years of violence. Rumors that they burned poppy fields endeared them to the United States and Pakistan. The Western press was generally positive in its coverage of the emerging movement, comparing the Taliban favorably to the discredited parties that led the jihad, and downplaying their religious zeal.[4]

The Taliban did not rest on their laurels after taking control of Kandahar. In December they promptly moved to occupy the adjacent provinces of Zabul and Uruzgan and faced little resistance. In January they invaded Helmand, a breadbasket province and poppy-growing center. They then expanded through other Pashtun areas, where some commanders joined them and others were disarmed. Along the way, the Taliban eliminated the ubiquitous roadblocks, imposed sharia-based civic order, closed girls' schools, and provided a rare unifying moment in the region's history.

By early 1995 they had reached Hekmatyar's strongholds south and southwest of Kabul and handily routed his forces. Hekmatyar, the ambitious mujahedin leader who had dominated Afghan politics and organized one of the country's most potent organizations, had to flee his base in Chaharasyab, leaving immense resources behind for the victorious Taliban. He would later become the token Pashtun in Rabbani's government before disappearing for a few years from Afghan political life in comfortable exile in Tehran. With little effort, the Taliban also swept through Paktya and Paktika provinces, which had been hotbeds of mujahedin resistance to Soviet and Afghan communists and were home to the Ghilzai Pashtuns.

Masud was initially delighted by the defeat of his old enemy Hekmatyar. He took advantage of Hekmatyar's predicament by attacking his Shia allies in March 1995, finally terminating efforts by the main Shiite party (Hizb-e Wahdat) to maintain a presence in Kabul.[5] The collapse of Hekmatyar's party and the Masud attack left the weakened Shia with no choice but to accept Taliban mediation and surrender their posts and heavy weapons to the Taliban. In the confusion that ensued, both Masud's troops and some of the Shiite troops attacked the Taliban forces instead of giving up their weapons. The Taliban, in turn, killed the head of the Shiite party, Abdul Ali Mazari, who was in their custody. Masud took advantage of the chaos by launching an all-out attack on both the Taliban and the remaining Shiite forces. He outmaneuvered both and pushed the Taliban out of Chaharasyab, Hekmatyar's old base, thereby putting Kabul out of the range of Taliban rockets. Masud finally controlled all of Kabul.

The setback at the gates of Kabul shifted the Taliban's attention to Ismail Khan's Herat-based fiefdom in the west of the country. They aggressively moved from Kandahar toward Herat and the strategic airbase at Shindand in March 1995, prompting Masud to airlift hundreds of fighters to assist Ismail Khan. Masud also contributed his air force to the effort to defend Shindand, subjecting the attackers to some ten to fifteen sorties a day. The Uzbek commander Dostum joined the fray by wresting a part of Badghis Province from a distracted Ismail Khan. The Taliban eventually halted their attacks after suffering hundreds of casualties.

Perhaps heartened by his troops' performance a few months earlier, Ismail Khan attacked the Taliban in August. He captured Girishk in what appears to have been a momentous thrust toward Kandahar, but the Taliban counterattacked his overstretched forces with astounding mobility. This attack forced Ismail Khan's fighters into a disorganized retreat that culminated in the fall of Herat on September 5 and the flight of Ismail Khan to Iran. The mobility of the Taliban troops and their tactical aptitude had taken the seasoned Ismail Khan by surprise and marked a new phase in the conflict. Not only were the Taliban now in control of more than half of the country, including some non-Pashtun areas; they also had acquired expertise in the tactics necessary to challenge their established rivals to the north.

Hekmatyar continued to squabble with Rabbani and Masud from his remaining base in Sarobi, thirty miles east of Kabul, but he finally joined the government as prime minister in June 1996. His situation was desperate: his support from Pakistan was vanishing, and his troops were ready to defect to the Taliban upon contact. Taliban troops indeed advanced with ease in areas inhabited by Ghilzai Pashtuns, taking Jalalabad and Hekmatyar's remaining stronghold in Sarobi. They then attacked Kabul in September 1996, entering the city on September 27 and dispatching their rivals back to their northern strongholds. The front line moved to the Shamali plains north of the capital, an area that would suffer immensely from fighting in the following two years.

The loss of Kabul, however, was not fatal for Masud. The master strategist managed an organized retreat under attack that allowed him to save much of his troops and weapons to fight another day. He also improved his odds for survival by retreating to more favorable terrain and destroying the southern entrance to the Salang tunnel, impeding a Taliban push toward the north. The Taliban occupied the area just south of the Salang and Panjsher in February 1997, including the provincial capital of Chaharikar, but veered toward the Hazarajat to pressure the Shia instead of pushing north.

With the capture of the capital, the Taliban controlled four of Afghanistan's major cities. They made their first attempt to seize the fifth, Mazar-e Sharif, in May 1997. Abdul Malik Pahlawan, the largely autonomous Dostum lieutenant whose area of control west of Mazar lay on the front line, defected to the Taliban on May 19, blaming his patron for the death of his brother. In the process he handed them Ismail Khan, who had taken refuge in the north via Iran after his rout from Herat. Dostum fled to Turkey after fighting broke out in Mazar. On May 25, Islamabad recognized the Taliban as the legitimate government of Afghanistan. Saudi Arabia and the United Arab Emirates did the same in the next two days.

Some Taliban forces were flown to Mazar while others were allowed free passage through the Hindu Kush mountains by Bashir Salangi, a Masud commander who shifted his loyalty to them. Some jubilant Taliban attempted to disarm Abdul Malik's troops and those of the Shiite militias in Mazar, but they faced stiff resistance. A hesitant convert to the Taliban cause, Salangi blocked their retreat and prevented reinforcements from reaching the Taliban in Mazar. Hundreds of Taliban perished in battle. Their foes imprisoned thousands of them, together with key leaders, and later had them murdered. Some three thousand surviving Taliban in the north withdrew to Konduz, where they occupied the airport and received reinforcements. The Mazar debacle embarrassed those states that had extended diplomatic recognition to the Taliban in anticipation of an ultimate victory, and it provided an opening for Masud to make a push for Kabul.

In spite of the Taliban's bold move of changing the country's name to the Islamic Emirate of Afghanistan and Mullah Omar's assumption of the title *Commander of the Faithful*—a title that claims authority beyond state borders—the Taliban seemed unsteady for the remainder of 1997. Masud advanced to within artillery range of Kabul. A Taliban push from Konduz toward Mazar faced fierce resistance. In September, Dostum returned from exile to replace his former betrayer Abdul Malik, whom he sent to exile in Iran. In the meantime, the Shia Wahdat pushed the Taliban to the western edge of Kabul.

The Taliban rivals who made up the Northern Alliance proved to be odd bedfellows, however. In Mazar, the forces of Abdul Malik, Masud, Dostum, and the Wahdat turned on one another. Their wild battles, looting of the offices of charities, and wanton murder of many civilians drove United Nations agencies and NGOs out of the city, depleted it of necessary staples, and made the once-irrelevant trade-off the Taliban offered—security in exchange for the acceptance of a strict social code—particularly appealing for the city's residents. In another indication of the fragmentation of the Northern Alliance, Hekmatyar's forces in the north of the country disarmed the Ismaili force of Mansur Nadiri that was allied with Dostum.[6]

In 1998, several meetings of high-level representatives of Afghanistan's six neighbors, plus America and Russia, did little to reduce conflict in the country, and the Taliban regained the initiative. They embargoed the impoverished Hazarajat, aggravating the effects of an already debilitating drought, and initiated a final assault on Mazar with approximately eight thousand troops. In August they vanquished Dostum and occupied Mazar. In September they moved on Bamyan. The Taliban exacted revenge for the massacre of their comrades in Mazar by killing large numbers of Hazaras and murdering Iranian diplomats in their Mazar consulate. These acts prompted Iranian mobilization of some two hundred thousand troops and skirmishes on the border. Now isolated and under military pressure, Masud retreated on several fronts toward the Panjsher and adjacent valleys. In 2000, Pervez Musharraf openly declared Pakistan's support for the Taliban and their summer campaign that wrested Taloqan from Masud, pushing him from his headquarters and cutting off his main supply lines from Tajikistan.

The Taliban now occupied more than 90 percent of the country. They faced only scattered guerilla resistance in the Hazarajat and the Uzbek regions. Masud, "the Lion of the Panjsher," resisted in his stronghold and executed some brilliant, but ultimately inconsequential, operations to expand his zone before he was assassinated by two al-Qaeda Arabs posing as journalists on September 9, 2001.

Many observers have attributed Taliban success to foreign actors. In this view, the movement was, in effect, Pakistan's creature—created, equipped, trained, and directed by the ISI (the powerful branch of Pakistani military intelligence) and funded by the Arab Gulf. Indian writers are particularly fond of such explanations, but some of the more savvy observers of Afghan affairs make similar arguments.[7] Anthony Davis provides a more potent version of this argument:

> It has become fashionable to portray the meteoric rise of the Taliban as stemming from the complex interplay of social and political conditions prevailing in southern Afghanistan . . . But the Taliban were pre-eminently a military organisation rather than a political movement. In the short space of two years, their numbers multiplied rapidly from a force of less than 100 men, to one of several thousand and finally to one estimated in late 1996 to number at least 30,000–35,000

troops with a functioning brigade and divisional structure. It was equipped with armour, a notably effective artillery arm, a small air force, an impressive communications network and an intelligence system. The organizational skills and logistical wherewithal required to assemble from scratch, expand, and maintain such an integrated fighting machine during a period of continuous hostilities are simply not to be found in Pakistani madrassas or Afghan villages. Covert Pakistani support for the Taliban can thus be inferred to have been fundamental if not to the movement's political inception then at least to its expansion as a regional and then national force.[8]

Barnett Rubin adds a political economy framework to this explanation of the rise of Taliban, arguing that "overcoming predation poses a collective action problem: each predatory actor benefits, while a larger but diffuse constituency would benefit from suppressing predation . . . Both social capital that strengthens networks of solidarity and investments or side-payments from groups benefiting from the suppression of predation can help overcome the obstacles to collective action. The Taliban both mobilized social capital created in madrasas to create a homogeneous leadership group linked to political networks in Pakistan and used assistance from Pakistan and Saudi governments and traders to build up a military force and buy off opponents."[9] There is little doubt that the Taliban benefited from substantial Pakistani support and Arab Gulf largesse. Yet such an explanation is too expedient, if only because the ISI and Arab donors fully backed another Pashtun organization—the Hizb-e Islami—for the three years that preceded the rise of Taliban, but with paltry results.

Pakistani support to the Taliban might have been substantial, but it could not possibly compare in scale with Soviet support for the Afghan communists or even the resources poured in by Western and other donors in support of the Karzai regime. And while Pakistan supported the Taliban, their rivals were vigorously backed by Iran, Russia, and India. The situation was hardly lopsided.[10] Gulf Arabs simultaneously supported a number of highly conservative Salafi figures with support among the Pashtuns, including Abdul Rabb al-Rasul Sayyaf, head of the Islamic Union (Ettehad-e Islami) and later a member of the Northern Alliance, and Mawlawi Jamil al-Rahman "Kunari" who headed his own Salafi "emirate" until defeated by Hekmatyar. None of them enjoyed the Taliban's success.

Another piece of evidence that undermines the "Saudi money" argument is that Saudi financial support to the Taliban became substantial only after July 1996, when the Taliban had already swept through most Pashtun areas.[11] Saudi aid dried up by September 1998 over the Taliban's refusal to give up Osama bin Laden. The Saudis also gave Masud and Rabbani $150 million in 1993–1994 after they distanced themselves from Iran, money that could have been used for purchasing the loyalty of many commanders if this were indeed the way to extend power in Pashtun areas, as the Taliban's rivals and some scholars have alleged.[12] The scale of donations given to the Taliban was also far from enough to dwarf aid given to their combined rivals. While Masud, Dostum, and Ismail Khan received massive support from Iran, Russia and India, the well-connected Ahmed Rashid estimates Pakistani support to the Taliban in 1997–1998 at a fairly modest $30 million.[13] It is hard to argue that the Taliban bought their way to power on $30 million a year when the Soviet-backed Najibullah regime barely managed to hang on by spending ten times this amount every month.

All else being equal, both sides would have been able to buy the loyalty of regional leaders. But such leaders do not make decisions based solely on money. At least early on in the conflict, "Saudi money" seems more likely to have been a rhetorical tool used by the

Taliban's rivals in attempts to discredit them and to explain their own failures. Moreover, accusations of association with "Wahhabis" has long been a tactic used to taint rivals in Afghanistan. At the same time, the political economy explanation does not explain why Hekmatyar, who also had exclusive access to young Afghan men in refugee camps and madrasas, strong connections, and comparable financing, was not able to maintain a stable constituency. Of course, before the rise of the Taliban, Afghans had suffered for years from the rapacious behavior of many local leaders.

Pakistani and Arab backing at a crucial juncture of Taliban organizational development probably assisted their rise. Yet it is impossible to prove that the Taliban would not have achieved similar results without outside intervention in Afghan affairs at this juncture. After all, in the past, Pashtun and other Afghan areas had experienced a large number of tribal upheavals and movements that were not encouraged or financed by outsiders, including various anti-British uprisings and the early mujahedin resistance to the Afghan communists and Soviets. It is too facile to explain the rise of the Taliban through outside assistance alone. At least part of the explanation of Taliban success must be found in what the Taliban *did.* Even Ahmed Rashid's powerful thesis, which almost reverses the agency relationship between the Taliban and Pakistan (the Taliban had a lock on Pakistani support because of their strong ties to many powerful Pakistani constituencies), does not spare us from having to look at intra-Pashtun dynamics to explain the rise of the Taliban.[14]

Another analysis of the movement focused on a purported power vacuum. Davis argues that "the speed with which the Taliban burst onto the Afghan scene stemmed from several factors, none of them military. Primarily, the Taliban expanded—faster than they themselves believed possible—to fill what was, in effect, a political vacuum in southern Afghanistan."[15] His use of the vacuum metaphor and the feelings he ascribes to the Taliban imply that Afghanistan was bereft of political organizations ready to immediately fill the void or willing to grow fast enough to do so. But Hekmatyar would have been perfectly happy to fill any void in the Pashtun areas long before the Taliban emerged. The reason he did not expand his area of influence is that there was no void to be filled.

Afghanistan was like the efficient world of Chicago economists: every area where poppy could be grown, traffic could be taxed, goods could be smuggled, and villagers could be exploited or mobilized was already controlled by local self-financed leaders who sometimes were even part of loose regional councils *(shuras)*. And if those many local leaders and their armed followers do not seem substantial enough, it is worth recalling that they are in many ways similar to those who bedeviled the Soviets; and they currently are providing an intractable challenge to the United States. The vacuum explanation also fails to explain why Hekmatyar's forces crumbled upon the Taliban's approach—Hekmatyar's organization was highly centralized and articulated, with almost all the trappings of a government.

Other explanations do not explain *how* the Taliban rose to power. Larry Goodson identifies five factors he believes explain the rise of the Taliban:

> First and most telling has been the shared Pashtun ethnicity of the Taliban and the majority of the noncombatant population in most of the area they have come to control . . . The next two factors in explaining the rise of the Taliban are interrelated. These are their emphasis on religious piety and the war-weariness of the Afghan civilian population . . . A fourth factor that explains the rise of the Taliban is money. Numerous knowledgeable observers of modern Afghanistan report that the Taliban used money to induce opposing commanders

to switch sides or surrender . . . Finally, the fifth factor that explains the success of the Taliban is Pakistani support. Support for the Taliban within Pakistan's government, army, and society is deep and multifaceted. Indeed, it is not incorrect to say that the Taliban are Pakistan's proxy army in Afghanistan, even though the Taliban leadership has not always followed Pakistan's preferences.[16]

Even if sufficient, necessary, and true, Goodson's list points merely to empowering and facilitating elements, elements that helped the Taliban execute the processes that were essential to their success. Facilitating factors do not an explanation make, but they provide the backdrop for the description of unfolding processes.

Hekmatyar's Hizb failed to overcome the same opponents the Taliban trounced, even though it enjoyed the exact same advantages. The Hizb touted itself as a Pashtun party after 1992 while still emphasizing its Islamist pedigree, forcing women to be veiled and limiting "un-Islamic" entertainment. The Hizb had access to more resources than it could reasonably use, as its many overstocked weapons depots clearly demonstrated. The Hizb also enjoyed generous Pakistani support through thick and thin for more than fifteen years. Although both the Hizb and the Taliban had the potential to take advantage of the same facilitating factors, the Taliban were much more successful. It is hard to argue that the Taliban expanded by buying off commanders with Arab and Pakistani money when, a few years earlier, Kandahari commanders expelled Hekmatyar from their area in spite of a very generous ISI offer to buy their support for a campaign to liberate the city under his leadership.[17] In this story, money is overrated.

Other observers ascribe the rise of the Taliban in Pashtun areas to the appeal of their aura of religious purity and law-and-order agenda in a land ravaged by bandits, smugglers, and other miscreants. "The Taliban have won support from a people sick of war. The three [*sic*] years since the Soviet army left have been three years of fighting between rival Islamic groups. Traditionally, religious students are held in high esteem. Other Islamic militias find it hard to bring themselves to shoot at them; the people find it easy to follow them. And the Taliban's advertised aim of establishing a government of national consensus, true to Islamic teachings, seems unchallengeable."[18] There is no doubt that the Taliban's appearance of piety and their law-and-order agenda were very appealing to the "people" in Pashtun areas. But how did this popularity translate into the ability to either defeat or co-opt the entrenched local leaders, who were benefiting from insecurity and exploitation? Afghanistan was not a liberal democracy for the will of the "people" to automatically translate into the emergence of a new regime.

The process through which the appeal of the Taliban's agenda translated into victories on the ground must be analyzed further. Antonio Giustozzi provides us with a hint that moves us along this line of reasoning: "In the end these young fundamentalists found it easier to root themselves in the Afghan countryside than the Islamists with their urban background, who continued to make up the thin upper crust of these parties. As the advent of the Taliban has shown, notwithstanding their military ineptitude, they could easily sweep away the Islamists from the Pashtun belt, thanks to their influence over the rank and file of the Islamist parties themselves."[19] Giustozzi's process-based argument—that the identity and creed of the Taliban undermined their rivals by causing defections among their followers—is compelling because it explains how different factors affect the preferences and behavior of specific actors.

Some argue that it is the Pashtun identity of the Taliban that mattered. Others suggest that the identity in question is Durrani as opposed to Ghilzai, but even this should probably be nuanced further because several Taliban leaders, including Mullah Omar, are of Ghilzai extraction.[20] David Edwards, who spent considerable time among the Pashtuns, probably best isolated the specific flavor of agenda-linked identity that made the Taliban acceptable to most rural Pashtuns. The Taliban, he notes, "consistently downplayed tribal or regional identities in favor of what might be called 'village identity' . . . In identifying purist culture and tradition with the Islam of the village, the Taliban were indirectly condemning the Islam of the parties since most of the party leaders were products of Kabul University or had worked for state-sponsored institutions. They were also putting themselves on a par with the people whose support they had to enlist if their movement was going to be successful."[21] While there should be room for some of the factors discussed above in an explanation of the Taliban's feat of mobilizing the Pashtuns on their way to control much of Afghanistan, their roles must be integrated into a dynamic process-based account. Pakistani and Arab Gulf support was helpful for the Taliban but not for others because the former used their support effectively to achieve their goals.

It therefore makes sense to explain the rise of the Taliban by comparing the perceptions, preferences, and strategies of the Taliban and their rivals. One deterrent to the adoption of such an approach is the dearth of accurate and useful information from the critical 1994–1996 period. The contested territory was not particularly hospitable for the very few scholars and journalists who cared enough about events in Afghanistan. Yet this is the only intellectually rigorous way to proceed.

The Taliban were able to co-opt or marginalize many established Pashtun elites by promoting defections among their local followers and by deploying their unique knowledge of Pashtun politics to diffuse opposition. These processes worked sometimes simultaneously and at other times independently. They were also *facilitated* by some of the factors identified above—exclusive access to a pool of madrasa students, a widespread desire for law and order, a desire for a Pashtun political comeback, support from various Pakistani agencies and constituencies, and financing from the Arabian Peninsula.

The Taliban's beginnings were not wholly unprecedented in Afghanistan. Several ephemeral Salafi-based movements, such as Jamil al-Rahman's emirate in Kunar, Mawlawi Afzal's state *(dawlat)* in Nuristan, and Mawlawi Shariqi's followers' tiny emirate in Badakhshan, had appeared before them. But they were all defeated by stronger rivals, including Hekmatyar's Hizb.

The Taliban's hundreds of small rivals in the Pashtun belt were not all organized along the same lines. Some consisted of independent self-financing bands that thrived on a combination of banditry, taxing traffic, smuggling, and small-scale production of poppy. Some commanders managed to develop networks of patronage and economies of scale in the same sectors. Such commanders maintained the loyalty of lesser commanders by providing them with resources they were well positioned to tap, including revenues from smuggling or rents from the faraway Rabbani regime or the closer Hekmatyar. Some commanders developed loose coordination and consultation councils where they conferred as equals, as in the Jalalabad shura. The only large centralized organization in the Pashtun belt was Hekmatyar's Hizb, with its Army of Sacrifice, some twelve thousand strong. Some local leaders tended to dominate their regions; others lived in a precarious rivalry with their neighbors. Many leaders maintained their followings through their ability to organize resource-generating activities, while others mustered support through a combination of kinship ties, religious authority, and a history of heroism during the jihad. Some were particularly aggressive and hated, others were not. This was a very complex landscape that provided the Taliban with various types of rivals in different configurations of power in each region they approached.

The Taliban calibrated their image and their message to successive Pashtun neighbors in a way that undermined the loyalty of a commander's following, thus simultaneously increasing his motivation to join the Taliban venture and reducing his ability to resist it. As Taliban forces approached the domain of a field commander or an area shared by rival field commanders, their presence automatically reordered the preferences of field commanders and their followers. The commanders' followers suddenly had an alternative to being part of a local group engaged in a precarious and brutish rivalry with others and that might have kept itself afloat through predatory behavior.

The Taliban occupation and management of Kandahar provided the Taliban with the base and credibility to launch their dramatic expansion. Their proposition to their Pashtun rivals' followers after they proved their mettle in Kandahar was particularly forceful. It consisted of a mix of the following: the Taliban provided moral clarity, a promise of a just and safe society stemming from a potent vision of Pashtun authenticity, and the satisfaction of being part of a momentous movement that could accomplish what became the stated goal of the jihad started in 1979—a just Islamic state that would incidentally also terminate non-Pashtun control of the capital. The Taliban alternative made the followers of commanders in their vicinity question the wisdom of resisting the Taliban when they seemed to be the credible providers of a better order. Followers whose loyalty to their commander was based on kinship or deep respect for his martial prowess or religious scholarship might have stuck by him longer or tried to pressure him not to resist the Taliban advance more than members of bands brought together by banditry or economic interests.

The limited options available to Pashtun commanders when the Taliban approached their region varied depending on their place in the local configuration of power, their size, their own Islamic credentials, and the cohesion of their own rudimentary organizations. Although not all field commanders and local leaders could realistically hope for the entire possible range of outcomes to their interaction with the Taliban, it is reasonable to assume that each leader would have ranked his theoretically possible outcomes in the following order of preference (higher first):

1. Maintaining local autonomy and control over local resources by successfully resisting the Taliban
2. Joining the Taliban as a client with a degree of autonomy while maintaining his organization's integrity
3. Being rewarded for surrendering local autonomy—money or joining the Taliban as an individual
4. Disbanding or disappearing from public view
5. Being defeated in battle
6. Being defeated by losing the support of his own troops and clients

Those who led tiny bands could not reasonably hope to resist the post-Kandahar Taliban; these generally disappeared from view. They would later be taken care of in the consolidation phase when the Taliban developed their polycentric system of shuras, morality police, and courts that enforced their order.

Established and independently financed commanders who controlled networks of patronage had the option to resist the Taliban but had to assess whether their client commanders (if any) and their troops would support them. Those who led patronage-based organizations that were kept together by more than money flows could opt to resist, while those who maintained loyalty solely through economic means probably could not rely on their clients to support them. Commanders who generated their revenues by lending their support to the Hizb, the Jamiat, or Ismail Khan, as opposed to the exploitation of local resources, might have perceived the Taliban as an alternative source of patronage. Leaders with Islamic and jihad credentials, including figures such as Jalaluddin Haqqani, were able to join the Taliban without losing face or might even have had a dominant strategy of joining them because of their ideological affinity. Weaker commanders in a regional power configuration or ambitious clients of stronger regional leaders could have found in the advance of the Taliban an opportunity to improve their local standing or to survive a precarious situation.

The mere proximity of the advancing Taliban was often enough to strain the elementary organizations and patronage networks of the local leaders the Taliban approached, forcing them to evaluate their options and attempt to preempt some of the worse outcomes by making gestures of goodwill, like Abdul Wahid of Helmand did. The Taliban astutely used their sophisticated knowledge of Pashtun politics to approach different local leaders in ways that convinced them that successful resistance (outcome 1) was impossible and to prompt them to either disband (outcome 4) or join them while sacrificing autonomy (outcome 3). The Taliban shaped the preferences of local leaders by (1) approaching the most vulnerable ones in a regional power configuration first, (2) approaching key clients before approaching their regional patrons, (3) carefully deciding which commanders to appoint or discard, and/or (4) calibrating their message to appeal to the majority of the local leaders' rank and file.

It made sense for the Taliban initially to approach the weaker and more vulnerable commander in the context of a regional competition and to prevent the creation of a coalition of former rivals from coalescing against their advance. A vulnerable commander at risk of elimination by his stronger local rivals was more likely to be willing to join the Taliban. In return, he offered them a foothold in his area and specialized local knowledge. The previously dominant commander then found himself as the weaker of two parties locally and had to face the difficult choices above, knowing that he was alone against the Taliban. The pressures in such dynamics often drove the weaker side to plead with the Taliban to support him, presumably in return for his loyalty. This is in part how Ghazni fell at the end of January 1995 after the Hizb attacked in an attempt to preempt Taliban advances. To resist this attack, Governor Qari Baba allied himself with the Taliban while Masud's bombers also attacked Hizb positions.[22]

The largest and most aggressive organization in Pashtun areas, Hekmatyar's Hizb, pushed more commanders toward the Taliban than any other organization. Davis reports that this pattern of defections also prevailed in Maidanshahr, which fell to the Taliban on February 10, 1995. Similarly, the Taliban defeated an established group led by Ghaffar Akhundzadah in Helmand by leveraging his local rivals in early 1995.[23]

Approaching key clients before confronting their patrons was another strategy that served the Taliban well in Pashtun-majority areas as well as with Pashtun clients of non-Pashtun patrons. An ambitious client could be tempted to switch allegiance in the hope of making up for an unsatisfactory relationship of patronage, to transplant his previous patron, or out of ideological affinity with the newcomers. Clients were also not immune to the Taliban's pull on their followers. Such defections often were damaging, not only because they caused a blow to morale, but also because commanders on the periphery of the patron's domain were generally entrusted with securing strategic areas that blocked the highly mobile Taliban from outmaneuvering their opponents.

Indeed, many of those commanders were both valued as clients and targeted for recruitment by the Taliban because of their strategic locations. One or more defecting commanders allowed the Taliban to control strategic heights that facilitated their first assault on Kabul.[24] A number of sources report that the decisive Taliban push toward Herat was greatly facilitated by the defections of Ismail Khan's Pashtun clients to the south of his domain.[25] In the north, several Pashtun commanders embedded among Uzbek and Tajik regional majorities (particularly around Konduz) also made the switch at decisive junctures.[26] The Taliban's second push toward Mazar was facilitated by the support of previous Hizb commanders from the area.[27]

The most famous defection by an ambitious client was that of Dostum's retainer Abdul Malik, who feared for his life after suspecting that Dostum had killed his ambitious brother, Rasul Pahlawan. But Abdul Malik's defection was also induced by Taliban promises of a government post and perhaps money, allowing Taliban forces to enter Mazar-e Sharif and rout Dostum's forces. Soon afterward, Malik turned against his Taliban allies as they tried to disarm him and then continued to attempt to seize Mazar. Malik's defection provides us with critical evidence that the Taliban's ability to marginalize or assimilate Pashtun leaders hinged on their ability to influence their followers. While the Taliban were able to draw even the best-organized Pashtun troops away from their leaders, the non-Pashtun Malik was able to switch allegiances at will because he was secure in the loyalty of his supporters. The Taliban forces in Mazar must have forgotten why their strategies worked in the past as they became accustomed to easy acquiescence to their monopoly on violence in Pashtun areas.

The Taliban also astutely used their sophisticated knowledge of the Pashtun landscape to decide whether to co-opt, discard, or assassinate different commanders. The Taliban co-opted local leaders who would not have tarnished their finely calibrated image as heralds of a better order and who could substantially add to their military potential. Jalaluddin Haqqani, the master guerilla leader and uncompromising learned scholar without independent ambitions, was the epitome of the co-optable commander. Those tarnished by a history of predation or loyalty to the Hizb or Jamiat were better discarded, and their followers recruited on an independent basis or disbanded. Ambitious commanders with a solid and large group of followers who could have put up strong resistance were sometimes targeted for assassination.[28]

The Taliban assassinated the prominent Durrani leader Abdul Ahad Khan Karzai, father of Hamid, in July 1999, and made several attempts on Abdul Haq's life before they ultimately succeeded after the United States entered the fray in Afghanistan. The assassination of Masud, with the help of al-Qaeda, was the ultimate coup. It could very well have led to the collapse of the Panjsheri resistance, absent American intervention. Of course, Taliban choices were not always flawless in this regard. They integrated highly trained former members of the communist Khalqi faction into their troops for their military capabilities, but discarded them by 1998 when they realized the damage the Khalqis caused them and found alternative sources of expertise.

The carefully scripted image and message of the Taliban were essential components of their successful expansion across Pashtun areas, and these were later tweaked, with somewhat lesser success, to win over other constituencies. The Taliban's image and message reduced the ability of rival commanders to rely on their followers' support in case they wanted to resist the Taliban advance. They prevented local leaders from coalescing against the Taliban the way they would have, had they been the forces of a client regime under the tutelage of a foreign power, such as the Soviets, British, and Americans, or anti-tribal Islamists like Hekmatyar.

The identity of the Taliban leaders and rank and file probably influenced how they were perceived and the credibility accorded to their message, but probably not in the way most observers believe it did. Identity mattered, not because of who the Taliban were, but because of who they were *not*. The Taliban were not hindered in their expansion within the Pashtun areas by being of urban background. They were not modernist Islamists with anti-tribal dispositions. They did not have a long record of ambitious expansion, nor could they be accused of being non-Pashtun. The Taliban's message and image would have been hindered by any such attributes. Kabuli urbanites (such as the Afghan communists) would have been perceived as expanding the power of a central government and of being culturally alien to rural Pashtuns. Modernist Islamists like Hekmatyar were perceived as planning to sacrifice local political and cultural autonomy in their effort to create a centralized and modernizing Islamic state. Established organizations that have attempted past expansion (like Hizb, Ismail Khan, and Sayyaf) clashed with many commanders in the past and therefore lost any pretense to neutrality.

If the Taliban's identity mattered because of who they were, as opposed to who they were not, one would not have expected Mullah Omar, a Ghilzai of unremarkable lineage, to have mustered support among the Durranis. Regardless of his ancestry, Mullah Omar was able to woo support across Pashtun areas because of the vision he and his organization articulated and their projected image as credible purveyors of this vision. The credibility of the Taliban's reputation could not be undermined because of who they were, but what really mattered were the message and the image, not the Taliban members' ethnic, tribal, or community *(qawm)* identities.

A critical component of the Taliban's image was that they were perceived as neutral in the context of ongoing Afghan conflicts. They also suggested at an early stage that they were not interested in wielding power themselves. The Taliban's perceived neutrality made them acceptable neighbors, allies, and intermediaries for many commanders who kept their options open. The way the Taliban approached commanders also leveraged the neutral role of religious figures in Pashtun tradition:

> Taliban sent religious envoys ahead to demand that local commanders disarm and dismantle roadblocks. Most duly did. Some even offered money, vehicles and weapons to help Taliban eliminate their rivals. But then Taliban pushed aside these collaborators too.[29]

The Taliban's strategies of manipulating regional rivalries and patronage ties would have proved much less successful if they had not been perceived as being neutral and promoting a selfless order. And when they tried to extend this advantage beyond Pashtun areas, they faced more skepticism by the minority groups they faced (for example, in the Wahdat-Masud conflict in Kabul).

The Taliban also leveraged cultural knowledge and affinity to project an aura of invincibility. This reduced the commanders' perception of their own ability to put up a challenge and the willingness of their fighters to go along. The use of cultural norms and symbols also provided assurances for those who would accept surrender or cooptation. There is no stronger evidence of the importance the Taliban gave to the preservation of Pashtun customary legal norms *(Pashtunwali)* than their willingness to shelter Osama bin Laden until the bitter end, the way a good Pashtun is expected to do. As one Taliban leader candidly acknowledged, Taliban leaders would have lost the respect of their followers, and consequently the organization's cohesion, if they gave up bin Laden.

With Pashtunwali came cultural assets that reduced the cost of Taliban expansion. As they expanded, the Taliban brought back collective memories of Pashtun uprisings and symbols that were well enshrined in oral culture. Reputation became a valuable asset to risk, thus committing those who declared their loyalty to maintaining it. And even a certain degree of susceptibility to rumors and superstition might have contributed to Taliban victories. Rumors circulated that those who fired on the advancing students were miraculously stricken with fear, incapacitated by unexplained bleeding, or fell into a coma. While there is no evidence that such rumors were decisive, no other force in Afghanistan than the Taliban could have inspired such fear in those who were religious and superstitious.[30]

The momentum of the Taliban amplified their message and increased both the perceived cost and the real cost of resisting them. The farther and faster they expanded, the more credible became their promises to usher in a better order. Their expansion also brought with it new recruits in the guise of co-opted commanders and individual volunteers, which made them an ever more formidable force. And the commander who saw dozens of others fall or surrender to the Taliban before him had a robust example of what would become of him if he tried to resist. By the time the Taliban reached Hekmatyar's base in Chaharasyab, their momentum had increased their ability to undermine rivals' followings to the point that even the Hizb's fairly well-organized and structured force surrendered to them without a fight. The same scenario repeated itself in Sarobi. Even the tenacious Hekmatyar, who had patiently built his organization over some twenty years of struggle, had to see his followers abandon him without even the pretense of a fight.

The Taliban perpetuated their monopoly on the use of violence in Pashtun areas by carefully disarming the forces of commanders they did not co-opt. They then maintained some control through a polycentric system of ruling shuras, a network of informants and dedicated followers, and a monopoly over the taxation of poppy production and smuggling.[31] The cost became too high for those Pashtuns who wished to organize resistance from scratch to challenge the Taliban.

To expand beyond the Pashtun belt, the Taliban had to tweak their message and adopt different strategies. In minority areas they could not rely on their ability to pull the rug out from under their rivals' feet by appealing to their followers. The Taliban therefore adopted a new mix of strategies: military attacks, assassination of leaders, buying the loyalty of key commanders, and co-opting embedded minorities (not only Pashtuns) within regional majorities. The Taliban also made efforts to appear nonthreatening to minority populations, including, initially, the Hazara. They added minority members to their governing shura, albeit with inconsequential portfolios, and recruited minority fighters in the north. Their results were mixed, however, particularly after they killed Mazari and violently retaliated for the massacres in Mazar.

This explanation of the rise of the Taliban suggests lessons for the current U.S. venture in Afghanistan and provides a basis to speculate on the potential for a greater revival of the Taliban. There is no hope for the state-building venture to succeed if the Karzai regime fails to sideline or overwhelm the now self-financed and entrenched Pashtun militias that reemerged after November 2001. The constitution, elections, institutions, and other trappings of a democratic society that have been absorbing resources and the energy of figures in the Karzai regime and their Western patrons are not key to mobilizing the Pashtuns and consolidating the state—they are illusory symbols of a state that normally should have developed after the government had become secure by weakening its potential military challengers.

Instead of focusing on creating the image of a state, the United States and its clients should have done what the Taliban did before them: dismantle rival power structures. Of course, the Taliban's knowledge of the complex Pashtun tapestry of power, the preferences of warlords and their followers, and their credible promise to bring back Pashtun greatness, allowed them to fine-tune their image, message, and strategies in a way that is impossible for the alien U.S. military and its minority or émigré clients to do. In fact, this window of opportunity closed a long time ago. The tools left at U.S. disposal are the use of brute force and patronage, both of which have proven to be self-defeating in the past.

Will the Taliban make a broader comeback? Some of the facilitating factors that preceded their rise persist, while others have disappeared. There still is a reservoir of dedicated talibs fueled by resentment at the U.S.-backed reversal they experienced, with intricate knowledge of the area's power structure, access to weapons, and some financial support. On the other hand, Pakistani and Arab state support has almost stopped, even if Pakistani covert backing may very well have resumed. Of course, things could change, and even overt Pakistani aid could resume in earnest, if Musharraf is deposed or the United States leaves the country. The Taliban could very well come back with a vengeance, if the United States decides to undermine militarized Pashtun local leaders by depriving them of their sources of income or decides to leave the Karzai regime to perish. The Taliban have some very good reasons to wait until the United States makes such fateful decisions.

The Taliban are likely to sweep through Pashtun areas again if the United States leaves Afghanistan in the next few years, given their continuing ability to provide the same compelling proposition to leaders and their followers, even without Pakistani support. However, a resurgent Taliban will most likely need Pakistani support and financing from sympathetic sources, if they are to reconquer non-Pashtun areas. A serious effort by the United States to weaken the many Pashtun local leaders and curb their production of poppy is likely to push them to covertly or overtly support the Taliban and other insurgents.

In this case, the Taliban could become only one of a number of organizations that will ultimately strive for influence in Pashtun areas. But the Taliban are resilient even as an insurgent organization—the group is not vulnerable to decapitation (Mullah Omar is only a first among many equals), and it is structured in a way that shields it from the many counterinsurgency shortcuts. Either way, the Taliban in one form or another will remain a player in Afghan affairs for some time.

Perhaps more important than its policy consequences, this narrative illustrates the kind of dynamics involved in the production of societal outbursts in some analogous contexts. The dramatic rise of the Taliban provides us with a rare opportunity (perhaps never to be observed again, given the gradual disappearance of similar societies) to observe the kind of processes that might have animated much greater ventures in the past. If my understanding of the processes underlying the rise of the Taliban is correct, then the power of great ideas should be coupled with an understanding of strategies and organizational features to explain historical events such as the Mongol outburst and tribal mobilizations in Afghanistan, Algeria, the Arabian Peninsula, and elsewhere. Some of those historical events produced or defeated empires, and it does not suffice to explain their early stages by referring to merely facilitating and empowering factors, as many scholars have done.

CHAPTER TWO

The Rise and Fall of the Taliban

Neamatollah Nojumi

Though the institutionalization of the Taliban's brand of Islam neither lasted nor developed into a viable state, the establishment of the regime had political implications far beyond Afghanistan. The persistence of this movement and its political and military operations more than six years after its removal from power reveals the extent to which the Taliban continue to draw on their regional and international support base, maintaining it as an outpost of global militancy. The rise of the Taliban had firm roots in the regional and international politics of the 1980s and 1990s. Their demise, too, depended upon crucial shifts in the international context.

In the late 1970s, Soviet aggression resulted in a coup d'état by the People's Democratic Party of Afghanistan (PDPA) and the subsequent Soviet invasion of Afghanistan. In combination with the Soviet intervention, the PDPA's socialist revolutionary reforms appeared to the Afghan masses as an assault on their traditional and Islamic values.[1] This understanding provoked both their religious sentiments and political conservatism as a rational means of self-defense, resulting in the formation of local resistance groups who identified themselves as mujahedin, those who wage jihad. The United States responded by supporting the resistance groups against the Soviet-backed communist government in Kabul; as a result, Afghanistan became an active battleground between the two superpowers. The Carter administration began forming alliances with other Islamic countries, chiefly Saudi Arabia, Egypt, and Pakistan, to support the Afghan mujahedin. This effort was significantly expanded during the Reagan administration and placed under the direct responsibility of the Central Intelligence Agency.[2] U.S. regional allies also contributed: Saudi Arabia matched U.S. financial assistance dollar for dollar, Egypt became the main military supplier and training ground, while Pakistan developed as the conduit of military and civilian assistance for the Afghan resistance fighters and refugees and engaged in training and recruitment. Pakistan's president general, Muhammad Zia ul-Haq, awarded his Inter-Services Intelligence (ISI) agency a monopoly over the distribution, training, and shipment of military and financial assistance to the Afghan resistance groups.[3]

The ISI focused on seven of these groups whose ideologies were generally in accord with General Zia's doctrine of Islamizing of Pakistani society. It granted special status to those who were either associated with, or supported by, the Jama'at-e-Islami Pakistan, the most powerful extremist group and Zia's ally in the government.[4] The moderate Afghan nationalist groups were encouraged to either accept the leadership of one of the seven or leave Pakistan. That the ISI was responsible for selecting and approving the leadership among the Afghan resistance changed the balance of power among the Afghan resistance in favor of extremists and conservatives.

For the first time in history, Afghan Islamists received official recognition and access to unchecked financial and military assistance. Yet this status served, in practice, as acknowledgment of the Islamists' authority outside of Afghanistan rather than among the resistance groups within Afghanistan. There the majority of the field commanders were not Islamist followers, though they were desperate for external military and financial assistance. As a result, the ISI favored Hizb-e Islami (Islamic Party), led by the extremist Gulbuddin Hekmatyar. It received the largest portion of U.S. assistance, which helped the group open its own military training camps and a large network of religious schools, where Islamic extremism became an integral part of the curriculum.[5]

In addition, Hekmatyar's party was among the first to include a significant number of foreigners trained in "jihad." This model was followed by other Pakistan-based mujahedin groups as funding from the Arab states and wealthy individuals of the Persian Gulf increased. Graduates of these schools received military training and were then sent to Afghanistan to expand the influence of these political groups based in Pakistan.[6]

Islamist leaders that were previously unknown now found access to international assistance through the ISI and were able to form extensive networks of armed political organizations. They were given free rein over millions of Afghans who were living in refugee camps, and the assistance they received was used to recruit and influence the refugee populations. Their connections with the Islamists in Pakistan allowed them to build bridges with other Islamists and conservative groups in North Africa, the Middle East, and South Asia and fundraising capacities in Turkey, Europe, and the North America, energizing the flow of activists and resources to Afghanistan as well as throughout the larger network of Islamists around the world.[7] Many centers that were run by non-Afghan Islamist activists in the United States, Canada, and Western Europe were involved in fund-raising and recruiting activities and often channeled donations mainly to Afghan militants and other Islamist groups in Pakistan. Hekmatyar's visits to the United States, Europe, and the Middle East via both official and Islamist groups, like the Turkish organizations in Europe, gained him notoriety and millions of dollars in donations.

In Iran, a similar process shaped the experience of some two million refugees. The Afghan Shiite Islamists and, to a certain extent, Sunni Islamists received direct and indirect military and financial support from the Iranian government. Iranian government agencies, including the Islamic Revolution Guard Corps (IRGC), the Intelligence Service, the Interior Ministry, and the Office of the President, as well as leading religious clerics, established, funded, and trained various groups.[8] The Shia groups (with the exception of Shura-ye Inqelabi-ye Etefaq-e Islami-ye Afghanistan and Harakat-e Islami-ye Afghanistan, which had been expelled from Iran) embraced Ayatollah Ruhollah Khomeini's vision of Islamic revolution, advocating the formation of an Islamic state as an alternative to communism and liberal capitalism for the Islamic world. During the Iran-Iraq war (1980–1988), some pro-Iranian Afghan Shiite groups recruited Afghan fighters to the front lines to fight against Iraq. In return, these groups received financial and military support and were allowed to transport captured Iraqi weapons to their groups inside Afghanistan.[9] In Iran, the Afghan Islamists received free office space, fuel, personal security, food stamps for their families, and permission to run businesses, all of which was restricted for the rest of the refugee population. These developments in both Pakistan and Iran prepared the ground for the ascendance of the Afghan Islamist militants once the Soviets were forced from Afghanistan.

The communist coup and Soviet invasion also reshaped local politics within Afghanistan. Afghan political culture has a long history of solving local social and political grievances via a traditional forum, the *jirga* or *shura* (council), composed of respected community leaders.[10] The two critically important aspects of these local councils are the notions of individual freedom and communal autonomy—democratic notions in traditional ways. Male members of the community could freely participate in the political process of the local forum, which functioned outside of the administration of the central government. But the communist takeover, the Soviet invasion, and the rise of the Islamists, disrupted this system. In the areas that were controlled by the Afghan communist regime and the Soviets, local communities were forced into conscription and government programs.[11]

During the first two years after the communist coup and Soviet invasion, moderate Muslims, democrats, and nationalist activists dominated the domestic front of the mujahedin.[12] But once the Soviets began destroying the internal social basis of the resistance through the massive bombardment of rural Afghanistan, where over 80 percent of the population lived, millions of people fled for their lives to Pakistan and Iran. This operation forced around half of the estimated total population of sixteen million into refugee camps in the neighboring countries. Suddenly the Afghan resistance groups fell short of ammunitions, food, medicine, and adequate training, and they became desperate for external support.

In Pakistan, aside from the seven groups recognized by General Zia's regime, the ISI had not allowed the formation of any moderate or democratic groups, and it denied aid and protection to prominent pro-democracy activists. However, these activists were able to gain major support among refugee communities via the reestablishment of the jirga forum. Prominent democratic leaders like Shamsuddin Majruh, a former philosophy professor, and Dr. Muhammad Yosuf, a former prime minister, began to offer a popular alternative to that of the Islamists—forcing the Soviets out of Afghanistan. Dr. Yosuf was a well-known and respected political leader who supported the return of the former king, Muhammad Zaher, from Rome. He advocated the formation of a loya jirga composed of representatives of the local communities and tribal leaders under the leadership of the former king to decide the fate of Afghanistan. To facilitate the return of the former king and establishment of a loya jirga, Majruh and Yosuf were active in the formation of traditional local jirgas among the refugees and across the border into Afghanistan. Majruh published a public-opinion survey collected from thousands of Afghan refugees in Pakistan. The poll showed that the majority of those interviewed favored the return of the former king. At the same time, large numbers of moderate Afghans staffed NGOs and engaged in humanitarian work, providing health and education services for the refugees.

This gained the Afghan moderates popularity among both refugees and the fighters inside the country. Yet this popularity made them the target of militants, who waged an indiscriminate campaign of harassment, kidnappings, and assassinations. Shamsuddin Majruh and many other prominent Afghan democratic leaders were assassinated in Peshawar, and many more were slain every day by the Islamists' terror groups, all while the Pakistani security forces, and particularly the ISI, turned their backs and denied them any protection.[13] Many others of this persuasion, including Dr. Yosuf, were forced to leave Pakistan for either North America or Europe.

The empowerment of the Islamists in Pakistan—the main support base for the Afghan resistance—and their access to international assistance, especially from the United States, enabled the Afghan Islamists to brutally suppress the moderate Muslims and pro-democracy resistance forces.[14] As a result, moderate political forces were caught between two fronts: the communists and Soviets, on the one hand, and the Afghan Islamist militants, on the other. Unfortunately, many of those who survived the first fell victim to the second.[15] This development gave the Islamists the guns and funds necessary to eliminate their political opponents and purchase loyalty within the Afghan resistance camps.

The environment in Iran produced similar outcomes. The only way Afghan refugees could receive permission to stay in Iran was through one of the eight Afghan Islamist groups authorized by Tehran.[16] Afghan Islamists such as Hizb-e Islami and Jamiat-e Islami and Shiite groups like Sazman-e Nasr-e Islami and Hizbullah received travel and business permits in partnership with Iranians connected to the regime.[17] Leading officers of these groups also were allowed to carry weapons for their protection and receive training at the Qods Forces base.[18] As in Pakistan, the moderate and nationalist Afghan political forces were denied access to rights and services that were easily accessible to the Islamists. The Islamic regime in Iran viewed Afghan moderates as *mili gara* (nationalist), a concept thought to be hostile toward Tehran's brand of Islam. As a result, the Iranian government jailed, harassed, or expelled Afghan moderates; some they handed over to the communist regime at the border with Afghanistan.

Under the watchful eyes of the Iranian security forces and the IRGC, the Islamist militants were able to build covert networks and act against Afghan moderates, who were often kidnapped from the border towns, transferred to border posts inside Afghanistan, and executed as "hypocrites [*monafiqin*]," "communist sympathizers," and "Soviet spies."[19] Moreover, Hizb-e Islami, Jamiat-e Islami, Sazman-e Nasr-e Islami, and Hizbullah could arrest Afghan moderates, accuse them of being communist sympathizers, and turn them over to the IRGC and Revolutionary Committees throughout Iran, including Tehran. These accused Afghan moderates were frequently held in jail and at the end of their terms deported directly into the hands of the pro-Soviet border forces in Afghanistan. Many of these Afghans were forced into the front lines against the other mujahedin forces or, if their identities were revealed, they were put in jail and sometimes executed.[20]

In the mid-1980s, the Afghan Islamists used international financial assistance to establish hundreds of religious boarding schools and recruited thousands of young Afghan boys among the refugees to these schools.[21] These boys were trained in an educational system that fit within the political ideology of the Islamists, including a requirement that the boys participate in military training, active engagement on the front line, and other militant activities.[22] Toward the end of the 1980s, the graduates of these schools became the leading preachers in thousands of mosques—on both sides of the Afghan-Pakistani border—that consistently expounded upon the necessity of militant warfare.[23]

These messengers gave the Afghan Islamists an extended arm with which to influence the local political culture via a centralized political system—similar to the one pushed by the Afghan communists—within the mujahedin-controlled areas. As a result, the traditional political culture of Afghanistan was suppressed in these regions, the decision-making process of the local jirga was disbanded, and the rule of military commanders and Islamists was imposed. In these areas, the Islamist armed groups established courts led by specially selected clerics who ignored both the legislated civil and criminal codes as well as customary law and instead enforced their restricted version of sharia rule over the local population. Women's public appearances were restricted, and simple amusements such as kite flying, pigeon flying, and music were prohibited.[24]

The political process in Iran was similar. Afghan refugees were not allowed to attend secular educational institutions. As a result, thousands of young Afghans, mostly Shiites, were enrolled in the Iranian religious schools and attended lectures by the leading clerics.[25] The Iranian clerics used many of these groups to form a pro–Ayatollah Khomeini camp among the Afghan Shiites, organizing them into political armed groups that were then deployed into the central highlands and surrounding areas within Afghanistan and commanded to suppress those Shiite Muslims that did not follow Khomeini's revolutionary doctrine. These groups killed thousands of moderate Shiites who had formed the major force against the communist regime and Soviet troops on several fronts.[26] Like the graduates from the religious schools in Pakistan, many Shiite disciples became leading preachers in the local mosques among the Shiite communities throughout Afghanistan and received funding from Iranian sources.

One of the more notable characteristics of the Afghan graduates of these schools was their lack of understanding of Afghan history. Having grown up at these schools, they were unfamiliar with the cultural norms, neighborhood traditions, and historical heritage of local communities. In 1984, for instance, a teacher at one such school told me that "nationalism and love for country is irreligious, Islam doesn't have boundaries, and we are fighting for the victory of Islam in the world."[27] In practice, the students were trained in, and lived through, the mandates of the Islamist political ideology to prepare them for "paradise" by resisting all those who thought, dressed, and behaved differently from how they were trained. Like the Afghan communists, the Islamists had also begun to rewrite history by condemning local traditions, especially the passive role of religion and the religious establishment toward the cause of the Islamic revolution and the creation of an Islamic state in Afghanistan.

Those Afghan boys who attended these boarding schools, most of them from the age of six or eight until the age of sixteen, were raised in a socio-psychological environment that had guided them to understand the world in black and white, which was out of context with reality.[28] Hekmatyar's group funded a religious boarding school system for boys whose parents were killed during the war. This school system was much like the Soviet model, where children were raised to put the interests of the state above culture, family, and individual. The Afghan sons of the martyred in Hekmatyar's schools were trained for the purpose of purifying society and taking revenge on those who killed their parents.[29] Toward this "holy" and "jihadist" goal, they were given extensive military training at a very young age and were exposed to notions of political violence. In 1992 these graduates formed a significant portion of Hekmatyar's well-equipped, well-trained military brigades known as the Lashkar-e Isar (Army of Sacrifice), who were deployed to the south of Kabul to take the capital. This army followed orders without any hesitation and indiscriminately bombarded Kabul, killing thousands of civilians. According to a local journalist, one of Hekmatyar's commanders, before ordering the bombardment of the city, preached to his troops: "We know that non-military people will be killed today; if they are good Muslims, God will reward them as martyred and send them to heaven . . . if they are bad Muslims, God is punishing them at the hands of his true believers [Lashkar-e Isar]."[30]

Notwithstanding their access to military and financial resources through these international networks, the Afghan Islamist leaders in Pakistan and Iran failed to offer a viable political platform that convinced the major mujahedin field commanders. The Islamists' rigid political ideology, arrogant claim to leadership, and especially their rejection of local Islamic traditions, which are deeply rooted in the people's understanding of culture and faith, turned many Afghans against them. These factors disillusioned the field commanders and led them to develop their own political and military organizations, both locally and regionally. This development was very effective in imposing organized pressure against the Soviet military front inside Afghanistan, but it built a sea of differences between the major field commanders and the political leaders waiting in the wings in Pakistan and Iran.

Following the Soviet withdrawal in 1989, Afghan society remained divided into two main factions: the Kabul government led by Najibullah, and the mujahedin groups led by several conflicting groups. The war that had raged continuously since 1978, resulting in the destruction of thousands of villages, the loss of a million people, hundreds of thousands wounded, and several million more displaced as refugees, brought about fundamental changes in the social, political, and economic structure of the country. It also impacted the traditional cultural pattern through which the local communities had lived for a major portion of recent Afghan history. Those who had remained in the country had lost their individual freedom and communal autonomy to the imposed governments as well as to the armed resistance groups. Those who took refuge in neighboring countries were influenced by the host culture, and the majority of refugees were kept in camps that were economically dependent on foreign aid and ruled by Islamists. As a result, the fate of the majority of the Afghan population fell into the hands of political groups, military factions, and international organizations. The population had no say in the leaders' dialogues, although each leader proclaimed that he represented the people of Afghanistan.

Islamabad rejected both the formation of a coalition government in Kabul and the broad-based government mandated by the United Nations. With the support of the CIA and Saudi financing, the ISI pushed for a military victory to install the Afghan Islamists in Kabul without informing major mujahedin field commanders.[31] In the meantime, Afghan Islamist groups were unable to fund thousands of their established religious schools; most of these schools were subsequently taken over by the Jamiat Ulema-e-Islam, another powerful and highly influential Islamist group in Pakistan. These competing factions nonetheless failed to form a national government, and their competition sparked a bloody civil war, which continued for two years. During this massive infighting, some thirty thousand people were killed and a hundred thousand were wounded; the capital was destroyed entirely.[32]

This chaotic social and political environment gave rise to a vacuum of leadership and gave momentum to the appearance of a political force that promised to stop the infighting and further destruction of the country. Led by Mullah Muhammad Omar, the initial Taliban group emerged in the southern part of Kandahar Province in 1994 as a local response to the former resistance and militia forces implicated in banditry, brutality against local residents, and offenses against the local values such as *nang* (reputation) and *namus* (local honor with respect to women). Mullah Omar was a veteran mujahedin commander and had previously headed a religious school in a remote district of Kandahar. Through their association and friendship with the Jamiat Ulema-e-Islam, headed by Mawlana Fazlur Rehman, the strongest coalition partner in the Benazir Bhutto government in 1994, Taliban leaders were brought to the attention of the Pakistani government, which put Ministry of Interior General Nasirullah Babar in charge of logistical support for the Taliban. This development enabled the Taliban to mobilize forces and take over the strategic province of Kandahar, rapidly expanding toward Herat and then Kabul.[33]

The rise of the Taliban was embedded in regional developments. Competition for access to the oil- and gas-rich states of the former Soviet Union in Central Asia added an economic component to Pakistan's policy toward Afghanistan.[34] Bhutto's regime viewed access to these Central Asian markets and the transport of energy as critical to Pakistani industry. Meanwhile, Hekmatyar's forces, backed by Pakistan, were failing militarily and politically to capture Kabul. Moreover, ISI support for Hekmatyar had already antagonized Islamabad's relationship with the Afghan mujahedin government led by

Burhanuddin Rabbani. The transportation of oil and especially gas from Turkmenistan, estimated to have one of the largest natural gas reserves in the world, via Afghanistan to Pakistan had already emerged as a possibility, given the fact that the transportation of goods through Afghanistan had started three years before.[35]

Pakistan thus became an important player in the construction of two giant pipelines. The U.S. oil company Unocal and the Saudi Delta oil companies sought contracts to build pipelines worth over $4 billion.[36] With help from Unocal's lobbying efforts in Washington, the United States gave the green light to Islamabad to go forward with supporting the Taliban, which had been introduced by Pakistan as a "traditionalist" stabilizing force in the chaos of Afghanistan. Delta directed the financing for the operation, which included several hundred Toyota pickup trucks that were converted into excellent military advance convoys.[37] The direct role of the United States was not clear until, in a BBC interview, Benazir Bhutto shed light on American involvement, admitting that her government had trained the Taliban in Pakistan with American financial assistance.[38]

Benazir Bhutto conceded that this group developed out of a joint venture among the Jamiat Ulema-e-Islam, Pakistan's Ministry of Interior, and the Pakistani merchants and trucking network.[39] During the 1980s, a transportation system involving hundreds of trucks was established to deliver aid to the Afghan resistance from the port of Karachi to Peshawar.[40] Controlled by elements of the Pakistani military, this system employed thousands of military members as well as some retired officers, and emerged as a lucrative business once the owners, drivers, and administrators became involved in the return shipment of narcotics from Peshawar to Karachi. Because the operation of these trucks fell under federal military authority, none of the local law enforcement agencies were authorized to stop or search these vehicles. The engagement of the trucking industry in narcotics converted the system into a "transport mafia." Once the Soviets pulled out of Afghanistan, this system became a joint venture with organizations from the private sector. The chief contractor on the government side—apart from a number of local godfathers who served in local governments—was General Nasirullah Babar, the father of Pakistan's "in-depth policy" toward Afghanistan. According to this policy, Afghanistan presented Pakistan with a strategic advantage in the event of a future war against India. Favoring the formation of a "friendly" pro-Pakistan regime in Kabul became the underlying strategy by the Pakistani government toward supporting the exiled Afghan Islamist opposition groups in the 1970s and 1980s and the Taliban in the 1990s.[41]

General Babar established the Afghan Trade Developing Cell, a government-sponsored unit to redirect the "transport mafia" toward transporting goods from Pakistan to Central Asia via Afghanistan.[42] The emergence of Afghanistan as an economic highway to the landlocked post-Soviet states in Central Asia offered a significant opportunity for the already established ground transport network in Pakistan. Within several months after the collapse of the pro-Moscow regime in Kabul, the trucking industry to Central Asia was booming. The mixture of shipping both goods and narcotics had expanded the local interests of opium producers, refinery owners, and thousands of merchants, as well as truck drivers, truck owners, and auto shops, just to name a few. At the same time, both politicians and the military establishment benefited from the high level of profit generated by this industry.

Yet the main obstacle to a continued boom within the industry was the absence of law and order: large numbers of checkpoints on the Afghan highways trafficked in collecting taxes, harassing owners and drivers, and forcing extortion payments; some armed groups also raped women and young boys.[43] One crucial stretch of highway, from the border town of Spin Boldak to Kandahar, was controlled by three notorious militia groups answering to Hekmatyar; here, merchants and truck drivers had to pay fees to these groups as well as pay the customs duties to the Kandahar government authority.[44] It was the same for significant numbers of shipments coming from the Persian Gulf states via Iran and then Herat to Pakistan on the same highway. Goods transported via Pakistan and Iran to Afghanistan fell under the Afghanistan Transit Treaty Agreement (ATTA), which was signed by the three countries prior to the 1978 coup. Under the ATTA, Afghanistan was entitled to have access to the Persian Gulf and the Indian Ocean via Pakistani and Iranian seaports. Shipments delivered from either Karachi or Iranian ports would be free of customs. Once goods arrived in Afghanistan, they were shipped illegally to Pakistan to avoid customs fees, taxes, and tariffs. But the roadblocks and checkpoints maintained by armed groups slowed the flow of goods and forced merchants to carry the burden of the unnecessary costs. Both the merchant communities and the transport owners were fed up with these armed groups and began looking for solutions.

In August 1994, a thirty-truck convoy bound for Turkmenistan and accompanied by several Pakistani officials, including Colonel Jawed Imam, an ISI field officer, was stopped at gunpoint by these notorious Hekmatyar commanders, in a locale where local communities sought an outlet for various grievances. Mullah Omar, then head of a local religious school, called his former military brethren to bear arms in the name of justice to provide protection to the locals, calling themselves "the Taliban." Suddenly the Taliban received significant support from merchants in Quetta and were unofficially supplied by local Pakistani border forces. In October a group of the Taliban captured Spin Boldak from Hekmatyar forces and seized significant amounts of weaponry. They then cleared the highway of roadblocks in the direction of Kandahar, released Pakistani trucks, and eventually captured Kandahar. They chose Mullah Omar as their amir, established their administration, and began receiving local and Pakistani support.

The main forces of the Taliban, including their leaders, were the students and graduates of the religious schools that were built during the Soviet occupation, mostly with Saudi financial support. After the Soviet withdrawal, these schools became part of an extended network of religious schools controlled by the Pakistani-based Jamiat Ulema-e-Islam. After the Taliban captured Kandahar and benefited from the rise of local support, their capture of massive amounts of weapons, and their close relationship with Pakistan, they decided to move against Kabul. The Jamiat Ulema-e-Islam mobilized thousands of Afghan and non-Afghan students, especially from the areas close to the border, into the training centers run by the Pakistani interior minister in support of the Taliban military adventure. Pakistani military officers were put in charge of the command and control of the Taliban forces by managing logistics and fuel, conducting communications, operating artillery, and providing air support. Pakistan's high level of involvement in planning and operations allowed the Taliban militia forces to advance rapidly toward Kabul and establish their institutionalized version of Islamic theocracy, the Islamic Emirate of Afghanistan, in September 1996.

The emergence of the Taliban's Islamic Emirate and its association with the Jamiat Ulema-e-Islam seemed to fit with what al-Qaeda leaders hoped to see in Afghanistan. Once the Taliban had captured eastern Afghanistan, where Osama bin Laden had taken up residence in early 1996 following his flight from Sudan, they benefited from his first investment in the Taliban regime—$1 million in cash, as an incentive for capturing Kabul.[45] Later, bin Laden established "special" ties to Mullah Omar, now the supreme leader of the Taliban regime and movement. Under Taliban rule, highways became secure, which resulted in significant incomes and encouraged al-Qaeda leaders along with numerous wealthy entities from the Persian Gulf states to invest significantly in this "transport mafia" network that was now operating under the Afghanistan Transit Treaty Agreement. The transport mafia shipped goods from the Gulf states via Pakistan to Afghanistan legally, and then reshipped goods back to Pakistan, Iran, and other Central Asian states illegally to avoid customs fees and taxes in countries that were at the receiving end. As a result, there developed a multibillion-dollar industry that paid for the Taliban's military adventures and produced significant profits for al-Qaeda and the militants in Pakistan, which in turn financed the growing number of religious schools across Pakistan and now Afghanistan. These religious schools attracted thousands of students from all over the Islamic world and influenced them in the Taliban and al-Qaeda brand of militancy and global warfare. These economic and political developments all occurred in what had become a black hole within the international system after the Soviet and U.S. withdrawal from Afghanistan.

At the same time, the Taliban movement was rooted deeply in the remote rural settings of southern—and to a certain extent eastern—Afghanistan, where many locals, such as village clerics, held rigid perspectives on urbanite culture. However, the Taliban's political ideology was also rooted vaguely in the traditional Deobandi school of Sunni Hanafi Islam. The local interpretation of Islam in these remote social environments dominated by clerics, as well as by a new breed of students trained in Pakistan during the 1980s and 1990s, also strongly influenced their ideology.[46] The Taliban leaders who elaborated their distinctive interpretation of Islam had rarely studied beyond a primary level. Such localized understandings were not shared by the greater southern society, and especially not by the urban sociocultural milieu of Kandahar, which had been famous for its contributions to the intellectual and artistic character of modern Afghanistan.[47]

Moreover, those who had studied in Pakistani religious schools were trained in a system that differed from the traditional Afghan system. Besides learning general subjects related to Islamic law, such as the *usul* (methods) and *fiqh* (Islamic jurisprudence), they were trained in the theory and practice of political concepts like jihad as "holy war" against the Soviets and the West. In reality, what they learned was a highly charged and politicized version of Islam that spoke of the expectation of a holy war around the world. Though some of the Taliban leaders claimed adherence to the Deobandi school of Hanafi Islam, their religious doctrines lacked the approval of any prominent religious leaders in Afghanistan or abroad, including other Deobandi religious scholars or the internationally respected establishment at al-Azhar in Cairo. These teachings in the Pakistani schools never mentioned Afghanistan's history, culture, or economy, or the importance of ethnic and religious coexistence in Afghanistan, even though the curriculum of these schools seemed broader than those taught in Afghan seminaries. Divorced from the social and political realities of Afghanistan, the Taliban resorted to brutal policies, such as banning music, arts, and literature. This mentality informed their apartheid-like treatment of women and, later, the destruction of historical symbols like the statues of Buddha of Bamyan.[48]

The Taliban's political ideology was also influenced by their rage toward the Afghan mujahedin leaders and some local armed groups, whom they criticized for failing to establish a central political institution. Thus they championed the establishment of an Islamic caliphate in Afghanistan. Their supreme leader, Mullah Muhammad Omar, proclaimed himself "Commander of the Faithful" *(Amir al-Muminin),* and the Taliban renamed Afghanistan an "Islamic Emirate." According to this formulation, all of the residents of Afghanistan were required to follow the rules of the Emirate and obey the orders of the Amir al-Muminin.[49] Anyone who refused would "be called a rebel according to sharia" and, for other Muslims, "it would be obligatory [*farz*] to execute him." Moreover, if the Amir called the people to jihad, "it was also obligatory for all qualified Muslims to follow his order and bear arms against those who are enemies of the Amir."[50] But the Taliban rejected other Islamists, such as Abul Ala Maududi, and criticized their political ideologies as a modern interpretation of Islam.[51] Some outside observers believe that this rejection was a result of their political affiliation with the Jamiat Ulema-e-Islam, a rival religious political party of the Maududi followers of the Jama'at-e-Islami.[52] Yet the Taliban also rejected the Islamic Republic of Iran and the Khomeini-led Islamic model on the basis of Taliban criticism of the Shiites.

For the first time in the history of Afghanistan, the Taliban began to institutionalize Islamism—in a top-to-bottom process—within the state bureaucracy and society at large. Prior to the establishment of the modern Afghan state, sharia had furnished the underlying framework of legal jurisprudence, and the entire judiciary was subordinated to the authority of the king.[53] The historical development of constitutions in Afghanistan illustrates that the state-legislated law *(qanun)* formed the highest source of the law, while its civil and criminal codes drew on the Hanafi jurisprudence of Islamic sharia.[54] But Afghanistan had never been ruled by clerics, and a clerical leader had never been crowned as the head of state. A new force in Afghan political life, the Taliban banned women from education and public participation, and even restricted their public appearances, depriving women and children of access to health care and basic welfare services.[55] Furthermore, the Taliban enforced bans on televisions, VCRs, satellite dishes, and the shaving or trimming of men's beards. They unleashed thousands of religious police under the Ministry for the Promotion of Virtue and the Prevention of Vice to implement such decrees. Public beatings of men and women, executions, stonings, and the amputation of hands and limbs became routine practices.[56]

The formation of the Taliban in a remote and rural area of Afghanistan, the training of a significant number of their leaders abroad, their exposure to a political ideology different from the indigenous patterns of politics, their long military and political march from Kandahar to Kabul, and their puritanical dictatorship all contain echoes of the Chinese Cultural Revolution. And like the Chinese communists who received aid from the Soviets, the Taliban looked to Pakistan in forging a movement and state.[57]

Yet what the Taliban movement lacked was a sophisticated ideological framework; their own ideas remained alien to many of the peoples of Afghanistan. In China, by contrast, the communists rooted their Marxist ideology in ways that generated social, political, and economic changes. This transformation gave the communists a broader popular base. Their establishment of collective farms, worker and student unions, and armed forces with significant political and military cadres enabled China to stand against Stalin's "forward Chinese policy."[58] The Chinese case highlights the significance of the Taliban's inability to remake the movement into a working bureaucracy.

As Hannah Arendt has noted, there are significant differences between a popular movement in opposition and one facing the challenges of governing once in power.[59] This suggests that there is a hidden contradiction within the nature of revolutionary movements that is often buried within the personal character and political ideology of its leader. Like many other revolutionary movements, the Taliban failed to differentiate between running a popular militaristic movement and administering a functioning state.

Mullah Omar and his six-man clerical council formed a system that was based on personal charisma. Meanwhile, the religious decrees that they issued provoked opposition within Afghanistan and beyond its borders. Many of their religious and political rulings even contradicted their ideological colleagues in Pakistan and broke with mainstream Deobandi thought.[60] UN representative Lakhdar Brahimi met Mullah Omar twice and found him to be "cut-off, entirely surrounded by people like himself, [and] very suspicious of intellectuals and the elite."[61] Omar's personal dogma and his rough interpretation of Islam and sharia law had a great impact on the conduct of the Islamic Emirate. Because Omar was the supreme power within the government and personally selected his loyal clerics as members of his inner council at the top of the regime, personal connections prevailed above pragmatic bureaucratic relationships, dooming the Taliban project to failure. A number of Taliban leaders, including Mullah Rabbani, who headed the Taliban government in Kabul, supported the formation of a broad-based government in Afghanistan, exclusion of bin Laden from the affairs of the Taliban, opening schools for girls, and the regulated return of women to work. But Mullah Omar rejected these positions, making the religious police autonomous from the government council in Kabul.[62]

A separate examination dedicated to analyzing the Taliban regime in terms of a totalitarian state would form an interesting discourse. Historical studies have shown that in totalitarian states the dominant political party and the government were combined while evolving into large bureaucracies. Within the infrastructure of the Taliban, however, key leaders of the government played both civil and military roles. They were often more loyal to the principle of the movement than to the state bureaucracy. Still, one resemblance between the to-talitarian system of government and that of the Taliban in Afghani-stan was the manipulation of power by a small group of leaders to di-rect the system based on their worldview. Anthony Downs identified this feature as a hallmark of totalitarian systems: "It makes it more difficult for persons anywhere other than at the top of the bureau-cracy to have a sufficiently wide grasp of the workings of the organi-zation to be able to manipulate the organizational structure for their own purposes, or to direct the organization's behavior in directions contrary to the wishes of the top leadership. Thus task routinization seems to have conflicting thrusts: It implies less arbitrariness and ca-priciousness on the part of supervisors, while at the same time it im-plies a reduced capability for persons not already in positions of sub-stantial authority to affect the character of the system."[63] Indeed, examining the Taliban phenomenon from a more scholarly perspec-tive by utilizing resources in sociology and political science, especially in the context of revolution and bureaucracy, requires much more depth. However, the above analysis indicates that the Taliban leaders lost their contact with the masses once their movement expanded and they were able to seize political power. As a result, they became isolated and they failed to understand the need for directing the af-fairs of the bureaucracy toward recovery from years of violence, wars, and destruction. Instead, they moved toward institutionalizing what they thought would be good for the Afghan masses.

Their lack of bureaucratic and managerial skill made them rely on their "puritanical morality" when formulating public policy. For in-stance, Taliban judges' lack of legal education and training, including in sharia law, was a major contributing factor in prioritizing their brand of moral theology over legal decisions. As a result, they viewed all affairs of state and society in terms of a framework of black versus white, virtue versus vice, Islamic versus un-Islamic. Throughout the entire reign of the Taliban, their government failed to provide public services or undertake any significant reconstruction project in Kabul or in their spiritual capital, Kandahar.

The Taliban's struggle against their opposition, especially the United Front (Northern Alliance) led by Ahmad Shah Masud, resulted in a large number of losses and casualties. The continued resistance, combined with financial difficulties due to UN and U.S. embargos, made the Taliban desperate to produce human and capital resources. Yet their ideological alliance with Osama bin Laden drew them in the orbit of al-Qaeda, making Afghanistan its headquarters, with thousands of Islamic extremists arriving in Afghanistan for military and ideological training. After the United States struck Afghanistan with missiles in 1998, bin Laden attracted enormous attention among the Islamists around the Islamic world, and al-Qaeda emerged as an international front for terrorist activities. On October 8, 1998, Ahmad Shah Masud warned the U.S. Senate Committee on Foreign Relations of the outburst of Islamist militancy in Afghanistan, stating:

> This is a crucial and unique moment in the history of Afghanistan and the world, a time when Afghanistan has crossed yet another threshold and is entering a new state of struggle and resistance for its survival as a free nation and independent state . . . Today, the world clearly sees and feels the results of such misguided [external interfering by our Cold War allies] and evil deeds. South-Central Asia is in turmoil, some countries on the brink of war. Illegal drug production, terrorist activities, and planning are on the rise. Ethnic and religiously motivated mass murders and forced displacements are taking place, and the most basic human and women's rights are

shamelessly violated. The country has gradually been occupied by fanatics, extremists, terrorists, mercenaries, and drug
Mafias. One faction, the Taliban, which by no means rightly
represents Islam, Afghanistan or our centuries-old cultural
heritage, has, with direct foreign assistance, exacerbated this
explosive situation.[64]

According to his aides, Masud launched a covert mission to collect
information about the activities of al-Qaeda, their military bases,
and bin Laden's hideouts in order to prepare his forces and develop
a long-term strategy for fighting the Pakistan-backed Taliban.[65] If
true, Masud would have understood that al-Qaeda was strengthening its roots in Afghanistan and transforming the Taliban government into a support system for international militancy and warfare
around the globe. Thus his warning to the U.S. Senate Committee
on Foreign Relations about al-Qaeda and the Taliban had critical importance that was neglected by the Clinton administration and members of the committee.

Al-Qaeda's military units were located on the front lines against
Masud's forces, and as the fighting continued, the Taliban became
more dependent on al-Qaeda's military and financial support. By the
end of 2000, al-Qaeda contributed around 30 percent to 40 percent
of the Taliban's core military forces.[66] Al-Qaeda's investments, including bin Laden's personal venture in the transregional trafficking
of goods and narcotics, created a lucrative network that attracted increasing investments by other Arab princes and personalities, including some Pakistani military officers, regional politicians, and businesses. In 2000, when sanctions were imposed by the United Nations
and the United States, and after Saudi financial assistance was dis-
continued in an attempt to pressure the Taliban to extradite bin
Laden to the United States, the "transport mafia" became the Tali-

ban's lifeline, requiring even greater monetary involvement by al-Qaeda and Persian Gulf countries. This development made the Taliban both militarily and financially dependent on al-Qaeda. By 2001, al-Qaeda controlled its own military and training camps in various parts of the country, notably in the eastern province of Nangarhar and the northern province of Konduz, and frequently overruled Taliban authority.[67]

The attraction of trafficking industries, combined with the expansion of the madrasas and the establishment of large numbers of training camps for international Islamist militants and their global warfare, put Afghanistan at center stage in the war waged by militant revolutionary forces challenging the existing international order. From the perspective of the al-Qaeda leadership, the geopolitical position of Afghanistan, as the link between Central Asia, the Indian subcontinent, and the Middle East, provided the Islamist militants with enough human and capital resources. The region was vulnerable to nonstate actors, and al-Qaeda pragmatically expanded its connections through regional and international networks.

In this regard, the Talibanization of Afghanistan was a first step toward the Talibanization of the region and the formation of a center of gravity, especially one that influenced Pakistan. Yet standing in the way of this achievement was the indigenous resistance of opposition forces led by Ahmad Shah Masud, who had been pushed into the northeastern corner of Afghanistan, where they controlled only about 20 percent of the country. As later information and analysis has revealed, militants viewed the attack on America as the spark for a global wave of support for the al-Qaeda brand of militancy in the Islamic world.

However, before this could be accomplished, any Afghan opposition needed to be eliminated so that the country would be controlled entirely by the Taliban and al-Qaeda. Masud's military skills and his art of command could have attracted support from Washington. Such backing for Masud could have rapidly developed effective leadership among the anti-Taliban Afghan forces. Therefore, on September 9, 2001, in a preemptive effort to avoid any direct U.S. military support for the opposition forces, al-Qaeda suicide bombers posing as journalists assassinated Masud, a man that the United States very well could have relied upon in the quest to end the Taliban's reign and possibly apprehend bin Laden. Two days later, on September 11, members of al-Qaeda hijacked four passenger planes, crashing them into the World Trade Center and the Pentagon, killing close to three thousand people, both Americans and people of other nationalities.[68]

The terrorist attack on U.S. soil converted Afghanistan into an active war zone between al-Qaeda's multinational fighters and the U.S.-led coalition forces. In early October 2001, the United States began an air campaign against the Taliban and al-Qaeda forces in Afghanistan, while the United Front forces in northern Afghanistan captured Mazar-e Sharif. Soon the rest of their forces, which had been positioned in the Panjsher Valley north of Kabul, moved against the Taliban and al-Qaeda forces in Kabul. In several major cities, such as Herat and Kabul, the city's youth, who were fed up with the Taliban and al-Qaeda, bore arms and freed city centers before the arrival of United Front and coalition forces.

In December, with the support of the UN and the United States, the anti-Taliban political groups mapped out the post-Taliban administrative structure for Afghanistan in talks held in Bonn, Germany. Under this accord, the delegates selected Hamid Karzai as the head of the Afghanistan Interim Authority (AIA) and placed Kabul under the protection of on an international military force—the International Security Assistance Force (ISAF). In December they formed the first post-Taliban, post-al-Qaeda transitional government in Afghanistan, headed by Hamid Karzai, and by June 2002, following the mandates of the Bonn Accords, a loya jirga of sixteen hundred delegates from around the country had convened. The delegates elected Hamid Karzai as president of Afghanistan, along with his proposed cabinet, for another two years. In December 2003 the delegates of the Constitutional Loya Jirga approved a new constitution and opened the way for a presidential election in October 2004.

The effects of Islamization on Afghanistan are far from over, and there still exist Islamist groups that hold substantial political and military power within and outside of the central government: The re-emergence of the Taliban in the southern and southeastern parts of Afghanistan, and their ability to organize cross-border military operations against the coalition and Afghan forces, not only threatens the stability of the newly established regime in Kabul, but has also given momentum to the Islamists in the government who have sought to influence laws and dominate branches of the government.[69] In fact, Islamist domination of local governments in the North West Frontier Province in Pakistan has, in effect, kept alive the internationally oriented support system for the Taliban and al-Qaeda. This influence, along with their integration of militants within the tribal belt via marriage and through the existing network of religious schools, has given them a comparative advantage and the mobility to survive military attacks by the U.S., Afghan, and Pakistani forces.

Like Pakistan's president Pervez Musharraf, President Karzai has barely escaped assassination attempts by the Islamist militants. This indicates that their networks are alive and active to a level that can pose serious threats against the national leaders despite the presence of thousands of sophisticated U.S.-led military units within the area. The Karzai government has become particularly vulnerable due to the shortfall in reconstruction programs and slow social and economic development, as well as the extension of Islamist militant opposition that resulted when Gulbuddin Hekmatyar and Muhammad Yunos Khales (another conservative Islamist leader) joined the militants' camp. The existence of powerful warlords who control their own private armies is also jeopardizing the ability of the Afghan government to provide physical and human security within the government-controlled areas.[70]

More than ten years after its emergence, the Taliban movement is still active, and its survival is strongly rooted in its regional and international support system, which extends beyond the geographic boundaries of Afghanistan, and in the shortcomings of Afghan reconstruction. The Taliban forces continue to use the extended networks of Pakistani Islamist groups. Local conflicts and the lack of progress in reconstruction have afforded the Islamist militants a center of gravity for recruiting human and capital resources. This movement must therefore be dealt with at both regional and international levels. Indeed, this new brand of global militancy continues to draw force from local conflicts. It reflects the weakness of the democratic movement within the Islamic world, deriving from Western neglect of the Islamic world during the Cold War, and the sluggish pace of political, social, and economic progress. The reemergence of the defeated Taliban and their growing influence among populations on both sides of the Afghan border are fueled by the deepening crisis of democracy in a region where its people suffer from a lack of political representation and the basic opportunities necessary to emerge from this crisis.

CHAPTER THREE

The Taliban, Women, and the Hegelian Private Sphere

Juan R. I. Cole

The society created by the Taliban in Afghanistan between 1996 and 2001 constantly evoked outrage and reactions of openmouthed disbelief in the Western press. Even the ayatollahs in Tehran issued a statement condemning the Taliban for defaming Islam by confusing it with medieval obscurantism. Because the Islamic Republic of Iran had long been called medieval itself by political opponents, this criticism of the Afghan government has a delicious irony. One key to comprehending the somewhat strident bewilderment that the Taliban provoked in many observers is the Taliban's reconfiguration of the public and the private in their quest for a pure Islamic countermodernity. I use the phrase *countermodernity* rather than *antimodernism* because the Taliban adopted some key motifs from high modernism and their power depended on modern tools (the state, radio, mass spectacle, tank corps, and machine guns mounted on Toyotas). They used these tools for purposes very different from the goals of the industrialized democracies, however, especially with regard to the private sphere. The public/private divide as drawn by modern liberalism affects everything from how power is attained and exercised to how women are treated. Did the Taliban strike outsiders as bizarre in part because they drew those lines very differently than most other contemporary societies?

The German sociologist Jürgen Habermas argues that the divide between public and private is a feature of modernity. He reports that the word *privat*, derived from the Latin, can be found in Germany only from the late sixteenth century, and that it initially referred to someone who was not an officer of the state. He says that institutionally, "a public sphere in the sense of a separate realm distinguished from the private sphere cannot be shown to have existed in the feudal society of the High Middle Ages." The power of the kings and aristocrats was "public" in the sense not of a sphere of society but of a status position. The lord "displayed himself, presented himself as an embodiment of some sort of 'higher' power." The arena in which power was represented to a wide audience was public, but was not characterized by public participation—it was public the way a stage play is, for a passive audience. The church was likewise "public" in this sense of open display of ritual and authority until proponents of the Enlightenment increasingly coded it as private from the eighteenth century forward.[1] Joan Landes draws attention to Habermas's emphasis on "features of visibility, display and embodiment, that is, an "'aura' that surrounded and endowed the lord's concrete existence." She argues that "staged publicity" was fundamental to absolutist society in the early modern nation-states. This re-presentative performance of kingly authority by a royal subject before an audience was not dependent on having a permanent location or on the development of a public sphere of communication.[2]

Habermas's use of a binary opposition between the "medieval" and "modernity" and his concentration on select areas of Western Europe create an ideological natural history of the public sphere that remains highly Eurocentric. His account obscures the ways in which power as representation, and religion as public, continued to characterize many societies in modernity. Rather than being conceived of as medieval throwbacks, such societies must be viewed as forms of alternative modernity. Even in the Soviet Union and the People's Republic of China, Lenin's vanguard theory allowed power to be exercised in the twentieth century by unelected bureaucrats, in part through massive military parades and other spectacles. In Bolivia and Greece, religion remained public, even as it was privatized in Turkey and Mexico.

What of the private sphere? Seyla Benhabib notes three meanings of the private sphere in modern political thought. She says, "First and foremost, privacy has been understood as the sphere of moral and religious conscience," referring to the separation of religion and state and the granting of individual autonomy in deciding such matters, which are "rationally irresolvable." The second is private enterprise, or the "non-interference by the state in the free flow of commodity relations." The third, she says, is the "intimate sphere"—"meeting the daily needs of life, of sexuality and reproduction, of care for the young, the sick and the elderly"—which she says are typically recognized by modern thinkers as belonging to the domain of the household. She points out that for many modern thinkers, a tension exists between their vision of a patriarchal domestic realm, in contrast to the values of equality and consent in the political sphere.[3] I will argue below that the Taliban stances on the first and the last of these three meanings of the private were the precise opposite of those Benhabib attributes to modern political thought.

As Landes and others have noted, Habermas did his early work on the public sphere before the wide impact of 1970s feminist theory, and he neglects the issue of gender. In retrospect, this lacuna is the most problematic, because all societies imbue the public and the private with overtones of male and female. Even a modern thinker such as Hegel could write,

> The ethical dissolution of the family consists in this, that once the children have been educated to freedom of personality, and have come of age, they become recognized as persons in the eyes of the law and as capable of holding free property of their own and founding families of their own, the sons as heads of new families, the daughters as wives. . . . The natural dissolution of the family by the death of the parents, particularly the father, has inheritance as its consequence so far as the family capital is concerned.[4]

The sons hold free property and enter the public sphere on the dissolution of the old family, whereas the daughters remain domestic, as wives. Hegel writes, "Woman, on the other hand, has her substantive destiny in the family, and to be imbued with family piety is her ethical frame of mind."[5] As Dorothy Rogers has argued, Hegel sees children as initially closer to the spiritual and feeling-oriented sensibility of women, but through education they gain a sense of objectivity and rationality and are prepared to enter the public sphere. She notes, "As anyone with even a hint of gender awareness can see, this leaves women conspicuously absent from public life, because as creatures ruled by feeling, they are unable to make this step from family life into civil society."[6] Hegel's vision was incontrovertibly modern, but he expressed a patriarchal version of modernity.

In Islamdom, as in Europe, the gendering of the public and private was never complete in either theory or practice. An idea of the private, as an inviolable domestic realm, existed in Islamic jurisprudence.[7] Moreover, since Muslim women, unlike European women until the mid-nineteenth century, most often owned property independently of their husbands, their property transactions and endowments had a somewhat public character, though these tended to be executed by male agents. As for social reality, it should be remembered that the vast majority of Muslim women have never veiled or been excluded from appearing in public. Peasant and tribal women worked outside their domiciles. In the twentieth century, millions of Muslim women have become physicians, attorneys, journalists, and members of other public professions. It is often not appreciated with what alacrity urban societies in countries such as Egypt, Tunisia, Iraq, Pahlavi Iran, and Pakistan adopted key elements of modernity, including changes in the status of women.

Afghanistan, which was much more rural and pastoralist and less urban than most of the Muslim world, had a far more limited and sectoral experience of modernity, mainly among the small urban upper middle and upper classes.[8] Early reformist measures taken by Amir Amanullah in the 1920s, such as improving the position of women, contributed to a popular backlash against that monarch.[9] The country was thrown into long-term upheaval by the 1978 Marxist coup and the Soviet invasion and occupation from 1979 to 1989, during which, again, the question of women's position in the public sphere was broached in a major way. A conservative approach to women was taken up by the Islamic guerrilla movement and implemented during the period of warlord infighting between 1992 and 1996. A vast Afghan diaspora in desperately poor refugee camps grew throughout this period, ultimately with some three million expatriates in Pakistan and two million in Iran. In the midst of imposed totalitarian utopias, war, upheaval, and squalid camp life, the ideals of personal autonomy and privacy so dear to the liberal tradition could have meant very little, though they continued to have a purchase among the small urban middle classes that remained.[10]

Radical Islamism is a response both to what its adherents see as the "incomplete" project of Islamization and to the inroads of liberal modernity. Although it draws on "medieval" motifs and imagines the medieval as a golden age, it is in many ways quite different from anything that actually existed in the medieval period. (Conceiving of Islamization as an incomplete process that now requires the technologies of the state to bring it to fruition is itself a form of high modernism.)[11] Radical fundamentalism in any religion challenges the emergence of a reasoned public sphere, favoring forms of authoritarian rule, patriarchy, and religious control. Power and faith are reworked as imposed spectacle rather than as discursive give and take. Like Hegel, radical Muslim fundamentalists code women as essentially subjective and private, and therefore excluded from the public sphere. They advocate a neopatriarchal countermodernity in which they actively combat those elements of the modern condition that contribute to the entry of women into the public sphere, including mass coeducation, mixed-sex factory and office work, women's entry into many professions, and consumerism and the consequent desire for a second income within the family. In Afghanistan, the Taliban feared the advent of such developments, given that few actually existed on the ground. By what techniques did they seek to accomplish the publicization of power and the male body, and the almost complete privatization of women? I will attend in particular to the few female Afghan voices we have for the Taliban period, referring to two memoirs and to material published in Persian on the Internet by the Revolutionary Association of the Women of Afghanistan (RAWA), a Maoist feminist Afghan group.

Let us begin with the question of the nature of the Taliban public realm.[12] As in medieval society, there was little in the way of a public sphere in Afghanistan under their rule. The "public" was coterminous with the power of the state and the somewhat personalistic and arbitrary implementation of its law. Although the Taliban advertised themselves as offering a strict interpretation of sharia, in fact they often presented it in a highly idiosyncratic manner that astonished mainstream Muslims. Habermas depicts two forms of political modernity in his work on the public sphere. In his ideal liberal democracies of the eighteenth and nineteenth centuries, power is exercised through public, reasoned discourse and by the ballot box. He admits that in post–World War II mass societies, however, corporate media have increasingly made power instead a matter of representation again (through political advertising and the monopoly over opinion mongering in the mass media by a relatively small number of talking heads). In mass society, democratic communicative procedures still exist, but they are powerfully subverted by the large corporations. Habermas thus posits two forms of possible political modernity, one liberal and the other employing modern technology to replicate the medieval sense of power as spectacle.

I would argue that the Taliban represent yet a third possibility, also visible in Khomeinist Iran in the 1980s: medieval motifs applied to the modern re-creation of power as representation (and employing some mass media, such as radio, to this end). The Taliban had no elections or public debates, and not even much of a press. The few newspapers published under their rule were heavily censored, appeared only intermittently, and because 90 percent of women and 60 percent of men were illiterate, could have had only a superficial impact in any case. Radio was the major manner by which the Afghan public was reduced to a mass, receiving instructions rather than engaging in democratic consultation. It was supplemented for smaller villages by the network of pro-Taliban clerics throughout the Pashtun regions. Afghanistan had conducted relatively few elections in the twentieth century, so the authoritarian character of Taliban rule was not new. However, their extreme clampdown surpassed the severity of most pre-1979 Afghan regimes.

The overwhelmingly Pashtun Taliban took and kept power by military means, instituting rule by militia, but their authority was enhanced by their religious charisma as holy men. (Pashtuns make up about 40 percent of the Afghan population.) In some ways their rule was analogous to that of the urban *lutis*, or ruffians, in the nineteenth century, when Muslim clerics, seminary students, and street gangs often took over cities in the area from Baghdad to Bukhara.[13] They ruled in part through power spectacle, through the use of captured Soviet tanks and artillery against other ethnic militias. The incessant Taliban warfare and feuding with other ethnic groups, such as the Shiite Hazaras and the Tajiks and Uzbeks (who formed the opposition Northern Alliance), demonstrated their power, as did events like the massacres of defeated populations in the towns of Mazar-e Sharif and Bamyan. The Taliban asserted control over the Hazara region, which had long resisted them and was inhabited by Shiite Muslims, whom they despised. They committed substantial massacres of Hazara civilians. In part, these conflicts and massacres driven by religious ideology reflected a breakdown in barriers to communication and transportation that had enabled heterodox groups like Imami Shiites and Ismailis to flourish in rural areas.[14] Modernity brought the highly disparate citizens of Afghanistan together, and the immediate result was not more but less freedom of conscience. Turkic Uzbeks fared little better. Some eight thousand noncombatants are said to have been killed in Mazar-e Sharif in 1998 alone, when the Taliban reconquered it.[15]

The Taliban's titular head, Mullah Muhammad Omar, claimed charismatic authority and eventually the Islamic caliphate itself. Mullah Omar came in many ways to be beholden to and threatened or manipulated by his Saudi guest, Osama bin Laden, the head of al-Qaeda and commander of the Taliban's 55th Brigade (its most effective fighting force, mainly Arab). Mullah Omar was reclusive and staged few public spectacles. His power circulated to the public through his representatives, the Taliban themselves, who were omnipresent in the streets and over Radio Voice of Sharia. He did, however, engage in one momentous piece of "staged publicity," just before his conquest of Kabul in 1996. Kandahar is the site of a mosque complex centered on a relic, the supposed cloak of the Prophet Muhammad, said to have been brought there by Ahmad Shah Durrani, who Afghans believe founded the modern Afghan state in 1747. Amir Amanullah had once also appealed to the charisma of the cloak in his failed bid to avoid being overthrown in the late 1920s. According to *New York Times* reporter Norimitsu Onishi, the shrine keeper said the cloak itself had been offered for viewing only twice before 1996: once to the country's former monarch, Zaher Shah, who is said to have averted his eyes at the last minute, and once to his former ally, the political leader Pir Sayyed Ahmad Gailani. In the spring of 1996 Mullah Omar requested permission to see it.

He not only viewed the relic, said to produce miracles, but insisted on bringing it out of the shrine for a public showing. This unprecedented public ritual produced a large crowd. Onishi writes,

> With the cloak in his possession, Mullah Omar went to an old mosque in the center of the city and climbed onto its roof. For the next 30 minutes, he held the cloak aloft, his palms inserted in its sleeves. According to residents of Kandahar who were present, the crowds cheered. Many lost consciousness. Many threw their hats and other items of clothes in the air, in the hope that they would make contact with the cloak. Most importantly, as other mullahs shouted, *"Amir-ul momineen!"* Mullah Omar gained the legitimacy he needed to pursue his conquest of the rest of Afghanistan.[16]

The cries of *Amir al-Muminin* (Commander of the Faithful) served as an affirmation that Mullah Omar had revived the caliphate, which had been abolished several times in Islamic history and then revived, most recently by Ottoman Sultan Abdülhamid II, around 1880. It was abolished by Mustafa Kemal Atatürk in 1924.

It was because of Mullah Omar's status as caliph, or prince of the believers, that Afghanistan under the Taliban was declared the Islamic Emirate of Afghanistan. Apparently bin Laden and al-Qaeda hoped to use this caliphal revivalism as a rallying point for Muslims throughout the world. Mullah Omar took his charge seriously, likening himself to the second caliph, also called Omar, and sneaking out in street clothes as his namesake had done to gauge the problems of the common person. (This sort of story was also told of some Afghan kings, and goes back to the depiction of Harun al-Rashid in the *Thousand and One Nights*.) He also began wearing a perfume said to be based on the same recipe as the one worn by the Prophet Muhammad. Despite his reputation as a recluse, Mullah Omar did circulate, virtually making his SUV into a sort of mobile office. Another press report quotes Mullah Omar's chauffeur. "After a time, he had so many supplicants that he could no longer maintain an office. 'Everywhere is my office,' he told Saheb [his driver]. 'I can issue orders from anywhere.' Saheb spent hours driving Omar around; after a time the car began to reek of a kind of perfume (probably camphor) which, Omar claimed, had been worn by the Prophet Muhammad himself."[17] Mullah Omar projected his personal authority through these forms of public display—the famed showing of the Prophet's mantle, symbolizing Mullah Omar's claiming to be his vicar, the circulating SUV office, the careful olfactory marking of himself as having divine authority through the Prophet's perfume (in Afghan folklore, the corpses of holy men in their tombs are widely thought to resist disintegration and to give off a sweet odor). But he more often marked his power by disappearing from public view and rationing access to himself.

The Taliban as a group, in contrast, were far from reclusive, and from the beginning employed public spectacle to rule. They announced their advent in Kabul in September 1996 from the minarets of mosques.[18] Like the eighteenth-century French monarchs who inscribed their justice on the criminal by drawing and quartering him, so the Taliban revived public executions as spectacle, as part of their implementation of power as public performance.[19] Even the tapes from music and videocassettes were torn from their casings and displayed on the goalposts of the stadium where executions were held. The ruined "bodies" of the offending magnetic tape media were made a spectacle, just as were the bodies of those human beings deemed criminal.

Journalist Jan Goodwin witnessed a Taliban spectacle early in 1998:

> Thirty-thousand men and boys poured into the dilapidated Olympic sports stadium in Kabul, capital of Afghanistan. Street hawkers peddled nuts, biscuits and tea to the waiting crowd. The scheduled entertainment? They were there to see a young woman, Sohaila, receive 100 lashes, and to watch two thieves have their right hands amputated. Sohaila had been arrested walking with a man who was not a relative, a sufficient crime for her to be found guilty of adultery. Since she was single, it was punishable by flogging; had she been married, she would have been publicly stoned to death . . . As Sohaila, completely covered in the shroud-like *burqa* veil, was forced to kneel and then flogged, Taliban "cheerleaders" had the stadium ringing with the chants of onlookers. Among those present there were just three women: the young Afghan, and two female relatives who had accompanied her. The crowd fell silent only when the luckless thieves were driven into the arena and pushed to the ground. Physicians using surgical scalpels promptly car-

ried out the amputations. Holding the severed hands aloft by the index fingers, a grinning Taliban fighter warned the huge crowd, "These are the chopped-off hands of thieves, the punishment for any of you caught stealing." Then, to restore the party atmosphere, the thieves were driven in a jeep once around the stadium, a flourish that brought the crowd to their feet, as was intended. These Friday circuses, at which Rome's Caligula would doubtless have felt at home, are to become weekly fixtures for the entertainment-starved male residents of Kabul.[20]

As in Foucault's old regime, these public punishments of miscreants inscribed the power of the state on the body of the offender. Afghan's twentieth-century monarchy had also staged such spectacles, including the gruesome trampling of adulteresses by an elephant. Unlike in absolute monarchy, however, the criminals here were considered to have sinned not against the king but against the holy law.

Mullah Omar and the Taliban claimed legitimacy as the guarantors of sharia, and said that it was their duty to conform the bodies of Afghans to its strictures. Thus, the back of the veiled fornicator was scourged by the whip (surely an erotically charged performance), and the hands of the thieves were detached, all before an audience of thousands. Sharia does not require, and perhaps even discourages, punishment as spectacle. The Taliban were not merely affirming their piety or their implementation of Islamic law as they saw it by their weekly show at the stadium; they were engaged in "staged publicity" that ritually affirmed their power and legitimacy. For this reason, watching the spectacles of punishment was not voluntary, and was even a family affair that exposed young children to the brutality. A young woman memoirist, Zoya, reports, "Near the stadium, we saw their patrols ordering shopkeepers to close down and go watch the ritual. I was surprised to see women taking their children with them, but [my friend] Zeba explained, 'They want their children to realize what will happen to them if they ever steal anything. They think scaring them is a good way to educate them.'"[21]

Despite Taliban claims, the public exercise of violence by the Taliban had more to do with power than with piety. Punishments were applied quite apart from the requirements of Islamic law. Latifa, a young Afghan woman, saw a group of women in long black veils being beaten bloody by Taliban in the street. Bewildered, she later made inquiries. "They were beaten because they were wearing white socks. . . . That is the color of the Taliban flag, and women do not have the right to wear white. It means they are defiling the flag."[22] This public thrashing, delivered to a group of hapless women in the street, upheld the castelike privileges of the Taliban and the sanctity of their flag (a modern instrument for the representation of the power of the state). Like the amputations and whippings in the stadium, it claimed a monopoly of symbolic power in the public sphere for the Taliban. Jan Goodwin reported another such state-related assertion of public power through violence. "After another man, a saboteur, was hanged, his corpse was driven around the city, swinging from a crane. Clearly, there is nothing covert about the regime's punitive measures. In fact, the Taliban insure they are as widely publicized as possible."[23] Sabotage against the state required not a quiet death sentence in a prison but a public hanging. Even a hanging in a single stationary site, like the stadium, was insufficiently public in this instance—the corpse of the miscreant had to be even further publicized by being swung from a crane mounted on a Toyota truck and driven around the city. The modernity of such a procedure should be underlined, since it is the combustion engine that makes practical the rapid touring of the saboteur's swinging cadaver. Likewise the bodies of former communist dictator Najibullah and his brother were left dangling from a traffic platform in bustling downtown Kabul for nearly two days in 1996. Goodwin alleges that they had been castrated, which would have been not a sharia punishment but an expression of Taliban power in their highly masculine public sphere.

The highly publicized destruction by the Taliban (apparently at the insistence of bin Laden and al-Qaeda) of the mammoth Buddhas of Bamyan in the spring of 2001 was not merely a statement of religious iconoclasm (graven idols are forbidden in the Taliban version of Islam). It also functioned as a further assertion of power by spectacle. The Taliban clearly enjoyed defying the outrage of the international community. The Buddhas had been in the past, and might have at some future point again been, tourist destinations, so the Taliban permanently destroyed this beacon for infidels. The Taliban were not the first Muslim iconoclasts to wreak damage on pre-Islamic art and monuments in Afghanistan, but they were the first to do it in so spectacular and systematic a manner.

Benhabib's three forms of modern privacy begin with "moral and religious conscience" and the autonomy granted the individual over these metaphysical matters, which are considered private because they are not amenable to public, rational resolution. That this issue comes first in her listing is no accident. She introduces the paragraph by saying that "first and foremost" privacy has been thus understood by modern political thinkers. Benhabib serves here as reporter for the modern, but of course each form of modernity has its own subtraditions. Raised in Kemalist Turkey with its militant governmental devotion to a sort of Jacobin tradition of forcibly divorcing religion from the state, it may be that Benhabib was influenced by her background to make this sort of privacy her keystone. (Most Americans would probably agree.) It is not clear that autonomy of moral and religious conscience would be quite as thoroughgoing or as central to modernity in the United Kingdom, for instance, where there is a blasphemy law on the books, or in Ireland or Greece.

Still, the centrality to "modern political thinkers" of this privatization of religion may certainly be conceded. The Taliban, in contrast, sought to deprivatize religion. This publicization of the sacred required that all men worship in public, and so it was decreed. "The decree saw scores of Taliban fighters armed with machine guns, lengths of hosepipe, and sticks forcing passersby into mosques for prayers on the first Friday after the Taliban arrived here."[24] The insistence that the five daily prayers be performed at the mosque had the effect of making the performance or nonperformance of worship a matter of public knowledge and concern. (In fact, by 1998 the pressure for universal male mosque worship had weakened considerably in Kabul, and the road blockades initially employed to require it had been given up.)[25]

Men were given six weeks to grow their beards to a hand's length and to trim their mustaches in accordance with a literal reading of sayings about the Prophet Muhammad's appearance. The young female memoirist of life in Taliban Kabul, Latifa, reported that her middle-class father complied with the new rule, grumbling, "My beard belongs to the Taliban, not to me!"[26] The religious state owned the beard of Latifa's father, which was thereby alienated from him insofar as he lost the autonomy to decide its trim. In Taliban terminology, what was *zaher*, or public, had to conform to their understanding of sharia as interpreted by medieval jurists. The beard was public, could be seen, and so required conformity.

Men's bodies became an arena of contention between globalizing consumer culture and Taliban localization. The popularity of bootleg copies of the film *Titanic* caused many young urban Afghanis to lionize Hollywood actor Leonardo DiCaprio. "The Titanic fashion wrought ravages, notably among the barbers," Latifa tells us. "Radio

Sharia announced that 28 of them were arrested and condemned for having given young men a Leonardo DiCaprio haircut."[27] Zoya also recounts the *Titanic* craze, noting that young men wearing the "Titanic cut" also risked harassment and beatings in the street. The Taliban called for the killing of Leonardo DiCaprio and his costar in the movie, Kate Winslet, should they ever come to Afghanistan, because the film celebrated love out of wedlock.[28]

The Taliban had a mixed record with regard to Benhabib's second notion of privacy as economic free enterprise. Under their rule, private trade between Afghanistan and Pakistan burgeoned. Pakistani journalist Imtiaz Gul reported, "The biggest supporters of the Taliban rule are the traders [and truckers]," because the Taliban had abolished the multitude of illegal checkpoints once run by the warlords. Truck drivers had been forced to pay bribes at each of the forty warlord checkpoints between Kandahar and the Pakistani border town of Chaman, whereas under the Taliban there were only two checkpoints, both legal, and the traders paid only official government taxes.[29]

Yet the Taliban strictly forbade the taking of interest on loans, the bedrock of the modern banking system. It had been a practice common even in the Muslim bazaar and among money-changers, justified by various legal workarounds *(hiyal)*. Islamic modernists such as the Egyptian jurist Muhammad Abduh (d. 1905) had allowed modern banking interest, but the Taliban rejected such modernist interpretations of Islam.

The Taliban sought to forestall the development in Afghanistan of a mass consumer culture and its publicization of the domestic and private spheres. Their policies produced what seem to be contradictions, insofar as they insisted on an extreme demarcation between private and public but at the same time attempted to extend the power of the state into the bedroom through their insistence on the ubiquity of Islamic law. In some ways they conducted a vast reprivatization of domesticity, a realm that they even more inexorably than Hegel assigned to women. Windows had to be painted black so that they did not reveal the private domesticity, especially unveiled women, within. In essence, the window had served as a potential hole in the dike of the public/private divide, and painting windows black patched the hole. Latifa complained bitterly of being thus deprived of a ground-level view of the street, but admitted that blackening the windows did have some advantages. It made it more difficult for the Taliban religious police to see the glow of the television screen within when her brother clandestinely set up a showing of Indian films on the family videocassette recorder.[30] Street-level windows were not traditional in Afghan buildings and were largely limited to fairly new upper-middle-class neighborhoods, so it was mainly families of Latifa's and Zoya's social class who were affected by this decree.[31]

The Egyptian journalist Fahmi Huwaydi pressed the head of the Ministry for the Promotion of Virtue and the Prevention of Vice about the nature of his work in 1998. This powerful agency had its own extensive funding from Wahhabi sources in the Gulf and was modeled on the similar Saudi corps of religious enforcers.[32] The minister, Mawlawi Qalamuddin, replied: "We do not spy on people. That is a matter forbidden by the divine law. Likewise, we do not enter anyone's house. Everyone is free *(hurr)* in his home. God will punish him for any vice he commits there. What concerns us is open vice *(al-munkarat al-zahirah)* in the streets or public places *(al-amakin al-'ammah)*. We see it as our responsibility to combat these vices because they harm the Islamic society we are seeking. In addition, our silence about them would be tantamount to encouraging the spread of vice."[33] In accordance with classical Islamic law, Mawlawi Qalamuddin acknowledged a sphere of domesticity as properly private. The privacy of domesticity was not entirely sacrosanct, however, because the divine law applied to all human behavior at all times. In actual fact, the public nature of sharia, and the application of sharia to even private acts, extended the reach of the Taliban state even into homes. Latifa notes that her neighbor's telephone went silent for a while, giving no dial tone. When the line was reestablished, however, Latifa's father hesitated to use it. "We know well that the Taliban listen to everything, monitor everything."[34] The lived reality of life under the Taliban contradicted Mawlawi Qalamuddin's insistence that the Taliban did not spy on private homes. Their deprivatization of society led to a panopticon where, whether justifiably or not, the populace felt under constant scrutiny and dared not commit speech crimes over telephone lines that may have become public. The Taliban employed the technique of circulation to impose this scrutiny, with the armed talibs constantly moving about the city in their pickup trucks.

Huwaydi reports the text of a decree by the Ministry for the Promotion of Virtue and the Prevention of Vice issued December 17, 1996, at the order of Mullah Omar, banning sixteen activities:

1. Temptation *(fitna)* likely to cause public disturbance and the baring of women's faces in public was forbidden. Taxi drivers were not to accept as fares women who wore a burqa but did not completely cover their faces, on pain of imprisonment. Women were not to walk in the street without a close male relative *(mahram)*.

2. Music was forbidden in shops, hotels, and automobiles, on pain of imprisonment and the closing of the offending establishment.

3. Shaving a beard was forbidden. A month and a half after this decree, anyone not bearded was to be imprisoned until his beard grew out.

4. Daily prayers were to be said in mosques. Shops had to be

closed at prayer time and vehicles had to cease circulating in the streets 15 minutes before prayer time. Shopkeepers open at prayer time would be jailed for 10 days.

5. Training pigeons and playing with birds were forbidden.

6. Drug trafficking was forbidden, along with the use of drugs.

7. Kite flying and betting on it were forbidden.

8. No image of persons could be displayed in shops, hotels, or taxis, since this was a form of idolatry.

9. Gambling was forbidden.

10. Letting one's hair grow out in the American or British fashion was forbidden. The agents of the Ministry for the Promotion of Virtue and the Prevention of Vice were to apprehend violators and cut their hair.

11. Taking interest on loans was forbidden, on pain of a long prison term.

12. Women were not to wash clothes on the banks of rivers. If found doing so they would be remanded to the custody of a male guardian and severely punished.

13. Music and dancing were forbidden at wedding ceremonies.

14. Drum music was forbidden. The ulama (body of clerics) would decide on the punishment for it.

15. Men were forbidden to tailor women's clothing or to take their measurements. If found doing so they would face a prison term.

16. Practicing astrology was forbidden. Astrologers would be imprisoned until they repented. Their books would be burned.[35]

I would argue that this list signals to us that we are in the presence of a way of thinking, an *episteme*, that differs significantly from that of liberal modernity.[36] The premises of the list are not immediately apparent, even to academics trained in Islamics. What logic drove Mullah Omar to issue these instructions in the first place? Many of these decrees forbade activities (music, dancing, pigeon flying, kite flying, gambling, representation of the human form, and astrology) that struck the Taliban as frivolous or impudent. The influence on them of the Wahhabi tradition is important here, because that branch of Islam views frivolity with the utmost disfavor. The public display of soberness is felt to indicate a private, inner piety, whereas public frivolity suggests iniquity in one's inner moral life. Soberness of mien was also a mark of authority for ruling cliques in Afghanistan, as the unsmiling portraits of most past Afghan monarchs suggests.[37] Pigeon flying and kite flying were both occasions for gambling (forbidden in Islam) and were probably banned partly for this reason. Other decrees, however, sought to close any connection between the public and the private. Thus, the baring of women's faces in public, the display of images of women (for instance, posters in shops hawking the charms of Bollywood actresses such as Neema and Madhuri), the male tailoring of women's clothes, and the public washing of the family's laundry, including unmentionables, by women, were all banned. In some cases the Taliban were simply reimplementing older statutes. Women washing clothes in the river was banned by the Kabul municipality in the 1950s, and tailors had for some time been under suspicion because of their mixing with and easy access to women.[38] I will return later to this concern with the extreme privatization of women. As Huwaydi notes, many of these decrees proved impractical to implement, or were so widely resisted as to remain only partially in force, if at all.

The Taliban ban on dancing at weddings extended public, state concerns into a sphere that might be considered private or at least semiprivate.[39] In Afghanistan, there was almost never mixed-sex dancing at weddings (unlike among the more secular middle-class Pakistani families, where cousins might dance together). Women would dance at their parts of the celebrations, and men at theirs. Even this sort of same-sex display of secular joy was banned, however, along with any playing of music.

In 1997 Latifa heard a woman wailing in the street below. She looked out her upper-story window to see the mother of Aimal lamenting as a group of three Taliban beat her son with the butts of their Kalashnikov rifles. Aimal had set up a showing for five friends of an Indian movie on a videocassette recorder at his home; somehow the Taliban had learned of it. They broke in, caught the boys in the act, and strung out the cassette tape. This "execution" of magnetic tape media seemed to give the Taliban special pleasure, perhaps because it restored what they saw as a breach in the wall of public and private, real and unreal. Inside its cassette, the tape was capable of illicitly displaying, in private, virtual human images and voice that ought to exist only in a real public sphere. Strung out in the street, the tape was pushed out of the private sphere permanently and inverted so as to be itself lifeless and public. The Taliban took the boys out in the street and made them beat one another in public, a humiliation for an Afghan youth. When Aimal was insufficiently zealous in beating his friend, the Taliban pulled him over and said they would show him how it was done. He died an hour later.[40]

Zoya tells a similar story as farce rather than tragedy. In her anecdote, once the offending family is pulled out of their home for viewing an Indian film and given a public lashing, the Taliban go inside. "When the family dared to return, they found the Taliban sitting around the television set watching and commenting on the film, which was still playing. The Taliban took a bribe from the family and did not arrest them."[41] These stories by middle-class urban women are about not the harshness of the law but its arbitrariness and unevenness of application. The Taliban regime opened all homes to invasion, it is being said, and could transform minor infractions into capital crimes or could elicit hypocrisy and bribe taking on the part of the young talibs.

The sense of being constantly under surveillance was reinforced by the ban on most media, which urban people continued surreptitiously to enjoy. "Zeba told me that the only time she could listen to her music tapes was before going to sleep, and she would keep the volume as low as possible out of fear that the neighbors would inform on her if they heard the offending sound." Zoya says that although photographs and television were formally forbidden, some families had illegal televisions sets (just as others had illegal videocassette recorders) and even satellite dishes with which they pirated signals (presumably they also had illegal signal decoders and were thus breaking international law as well as the Taliban version of sharia).[42]

Like in Anglo-Saxon law (and unlike the general continental European legal tradition), the Taliban interpretation of sharia did not recognize a right of privacy where lawbreaking is concerned. Thus, in 1986 the U.S. Supreme Court upheld Georgia's sodomy law by a 5-to-4 vote, insisting that consenting adults have no constitutional right to private homosexual conduct. Goodwin reported of Afghanistan, "Earlier that same week, three men accused of 'buggery' had been sentenced to death by being partially buried in the ground and then having a wall pushed over on them by a bulldozer, a bizarre and labor-intensive form of execution dreamed up by the supreme leader of the Taliban, the 36-year-old Mullah Muhammad Omar."[43] This execution was another example of grand spectacle aimed at making public the power of the Taliban state. But Goodwin is wrong that it was thought up by Mullah Omar. Rather, throwing a wall down on gay people is recommended in some very obscure sayings attributed in the medieval period to the Prophet Muhammad. The Taliban delighted in finding the more extreme and unlikely of such sayings and then attempting to put them into force (most often for the first time in Islamic history, underlining again that they were engaged in a form of countermodernity rather than in reviving medieval forms). The execution also had the effect, however, of reinforcing the extension of sharia into the realm of even private behavior.

The Taliban not only attempted to push (law-abiding) domesticity relentlessly into the private realm, but also coded the female body as inherently private. The neoprivatization of women formed a key goal of Taliban policy, as is clear in the autobiographical accounts of Latifa and Zoya. The Taliban's insistence on gender segregation was hardly new in Afghanistan, especially in Pashtun society. But because they imposed this norm on urban societies such as Mazar and Kabul, and because of the extremes to which they took it there, it seemed more draconian to city dwellers than in the past. Interestingly, this plank of their platform seems not to have stood out for some male Afghan observers. Of the nineteen goals that Abdul Hamid Mubarez attributes to the Taliban with regard to establishing a religious state, only one concerns women, and that is the imposition of full public veiling.[44] It is precisely because women are so little noticed in Persian and Urdu accounts of the Taliban by men that it is important to look at the small amount of autobiographical material we have from Afghan women in order to grasp some of the subjective implications of this reprivatization program. In male conversations, such as those Huwaydi conducted with Taliban officials, the reality of women's life under the Taliban is often obscured by talk about ideals.

Taliban policy toward women reversed that of the communist government of the 1980s. Val Moghadam has discussed the improvements in the lives of (mainly urban) women during the communist period in the 1980s. Women fought in the Revolutionary Defense Group militias and even served as commanders. A few served as delegates to the loya jirga, the national assembly. Moghadam saw women working in factories, including as supervisors of men and as union activists. Women were employed in the national airline, as unveiled newscasters, and in youth and peace organizations. It should be remembered, however, that most rural women's lives were little touched by the changing regimes, except insofar as they got caught up in the fighting. In 1979, according to International Labor Organization statistics, only 313,000 out of 6.2 million Afghan women were counted as economically active, and only 13,000 worked as professional and technical workers. In 1975 the enrollment rate among girls for primary and secondary school was only about 10 percent. The literacy campaign of the communist government in the 1980s led, by 1988, to 233,000 girls studying in schools and about 7,000 in colleges and universities. In contrast, few girls among the millions of refugees in Pakistan were provided any education.[45] When the Islamist government of Burhanuddin Rabbani came to power in 1992, it began the process of rolling back women's rights and immediately forbade women to drive. The Taliban were even more repressive of women. The urban and small-town women who remained in Afghanistan working in textiles or professional positions bore the brunt of Taliban neopatriarchy.

The Taliban announced a policy of closing girls' schools and of confining women to their homes. Mawlawi Said Shahidkhayl, the Taliban undersecretary of education in 1998, explained the regime's policy toward women to Huwaydi: "The education of girls requires a jurisprudential ruling (fatwa) that would fix its path and its limits. As for women working outside the house, the text concerning that is clear and the matter is incontrovertible. For when the Koran says 'stay in your houses' [33:33; the feminine imperative is used], the issue requires no further discussion and we have nothing to do but obey."[46] The undersecretary insisted that the formal ban on girls' education was not a fixed policy, but rather a temporary measure. The insistence that women remain within the four walls of their homes, however, was not only rigid policy, he said, but the divine law and so beyond discussion. Huwaydi pointed out that the verse about women staying in their homes concerned only the Prophet's wives and had to do with specific social arrangements in the Prophet's Medina, and that the Egyptian ulama held that it could not be generalized to all Muslim women. Indeed, it is preceded (33:32) by the clear statement to the wives that "you are not like any other women." Mawlawi Shahidkhayl insisted that the generalized import of the verse was upheld by all the prominent Afghan ulama (he meant those of the neo-Deobandi school, influenced by Wahhabi ideas from Saudi Arabia, who supported the Taliban).[47]

When Huwaydi quoted to him a saying of the Prophet Muhammad that seeking knowledge is a duty for every Muslim, Mawlawi Shahidkhayl said that there were two possible responses to this point. One was that the saying specified only "Muslims," using the male form of the word, and did not mention any female Muslim *(muslimah)*. He acknowledged that in Arabic grammar the male was most often considered to encompass the female, but he said that some among the Taliban took the failure to mention the *muslimah* specifically as an indication that she was not intended by the saying. He insisted that he himself did not belong to that school, and favored some form of women's education if it could be accomplished properly. He expressed dismay at the state in which the Taliban had found girls' education when they took Kabul, which could not have been pleasing to God. "Some classes were coeducational, and the curricula were the furthest thing possible from the Sharia of God." He said the girls knew nothing of their religion and "had no interest in their roles as wives, mothers and mistresses of the family." He said the appearance of the girls, the nature of the teaching staff, and the condition of the buildings all required extensive review.[48]

When Huwaydi pressed him as to whether there was any scriptural basis for forbidding men to teach women, Mawlawi Shahidkhayl said the Taliban were opposed to the mixing of the sexes in principle. "Anyone who is assailed by doubt concerning our stance on this matter has only to follow what the newspapers have published about the story of President Clinton and Monica Lewinsky. I have no doubt that it is repeated in one form or another in every government office where women and men mix." Huwaydi says that the mischievous mullah fell silent for a moment, then said, laughing, "I do not say that it is repeated exactly. But note that I used the phrase 'in one form or another.'"[49]

Mawlawi Shahidkhayl gave two examples of the way in which the Taliban had improved women's position and restored for them their human rights. He described the decree of Mullah Omar issued in September 1998 regarding a tribal custom. It was customary, he said, that when one Afghan man killed another, the clan of the offender would present a woman or several women to the clan of the victim as compensation, so as to avoid a blood feud. Mullah Omar ordered this practice halted because it "was contrary to the teachings of Islam, which bestows respect on women. It is therefore impermissible that they be given away or used as compensation." Likewise, there was another tribal custom, concerning widows. When a woman's husband died, the clansmen of her late husband would marry her off to another of their men, willy-nilly. Mullah Omar insisted that widows had the right to choose their own husbands, from another family or tribe if they so desired.[50] The Taliban saw themselves as recognizing the personhood and private autonomy of women in a far more thoroughgoing manner than was the case in Afghan tribal custom. They saw themselves as Islamic modernizers in an oppressive tribal environment (and it is true that the Taliban discouraged tribalism, at least in their formal discourse).

What Mawlawi Shahidkhayl neglected to say was that the reform allowing widows to remarry outside their husbands' clan had been passed by Amir Abdul Rahman (r. 1880–1901) and was not a new step at all, though it did partake of a history of modernist reform-ism.[51] Even the decrees passed by Amanullah in the 1920s went much farther. That such decrees had to be reissued by various governments over the past century suggests the resilience of Pashtun tribal practice with regard to widow remarriage and the unstable character of modernity in this setting. In his justifications for the Taliban, Mawlawi Shahidkhayl highlighted how anti-tribal their more universal, Islamic ideology was, and he denied that they were misogynists. Numerous eyewitness accounts of actual Taliban behavior on the ground, however, show that hatred of women informed many policies and incidents. Many Taliban were orphans, brought up in all-male radical Islamist seminaries, and so they grew up without much knowledge of or respect for women. Many had been refugees or displaced persons, deprived of the usual male sources of self-esteem, and for that reason perhaps they needed to feel superior to, and even to practice sadism on, women. Denied an ordinary private life in the camps and seminaries, and now in the ranks of their militia, many had scant respect for others' privacy.

Mawlawi Shahidkhayl insisted that, given how the Taliban actually "improved" women's conditions, there could be only one reason the Western press so excoriated their policies toward women. It was not that the Westerners really cared about women, he opined, but rather that they hated Islam. "The Koran informed us fourteen centuries ago that they will never be pleased with us until we follow their religious community *(millatahum),* even in the pattern of life and the manner of living it."[52] The Taliban policies on the privatization of women, then, were seen by some officials as a form of Islamic nativism, a refusal to adopt a globalizing Western "pattern of life."

Despite Mawlawi Shahidkhayl's equivocations, the first step the Taliban took once they captured Kabul was to close the girls' schools.[53] Within three months, the Taliban had closed sixty-three schools, affecting 103,000 girls and somewhat more boys.[54] Soon after the fall of Kabul there were reports of women being sentenced to public beatings at the bazaar for not completely veiling their faces.[55] Zoya reports:

> [Women] were banned from appearing on the balconies of their houses. They could go outside only if they were accompanied at all times by a *mahram*, a close relative. They were banned from working. At certain times during the Ramadan month of fasting, they were simply not allowed on the streets. Women who were sick could only be treated by women doctors. Girls could not go to school—according to the Taliban, schools were a gateway to Hell, the first step on the road to prostitution. Women were not allowed to laugh or even speak loudly, because this risked sexually exciting males. High heels were banned because their sound was also declared provocative. Makeup and nail varnish were banned. Women who failed to respect such edicts would be beaten, whipped, or stoned to death.[56]

In the week after the Taliban took Kabul, women doctors were confined to their houses and denied permission to go out (Latifa's mother was among them).[57] Zoya points out that women patients suffered as a result, since they could not be seen by male physicians, and she says that a religious rationale was given for women being a sort of martyr if they died from lack of treatment. "The women suffered more than the men, because the Taliban would not allow them to be treated by male doctors. For the Taliban, if a woman was sick, it was better for her to die than to be treated by a man. If she refused to let a male doctor touch her, she would be certain of going to Heaven. If she let herself be treated by him, she would be condemned to Hell."[58] She described a woman at the hospital she visited who said she could not afford medicine because she was not allowed to work, and had waited days to see one of the few female physicians on staff.

The Taliban rules hit working-class women, especially single women, orphans, and war widows, especially hard. The twenty-year-long war had left as many as thirty thousand of them without male relatives able and willing to support them. Zoya complained, "I could only think that for many war widows the rule that they could not go out without a mahram was a tragedy. It meant that they could not leave their houses and had no way of earning a living apart from begging in the streets and risking a lashing from the Taliban, or turning to prostitution."[59]

The accounts by Latifa and Zoya, despite their value in giving us a private, insider's view of the impact of these policies on educated urban women, often neglect to distinguish between social reality and stated Taliban policy. By 1999, for instance, CARE had convinced the Taliban to allow Afghan women to distribute food aid on its behalf to the war widows. Thus, not all of them were left to starve or sell themselves, although no doubt some were. Likewise, there were at least some female physicians in government clinics to see women (far too few for the need, and the official ban on female education impeded the training of a new generation). By 1999 some thirty thousand girls were being quietly home-schooled or taught in segregated mosque school classes. The numbers are small and the classes were rudimentary and technically illicit (and could bring punishments), but it is important to stress that Taliban policies were not applied consistently and that the Taliban did not have the manpower to implement every policy they announced.[60]

For middle-class urban women with male providers, the strictures had less dire economic consequences, but they still came as a shock. Latifa says she tried on what in Pakistan is called the "shuttlecock" burqa for the tiny mesh that covers the face even as the rest of the body is completely enveloped in cloth. She found she could barely breathe and was rendered clumsy. "I left there humiliated and furious. My face belongs to me. And the Koran says that a woman may be veiled, but has to remain recognizable." To Latifa's dismay, around the spring of 1998 Mullah Omar decreed that the mesh of the burqas then in use was too large and must be made finer, even further limiting women's ability to see their surroundings when outside. The new confinement to a small interior space, and the end of school and socializing, drove Latifa into ennui and depression. "My head is empty of projects. Sometimes, I make a tour of the cell."[61] She ultimately fell physically ill with pleurisy and had to be taken to Pakistan for treatment, where she was diagnosed with depression. She also saw her mother, a physician, decline into deep depression from being confined.

RAWA insists that suicide among women rose significantly under the Taliban as a result of depression induced by cabin fever. They cite not only being kept within four walls but also the various assaults on women's honor and feelings of helplessness as driving this phenomenon, which often took the form of self-immolation. They give the example of Lida "Umid," age 20, who, in April 2000, doused herself with gasoline and set herself on fire out of depression under Taliban rule. They report that she was unable to get medical care in her home city of Herat because no female physician was available. The family rushed her to neighboring Iran, but she died of her self-inflicted injuries.[62] RAWA's anecdotal information is confirmed by the results of a health survey of Afghan women conducted in 1998. The report on the Physicians for Human Rights survey explains:

> Participants in the health and human rights survey also reported extraordinarily high levels of mental stress and depression. 81% of participants reported a decline in their mental condition. A large percentage of respondents met the diagnostic criteria for post-traumatic stress disorder (PTSD) (42%) (based on the *Diagnostic and Statistical Manual of Mental Disorders,* Fourth Edition) and major depression (97%), and also demonstrated significant symptoms of anxiety (86%). Twenty-one percent of the participants indicated that they had suicidal thoughts "extremely often" or "quite often." It is clear from PHR's forty interviews with Afghan women that the general climate of cruelty, abuse, and tyranny that characterizes Taliban rule has had a profound affect on women's mental health. Ninety-five percent of women interviewed described a decline in their mental condition over the past two years.[63]

The educated middle class in the cities appears to have experienced alienation and boredom as a result of the extreme privatization of the female body. These women did not see Taliban policy as achieving a new, pure Islamic society; instead, they saw it as unreasonably restrictive and as stunting their sense of personhood, even driving them to consider or commit suicide.

Latifa freely admits that fear of the Taliban drove her to stay inside and risk this depression, while some of her friends were more adventurous. Fahmi Huwaydi, the Egyptian journalist, was surprised to see gaggles of unaccompanied women on Kabul streets in 1998, and this sight is reported by Western journalists as well.[64] Presumably these were working-class women who had no choice but to go out to beg or engage in illicit labor.

Latifa had good reason, even ghoulish reason, for caution, however. Goodwin tells us that Radio Voice of Sharia announced that "225 women had been rounded up and sentenced to a lashing for violating the dress code. One woman had the top of her thumb amputated for the crime of wearing nail polish." Zoya reports that she was whipped on the hand in the streets of Kabul by an elderly talib because her hand had inadvertently come out from under the veil while she was walking. "When I turned I saw a Taliban [*sic*] with a lash in his hand. 'Prostitute!' he shouted at me, the spittle spraying his greasy beard. 'Cover yourself and go from here! Go to your house!'"[65]

The strict privatization of the female body made women's presence in public always problematic for the talibs. Zoya tells of finding a woman distressed in the street. She tried to comfort her and asked why she was distressed. The woman said her mother had an asthma attack and rushed to the hospital. While there her condition worsened because of her burqa, which she removed to fight for breath in the ward. A talib "had burst into the ward and given her mother forty lashes while the daughter watched, helpless to intervene. The nurses had done nothing to stop the beating."[66] Zoya implies that once the Taliban had coded even a hospital waiting room as "public," they were led inexorably to forbid the open appearance of the female body and face there and to beat an asthmatic when she unveiled. The complete privatization of women's bodies aimed at in Taliban ideology, she suggests, inevitably leads to irrational injustices and to the disorientation of women.

As with other forms of illicit behavior, the Taliban dealt with the problem of women who contravened their laws in part by use of spectacle. Spanish journalist Ana Tortajada was shown a video by women activists of a staged punishment of a woman, this time an execution. She says that a woman, Zarmina, was accused of having murdered her husband, though there was no real proof that she was the murderer. Once she was brought to the soccer stadium in Kabul and it became clear that she would be executed by the Taliban's summary justice, the family of the deceased exercised their right in Islamic law to pardon the accused in return for a payment of money. The Taliban officials, however, discussed the matter in the middle of the stadium and announced that, in spite of everything, they would proceed with the execution, for which they had forcibly assembled a large crowd, including children:

> They bring Zarmina to the arena, sitting in the rear of a van they had found, escorted by two other women. Taliban women. All three were covered in blue burqas. They lead her to the site of the execution, on the green of the soccer field. They order her to crouch. Zarmina turns her head back and through the burqa, which at that moment covers her entire body, says something to her executioner, who is leaning against a large cannon. Her head bends again and they shoot her in the nape of the neck. Her body collapses. The lower part of the burqa parts and displays her legs openly, covered in wide printed trousers. The Taliban women hasten to cover back up the lifeless cadaver with the burqa. Zarmina's seven sons attended her execution. The surround-sound of the recording preserves the reaction of the public: weeping and lamentation.[67]

This particular spectacle underlines the extreme patriarchy of the Taliban interpretation of the law. Tortajada's account implies that they were unreasonable in disregarding the willingness of the murdered husband's family to accept blood money in lieu of the execution. The effrontery of a wife who allegedly kills her husband drives them to make an object lesson of her. The spectacle is daring, insofar as in disciplining the rebellious female body the Taliban also risk exposing it. The pistol shot disorients the executed body, throwing off the burqa from her legs and displaying her forbidden trousers. Even in death, she must immediately be covered, the privacy of her body restored because it remains female even if a corpse.

The radical Islamist regime of the Taliban affords an extensive view of the logic of Muslim fundamentalism regarding the public and private spheres. I have argued that the Taliban deprivatized several life-worlds, "publicizing" power, religion, and the male body. The Taliban's techniques were spectacle, circularization, corporeal punishment, and informing and surveillance.

The Taliban, like Afghan leaders before them, employed exhibition to project their power. Mullah Omar's display of the Prophet's cloak is an example of such staged spectacles. The forcible rounding up of thousands to serve as an audience for executions of gays, thieves, adulteresses, and other offenders against the Taliban moral order underlined the public nature of power and the manner in which even private acts could constitute public offenses. Another repertoire of power consisted of circulation—the constant movement in the streets of talibs seeking evidence of public infractions or of private indiscretions. As in the state of Georgia in the United States, so among the Taliban, there was no guarantee of privacy within one's own home, despite official Taliban denials of domestic spying. The circulation of a Toyota truck through the streets of Kabul with a corpse swinging from its winch served as an alternative to the stadium, but was equally public, and it also exemplified the technique of circulation.

Religion, too, was to be completely public, as Habermas argues it was in Europe before the eighteenth century. As soon as they took Kabul, the Taliban insisted that all residents had to say their five daily prayers, the men in mosques. Likewise, men were given six weeks to grow out their beards to a hand's length and to trim their mustaches. The rendering public of religion made common property of every religious act, including a man's pious beard and his ritual worship. In both instances, his body had a choice— to conform to the Taliban reshaping of religion, or to be tortured for not complying. This publicization of the male believer's body resulted in individuals becoming alienated from parts of themselves, as with Latifa's father, who lamented that even his beard no longer belonged to him. His beard was *zaher,* open and apparent, and therefore public property.

Likewise, the gendered character of the public and private spheres, with women confined to the private, is even more developed in Taliban thinking than in Hegel. The expansion of the public realm of power, religion, and morality by the Taliban had the effect, in addition, of shrinking the private sphere and further constraining women. Some fundamentalists accomplish this project through thoroughgoing veiling, which is aimed at disguising women's presence in public. In essence, full veiling allows the private character of women to be made portable. Like scuba divers who bring along oxygen from a land-based style of life when they invade the underwater sphere, veiled women transport their privacy along with them when they go out onto the street. Some radical fundamentalists are not satisfied with this solution, because it still allows a certain kind of trespass by the feminine into the male public sphere. Thus, the Taliban largely excluded women from going to school, and for the most part from working outside the home. The 40 percent of women who had worked for a living in Kabul before the Taliban took control of the city in 1996 were at best thrown on the mercy of the international aid agencies and at worst cast into unemployment and penury, sometimes even reduced to begging or prostitution by the Taliban, who professed the ideal of a complete exclusion of women from the public sphere. Many fell into depression from being immobilized in their small apartments, and some committed suicide. Even literacy in modern societies had allowed women to trespass in the public sphere. Women journalists and editorialists attained a public voice through literacy and print. The Taliban solution to this further trespass was to deprive women of the little literacy they had attained. Of course, there was not much of a press for women to publish in under the Taliban, even if they had they been able to. The press was too much a part of the secular public sphere of reasoned communicative action, and was itself largely abandoned, along with most television and videocassettes. The only mass medium regularly allowed was Radio Voice of Sharia, carefully controlled by the Taliban, on which no female voice was ever heard. Radio, along with the sermons of pro-Taliban clerics, constituted the Afghan populace as a mass receiving instructions rather than as a public engaged in debate.

The Taliban project was tinged with medieval romanticism, in which supposedly traditional practices were exalted over the West of independent women like Monica Lewinsky and Kate Winslet. It was above all, however, a form of countermodernity. It envisaged itself as a pure form of Islam capable of overcoming the intertribal fighting and the devaluation of women as persons that had plagued Afghanistan in the past. As a nativist countermodernity, it rejected both major foreign forms of cultural imperialism—Marxism and liberalism. It represented itself as at once authentically Afghan and universal in its aspirations, as witnessed by Mullah Omar's claim to the caliphate. At the center of the project was an alternative conception of how to draw the line between the public and the private.

The Taliban regime fell late in 2001 to American special forces and air raids, which were aided by the forces of their equally Islamist foes, the Northern Alliance. Some journalistic observers assumed that everything therefore had changed in Afghanistan. They were puzzled over time that many women continued to wear the burqa, unaware that veiling is a highly classed and regional practice, and that for some women its guarantee of privacy was welcome or too familiar to abandon.

On November 11, 2002, the new Hamid Karzai government announced that twenty women were being released from prison because the facility did not meet international standards. Most of these women had been jailed under the new regime. Some of them were imprisoned for "violations of Shariat laws." One had been jailed for having eloped with a man her family did not want her to marry; another had been turned over to the police summarily by a son-in-law who accused her of theft. In provinces such as Herat, moreover, Taliban-like practices of gender segregation had largely returned after the Americans' war ended. In January 2003, Afghanistan's chief justice ordered the closure of five cable television stations in Kabul and insisted on an end to coeducation for girls and boys. Not everything had changed, after all.

CHAPTER FOUR

Taliban and Talibanism in Historical Perspective

M. Nazif Shahrani

The seeds for the emergence of the Taliban and Talibanism were sown during Afghanistan's creation a century before the Soviet invasion of 1979. At the height of the "Great Game" in Central Asia, British India and tsarist Russia established a Pashtun-dominated buffer state. Between 1880 and 1980, this Pashtun nation-state received support from outside powers, principally the British and Soviets, to pursue a modernizing project of internal colonialism. These tribal policies and practices gradually transformed ethnic and cultural differences among the peoples of Afghanistan into articulated forms of social fragmentation. During the 1960s and 1970s, these societal cleavages gained ideological scaffolding among the newly educated youth and led to the Soviet-backed communist coup of April 1978. Communal tensions rose to the surface after the collapse of the autocratic monarchy in 1973 and the puppet communist regimes by 1992. Further aggravated by prolonged war and increased outside interference, they ultimately enabled the creation of the Taliban militia and the brutal policies and practices of Talibanism.

The intercommunal wars that spiraled out of control following the mujahedin military victory in April 1992 were in fact the virulent manifestations of Pashtun-dominated nation-state building policies shaped by decades of Cold War politics in the region. The rise of the Taliban and Talibanism may be best understood within the context of the troubled history of the "modern" Afghan buffer state, perpetually indebted to foreign patrons and consistently hostile toward its subjects in general, and to the Turkic- and Tajik (Persian)-speaking peoples of western, northern, and central Afghanistan in particular.

After the victory of the peoples of Afghanistan against the Afghan communist regimes and their Soviet patrons in the jihad of the 1980s, the situation in Afghanistan quickly dissolved into a bitter interethnic and sectarian war of all against all. Various attempts to explain why Afghan mujahedin did not, or could not, translate their signal military triumph into national political success have for the most part ignored the legacies of Afghanistan's history and political culture while focusing exclusively on the role of recent external forces. Zalmay Khalilzad and Daniel Byman claim:

> As the United States departed [following the withdrawal of the Soviets in February 1989], a vicious civil war spread throughout the country. Once the Soviet-backed regime fell, war, anarchy, and fragmentation followed. The conflict became increasingly one of ethnic and sectarian groups, particularly Pashtuns, Tajiks, Uzbeks, and the Shi'a Hazaras. . . . The war also became a proxy war between Iran and Pakistan, with each power backing different factions.

The role of outside powers and foreign forces in the factional violence since 1992 has been amply documented.[1]

What is often left poorly explored and little understood are the internal dynamics of the conflict, both before and after the Soviet withdrawal.[2] Why did Afghanistan's major ethnic communities turn their guns against each other? Does this unusually intense communal violence "stem [only] from the Soviet occupation and the [peculiarities of] the U.S.- and Pakistani-backed resistance"?[3] Alternatively, could these post-jihad intercommunal conflicts have deeper historic roots within the political culture of the "modern" Afghan state and society? Why the sudden appearance of the Taliban tribal militia in Kandahar and their rapid transformation into an extremely harsh and violent movement insistent on reconquering all other areas? What were the Taliban and their opponents fighting for or about? Could it have been just another, more violent, case of struggle for the control of state power? Or was it, as the Taliban claimed, purely a religiously motivated movement trying to establish the rule of "true" Islamic sharia?

More significantly, why did the non-Pashtun peoples put up an unprecedented and tenacious resistance against the Taliban while most of the Pashtun in southern and eastern parts of the country and all recently resettled Pashtun in the north joined them with such enthusiasm? Was the rise of the Taliban, with their harsh religious and political policies and practices, what Peter Marsden refers to as the "Taliban Creed" (and what I call Talibanism), an expected manifestation of recognizable historical patterns in the country? Or was it an aberration, a product of the novel circumstances of post-jihad Afghanistan?

If it was not a novelty, then it must be explained within the parameters of Afghanistan's contemporary social history and political culture. In order to understand the structural dynamics of the rise of Talibanism, one must consider not only the effects of the mobilization of the peoples of Afghanistan during the jihad from 1978 to 1992 and the subsequent internecine warfare among mujahedin factions between 1992 and 1994. Three historical factors also had an enormous impact: the Pashtun ruling elite's role in laying claim to state-building projects by and for Pashtuns; the legacies of kin-based and person-centered Pashtun tribal politics; and long-simmering ethnic cleavages resulting from state discrimination that predated the current two-decade war.[4]

According to Marsden, the appearance of the Taliban in October 1994 "coincided with an initiative by the government of Pakistan to dispatch a trade convoy through Afghanistan, via Kandahar and Herat, to Turkmenistan." When the convoy crossed the Afghan border post at Chaman on its way to Kandahar, "it was attacked by an armed group. Immediately, another group came to the rescue and fought off the attackers. These were the Taliban."[5] After the safe passage of the Pakistani convoy, Mullah Muhammad Omar and his followers attacked Kandahar, one of the two most conflict-ridden and anarchic urban centers in the country (the other being Kabul) since the fall of Najibullah's government in April 1992. They took the city without resistance, quickly disarmed the population, and reportedly gained considerable popularity for bringing a semblance of security and order to the long-troubled city.[6]

Shortly thereafter, the Taliban captured most of the southern and southeastern Pashtun provinces without resistance and were welcomed by their Pashtun tribesmen as liberators. Emboldened by their rapid military successes, thanks to the infusion of considerable amounts of cash, weapons, fighters, and technical support from their foreign patrons (Pakistan, Saudi Arabia, and Osama bin Laden's al-Qaeda terrorists), their agenda expanded to bringing all of Afghanistan under their control by means of military force. Thus they systematically attacked Herat, Mazar-e Sharif, and the entire northern, central, and northeastern parts of the country, areas that were inhabited mostly by the non-Pashtun communities and, since 1992, had remained relatively peaceful. In the fall of 1995 the Taliban assaulted Herat. The city fell without a fight because the people of the western provinces had been disarmed by their own leader, Ismail Khan, shortly after the mujahedin victory of 1992. However, the Taliban met with stiff resistance in other non-Pashtun territories, particularly in the Shamali plain just north of Kabul, in Hazarajat, and in northern Afghanistan (also known as Afghan Turkestan).

By the time the Taliban captured Kabul in September 1996, "the Taliban Creed" consisted of a number of significant elements. According to Marsden, they sought "the purification of Afghanistan" and were committed, in the words of Mullah Muhammad Omar, the Taliban supreme leader, to ridding Afghanistan of "corrupt, Western-oriented time-servers." These were aims to be achieved by military conquest, punishing any resistance with extreme violence, including large-scale massacres and devastation of communities. In a Radio Voice of Sharia broadcast of November 5, 1996, the Taliban asserted that they "emerged from the masses . . . to deliver their compatriots from pain and hardship, to ensure complete peace and security across the country by collecting weapons, by doing away with feudal principalities here and there in the country and by creating a powerful Islamic government in Afghanistan." They deemed justifiable the removal of the mujahedin government "as having failed to adhere to the standards expected of an Islamic state"—that is, not enforcing the *hudud* punishments fixed by the sharia, not restricting the human rights of girls and women, not strictly enforcing *hejab,* and not forcing men to grow beards to a prescribed length, among other things.[7] The Taliban leadership and rationale, according to their spokesman (and later foreign minister), Wakil Ahmad Mutawakkil, as reported in the Arabic magazine *Al-Majallah,* were

based on the advice of the Amir Al-Muminin [Commander of the Faithful] . . . [and so] . . . consultation is not necessary.

We believe that this is in line with the Sunna [practices of the Prophet of Islam]. We abide by the Amir's view even if he alone takes this view . . . There will not be a head of state. Instead, there will be an Amir Al-Muminin. Mullah Muhammad Omar will be the highest authority, and the government will not be able to implement any decision to which he does not agree . . . General elections are incompatible with the shari'a and therefore we reject them. Instead, we consult with eminent scholars who fulfill certain conditions.[8]

Their foreign patrons generously supported the major components of "the Taliban Creed"—a form of personalized, sovereignty-based, paternalistic tribal politics, legitimized by an extremist interpretation of sharia in support of a state-building project undertaken on behalf of their Pashtun tribesmen on both sides of the Afghan-Pakistan border.[9] Yet this Taliban creed is also firmly rooted in the history and political culture of the rulers of the modern Afghan nation-state.

Autocratic and paternalistic politics have formed the cornerstone of Pashtun tribal, social, and political organization and have been the defining attribute of Afghan politics since the creation of the Pashtun-dominated state in the mid-eighteenth century by a charismatic and able Abdali Pashtun chieftain, Ahmad Shah Durrani (r. 1747–1773).[10] Eric Wolf has pointed out that such kin-based polities have "Achilles' heels" and "diagnostic points of stress" because a chief or leader "draws a following through *judicious management of alliances and redistributive action,* [but] he reaches a limit that can only be surpassed by breaking through the bounds of the kinship order [itself]." To overcome these limitations, Wolf suggests, the leader "must gain independent access to reliable and renewable resources [material, monetary, and ideological] of his own."[11]

Addressing this serious limitation of political economy in Afghanistan has been made possible, however briefly, by two primary means. During the eighteenth and nineteenth centuries, it was through the fruits of waging jihad, initially against non-Muslims in the Indian subcontinent, and then internally against the non-Pashtun communities with the aim of imposing a form of internal colonialism. In the latter parts of the nineteenth and twentieth centuries it was through foreign subsidies from real or potential enemies of the nation. The effectiveness of both of these strategies, however, has proved thus far to be not only episodic and transient, but also intensely problematic for the Afghan government's nation-building project itself.[12]

Indeed, Afghanistan has paid a heavy price for its failure to resolve this serious problem of political economy. The primary reason for the failure has been the unwillingness or inability of the leadership to shift from a tribal political culture anchored in person-centered, sovereignty-based politics to a broader, more inclusive, participatory national politics based on the development of modern and democratic national institutions and rules of governance. With rare exceptions, rulers of Afghanistan have consistently preferred to depend on foreign patrons to rule, instead of gaining the loyalty and trust of their own people and relying on the internal resources of the nation, both human and material. As a result, during its 250 years of statehood, Afghanistan has suffered through at least 100 years of fratricidal wars of succession and pacification (often called "jihad" by the contestants) with devastating consequences and painful legacies.[13] These bloody internal conflicts have facilitated—and even invited—foreign interventions by the British, Russians, Pakistanis, Iranians, and now the Americans and their coalition partners.

Even when dressed up with ideological justifications, whether Islamist, nationalist, socialist, secularist, or democratic, these struggles have not been fought for or against any ideological or institutional causes. Instead, they have pitted specific individuals, families, and clans or ethnic, linguistic, and sectarian communities against one another because of personal loyalties, albeit often rapidly shifting and commoditized ones. To illustrate and stress the continuities of the constitutive principle of this state—society relationship, let us examine a formative period in the history of state building in Afghanistan.

The credit for the creation and consolidation of the modern nation-state of the "Afghans"—more specifically, of the Pashtuns, the alleged majority ethnic group in the country—is generally bestowed upon a prince of the Barakzai clan of the Durrani tribe of the Pashtun, Abdul Rahman Khan. Favored by the officials of British India, Abdul Rahman Khan was picked from among scores of warring contenders for the Kabul throne and installed as the amir of Afghanistan. Between 1880 and 1901, the British provided him with considerable military, financial, and technical support to embark on a project of nation building in an environment somewhat reminiscent of the post-Taliban situation. During his two-decade-long reign of terror, the amir, like his Taliban successors a century later, indulged in bloody military conquests to establish the sovereignty of his centralizing monarchy.

The political ideals and practices of Amir Abdul Rahman Khan, the founding hero of the modern Afghan (Pashtun) nation-state, its governance rules and practices, and its hegemonic discourses, have been preserved in a two-volume autobiography, allegedly dictated by him to his scribe, Sultan Mahomed Khan. This work served as a kind of "Mirror for the Afghan Prince," with a profound impact on contemporary Afghan political culture.[14] In this "Mirror" he uses the metaphor of "building a house" to justify his brutal methods of nation building, stating, "It was necessary to clear that house of all the injurious scorpions existing in it, scorpions that formed a great obstacle in the way of peace and progress. . . . I mean that I had to put in order all those hundreds of petty chiefs, plunderers, robbers, and cut-throats [that is, the current "warlords" in Taliban and post-Taliban parlance!], who were the cause of everlasting trouble in Afghanistan. This necessitated breaking down the feudal and tribal system, and substituting one grand community under one law and under one rule . . . [and] one united kingdom." He also claims that his violent poli-cies transformed some of those "scorpions," the tribal chiefs, "from bitter enemies into warm friends[!]" whom he placed "in high posi-tions and offices under [his] Government."

Those who did not submit to his rule were killed or forced out of the country. Hence he proclaimed, "There is not a man, from a chief to a beggar throughout the whole country of Afghanistan, who has such a power, as to offer resistance to my Government, or after my death, to my successors."[15] Indeed, by the time of his death at the dawn of the twentieth century, he had earned the title *Iron Amir* from his British colonial patrons for his brutality against his own royal subjects *(atiba/ruaya)*. He justified military rampages against his pre-sumed enemies, the disloyal subjects, by charging them with heresy or castigating them as "bad Muslims," much like the practices of his recent successors, the Taliban band of terrorists.

Abdul Rahman was chosen by the British for the throne of Kabul, not by any loya jirga, or grand assembly (the institution that observ-ers of the post-Taliban period have identified as the ostensibly *tradi-tional* means of choosing the national leader). His rendition of the lore of an earlier loya jirga that marked the rise of Pashtun tribes to political ascendancy in the region is highly informative of his own view of the nature of this cherished national institution, however. He recounts that when, in 1747, the representatives and chiefs of the various tribes and clans of Afghanistan, meaning the southwest-ern Pashtun tribes, convened in a shrine in the city of Kandahar to choose a king, each insisted that his own claims to the throne were greater than those of others, and that he would not submit himself to the rule of any of the others. After a long dispute . . . they were no nearer to the issue [of electing a King] then when they started, [so] a holy man, named Saber Shah . . . [placing an ear of wheat upon the head of Ahmad Khan, the chief of the weakest clan (Sadozai)] said: 'You need not quarrel, Ahmad Khan is the proper ruler for the kingdom . . . Having agreed upon this, they all took pieces of green grass in their mouth as a token that they were his very cattle and beast of burden, and throwing around their necks pieces of cloth in the shape of ropes, as a sign that they were willing to be led by him, they submitted to his rule, and gave him the powers of life and of death.[16]

The constitutive value of the Iron Amir's advice to his descendants and political successors cannot be underestimated, as evidenced by how closely it has been adhered to by Afghanistan's rulers over the past hundred years.

Another passage from the "Mirror" may shed some light on both the amir's problematic view of a "constitutional" or "representative government" and why the latest successors to his throne in Kandahar (Mullah Muhammad Omar) and Kabul (President Hamid Karzai, during the Constitutional Loya Jirga) so strongly resisted the demand for a parliamentary system of government. Abdul Rahman maintained:

The first and most important advice that I can give my successors and people to make Afghanistan into a great kingdom is to impress upon their mind the value of *unity;* unity and unity alone, can make it into a great power. . . . I have arranged matters during my lifetime in such a way, that all the members of my family and the Afghan [Pashtun] people acknowledge the supremacy of my eldest son [his successor to the throne, Amir Habibullah]. . . . The foundation stone of a Constitutional Government has been laid by me; though the machinery of a Representative Government has not taken any practical shape as yet. . . . There are three kinds of representatives who assemble in my court . . . These three classes are called *Sirdars* [elders of his own Barakzai Pashtun clan] . . . *Khawaninin Mulki* [other tribal and local leaders], and Mullahs. . . . This constitutional body has not yet attained the ability nor the education to qualify it for being entrusted with authority of any importance for giving sanction to Bills or Acts of Government. . . . I must strongly urge my sons and successors never to make themselves puppets in the hands of . . . representatives of constitutional Government; they must always reserve to themselves the full power of organizing the army and keep it in their own hands, without admitting any right of interference by their constitutional advisors. And, further, they must keep the power of vetoing any reforms, schemes or bills passed and sanctioned by their Council or *Durbar* [courtiers] or Parliament.[17]

The discourse of "unity" in this passage refers above all to the unity of the royal family and their clan elders, the Barakzai Sardars, and then to that of the Pashtun tribes as a whole, a phenomenon that has remained an important aspect of the political aspirations of the ruling elite. The discourse of unity has also been employed repeatedly as a powerful weapon against the non-Pashtun movements advocating local autonomy or community self-governance within the unitary Afghan state. For example, the amir wrote, "I often say to my personal friends among the courtiers: 'What unhappy life we all lead! All the time you are in my presence I keep on watching to see which of you, owing to your stupidity, may attack me. And, on the other hand, your anxiety is so great, that you leave your wives and children in suspense, anxiously wondering which of you may possibly be hanged for your own offences, or for intriguing with your colleagues and so-called friends.'"[18] Thus another persistent legacy of the political culture of the Afghan state, further aggravated by the years of national discord, has been contempt for the people (portrayed as cattle, beasts of burden, and chattel) and suspicion toward government officials and political associates.

The most powerful legacies of the Iron Amir's "Mirror" for building a centralized nation-state structure in multiethnic Afghanistan, with all of its attendant twentieth-century disasters for the suffering people of the country, have been a number of political practices that form the most significant features of Afghanistan's contemporary political culture. These include personalized and sovereignty-based dynastic rule from Kabul, dominated by the Barakzai clans of the Durrani, allegedly on behalf of all Pashtun tribes. Expressed in the mantra of national unity, a conservative, even reactionary, interpretation of Islam in turn buttresses the legitimacy of this form of government.

Preservation of the absolute monarchy established domestically by "the help of the sharp blade of the sword" and "with the sharp blade of the pen by communicating with the neighboring Powers" remained the supreme goal of the rulers of Afghanistan.[19] In 1923 Amir Amanullah, the grandson of Amir Abdul Rahman Khan, introduced the first Afghan constitution. In 1931 the second constitution, introduced by Muhammad Nader Shah, the father of the last Afghan monarch, Muhammad Zaher, legitimated the conveyance of the throne from the Iron Amir's line to him and his descendants.

Both documents affirmed the absolute power of the monarchs, although both also provided for partly appointed and party elected Consultative Councils. In both cases, the loya jirgas were expected to be summoned only to vote "yes" or "no" on what was presented to them by the king; they "then adopted the majority vote as the unanimous decision by all present."[20]

A loya jirga convened to ratify the constitution of 1964 was the first such body, composed of some 442 members (352 of them elected and the rest appointed), that was allowed not only to accept or reject the entire draft but also to discuss and amend the articles. The framers of this constitution (a 7-member Constitution Committee and a 24-member Constitution Commission) were instructed to draft a document more appropriate to both the changing times and the altered dynamics of the royal family. Due to serious family quarrels at the time, the new national charter was to keep close relatives of the king, who had dominated the government for three decades, out of governmental affairs. It also had to create an independent judiciary, give priority to modern legal codes over those of the sharia on certain issues, extend and clarify the rights of the people (*atiba*, or subjects), encourage and expand the possibilities for local self-government (in Article 110, which was never enacted), and address other matters to convince the non-Pashtun peoples that "they were no longer to be dominated by the Pashtuns."[21]

The most significant articles of the constitution of 1964 also guaranteed the right to form political parties, freedom to print and publish free of government supervision, universal suffrage, and equal social status for women. Compared with the previous two constitutions, this one was considered more liberal and forward looking. Like its antecedents as well as its successors under Daud Khan in 1977 and Najibullah in 1990, however, this constitution was a product of the initiative and direction of each of the rulers. For the most part, the validity of these documents did not outlast the reign of the person who promulgated them. To a large measure, the only parts of all the previous constitutions of Afghanistan that were adhered to were those having to do with the rights and duties of the rulers and their governments, always at the expense of the constitutionally guaranteed rights of their subjects, the peoples of Afghanistan.

Since the onset of modern state-building efforts in Afghanistan, successive governments have inflicted extraordinary brutality and violence upon large segments of society, including, at times, non-Durrani (primarily Ghilzai) Pashtun and especially non-Pashtun groups (particularly Shia Hazaras, Uzbeks, Turkmen, and Tajiks). The history of the pre-Taliban state's hostile relations with the Shia Hazara communities has recently been documented and analyzed.[22] Unfortunately, with minor exceptions the policies and practices of Afghan governments toward the Turkic- and Tajik-speaking peoples of Afghan Turkestan have not yet received the systematic attention they deserve, especially from the perspective of these peoples themselves.[23] The story of the exiled amir of Bukhara, Amir Sayyid Alim Khan, and some half-million Uzbek and Tajik émigrés *(muhajirin)* who took refuge among their own ethnolinguistic communities in northern Afghanistan following the fall of Bukhara to the Soviets helps illustrate the troubled nature of the Afghan Turkestanis' relationship with the oppressive policies of the Afghan state.

Confronted by the Soviet army on the eve of August 27, 1920, Amir Alim Khan's poorly trained and inadequately equipped forces staunchly defended Bukhara, until August 31. Daunted by the superior military technology of the Bolsheviks, the amir retreated to the eastern mountainous parts of his domain, yet continued to fight. In his futile effort to defend and liberate Bukhara, the amir counted, rather naively, on military and financial help from his royal "brothers" King George V of Britain and Amir Amanullah of Afghanistan. In a written request dispatched on October 21, 1920, from his new head-quarters in Dushanbe, he asked Britain to provide one hundred thou-sand pounds sterling in cash as "a state loan," twenty thousand rifles, thirty heavy guns, ten airplanes, and the necessary ammunition. De-livered by his emissaries to the British consul-general in Kashghar (in eastern, or Chinese, Turkestan) and communicated to Delhi and London, his request apparently fell on deaf ears. Similarly, the amir of Bukhara's urgent plea for military assistance through his gift-bearing representatives to King Amanullah also produced no arms. Instead, Amanullah invited Sayyid Alim Khan to come to Kabul for an urgent consultation on how best to address the tragedy of Bu-khara.

Suspicious of the true intent of an Afghan king who offered advice but refused to supply arms, and faced with the threat of the ap-proaching Red Army, Amir Alim Khan was reluctantly forced to leave Dushanbe and cross the Oxus (Amu) River on March 4, 1921. He then proceeded with his large entourage to Kabul, where he was given polite hospitality and kept under constant surveillance by King Amanullah's regime. The amir of Bukhara's clandestine attempts to purchase arms from British India for his guerilla forces, which con-tinued to fight in eastern Bukhara until at least 1931, were thwarted and stopped as soon as they had begun. Later, during the Second World War, when some of his close associates attempted to contact German agents in order to organize an anti-Soviet Turkestani resis-tance unit, the Afghan authorities once again aborted the plan, fear-ing Soviet retaliation.[24] The story of the amir of Bukhara and the half-million of his subjects who voted with their feet against commu-nism and the Soviet occupation of their land, following the model of the Prophet of Islam into *hijrat* (exile or separation from their home-land to avoid religious persecution), has for the most part remained untold.

Indeed, until the demise of the Afghan central government and the rise of the anticommunist jihad, their tragic stories were, for largely political reasons, untellable, and have thus remained unexplored. Some of the critical issues that need to be addressed concern the consequences—social, economic, cultural and political—for those who were forced to choose exile. How did they make sense of the events that led to the fall of Bukhara into the hands of Russian Bolsheviks and their local collaborators? How did the exiles respond to the challenges that confronted them in Bukhara as well as in Afghanistan? What did they say or write, or did they decide not to say or write (or were they unable to say or write), about their experiences of exile?[25]

At the outset of the Bukharan crisis, there appears to have been much genuine support and heartfelt Islamic concern and sympathy on the part of the young reformist king of Afghanistan, King Amanullah, and especially among the peoples of northern Afghanistan who received the bulk of the Bukharan exiles. The great majority of the Central Asians who came from villages north of the Amu River settled in rural areas of northern Afghanistan, joining either existing Uzbek and Tajik settlements or founding new ones. Urban refugees chose mostly to settle in towns and cities, primarily in the north, as well as in the western city of Herat and the capital, Kabul. Popular sentiment among the victims of Bolshevik aggression, especially local Tajik, Turkmen, and Uzbek communities who offered assistance, remained unchanged. At the official level, however, Afghan attitudes turned increasingly inhospitable toward the exiles, especially after the outbreak of civil war in Afghanistan and the subsequent change of regime in 1929. Afghanistan's oppressive political climate, compounded by its impoverished economy, kept the Central Asian muhajirin pining for Bukhara and Turkestan.

The great majority of those Turkestanis who chose exile may not have been at the center of politics in Central Asia. But their very choice of exodus as an act had a political nature. This fact was by no means lost on the people of the region, especially their hosts in the Afghan government. King Amanullah, who had "invited" the amir of Bukhara to Kabul under the pretext of consultation and formulation of a joint strategy, had in fact tried to prevent the amir from orchestrating any effective political and military activities supporting his Basmachi warriors across the Afghan border.[26] In the meantime, the British allegedly instigated internal rebellions, initially by eastern Pashtun tribesmen, against the reformist policies of King Amanullah. The king's inability to deal with the rebellions gradually dragged the country into the bloody civil war of 1929, forcing Amanullah to abdicate.

During a nine-month interregnum, a new Tajik ruler, Amir Habibullah Kalakani, occupied the Afghan throne. Unlike King Amanullah, this new Tajik ruler publicly advocated support for the amir of Bukhara and his Basmachi fighters and expressed his willingness to help liberate Bukhara from the Soviets. The amir of Bukhara and the local supporters of his cause, most of the Uzbek and Tajik peoples of northern Afghanistan, welcomed the unexpected turn of events. A number of Amir Alim Khan's able commanders began to organize fresh resistance units from among the exile communities, as well as from local Afghan Uzbeks and Tajiks, to start fighting the Soviets again. Among these fighters was a very well-known Basmachi commander, Mullah Muhammad Ibrahimbek Laqay, who had temporarily stopped fighting the Bolsheviks in the late 1920s due to lack of arms and ammunition. This new twist in the politics of Central

Asian exiles made the Russians understandably nervous, while British India was equally concerned about the Islamist politics of the new Tajik ruler in Kabul.

Backed by financial and military aid from British India, a large militia force of Pashtun (Pathan) tribesmen from the North West Frontier Province of British India and eastern Afghanistan was mobilized and led by a distant "cousin" and former minister of war of King Amanullah, General Muhammad Nader Khan. This terminated the short-lived reign of Amir Habibullah Kalakani. The first Tajik ruler of Afghanistan was publicly humiliated and hanged. In October 1929 a new Pashtun dynasty, that of the Mosahiban family, led by Muhammad Nader Shah, was established. At the same time, Moscow soon exerted pressure on the newly installed, pro-British monarch. The new Pashtun rulers in Kabul responded positively to Stalin and demanded that the amir of Bukhara cease all military activities, disarm his men, and order Ibrahimbek Laqay to turn himself in to the Afghan authorities in Kabul immediately. The amir of Bukhara complied. Ibrahimbek Laqay agreed to halt his military activities and disarm, but refused to turn himself in to the authorities or go to Kabul.

In retaliation, the Afghan government sent thousands of Pashtun tribal *lashkar* (militia) to northern Afghanistan to hunt down suspected Central Asian fighters and their local Uzbek and Tajik supporters. According to recently published eyewitness reports, the government of Nader Shah also offered an undisclosed amount of money for every severed head of Ibrahimbek Laqay's Uzbek fighters delivered to the local government authorities.[27] This policy of the new Mosahiban dynasty unleashed months of bloody war in northern Afghanistan in 1930 and 1931 between the anti-Soviet Basmachi guerillas, their local Uzbek and Tajik supporters, and the Pashtun tribal mercenaries roaming the area. This state-sanctioned attack on

Central Asian exiles resulted in countless killings of innocent people and the plundering of local, mostly Uzbek, communities by the
southern Pashtun tribal militia as well as by some local mercenaries who joined them. This unholy war by the Afghan government
also drove many Central Asian Basmachi fighters across the Amu.
Among them was Ibrahimbek Laqay, who was captured by the Soviets in 1931, tried, and executed a year later.[28]

With the capture and execution of Ibrahimbek Laqay, the Soviet
regime finally declared its total victory against the Basmachi movement, and with that death the émigrés' prospects for the recapture of
Bukhara turned bleak. In an effort to end the exiles' hope of continuing their armed struggle against the Soviets, a public conspiracy of silence regarding official policy toward them was put into effect by
the Afghan government and meticulously enforced. Between 1930
and roughly 1980, the identity, social visibility, and cultural presence
of Central Asian exiles (referred to as *Bukhara-i*, "from Bukhara";
Farghanachi, "from Farghana"; or collectively, especially if their place
of origin was not known, as *Pan-e Darya-ye*, "from the other side of
the Amu River") and those of their northern co-ethnics, the Uzbeks
and Tajiks, diminished in national political life.

Indeed, these Uzbek, Turkmen, and Tajik populations were confronted by an official policy of suspicion and contempt, and an ethnic
politics of oppression and internal colonialism, by successive Afghan governments. A massive and systematic resettlement of Pashtun tribesmen to Afghan Turkestan from the southern frontier areas
began in the 1930s and continued well into the 1970s. In this process, government officials forcibly confiscated hundreds of thousands
of hectares of fertile, cultivated, and prime pasture lands from the local Uzbeks and Tajiks and distributed them among the Pashtun set-
tlers *(Naqelin)*.[29] Reminiscent of the Russian policies of colonization
in the northern steppes of Muslim Central Asia, which turned local

Kazakh and Kyrgyz herders into the virtual indentured serfs of their new colonial superiors, most of the dispossessed peasants in northern Afghanistan were also made to serve their new Pashtun masters.

According to some recent print media revelations based on the oral accounts of local informants, land appropriations and demographic aggression were also accompanied by considerable destruction of cultural artifacts. A well-known ultra-Pashtun nationalist governor-general of the area, Wazir Muhammad Gul Khan Muhmand, destroyed architectural, archaeological, toponymic, and literary texts, especially rare manuscripts in Persian and Turki or Chaghatai (literary Uzbek) written by locals.[30] Through administrative fiat similar to Stalin's policies of "national delimitation" in Russian Turkestan, the widely used term *Afghan Turkestan* in reference to northern Afghanistan and Qataghan (a large Afghan province named after an Uzbek tribe inhabiting the area) was effectively removed from official use. Pashto names replaced countless Uzbek and Tajik place-names throughout Afghan Turkestan. In the face of such adversity, Central Asian exiles and local inhabitants appear to have adopted a strategy of self-censorship. Collectively and individually, they sought minimal exposure of their cultural and emotional expressions.

Despite the overwhelming desire, at least on the part of urban Central Asian exiles, to leave Afghanistan for the less oppressive environments of the Indian subcontinent, Saudi Arabia, Turkey, and the West, very few managed to do so before the 1980s. When the long-anticipated Soviet military intervention materialized in support of the Ghilzai Pashtun-dominated Afghan communist regimes in 1979, the Central Asian exiles, along with millions of other Afghans, were once again driven into refugee camps across the Pakistani and Iranian borders, adding fresh salt to old emotional wounds. Many Turkestani and Bukharan exiles immediately joined the ranks of the

Afghan mujahedin, forming their own resistance groups to fight their old enemy, the communist Russians.[31]

More important, the radically altered political environment of the populist jihad—and the collapse of Pashtun-dominated central authority in Afghanistan—opened unprecedented military, political, and cultural opportunities for all the peoples of Afghanistan. The real essence of the altered conditions in Afghanistan, especially for the Central Asian exiles and the Turkic and Tajik peoples of Afghan Turkestan, proved to be their newly found freedom of political self-expression. The only major Pakistan-based Afghan resistance organization headed by a Tajik from Badakhshan province, the Jamiat-e Islami, published for the first time the *Memoirs of the Amir of Bukhara, 1910–1920* (*Tarikh-e Hozn al-melal*, or *History of the Sorrow of Nations*) in a monthly journal, *Mesaq-e Khun*. The complete *Memoirs* were later reissued several times in a single volume by different organizations and developed a very wide circulation. Utterly absent from the print media of Afghanistan since at least 1930, the history and struggle of the Basmachi movement and its major leaders, including Ibrahimbek Laqay, began to be written about in the Afghan mujahedin publications. The new situation offered the educated Bukharan exiles the opportunity not only to reveal what was previously written about their struggle and to retell their personal and collective stories of prolonged suffering, but also to reclaim their suppressed identities and express creatively their past sorrows, present challenges, and future hopes and aspirations in a burst of literary production—narrative histories, versified histories and memoirs, poetry, and more poetry, one of the most effective culturally recognized means of political and personal expression in Central Asia.[32]

The defeat of the Soviet army of occupation in 1989 by the Afghan mujahedin, the unexpected implosion of the Soviet empire in

1991, and the subsequent collapse of the communist regime in Kabul in 1992, have all had further important consequences for the phenomenal growth of literary production about the experiences of Central Asian exile communities in Afghanistan, as well as the experiences of the peoples of Afghan Turkestan under internal colonial rule. These developments have included, first, renewed efforts by independent researchers and governments of the newly independent states of post-Soviet Central Asia to rewrite the much-distorted history of their peoples in general, and those of the Basmachis and Central Asian exiles in particular; second, the emergence of an independent political movement, the National Islamic Movement of Afghanistan (Junbesh-e Milli-ye Islami-ye Afghanistan), headed by the Uzbek strongman General Abdul Rashid Dostum, which gives voice to the long-silenced Turkic-speaking peoples by supporting new publications and broadcast media focusing on the history, identity, and politics of the peoples of northern Afghanistan, including those of the Central Asian exiles; and third, the establishment of small but enterprising communities of Central Asian exiles in Turkey, Saudi Arabia, Europe, and the United States, who are also active in the production of new literature about their own history and experiences.[33]

Afghan rulers have utilized the discourses of Islam, tribe, kinship, and Durrani kingship, officially expressed in a crude ideology of Afghan (Pashtun) nationalism, to hold together myriad linguistic, sectarian, and tribal groups in virtual subjugation within a buffer state. Resistance and popular revolts against the state were repeatedly crushed with weapons and money provided for the governments by outside colonial powers—initially Great Britain and later the Soviet Union. These efforts did not disrupt the kin-based, personalized politics, however. Instead, the contradictory policies and practices of

nation-state building in Afghanistan have promoted a political culture of person-centered politics to the virtual exclusion of nurtur-
ing broader and more inclusive national ideologies, institutions, and
moral principles. I would therefore argue that the rise of the Taliban
movement during the post-jihad crises of succession, with its distinctive form of Islamic extremism, or Talibanism, was the natural
culmination of a long history of internal colonialism and a Pashtun-
dominated political culture.

A number of significant legacies of this culture haunt Afghan politics even in the current post-Taliban environment, and may do so
well into the distant future. First, government-appointed officials'
consistent policies and practices of political mistrust toward the great
majority of Afghan subjects have led the Afghan people to distrust
politics and politicians. Such prolonged experiences have in turn severely weakened traditional communities of trust *(jamaat)*, entities
akin to *civil society*. And it has caused the general erosion of trust as
"social capital" in Afghan society beyond the circles of family and
close kinsmen or one's own ethnolinguistic or sectarian group.

Second, autocratic and paternalistic politics have encouraged the
commodification of loyalties, the creation of a political economy of
dependency and patron-client relationships at all levels of Afghan
society, including the increasing dependence of the government, parties, and movements on foreign aid and foreign patrons. This situation has been further exacerbated by the interethnic and intertribal
conflicts throughout more than two decades of devastating war in
which all strata of society depended on economic and military assistance from numerous governmental and nongovernmental prox-
ies. This political and ecological condition of continuous warfare has
also introduced a new weapon into the arsenals of political combatants. Rivals have utilized access to a thriving print and electronic
media—inside Afghanistan, in Afghan refugee communities around

the world, as well as through the BBC, the Voice of America, and Radio Free Europe/Radio Liberty services in the Dari and Pashto languages—to vilify and demonize their opponents. These pervasive attempts at mutual character assassination of the "other," defined increasingly in ethnic terms, have left no room for constructive dialogue to devise common tactics and strategies for the realization of shared national goals, and have led to the inevitable escalation of political contests into violent military conflicts, increasingly justified by adherence to religious extremism and Talibanism.

Third, personalized politics have placed all ideologies (Islamic and others) and moral principles at the service of preserving the self-interest and protection of personal, familial, tribal, or ethnic group honor. This has resulted in serious discrepancies between the public policy pronouncements of the contending groups and their actual practices, including President Karzai's post-Taliban regime. The rising production of opium poppies and the manufacture, sale, and trafficking of illicit drugs in the areas formerly under Taliban control, and now under the coalition forces of NATO-ISAF, may prove a case in point.

Fourth, the treatment of non-Pashtuns as mere internal "colonial" subjects (not citizens) to be reconquered and ruled over by a strong centralized government, including the Taliban and now the post-Taliban regime in Kabul, has produced a deep sense of continued alienation, resentment, and distrust.[34] Traditionally, official national histories have depicted non-Pashtuns' role as negligible, and their participation in national politics remains purposefully marginalized. Through a well-established policy of demographic aggression, ranging from resettlement of Pashtuns in non-Pashtun territories to underestimating the actual size of "minorities" by administrative means, their political representation in national assemblies has been severely curtailed.[35]

At the same time, these non-Pashtun groups have been subjected to excessive extraction by taxation, appropriation, looting, and other extrajudicial exactions. Painful historical memories of oppression and injustice spurred the non-Pashtun minorities in Afghanistan into fighting with determination against the Taliban and Talibanism in the hope of preventing the country from returning to the status quo ante of the pre-jihad period. Unfortunately, the defeat of the Taliban by U.S. forces and their coalition partners, followed by the installation of a handpicked post-Taliban government, has not diminished the continuation of some of the core political/tribal policies and practices of Talibanism.

Finally, the ultimate product of Afghan political culture was the rise of the Taliban militia movement, in particular the anti-Shia, antimodern, anti-Western, antiwomen, and especially antidemocratic policies and practices of its enigmatic, increasingly apotheosized leader. On April 4, 1996, the Taliban's "divinely ordained" reclusive leader, Mullah Omar, was proclaimed the Amirul Muminin by a gathering of some twelve hundred mullahs in Kandahar, the spiritual capital of Talibanism. As the Amir al-Muminin, he was the ultimate source for articulating and enforcing the "new" Muslim orthodoxy (and orthopraxy) of Talibanism in Afghanistan—the basis of his legitimacy. The essence of Talibanism, relying on the Taliban's particularistic interpretation of Islam, seems to be to deny "the division of society into divergent interests, whether economic, ideological, or what have you." Religion has "become a means to hide these divisions . . . [and] is mobilized in order to avoid the creation of institutions that can express social and ideological differences within the community."[36] Like Afghanistan's past rulers, the Taliban have tried to maintain the fiction of the national homogeneity of their *umma*, or nation, for example, by equating the names *Pashtun* and *Afghan*, which are synonymous in popular usage, and have "attempted to negate the reality of conflict and resistance by political suppression of dissent in the community."[37]

The Taliban have portrayed themselves as the bearers of peace and "true Islamic justice" in the country, a justice bound by the harshest punishments *(hudud)* in the sharia. Among these tenets were the amputation of the limbs of thieves, the stoning to death of adulterers, and public execution of murderers by the victims' relatives in sports stadiums filled with thousands of spectators. Their real claim to infamy came from the imposition of "gender apartheid" directed against the girls and women of Afghanistan.[38] This collective self-image of Talibanism was further buttressed by their foreign Muslim allies—conservative and radical Muslim political organizations in Pakistan. These include, among others, two factions of the Jamiat Ulema-e-Islam led by Mawlana Fazlur Rehman and Mawlana Samiul Haq, the two rabidly anti-Shia terrorist groups, Sipah-e-Sahaba and Harkatul Ansar, as well as bin Laden's military organization, al-Qaeda. True to the nature of person-centered tribal political culture, the positive "Islamic" self-image projected by the Taliban has been solidified by demonizing the Muslim character of their many opponents.[39] Ironically, many of those being damned were in fact well-known heroes of the anti-Soviet jihad. In post-Taliban conditions, the undermining of mujahedin leaders, big and small, who opposed the Taliban, with the now-familiar Taliban-Pakistani accusation of "warlordism" persists mostly unabated.

The ascent and triumph of Talibanism, fleeting as it was, fit well within the structural patterns and dynamics of wars of succession that Afghanistan has experienced in the last one hundred years. The mysterious beginnings of the Taliban and their quick adoption by interested foreign powers—in this instance, Pakistan and Saudi Arabia—have had major precedents in Afghan history.[40] The economic support of foreign Muslim sponsors made it possible for the Taliban to rent loyalties from a huge chain of economically desperate local commanders within the country. By extending official recognition to the Taliban regime, these external patrons also condoned the Taliban version of Islamic extremism as well as facilitated the recruitment of foreign fighters (Pakistanis and others) from Muslim "seminaries" (madrasas) in Pakistan and beyond. Ironically, the Bush administration now regards the two principal patrons of the Taliban and Talibanism as close allies of the United States in the fight against global terrorism, including against al-Qaeda and Taliban terrorists.

What distinguished the Taliban and the rise of Talibanism at this juncture in the history of Afghanistan was the radically altered political, ecological, and economic conditions, both inside Afghanistan and in the region, following the collapse of the Soviet Union. The presence of multiple, competing foreign Muslim sponsors, with their divergent or conflicting agendas, has proved to be ideal for the emergence of an extremist militia organization such as the Taliban within the tribal political culture of the Pashtun in Afghanistan as well as currently in the North West Frontier Province of Pakistan. Indeed, these same realities in the region also fueled the wars of resistance against Taliban hegemony, forcing the Taliban to resort to increasingly violent policies and practices against women, Shiites, and the non-Pashtun ethnolinguistic communities. Any comprehensive attempt to bring a just and lasting peace for all the peoples of Afghanistan must seek to find a long-term solution to the tragic consequences of the history of state and society relations in this beleaguered country. Sadly, the post-Taliban political trends, at least so far, do not appear very promising, to say the least.

CHAPTER FIVE

Remembering the Taliban

Lutz Rzehak

The reign of the Taliban is over, but what remains? How Afghans re-call the past and preserve memories of the Taliban era are questions of crucial importance. The civil war and the Taliban are still part of individual experience today. Political alignment, ethnic affiliation, and, not least, personal histories shape the varying ways in which Afghans assess the Taliban and their way of governance. Recent events in Afghan history are often recalled in ways that transform stories about the past into meaningful history for the present.

In Afghan society, the written word is an important, but not all-embracing or constitutive, element of social communication. One must look instead to the oral transmission of knowledge. This mode of transmitting knowledge about contemporary Afghan history con-forms to distinct forms of traditional folk literature, reworking indi-vidual experiences into a collective one adapted to the construction of cultural memory. Popular poetry, songs, prayers, storytelling, and other, more casual, forms of communication reveal how Afghans adapt particular rhetorical patterns to construct oral accounts of recent history, including that of the civil war and the reign of the Taliban, to shape popular opinion in the present. Drawing on historical narrations and songs from early periods of Afghan history, the first part of this essay reconstructs the established tradition of folklore. The second then compares these traditional genres with new kinds of folklore in order to show both continuity and change.

I take my material from interviews and participatory observation conducted during trips in 2002 and 2005 to the southwestern province of Nimroz. Ethnically, the southwestern part of Afghanistan is inhabited by Baluch, Persian-speaking groups (Farsiwan, Tajik, Parahi, Anardarahi, and others), and Pashtuns (mostly of the Ghilzai tribe, who also use Persian as their primary language in this region). Persian is the main language of administration and education in Nimroz Province, whereas Baluchi may be used, along with Persian, as the lingua franca in everyday communication, even by non-Baluch people. During both trips I lived in the household of a Baluch family, which provided me the opportunity to follow casual communication in everyday life.[1] The members of this household belong to the Baluch Shayrzi tribe. They have close marriage ties with the Nurzi tribe, whose members may identify themselves either as Baluch or Pashtuns.[2] My hosts had largely been stock farmers until the catastrophic drought that began in 1997—an occurrence that many interpreted as divine punishment for the crimes of the Taliban (an interpretation reinforced by the ending of the drought in the winter of 2002–2003, one year after the collapse of the Taliban). Locals then shifted to earning a living through trade and occasional jobs, including cross-border drug trafficking. None of my hosts was associated with the Taliban movement, and no other informants admitted to having been. However, drug trafficking necessitates involvement with the producers and suppliers of drugs, who in this case are usually Pashtuns from Helmand Province and who may have been associated with the Taliban.

The greater part of Nimroz is desert and remains uninhabited. The majority of the population lives in the southwestern part of the province where the Helmand River forms a delta on both sides of the border of Iran and Afghanistan and flows into a large lake without an outlet *(the Hamun-e Helmand)*. Thus, expansive deserts separate all of the important settlement areas of Nimroz from the central parts of Afghanistan. Both in Afghan Nimroz and on the Iranian side of the border the population consists mainly of Baluch, who maintain close cross-border family ties with each other. Like many Pashtun tribes who live near the border with Pakistan, the Baluch belong to the "free tribes" *(qabayil-e azad)* of Afghanistan and enjoy some privileges, especially in frontier affairs. Officials tolerate the fact that many of them have two identity cards, a *tazkira* from Afghanistan and a *shinasname* from Iran. Some Baluch have Pakistani documents as well. They can cross the border easily and almost without restriction. In 2004 a new bridge was built over the Helmand River near Zaranj, and an international checkpoint was opened there; however, Baluch use neither the bridge nor the checkpoint. Only a hundred meters away, and still in plain view of the border officials, they cross the river that forms the frontier by boat—without any control. Even some members of the local administration of the province are said to keep two households, one in Afghanistan and another in Iran. Situated seven kilometers from the border with Iran, the administrative center of the province is Zaranj—a young town that was founded in 1970 and that, for this reason, may also be called Shar-e Naw, or "New City," by local people.

According to local informants, the Taliban conquered the province of Nimroz twice. In January 1995, Taliban military units took the city of Dilaram in the southwestern part of Farah Province.[3] This point is strategically important for Nimroz, because here one has to leave the main circle road that connects Kabul, Kandahar, and Herat in order to enter the province.[4] When the Taliban appeared in Dilaram, the local mujahedin government of Nimroz started negotiations with them. Both sides agreed that Taliban troops would not enter the province of Nimroz as long as it remained unclear which group would hold power in Kabul. If the Taliban succeeded in taking Kabul, the mujahedin would hand Nimroz over to them without resistance. People say that the Taliban ignored this agreement and entered Nimroz Province only a few days later. Local mujahedin forces under the leadership of Karim Brahui did not resist and withdrew to neighboring regions in Iran.

Soon after seizing Nimroz, the Taliban appointed a governor (*wali*) with a certain standing in local society. His name was Hamidullah Niyazmand, and he is said to belong to the Baluch Brahui tribe, the same tribe as the leader of the local mujahedin, Karim Brahui. The ancestors of Hamidullah Niyazmand had formerly lived in Nimroz, and some people still remember that his father worked as a mullah in some villages of the province. Hamidullah Niyazmand himself grew up and was educated in Pakistan and spoke neither Baluchi nor Persian. Under his rule Urdu became the official language of provincial administration, and only Pashto was accepted along with it. Baluch and Persian-speaking persons who applied to local officials and did not know Urdu or Pashto were turned away. However, people remember that Hamidullah Niyazmand was quite acquainted with local traditions, and that their customs were widely respected at this time.

Later on, Hamidullah Niyazmand was replaced by a new governor named Mullah Ghani. People remember that in the main he followed the same principles of governance as his predecessor. He did not rule for a long time, because in the meantime local mujahedin forces managed to summon up their strength and attack the Taliban on three sides. They reconquered Zaranj quickly and ruled again for some weeks. But when the Taliban captured Herat on September 5, 1995, and the strong mujahedin leader of Herat, Ismail Khan, fled to Iran, Taliban forces started a new attack on Zaranj. Once again the local mujahedin of Nimroz did not offer any resistance and, like Ismail Khan, withdrew to Iran, as they had done before.

Locals remember all subsequent Taliban governors as very hostile and barbarous persons who came from Pakistan and did not have the faintest idea about local customs. Sher Malang spoke Pashto, but persons who met him say that they heard only rude things from him. During his reign the local library, with more than fifteen thousand books, was burned down. Locals in Nimroz believe that Sher Malang, who wielded a stick and struck people with it, considered them to be Shiites due to their close relations with persons on the Iranian side of the border. They also recall that Sher Malang and his men had an order from the Central Council (*shura*) of the Taliban in Kandahar to kill all males in Nimroz and to marry all females in order to put an end to this kind of "unbelief." Undoubtedly there were cases of violence, but no mass executions or forced marriages are reported.

The successor to Sher Malang was Mullah Muhammad Rasul. Locals say that he was a close associate of Mullah Omar. Mullah Muhammad Rasul tried to bring cross-border trafficking under his control and to amass a personal fortune in the process. Under his rule, massive economic pressure was added to ethnic and religious discrimination. The Taliban confiscated land, private houses, and shops. Drug smuggling was the main source of income for the local Taliban at the time.

Mullah Muhammad Rasul founded a new city called Ghurghuri

seventy kilometers to the northeast of Zaranj in the middle of the desert in order to draw the local population away from the frontier regions with Iran. He declared Ghurghuri the new administrative center of Nimroz and moved all local offices to this city. There had been some Pashtun settlements in the region of Ghurghuri before, and people believe that the Taliban clearly felt safer in a Pashtun environment. The Taliban did not succeed, however, in moving the population of Zaranj to the new city.

When U.S. troops carried out an air raid on Zaranj on November 13, 2001, Mullah Muhammad Rasul fled, together with other Taliban. People say that they all went back to Pakistan. Local mujahedin forces soon returned from Iran. They let the Taliban flee and came into power without fighting. The former governor of the local mujahedin, Karim Brahui, has once again become the governor of the province.[5]

Oral transmission of history is a general phenomenon, but in a country like Afghanistan it is of special importance. The Persian language, officially called Dari since the 1960s in Afghanistan, has more than a thousand-year tradition of writing and literacy. Historiography has been an elaborate genre of Persian literature from the very beginning, and it has served as a model for historical writing in many other Islamic languages. This applies especially to Pashto, which has, at a minimum, a five-hundred-year-old tradition of writing.

For social communication, however, Afghans do not necessarily confine themselves to these very sophisticated and highly elaborate forms, styles, and genres of writing. This is not only related to a comparatively high rate of illiteracy. In many spheres of Afghan everyday life, writing is often less important than in most other societies. Consequently, Afghans tend to attach more importance to the spoken word. Eloquence, poetic talent, narrative art, and other rhetorical gifts are held in high esteem. Beauty of language is not seen as a superfluous ornamentation of oration. Rather, language is a thing of beauty. The aesthetic of oration holds much power of persuasion.[6]

This also applies to the transmission of knowledge in everyday communication. There is a lively tradition of storytelling in Afghanistan.[7] Narratives, legends, tales, and stories are told for entertainment and for education as well. Popular knowledge of Islam is transmitted in narratives of the lives, extraordinary adventures, pious deeds, and attributes of the prophets and saints.[8] Similar narratives of historical events transmit common knowledge of history.

How does this transmission of historical knowledge work? The following story is very popular in Afghanistan. It is about Amir Abdul Rahman Khan, who ruled from 1880 to 1901 and who is widely known as the "Iron Amir."

One day a woman came to the court of Amir Abdul Rahman Khan and said: "A man kidnapped me, brought me to his home and assaulted me." In order to show that a man would never assault a woman without any reason, Abdul Rahman Khan ordered his men: "Bring needle and thread!" His servants brought needle and thread. Abdul Rahman Khan took the needle into his hand and gave the thread to the woman. Then he said to her: "I will turn the needle and you will thread it." As much as the woman tried to thread the needle, she couldn't get the thread into the eye of the needle. Finally she said to Abdul Rahman Khan: "Keep the needle still so that I can thread it!" The Amir became really angry now, and he said: "I see, you also stayed still so that this man could assault you. If you would have turned and moved like I turned the needle now, this man could not have assaulted you." He surrendered the woman to his men and said: "Bring her into

prison because she made fun of the men." Thus his men imprisoned the woman.[9]

It is unclear whether the incident reported in this story really happened or not.[10] This story is nonetheless well known among Afghans,
and it can be classified as belonging to the traditional folklore of Afghanistan. The story not only keeps alive the memory of Amir Abdul
Rahman Khan as a hard-hearted and intransigent ruler. It has another and more important message as well: in a country where women
are not even allowed to testify in court, they have no opportunity to
appear as plaintiffs unless they want to be accused themselves.

In many languages of Afghanistan this kind of short prose story
recounting more or less concrete historical events is called *riwayat,*
which means both "metaphorical short story" or "narration," on the
one hand, and "tradition" or "transmission," on the other.[11] In Persian
(Dari) and Pashto, the words *hikayat* and *qissa* may also be used to
describe short stories of this kind, which, however, are not necessarily
about specified historical incidents. The same can be said for short
stories called *nakl* in Baluchi. Persian formulas like "once," "one day"
(roz-e, yak roz, yak waqt), or "the matter is that" *(hal in ast ki),* and
their equivalents in other languages of Afghanistan are typical introductions to this kind of short prose story on more or less specified
historical events in contrast to real fiction, as in fairy tales, which usually start with the formula "Once upon a time" *(yak-e bud, yak-e
nabud,* literally: "there was, there was not").[12]

Reports on historical events transmitted successfully in the form
of riwayat belong to a type of text in which each part has a clearly
defined function for the structure and meaning of the entire text.
Stories are generated when singular events are correlated to each
other, not only temporally and causally, but by a final idea, which
shows common features of finality and imparts a metaphorical idea.

Power of persuasion is thus emotional and aesthetic, rather than merely logical. Moreover, not only do these stories help keep in memory a particular historical event and the meaning attributed to it; they also present a narrative pattern for successful transmission of this historical knowledge. In short prose stories like riwayat, historical knowledge is always handed down together with the narrative form for transmission.

Historical events preserved and transmitted in cultural memory by means of well-established genres of folk literature like riwayat usually date back to older periods of history. These events do not belong to the individual experience of the persons who tell these stories or who listen to them today. No one can prove that an incident reported in such stories actually happened or not, and there is no need for such proof, because the main message of a riwayat is its metaphorical meaning and not the story behind it.

Stories in the genre of riwayat are always *meaningful stories* about the past that were successfully kept in cultural memory in order to become meaningful history for the present. Cultural memory, as it is transmitted in these genres of folk literature, is based upon specific codes of narration, on the one hand, and becomes supra-individual experience and objective culture, on the other, because it no longer depends upon the experience lived within individual biographies.[13] In a society where an aesthetic model of language is held in high esteem, stories in the genre of riwayat, together with other genres of literature, define the basics of cultural identity.

The civil war and the reign of the Taliban also belong to the past, but they are still part of the individual experience of most people who live in Afghanistan today. Remembrance of these events belongs to communicative memory: all participants who have a stake in this common discourse have more or less equal rights to form opinions based on the experiences of individuals, kin-groups, tribes, or other social groups. Yet transmission of this experience cannot be subject to those strong codes that are characteristic of traditional genres of folk literature, nor can this individual experience be transformed into supraindividual or collective experience as easily as was the case with traditional folk literature on historical themes.

It is almost a commonplace in contemporary rhetorical theory that the background and intention of a speaker as well as the audience and the context of communication are crucial determinants of rhetorical choices. When a foreign scholar conducts an interview and asks a person for memories about the Taliban, this person will choose other rhetorical and argumentative patterns than would be used in habitual communication with friends and relatives. In interviews, more literate persons tend to give a chronological account of the events, including temporal and causal links and putting personal experience aside.

Once I asked a person to tell me how the Taliban came to Nimroz. The interviewee had studied at Kabul University. People said that he was an officer in the intelligence services in Nimroz and neighboring provinces, which represented a sign of education in their eyes.[14] He started his narrative with a report of the well-known political events of 1978. Then he gave a detailed chronological account of the civil war and its international ramifications. I am sure he would have finished with the American attacks against Afghanistan after September 11, 2001, if we were not interrupted. In his lengthy response he never said a word about himself.

Less literate and illiterate persons tended to confine their narration to particular events without chronological specification. Every narrative could be given an imaginary headline that clearly captures what the story is about, such as "How I was forbidden to speak my language at the governor's office," "How the Taliban burned down the library," "How the Taliban tried to frighten us away from Zaranj," "How the Taliban raped Iranian boys," "How my brother was arrested for possession of firearms," and so on. Substituting the part for the whole, such events were reported to represent a certain aspect of this period of history.

Phrases like "one day" or "once" (*yak maughe* in Baluchi; *yak roz* in Persian) were typical openings for such narratives. Informants frequently used phrases such as "for example" *(masalan)* or "this is how the Taliban were" (*ame raz atant taliban* in Baluchi; *intur budand talibha* in Persian) to show that a particular event stands for a general idea. In Persian (Dari), people can express their attitude toward the Taliban by choosing a corresponding plural suffix. In Pashto the plural of *talib* is always *taliban,* whereas in Persian one can say either "taliban" (with the suffix *-an*) or "talibha" (with the suffix *-ha*). The suffix *-ha* is universal and applicable to any class of noun. More limited in application, the suffix *-an* may denote humans, is more literary, and can be used especially if one wishes to express respect. Thus the plural of "compatriot" *(hamwatan)* or "my dear" *(aziz)* is always expressed as "hamwatanan" or "azizan." No one would say "hamwatanha" or "azizha." Conversely, in Persian, people tend to prefer the form *talibha,* because *taliban* (with the suffix *-an*) would pay too much tribute to the Taliban.[15]

Usually interviews were conducted at gatherings in the guestroom of a private house. Other persons listened to the interviews, and communication could easily turn into common discussion. Once I asked a person whose name was Dastagir to tell me how he was arrested for possession of firearms. He had once mentioned the fact before. Instead of telling this story himself, Dastagir asked his brother to tell me how he was arrested under the Taliban.

> The time of the Taliban was a time when, for example, the Taliban came to Nimroz. Then they found out that Dastagir

had a firearm. One Talib took Dastagir and brought him to the intelligence agency. He hit Dastagir so much that his body became completely green. He said: "I swear to kill you. You must give up the firearm." [*Addressing Dastagir:*] You gave up the firearm. Then you sat at home for some months until you healed. When you healed the Talib [came again and] said: "Do you have other arms?" He [Dastagir] said: "No. God forbid! It was only one. I gave this one to you." And so his life continued on then. People, for example, were much afraid of the government at this time. Especially Persian-speaking people and Baluch. If you knew Pashto you could do everything. You could go to every office, if your language was Pashto. You could do everything. Nobody asked where you were coming from and where you were going. If you spoke Persian or Baluchi they thought you were cursing at them. This is how they were.[16]

The narrative was not limited to the incident when Dastagir was arrested. Recounting this event, the narrator tried to represent a more general aspect of the Taliban era, defined by the fact that Baluch in general faced discrimination, whereas Pashtuns enjoyed many privileges only because they were Pashtuns and because they knew Pashto. This informant presented this idea here in a very direct way without sophisticated rhetorical approaches, but Dastagir asked his brother Gholam Nabi to tell this story because his brother was a talented narrator. He knew that Gholam Nabi would tell this story better than he could have done himself.

Gholam Nabi has worked as a shepherd most of his life and is well acquainted with the tradition of storytelling. He is completely illiterate, but almost every evening one can hear the men and women of his house laughing at his jokes and droll stories. The oratory of such persons is held in high esteem. People not only listen to them when they tell traditional folk stories, but, as we have seen, narration about events from the recent past can also be delegated to such experienced storytellers, who are appointed as *guardians of narrative memory.*

Such experienced narrators know exactly what people expect from them. Sometimes they even try to generate stories that follow the structure of the well-established genre of riwayat when they are talking about events from the recent past.[17] Usually such narratives still show certain rhetorical deficits. However, the following example demonstrates that the same experienced narrator, Gholam Nabi, not only recounted an event from the recent past, but intended to give the reported incident a more common idea and to entertain his audience at the same time. The narrative was also recorded during casual conversation in a private guesthouse.

> Once a Baluch married his daughter to a Pashtun. This happened some years ago, twenty years ago. Well, the Pashtun came here, he was working and then he married, started a family. Then he took his wife and went to his homeland. I don't remember where this was, in [the province of] Helmand, in [the province of] Kandahar, or in [the provincial center of Helmand] Lashkar Gah. Well, he took her and went away . . . He brought her away one or two years after the wedding. Later on the father also set off. [He said to himself:] "I'll see how my daughter is—if she has not died, if she is still alive, if she was not imprisoned, how she is doing." Well, the man set off. At that time there were not so many cars and such facilities, just a camel or a horse. One night he stopped here, one night he stopped there, he traveled for several days and nights. Well, he went to the place where the house of his son-in-law was. He came to the village and asked: "Where is the house of that person?" One [person] said: "It is here." Another

[person] said: "It is there." And the poor man was so exhausted. Finally he found the house. Well, he found the house and went there. He saw his son-in-law and his father. They all welcomed each other. Then they went into the house. They gave much bread and tea to him. Well, so he was sitting there. One night went by and a new day began. Then he said: "I came to my daughter. I want to meet my daughter and to know if she is okay, how her life is, if she is doing well or not." [The Pashtun] said: "We still have time. You will see her." More days went by. A long time later the Baluch said: "I didn't come to you. I don't want to see you. I can well do without seeing you. I came to see my daughter." [The Pashtun] became embarrassed. First he said: "That's not our custom. We are not allowed to show our wives to anybody, no matter if he is her father or somebody else." Then the man said: "But she is my daughter. I cared for her, she slept at one place with me, she got up with me, and after all she is my child! And now you are hiding here from me." The Pashtun said: "I do not hide her. You may meet her behind a curtain." Then they hung a curtain in the room. The girl was sitting on one side and her father on the other side. Well, they welcomed each other and enquired after their health. The father asked his daughter how she was doing, how her life was. The girl said: "You see how I am doing, don't you? Why are you asking?" Then the old man went away from his daughter. He got on his old jackass and came back. This is the way the Pashtun did. Over. The program is over. [*Laughs*][18]

This incident was reported like an ethnic joke to stereotype Pashtun men as strong and uncompromising guardians of their daughters and wives. Often this stereotype serves as an explanation for the harsh policy of the Taliban toward women in all parts of Afghanistan where they had power. In Nimroz, where a considerable number of Baluch give their daughters to Pashtuns in order to strengthen economic ties for drug trafficking, this was indeed a true-life story that had another very topical message as well: never give your daughter to a Pashtun unless you don't want to see her anymore.

When Gholam Nabi told this story, he obviously tried to follow the pattern of traditional folk stories. The main protagonist remained anonymous. In this case the name of the protagonist was not important for the final idea of the story. The fact that he was Baluch is sufficient information. All singular events of the plot were combined in precise chronological order. The narrator included details that were not necessary for the plot, but that aimed to affect the listeners emotionally and to keep them in suspense—for example, when he mentioned how the Baluch became exhausted when he was searching for the house of his son-in-law, his characterization as a "poor man," or the pitiful statement that the Baluch came back on an "old jackass," although at the beginning it was said that he traveled by horseback or camel.

Gholam Nabi told the whole story nearly to the end in Baluchi. When he said the last sentence (still in Baluchi), "This is the way the Pashtuns did," he looked into the faces of the listeners and felt that they were expecting something more. Then he suddenly switched to Persian and added a phrase ("Over. The program is over") that all persons in the audience knew from Iranian television. He even said this phrase with the typical pronunciation of Iran, one that sounds quite funny from the lips of an Afghan. This code-switching created the punch line that the story itself was missing, but that people nonetheless anticipated. The story had a rhetorical deficit, and the experienced narrator knew how to compensate for it. Here the payoff of the joke was in the narrator's performance. This story can thus be regarded as a riwayat in nascent state. For successful transmission in the tradition of riwayat, the story still needs a punch line that would express the metaphorical idea and that would be an irredeemable part of the narrative structure of the story.

The following narrative about an incident that happened during the reign of the Taliban was given by a Persian-speaking officer of the local intelligence agency at a gathering of elders and tribal chiefs in a private house. It also contains a riwayat in nascent state, but this riwayat remained imperfect for other reasons.

The matter was that in sixty . . . eighty one [A.D. 2002] I went to Kabul. I joined a tribal meeting like we are sitting now. [There was] a doctor whose name was Doctor Abdullah and who was from Kabul, of course, and I was acquainted with him before. . . . In the course of our meeting he said: "At the time of the Taliban," he said, "one Friday I left my home to go to a mosque and say the Friday prayer and to go to the house of my daughter after the Friday prayer." He had married off his daughter, and "every week," he said, "on Friday I went to see my daughter always." "When I was walking on the way," he said, "there was a congregation, a prayer; I went to join the prayer, the Friday prayer. I said my prayer, the Friday prayer. The prayer was finished and I left the prayer. I was walking on the way [again] in the direction of my daughter's home." It happens that in Kabul at some mosques the prayer lasts ten to fifteen or twenty minutes up to half an hour, it may differ from other mosques. He said, "When I was walking on the way there was another mosque with a congregation, people were standing and praying." "The Taliban were standing with whips and bludgeons and said to me: 'You didn't say your prayer.' I swore: 'Leave me! I have said my prayer at that mosque already, but at that mosque the prayer was ten minutes earlier.'" Well, he said: "They whacked me so much and they said: 'You must say your prayer. You didn't say your prayer. You are lying.'" He said: "I went again to this mosque. I had performed twelve bows of the afternoon prayer at that mosque, and I performed twelve bows at this mosque." "The prayer was over. When I was walking on the way I came to a third mosque, where people were praying, and a Talib was standing there with whip and bludgeon. He said: 'Look at this guy, who is not praying now, who does not go to mosque, does not join the prayer. He has forsaken God.' I said: 'Leave me, because I have said my afternoon prayer at one mosque already, a second time a Talib criticized me, and I said my prayer at a second mosque. Now you are asking me for the third time to say my prayer.'" He said: "They whacked me so much and said that I had to say my prayer." He said: "I was offended, and I said that I wouldn't say my prayer." "Three or four persons," he said, "took me and brought me to the local commander, to that commander of the Taliban whom they had at checkpoints. He asked me: 'How many bows is a prayer?' I said: 'For Muslims an afternoon prayer is ten bows, for Taliban thirty.' He [the commander] said: 'Why is a prayer for Taliban thirty bows?' [I answered:] 'It is thirty bows because I have said my prayer two times and performed twenty bows, and now you are forcing me to say my prayer for the third time.'" Well, he said: "He whacked me so much there. He hit the whip upon my foot, on my back and on my shoulder. Finally white bearded men came and rescued me from their hands, freed me." He said: "When I was freed from the Taliban I swore to God that I wouldn't pray at all as long as the Taliban were ruling in Afghanistan, that I would never turn my face in the direction of the Qiblah." "Finally," he said, "I came home and told my wife, my children and my family what had happened. We decided that we had to leave Afghanistan." "We felt impelled to do so. We went to Pakistan. I lived in Pakistan, in Peshawar for three, four, five years up to the time when the Taliban disappeared in Afghanistan. Then I came, I came back to Afghanistan." "Now I am in Kabul," he said. He is an official servant. "I am a clerical worker," he said, "at the ministry of education. I am working there. My father was religious [Muslim], I am religious [Muslim], I say my prayer five times, and I go to mosque, because the fury which I had with the Taliban, is over now when the Taliban have disappeared."[19]

The main intention of the narrator was to describe the fate of one of his friends under the Taliban. He wanted to show how this friend, who had always been a good Muslim, lost his faith in God under the Taliban because they treated him as an unbeliever and forced him to pray again and again although he had done his prayer already voluntarily. In order to prove the authenticity and validity of the incident, the narrator mentioned the name of his friend and explained in detail where he had heard what had happened to his friend, what his friend had done, and what he had thought before and after this incident.

This narrative contains a part that could be told separately without mentioning the name of the protagonist. It recounts how ignorant Taliban forced a good Muslim to perform his afternoon prayer three times. The metaphorical idea of this story is given in the phrase "For Muslims an afternoon prayer is ten bows, for Taliban thirty." The number of bows is prescribed for each prayer in a canonical way, and for Muslims it is not subject to discussion or interpretation. Saying that for Taliban an afternoon prayer is thirty bows instead of ten, the narrator expresses the common idea that the Taliban had a very strange understanding of Islam and that they forced people to practice a faith that was not their own.

This part can be seen as a successfully generated story that follows the narrative pattern of traditional riwayat. It contains a metaphorical idea that can reflect collective experience, because it resonates with elements found in many individual biographies of the last decade in Afghanistan. Of course, the narrator would not have related the story of his friend if it did not contain an idea that all of his listeners could share and that was expressed, moreover, in a rhetorical way that could meet the aesthetic expectations of the audience.

The tradition of storytelling and especially the genre of riwayat seem to be suitable to combine individual experience about the reign of the Taliban and other events from the recent past into common experience that in the future can become collective experience and memory. Experienced narrators who are well acquainted with the traditional genre of folk stories are appointed as guardians of historical knowledge. They are able to present their narrations in a pattern where every part of the text has a clearly defined function for the structure and meaning of the entire text. Thus stories can be generated that show common features of finality and that are aimed to impart a metaphorical idea about the recent past. The narrative structure of these stories still seems imperfect, but in general a narrator knows that he should tell a story where an idea that is acceptable for the collective memory can be handed down together with the narrative form of transmission.

A similar narrative strategy appears in a manuscript written in Persian by a local intellectual named Abdul Rahman Pahwal about the reign of the Taliban in Nimroz.[20] The manuscript gives a largely chronological summary of the events that took place from the emergence of the Taliban until the end of their rule in November 2001, though sometimes the author refers to earlier events dating back to the 1950s. From a regional point of view, the main focus is Nimroz Province. The author often does not mention when a particular event took place, because the date was not important for his way of re-counting history. He does not intend to give a complete chronologi-cal account with all temporal and causal links. For Abdul Rahman Pahwal, many events were worth being preserved and kept in mem-ory because they could represent a more general feature of the reign of the Taliban. Thus, following the example of riwayat, he also gener-ated more or less metaphorical short stories where the main message is more important than the concrete story behind it.[21]

Together with prose stories, poetry is another important genre of folk literature intended to keep events and experiences from the past in memory. Epic poems like the Persian *Shahnama* or the classical po-ems *(shayr)* of the Baluch present legends about the origins and acts of great national heroes from the dim and distant past. However, in Afghanistan there has always been a lively tradition of composing poetry and songs about events from the recent past as well. The French scholar James Darmesteter was the first European to notice the importance of these historical songs in Afghanistan. When he published a collection of historical songs from the Pashtuns in 1888–1890, he was confident that no serious history of Afghanistan could be written without taking notice of these historical songs. In the foreword to this edition he pointed out, "The British historian Kaye wrote a book about the first British-Afghan war, but he did not men-tion the songs of the Pashtuns at all. He probably didn't even know that these songs existed. Imagine that a historian would write a book about the French revolution without knowing the Marseillaise."[22]

Indeed, in some historical songs, events from the past are recounted with so much detail that one can outline the essentials of what happened, when, and where. In contrast to written literature on historical subjects, historical folk songs of this kind are mostly dedicated to local events that belong to the historical knowledge of a tribe or of a single region alone. A Pashto song about the outbreak of the third Anglo-Afghan war in 1919 illustrates this point. In the genre of *charbayta* (Persian: *chaharbayti;* literally, "four verses"), this song was recorded by the Afghan scholar Abdullah Bakhtani in the early 1960s in Laghman Province, east of Kabul.[23] Of course this war was far from being a local event, but this song presents a quite comprehensible picture of how fighting took place in the region of Laghman. Moreover, the song conveys an interpretation of the causes of the war.

Refrain:

Ghazi Pacha ["the king, religious warrior" (King
    Amanullah)] is the ruler of all of Afghanistan.
Even in London the *parangi* [the British] are afraid of
    him.

Verses:

The *parang* was unfair in Peshawar;
Indians, Sikhs, and Muslims lost their houses [there].
Then *Ghazi pach* [King Amanullah] announced his decision.
And he sent his troops [from Kabul] against them.

Our weapons droned and were accompanied by thunder
when the *parang* sent bombs from the sky.

Our fallen heroes were beautiful like roses,
[but] uncountable was the number of *parang* whom they
    had killed.

Sardar Muhammad put on the uniform of the commander
    in chief.
Coming from Dakka he rushed to Jalalabad.
Brigadier Anwar was with him.
Both made a deal and appropriated the treasury.

From the bridge near Dargunt the way [of the troops]
    goes upward, oh my Lord!
First comes Charbagh, then [comes] Mandrawar, and
    then the town of Torgaray,
And in Qala-ye Seraj the sardar holds power.
A brave man lives there—Muhammad Zaman.

Let God give power to our ruler!
Let his throne become even more powerful!
Muhammad Yaqub will praise him everywhere.
Praise to the Almighty, who gave us the true faith.[24]

Like most *charbayta,* this song starts with a refrain (*sar* or *kasr*), which
is followed by usually five or six verses *(band).* In the first verse we
hear that the war broke out when King Amanullah sent his troops
to punish the British for quelling a riot in Peshawar in 1919. As
we know, the real reason for this war was a letter in which King
Amanullah demanded that the British viceroy in India recognize the
independence of Afghanistan. Nevertheless, the explanation given in
this song must be regarded as a true historical fact as well because the
complex diplomatic background to the war was obviously unknown

in the remote mountainous province of Laghman. On the other hand, the striking news of a bloody uprising in Peshawar, which really did take place at the same time, could spread like wildfire even without any modern mass media.[25] It is not surprising, therefore, that people thought this incident had caused the war against the British aggressors.

In the second verse the author remains close to historical detail, hinting at the fact that the British for the first time used bombers in the war and that they were superior to the Afghans in technical equipment. The third verse recounts how Sardar Salih Muhammad Khan from Dakka became the commander in chief of the Afghan army and how he stole the treasury together with Brigadier General Muhammad Anwar Khan from the Asaki tribe, thereby misusing their official positions. This is a verifiable detail as well. Sardar Salih Muhammad Khan was, in fact, later imprisoned.[26] In the fourth verse the local color becomes salient in a very special way. It describes the route along the river Alingar to Qala-ye Seraj (the former center of the province) that local troops took during the war. The last verse contains praise of God and King Amanullah. The author's name, Muhammad Yaqb, is mentioned here as well.

The information about historical events presented in these songs remains close to verifiable details, without further metaphorical meaning or other symbolic features. Sometimes the date may be included as well. The protagonists are not idealized, but described as honorable or contemptible persons. The language is rather prosaic, the form inflexible.[27] It is a special feature of these songs that they deal with local events or present a local interpretation of an event. This can be explained by the practice of performance. These songs were performed by their authors. They sing these songs for a limited local audience, and none of these songs is composed for written transmission or for recording, of course. The local viewpoint of the author and his audience define the local perspective of the songs.

Most songs of this kind deal with fighting and war, be it tribal feud or war against foreign invaders. The meaningful messages handed down and kept in the cultural memory with these songs can be seen in the maintenance and strengthening of the fighting spirit. Thus the British wars against Afghanistan inspired Persian authors as well. Many of them composed battle poems *(jangnama)* in the tradition of the epic poem *Shahnama*. The most famous of these battle poems from the nineteenth century are the "Poem about Akbar" *(Akbarnama)* by Hamid Kashmiri and the "Poem about the Battle of Kabul," written by an unknown author from Kabul. Hamid Kashmiri even used the unique meter of the *Shahnama* in his poem.[28] The fact that the British also hired Persian poets to compose similar poems advancing British military interests reflects the popularity of these battle poems and their importance for wartime propaganda.[29] Other historical songs are about local feuds, heroic victories in the traditional game of buzkashi, or other domestic happenings. Songs about disasters such as earthquakes and floods are meant to express pain and sorrow and can be interpreted as prayers of supplication or invocation.

Originally these historical songs were as ephemeral as the lives of their authors and the events they describe.[30] When a song contained a verse of high poetic quality, this part could be handed down by oral transmission and become common folk heritage. Other authors may incorporate such verses into their own poems later on. Today we know selected songs about historical events from the nineteenth or early twentieth century only because they were collected and written down by linguists, ethnologists, or folklorists. Although European scholars made the first of such publications, by the 1960s Afghan intellectuals also became interested in folklore and did their own linguistic and ethnological fieldwork. They gave these songs a second life as the folkloric heritage of Afghanistan that is no longer transmitted orally but kept in memory in written form.

The tradition of writing songs about current events is still alive in Afghanistan today. Local authors and singers can be found in every part of the country. Most songs about the recent past are songs about the wars that dominate the recent history of Afghanistan. They have a lot in common with older historical songs in terms of form and substance. As in the past, they are performed by their authors at concerts for a limited audience, but today performance and transmission are not limited to live concerts.

The first song about the civil war that I heard during my visit to Afghanistan in 2002 was an invocation performed by a young man. When I asked him if he wrote this song himself, he answered that he knew this song from a tape recording and that it had been written by a local singer, Zaher Baluch. Although he had never been at one of Zaher Baluch's concerts, he had heard him singing on television and in radio broadcasts. Like many other Baluch, he owned more than one cassette with recordings of this singer.

In this song *(liko)* the singer appeals to local saints, begging them to stop the war. Khajgir, Ghaltan, Amiran ("the Amirs"), Shai San, Bala Nosh, and Mir Iqbal are the names of saints whose graves are famous places of pilgrimage in southwestern Afghanistan. Invocations are a very popular genre of folk literature in Afghanistan, and it was no coincidence that, of all songs, this young man sang this one.

> O holy Khajgir! Help us, holiest of all saints!
> O holy Ghaltan. O holy Sultan!

Hoist your flags! Afghanistan was destroyed.

There is much war and bloodshed in the land of the Afghans.

All this war and dispute comes from America.

O holy Khajgir! Eliminate our hatred!

Destroy the enemies with your spear!

Bring peace to the land of the Afghans!

Muslims are fighting for money and dollars.

One says seven, the other says eight.[31]

Land of Afghanistan, you are unprotected.

We remember the saints, Khajgir and the Amirs,

Shai San and Bala Nosh, bring the war to an end!

Sayyed Mir Iqbal, don't forget about us![32]

Electronic media have radically changed the way modern historical songs are transmitted. In the bazaars of Afghanistan one can find hundreds of cassettes and compact discs (both audio and video) with recordings by local singers. Sometimes songs about the civil war are transmitted via radio and television as well. Especially in the first year after the fall of the Taliban, one could hear such songs on radio and television as an expression of joy about the newly resumed liberty. Modern electronic mass media have created a secondary mode of oral transmission.

Afghans nonetheless treasure the merits of live concerts. The following song was recorded in 2002 during a concert by Zaher Baluch in a private home in Zaranj. From Zahedan in the Iranian part of Baluchistan, Zaher Baluch is the most famous Baluch singer in Afghanistan. Since the Baluch do not recognize the frontier between Iran and Afghanistan, events from Afghanistan are as topical as what happens in the Iranian part of Baluchistan for Zaher Baluch. Some

Pashtuns from Helmand and Kandahar provinces were also present at the concert and were obviously trading partners of the host. Guests ordered songs from Zaher Baluch, writing their wishes on small sheets of paper, which were passed on to the singer. Although the following song *(liko)* had been ordered from the very beginning of the concert, Zaher Baluch sang it only when the Pashtun guests had left the concert. He apparently did not want to offend them. The song is about the famous mujahed, Ahmad Shah Masud, who managed to resist the Taliban until his death at the hands of Arab terrorists on the eve of September 11, 2001. Popular mass media may disseminate such songs widely throughout the country, but not all Afghans endorse the messages they convey. Only those persons who have struggled on the same side of the front line or who share the same political experience can embrace the themes of a battle song. This applies to the following composition about Ahmad Shah Masud in a special way.

Refrain:

Masud, the hero, commander of Panjsher

Verses:

Masud, the hero, declared [war] on the Russians.
Afghanistan must not be ashamed of him—Masud, the
    hero.

He warned the Russians with his struggle and with his
    physical appearance.
He hit the Russians and he killed them, [he] made them
    look foolish before the whole world—Masud, the
    hero.

Masud was a lion *(Sher)* in the valley of the five lions *(panj Sher)*.
He hit the Russians and made their eyes cry—Masud, the hero.

Brave Masud frightened the Russians away.
He had a hundred commanders [in his power] against the Russians—Masud, the hero.

When the brave Masud, commander in chief of the jihad, hit the Russians,
the whole world was looking at Afghanistan—Masud, the hero.

But then two brothers, Afghans [Pashtuns] and Tajiks made the day turn dark.
The enemy misused his friends and brothers—Masud, the hero.

Being masked as journalists these two terrorists came,
and [they] killed Masud, those wild animals—Masud, the hero.

God called Masud to himself. He said Goodbye to this world.
May God let him meet his fate! May God reward him with virgins (horis) and slaves—Masud, the hero.

Ahmad Shah Masud inflamed our hearts.
May our pure Lord forgive you all your sins—Masud, the hero.

> May Allah be close to you. Paradise will be your destiny.
> May your head be higher than the throne of the Lord on
>   the Day of Judgment—Masud, the hero.[33]

This song about Ahmad Shah Masud was written in the same pattern as traditional historical songs. It consists of a refrain repeated after every one of the ten verses. Like older historical songs, it gives a more or less detailed historical account of the struggle carried out by the main protagonist. Verses 1 to 5 treat the war of the mujahedin against the Soviet invaders. Masud is introduced here as the outstanding leader and army commander of all mujahedin. This can be seen as a legitimate interpretation because in 1992 Masud was appointed as minister of defense in the mujahedin government. Verse 6 hints at the civil war that broke out sometime later, concluding that foreign enemies brought the ethnic war to Afghanistan. In accord with the actual chronology of events, the terrorist attack against Masud is described in verse 7, even noting that the terrorists came in the guise of journalists. Verses 8 through 10 celebrate the main protagonist in traditional forms of praise.

In contrast to traditional historical songs, however, the events described in this song are not limited to one region only. Today news of all kinds is spread by modern mass media, and people are integrated into the political life of the country in quite novel ways. Their view is no longer confined to a single region. Zaher Baluch performed this song on Kabul television with great success. Far from Kabul, many Baluch knew the refrain and some verses. For them this song about Masud was a hymn about the end of a lengthy war. It figured as a kind of Afghan "Marseillaise." Common fate and historical experience forged shared heroes such as the protagonist idealized in this song. In 2002, Masud was regarded as a national martyr *(shahid-e milli)*, at least for all non-Pashtuns.

When I visited Nimroz again in 2005, however, I didn't hear this song. I brought my hosts a compact disc with songs of Zaher Baluch that I had recorded two and a half years before. This present was very welcome, and my hosts listened to the CD more than once. But usually they skipped the song about Ahmad Shah Masud and preferred the lyrical and epic songs. Today modern electronic media may preserve historical songs forever, but in the communicative memory of the people they are still as transient and ephemeral as the events these songs recount.

There is another important dimension of the role played by mass media in shaping communicative memory in Afghanistan. Concerts by local singers are organized in private houses. On such occasions, many guests are invited and feasted. People regard such concerts as meritorious deeds. As mentioned above, guests can order songs and write their wishes on small sheets of paper. Before a singer performs a song ordered by some guests, he gives a short introduction noting the identity of the guest who ordered this song and also offers a prayer of supplication for the host.[34] When recordings of a concert are sold later in the bazaar, the name of the host is spread together with the songs. Such acknowledgments increase the patron's reputation as a generous and noble person. Thus the songs are preserved and kept in memory together with the name of the singer's benefactor.

As in the past, songs about the past and present remain very popular in Afghanistan. Like their predecessors, these songs capture detailed chronological accounts of historical events. And some of these songs are still intended to inspire a fighting spirit. In contrast to the past, however, historical songs are now spread by electronic media as well and may be preserved for ever. Yet the popularity of historical songs is still as fleeting as the events they depict. In a context marked by widespread war-weariness, songs that convey invocations and prayers of supplication enjoy special popularity. The same applies to satirical songs that ridicule, in equal measure, all political parties and military groups.

CHAPTER SIX

Fraternity, Power, and
Time in Central Asia

Robert L. Canfield

I am struck by the rustic appearance of many of the movements that arose in the early 1990s along the frontier of the collapsing Soviet Union, the Taliban being but one of them. As Yugoslavia broke apart in the 1990s, Serb militiamen fighting their Croat and Bosnian neighbors adopted the appearance and demeanor of the *hajduks*, fourteenth-century anti-Ottoman mountain brigands, bandits, and highwaymen. They wore the oval field cap and full beard of the hajduk as a deliberate pose, projecting an image of the rural against the urban, the sectarian against the secular, the communal against the civil.[1] Similarly, the anti-Russian insurgents in Chechnya appeared, at least to their enemies, to be semiliterate thugs capable of abduction and large-scale murder.[2] In Uzbekistan, Juma Namangani, leader of an antigovernment force, affected a Robin Hood image, reportedly holding rich hostages for ransom but paying peasants $100 for one sheep.[3] In Afghanistan the mujahedin who fought the Soviets in the 1990s and turned against each other in the 1990s were largely rural in composition and perspective. All such movements—in the former Yugoslavia, in the Caucasus, in Central Asia, in Afghanistan and Pakistan—represented a distrust of urban society, civil institutions, and the secular world. But whatever the similarities among these movements, each was distinctive, arising out of local and particular tensions. For the activists with a Muslim background, Islam provided the vocabulary by which to answer Western culture and especially American hegemony, which was looming over them.[4]

These groups coalesced in a geopolitical context that was changing on a scale not seen since the major refiguring of political identities of the eighteenth and nineteenth centuries. As the Holy Roman Empire was expiring, the "interlinked certainties" of previous centuries lost their salience, and so, in the words of Benedict Anderson, "a search was on . . . for a new way of linking fraternity, power and time meaningfully together."[5] Anderson refers to the nationalism that would rise in the nineteenth century to enthrall the European political imagination. In our time a similarly grand refiguring of the political imagination has been taking place in the wake of the Soviet Union.

The declining cultural order that Anderson was referring to was one in which a concept of "fraternity" was based on religious affiliation (such as Christendom or the Muslim *umma*); on a conception of "power" in which monarchs had the right to rule "by some form of cosmological (divine) dispensation"; and on a presumption of "temporality" that fused "cosmology and history." The modern concept of the "nation" replacing the old political mentality would construe collective interest groups as localized and bonded by a sense of common history. A "nation" was a collective body that had a place, a distinguishable tradition, and an ancestry; it was a kind of "race" that shared lifeways and traditions of thought.[6] And it was preeminently a moral entity. Loyalty to the nation, nationalism, says Bruce Kapferer "makes the political religious . . . The nation is created as an object of devotion . . . the political is shrouded in the symbolism of a 'higher' purpose."[7] Even the most secular nations demand sacrifice—"supreme" sacrifices—for the collective good, a notion represented, for instance, in national cenotaphs and tombs to "Unknown Soldiers."[8] The rise of this new cultural "certainty" was paralleled by changes in the economy, specifically, Anderson claims, the rise of print capitalism, which grew as economic connections with the wider world enlarged, enabling dispersed speakers of a common language to envision a common moral bond. New imaginings were accompanied by new opportunities.

In the last couple of decades, long-established "certainties" are similarly being replaced—or at least challenged—by new conceptions of shared interest driven by a "search" for new social conventions where the old ones no longer apply—the difference in our time, though, is that, unlike the earlier transition, which was a slow process over a couple of centuries, the transition has been abrupt, marked by the sudden demise of the Soviet Union. Although it was a quiescent death (a brief announcement by Gorbachev on Christmas Day 1991), the aftermath for the peoples around its frontiers (not to mention inside them) was cataclysmic. In material terms, the flow of goods and information that had nourished the great imperial community dried up. "The abolition of the convertible ruble . . . disrupted trade, while the closure of Moscow's financing facilities drained the monetary lifeline of entire nations . . . The drawing of new borders between newly-formed countries severed ancient trade routes, blocked irrigation systems and hindered agrarian commerce."[9] The political consequences were no less disruptive, for the demise of the Soviet Union left a vacuum of politico-moral terms by which political groups could identify their interests. In the previous paradigm of political oppositions, communism, or at least Marxism, had provided the world with the most trenchant response to Western capitalism. Communism was international in its claim and moral in its appeal to the oppressed peoples of the world. For half a century, communism or Marxism (in various forms) provided the analytical critique by which to reject capitalism as a way of life.

In the absence of the political rhetoric of the Cold War, the terms by which alliances could be secured were now, in the early 1990s, unclear, and precipitated in the ripple of political and military contests that broke out all along the frontier of the empire. The established certainties of former times—East and West, capitalist and communist, contraries by which the world had been polarized—had vanished. The "search" for a new grand paradigm of political categories linking notions of fraternity, power, and time was now "on." What Nazif Shahrani said about the peoples of Central Asia in the early 1990s was likewise true for all the peoples along the frontier of the former Soviet Union: they "are facing serious spiritual crises and are desperately in search of meaning and a moral compass."[10]

In the early period after the collapse of the Soviet empire, nationalistic—actually, ethnonationalistic —ideologies came to prominence as various "nationalities" all along the frontier of the expiring Soviet Union began to assert themselves. In Afghanistan, when the war between Afghan communists and Afghan mujahedin finally ended, the politico-military organizations that had prosecuted the war against the Soviets fought it out among themselves, and because they had been rather loosely formed along ethnic lines—as Hazaras, Tajiks, Uzbeks, or largely as a Pashtun tribe—their struggle simply confirmed the fighting groups as ethnonationalist political bodies.[11] The rise of the Taliban reflected the ethnonationalist bias of the times, for they were Pashtuns, but there were also at work other forces, international and global, that imposed upon their political situation other politico-moral demands. Western secularism would threaten established social conventions among Central Asian Muslims—in confrontations that would stimulate forces and reactions of their own. The gathering importance of the Taliban and their incorporation into a wider network of similar-minded Muslims reflected a shift in the possibilities for meaningful cultural linkage that was taking place among Muslims in the region generally.

The new politico-moral orientation that emerged among some Central Asian Muslims expressed their distinctive problem with the ineluctable advance of Western hegemony. Islamism provided the moral critique by which to reject the overwhelming infusive and expanding presence of Western culture. Rejecting the West on grounds other than Marxism or communism, the Islamist critique is nevertheless like the communist/Marxist critique in that it is a moral view that resolutely stands apart from, even rises up against, Western culture. Islamism resonates for a variety of Muslim groups because, while encompassing their specific, local, and individual problems, it presents them as particular manifestations of a general problem, enabling the various groups to envision a common problem and collectively join a common cause.

The Taliban were a cultural body that arose in particular circumstances but were gradually brought into relation to other similar groups in the Muslim world. They changed in their perspective and cultural practice as the wider geopolitical field was transforming, acquiring new cultural features through the infusion of personnel and perspectives from several groups. I here describe the transformation in the political consciousness of the Taliban as other groups joined them. I do so only speculatively—or rather, as a kind of problematic, as a set of issues ideally to be examined, if I had access to the right people. I describe each of the groups allied with or embedded in the Taliban as a social entity marked by a particular way of defining the situation, with a particular sense of the past and a particular sense of commonality. Each, that is, had its own way of linking fraternity, power, and time. Each also had financial and material sources that enabled them to exist and expand. Somehow, there was money, there was materiel, there was moral encouragement—from sources only now becoming known. The groups that fused with the Taliban brought with them certain distinguishable features that their members shared to some degree. I examine the various groups and influences that shaped the Taliban movement in various stages, noting the changes in composition and sociopolitical ambiance that each group contributed to it. I trace these developments more or less chronologically, in the effort to disentangle the strands of influence that have made the Taliban what they are. The examination will expose an enlarging mesh of connections and influences that produced a contemporary social entity that the "original" Taliban would never have imagined.

By "original" Taliban I mean, of course, the small band that early in 1994 took up the cause against abusive commanders in Kandahar. They were acting to bring order in a time of anarchy. They knew each other and acted in response to the counsel and directives of their teacher, Mullah Muhammad Omar, and his seasoned colleagues. Sickened by the internecine fighting and inhumanity of previous years, they and most of the peoples of Afghanistan had turned away from the mujahedin leaders. Their perspective was local, their horizons were limited, and their concerns were immediate. They had no grand pretensions. Most interesting now, in retrospect, is what was *not* on their minds: they had no interest in, and perhaps no knowledge of, the hardships of the Palestinians or Kashmiris, or Muslims elsewhere. And they had no particular concern with Western culture. They were preoccupied with local problems.

To the original Taliban were soon added a body of young men from Pakistani madrasas (religious schools) eager to bring stability to the society. There was a great hunger for order, after fourteen years of civil war, and they wanted to help. These young men, perhaps more than those in the original group, had had little family life. Trained in the Deobandi tradition in schools financed by Saudi Arabia, these young men were educated to think of their participation with the Taliban as a jihad—a struggle against evil in the world—even though their opponents were other Muslims. Like the original Taliban they would have been inspired by narratives of Muhammad's struggle to bring good into the world. It was a moral cause with which devout Muslims could identify. Their horizons were presumably narrow in a different way than those of the "original Taliban": they probably had heard about the Muslim cause in Kashmir, they probably did not know much about problems in the Middle East, and they knew, Ahmed Rashid says, little about Afghanistan's past. They were, rather, better informed on the great exploits of Muslims in the first few centuries of Islam.[12]

If not along with this group, then soon after it, came Pakistani officers. We know that Pakistanis were offering military advice quite early. Two factions of Pakistani military men were represented. General Nasirullah Babar appeared in Kandahar at the behest of the recently elected prime minister, Benazir Bhutto, and represented the interests of the Deobandi madrasas where many Afghan Taliban had been educated.[13] Representatives of the Pakistani Inter-Services Intelligence Directorate (ISI), many of whom were informally associated with the Jama'at-e-Islami party, also made contact with the Taliban. Both groups of Pakistanis brought a new perspective to the Taliban. For them Afghanistan was never the only front: there was also Kashmir, and the endless struggle with India; and there were other fronts, in Punjab, Uzbekistan, and Chechnya.[14] Lieutenant General Hamid Gul, head of the ISI, soon after the Soviet defeat in Afghanistan put this perspective into words: "We are fighting a jihad and this is the first Islamic international brigade in the modern era. The communists have their own brigades, the West has NATO, why can't the Muslims unite and form a common front?"[15]

Most of the Pashtun Islamists who joined the Taliban had participated in the war against the Soviets as members of the military organizations supported by Pakistan. As the Taliban happened to be Pashtun, it is likely that some former mujahedin joined them because of their ethnic type. These would have been men formerly associated with the anti-Soviet Pashtun organizations led by such men as Abdul Rabb al-Rasul Sayyaf, Gulbuddin Hekmatyar, or Yunos Khales, warriors left over from the anti-Soviet war—left over in the sense that they were still unemployed, still available for hire. The alternatives for many former mujahedin were limited, and the Pashtuns with chauvinistic leanings had become alarmed that Kabul was under the control of non-Pashtuns (1992–1996), a circumstance scarcely known in Afghanistan history. So, in addition to the sense that this was a good religious cause, some Pashtuns were motivated by a kind of ethnonationalism. Indeed, the trend toward the formation of ethnonationalist military organizations was already established by other political parties: the Hizb-e Wahdat-e Islami-ye Afghanistan of the Hazaras, Jamiat-e Islami-ye Afghanistan of the Tajiks, Junbesh-e Melli-ye Islami-ye Afghanistan of the Uzbeks. As the original Taliban were Pashtun and those young men who raced in from Pakistan were Pashtun, the movement was growing incidentally as a Pashtun movement, a fateful development.

I include in this group another kind of Pashtun about whom little is known: the former communists. We know that some communists, such as General Shahnawaz Tanai, had joined the mujahedin in March 1990, well before the collapse of the communist regime, but many more former communists apparently joined later.[16] I have heard (from reputable sources) of formerly zealous communists who became Taliban, with no fanfare: They simply put on turbans, grew beards, and joined the cause. Certainly the communists, who had been so prominent in the 1980s, vanished from the scene. Those who were not executed or had not fled the country just blended in.

In spring 1996, twelve hundred Pashtun religious leaders converged on the city of Kandahar, "the biggest gathering of mullahs and ulama that had ever taken place in modern Afghan history."[17] They had been called together at a time when the leadership of the Taliban by Mullah Muhammad Omar and his colleagues was being questioned. Affairs had not gone well for some months: after advancing quickly in many localities in the south and west, the Taliban had been unable to take Kabul from the Tajiks commanded by Ahmad Shah Masud. Some of their members wanted to negotiate with the Tajiks, some were questioning the leadership of Mullah Omar. The movement was stalling. In this context the Pashtun clergy had been invited to help broaden and firm up support for the Taliban.[18]

The Kandahari establishment—the elders of the city and the local religious leaders—was of course partial to their own, the founder of the Taliban. With their encouragement, in an act of spiritual daring, on April 4, 1996, Mullah Muhammad Omar entered the shrine housing the sacred cloak of Muhammad, brought the cloak to the roof of the shrine where all could see, and ceremonially wrapped himself in it. His Kandahari supporters proclaimed him "Amir al-Muminin" (Commander of the Faithful) and formally offered him their allegiance *(baiat)*, setting the stage for the others also to offer allegiance.[19] This public act was a claim to legitimacy, the right to lead the now-powerful organization of the Taliban, but it also entailed a broader moral claim. If this was a religious cause for the

Taliban, it was now declared a holy cause for Muslims generally, the leader being, of course, Mullah Muhammad Omar. This was the cause of God. That the Tajiks they opposed in Kabul were also Sunni Muslims was no longer significant; they were the enemy, and for the Pashtun Muslim community this was now an explicitly religious war, no less than the ones before it—but now, with ethnonational nuances.

In May, scarcely a month after this redefinition of the Taliban cause, Osama bin Laden arrived with a planeload of "Arab-Afghans." These were old hands at jihad, and they brought with them a cosmopolitan perspective on the situation of Muslims in the world. Bin Laden and his colleagues had already been involved in what the CIA called "terrorist camps" in several countries: Somalia, Egypt, Sudan, and Yemen as well as Afghanistan. Once ensconced in Afghanistan, bin Laden began to cultivate Mullah Muhammad Omar, moving to Kandahar in 1997.[20] It was a fateful bond.

The Arabs were Wahhabis with an agenda of their own—to overturn the Saudi government, to reestablish Wahhabi dominance in the Middle East, and eventually to reestablish the caliphate. This outlook, this new definition of the situation, markedly changed the nature of the Taliban. Historically, before the Soviet-mujahedin war, among the Afghanistan peoples there was no tradition of strident anti-Westernism (a century-old distrust of the British excepted)—nothing like the well-articulated resentments that had long moldered in the Middle East and South Asia. Of course, the war with the Soviets intensified their loyalty to customs they regarded as Islamic, but it seems to have been later, under the influence of their Arab and Pakistani colleagues, that the Taliban turned against the West. "Until [bin Laden's] arrival the Taliban leadership had not been particularly antagonistic to the USA or the West," says Rashid, but they became "increasingly vociferous against Americans, the UN, the Saudis, and Muslim regimes around the world" as they came under the influence of the Arabs. "Their statements increasingly reflected the language of defiance Bin Laden has adopted and which was not an original Taliban trait."[21] Not Taliban, not Afghan of any sort. It is true that in the 1980s an antipathy against the non-Muslim world was taking root in the public discourse as the Afghanistan mujahedin fought the Afghan communists, but it was the Arabs who gave it a strident anti-Westernism. Now, in the 1990s, the Taliban were mouthing Islamist critiques formulated elsewhere (in Egypt by Sayyed Qutb and in South Asia by Abu'l Ala Maududi) to explain the frustrations of the peoples of Afghanistan. Islamism was now the meaningful vocabulary of fraternity, power, and time for the Taliban.[22]

This was the beginning of Arab dominance in Afghanistan. Now the views of the more moderate Taliban were suppressed.[23] The Taliban became more zealous for what they considered Islamic practice, enforcing it by their newly established Ministry for the Promotion of Virtue and the Prevention of Vice, which had been modeled after the Wahhabi Mutawwin of Saudi Arabia. Taliban leaders began to present themselves to outsiders as more "official" by flourishing personal business cards.[24] "The Arab-Afghans had come full circle. From being mere appendages to the Afghan jihad and the Cold War in the 1980s they had taken center stage for the Afghans, neighboring countries and the West in the 1990s."[25] They formalized their cause in February 1998, when they formed the "International Islamic Front for Jihad against Jews and Crusaders" and declared war against the United States. In his announcement, Osama bin Laden situated this organization on a world scene: "The people of Islam [have] suffered from aggression, iniquity, and injustice imposed on them by the Zionist Crusaders alliance and their collaborators." He added that "their blood was spilled in Palestine and Iraq" as well as in Lebanon, Tajikistan, Burma, Kashmir, the Philippines, Somalia, Eritrea, Chechnya, Bosnia-Herzegovina and Indonesia.[26]

This broadening of the Taliban's imaginative world, however, has been fostered not only by Osama bin Laden and the other Arab-Afghans but also by the Pakistan military establishment itself. As early as the 1970s Pakistan's military leaders were promoting Islam for strategic reasons, so it was no surprise that in the 1980s, when the CIA entrusted to Pakistan's ISI the management of money and materiel for anti-Soviet Afghan mujahedin, the ISI favored Islamist organizations.[27] As it turned out, its biases went further: the ISI supported "only those factions that were both anti-Western capitalism and anti-Soviet socialism."[28] When the ISI, with the concurrence of the CIA, recruited Muslim youths from all over the world for the holy war against the Soviets, the training they received had "strong anti-US overtones."[29] And after the Afghan-Soviet war, certain Arab-Afghans being sought by the United States government for their involvement in attacks against Americans elsewhere were protected by Pakistani officials who helped them obtain fake passports that enabled them to return to their countries of origin, where many of them continued their jihadi activities. Loretta Napoleoni claims that after the anti-Soviet war, "the ISI continued to export Islamist warriors from Pakistan to Central Asia and the Caucasus . . . A stream of covert operations was launched in Central Asia . . . [where] the ISI played a pivotal role in supporting Islamist armed insurgencies."[30] Bin Laden's International Islamic Front, formed in 1998, became an umbrella organization for various militant activities coordinated by Pakistan's Lashkare Taiba, an organization whose purpose, according to Mariam Abou Zahab and Olivier Roy, was "to Islamize Kashmir and India, then embark on global conquest with a goal of restoring the Caliphate."[31]

Militant Islamists were active in Pakistan's military, and in 1995 a clique of Pakistani officers attempted to overturn Benazir Bhutto's government in order to install an Islamic caliphate. The coup attempt failed and the leaders were put in prison, but the tolerance for militant Islamists in high places is suggested by the way General Pervez Musharraf dealt with the coup leaders after he seized power in 1999: he released them and allowed one of them to go immediately to Afghanistan to become a close advisor to Mullah Omar. General Musharraf effectively duplicated this behavior in 2002, when—under United States pressure—he "banned" several Islamist parties but then protected their leaders. The chiefs of Lashkare Taiba, Jaishe Mohammed, and Harkatul Mujahideen (all militant Islamist organizations) "were whisked away to the safe houses of Pakistan's intelligence service" where they were supported with sizable stipends for most of the year. "Once freed in 2003, the terrorist leaders barnstormed around the country, recruiting volunteers for Jihad in Kashmir, Afghanistan and even Iraq. Some of the rallies were conducted on military property, addressing Pakistani troops . . . Hafiz Saeed [leader of Lashkare Taiba] was allowed to address a 150,000 strong rally."[32]

If anyone in a prominent military position exemplifies Pakistan's official tolerance, if not support, of militant Islamism it is Lieutenant General Hamid Gul, former head of the ISI, whose involvement with various Islamist causes has gone unchallenged over many years. Hassan Abbas describes General Gul as "a loudly religious man without a beard" whose "religious ideals robbed him of objectivity."[33] Between 1988 and 2001 Gul was bin Laden's principal Pakistani adviser.[34] After the attack of September 11, 2001, he blamed Israelis and "elements within the U.S. government" for wanting "to subjugate the Muslim world and for this they needed a pretext and cause célèbre to justify their actions in Afghanistan."[35] He has declared that an Islamist nuclear power would eventually form "a greater Islamic state along with a fundamentalist Saudi Arabia after the monarchy falls."[36] In February 2004, he participated in a secret meeting to plan a coup d'état against President Musharraf, who would be replaced by Dr. Abdul Qayum Khan, the engineer who sold nuclear secrets to America's self-avowed enemies. Gul revealed the plot later that summer, stating that he "was assembling 'a strong team of faithful Muslims to take control of the country to serve the nation and the Muslim world with true Islamic spirit.'"[37] All this without consequence. Gul is still said to be active: In April 2007, Afghan police captured a young man with a bomb strapped to his body who claimed that General Gul "was financing and supporting the project" of training and equipping suicide bombers.[38]

It seems incredible that General Gul could be so openly involved with Islamist causes without official sanction. There is an "organic and symbiotic nexus between al-Qaeda and the Pakistani jihadist groups," says conservative journalist Arnaud Borchgrave.[39] Stephen P. Cohen, the authority on Pakistan's army, says, "Radical Islam certainly has found a home in Pakistan. Radical parties are profuse, and terrorism is an oft-employed tactic." Cohen further notes, "It has almost always been the state, especially the Pakistani army, that has allowed most radical Islamic groups to function on a wider stage—equipping and training them when necessary and providing overall political and strategic guidance for their activities."[40]

The American demand in September 2001 that Pakistan withdraw all support for the Taliban in order to have a credible involvement in the "war on terror" forced the Pakistani leadership to turn against its own well-cultivated practice. The reversal created a conflicted and contradictory leadership. Even after agreeing to American demands, the government was allowing the Taliban to be active. General Nasirullah Babar, interior minister under Benazir Bhutto, "confided to friends that since the Taliban were becoming a menace inside Pakistan, he had decided that the only solution to the problem lay in giving the extremists their own country."[41] Pakistan wants the Taliban to survive, says a confidant of Musharraf: "I think they want a weak government [in Kabul] and want to support the Taliban without letting them win . . . We are supporting them to give the Americans a troubled time . . . All the administrators of madrassas know what our students are doing. . . . The heart of this government is with the Taliban. The tongue is not."[42] This is the source of extreme militant Islamism in Pakistan itself. "The strength of religious extremism till now, has been derived from state patronage rather than popular support. The groups that are currently paralyzing the country were the creation of the late and unlamented Gen. Muhammad Zia ul-Haq."[43]

Does this duplicity entail a risk? Stephen P. Cohen believes not much: "Although the army has a long history of using radical and violent Islamists for political purposes, it has little interest in supporting their larger agenda of turning Pakistan into a more comprehensively Islamic state. Pakistan's political, institutional, economic, and social decay will have to accelerate before radical groups emerge as a independent political force." His own statements, however, give reason to wonder, for Pakistan's policy has nourished conflicts within the country. "Today, sectarian violence rages throughout Pakistan . . . Numerous sectarian battles have broken out among Sunnis, with pitched battles between Barelvis and Deobandis, often for control over Karachi's mosques."[44] Tariq Ali believes the situation has become perilous: the Islamist schools that Pakistan has tolerated and fostered, he says, "were nurseries designed to produce fanatics . . . Agents from the government's . . . ISI provided training and supervision and observed the development of the more promising students . . . who were later picked out and sent for more specialized training at secret army camps." "The dragon seeds sown in 2,500 madrassahs [have] produced a crop of 225,000 fanatics ready to kill and die for their faith."[45] Whatever its outcome will be, this duplicitous policy has made Pakistan the real epicenter of the war on terror.

Such were the influences that formed the Taliban as a movement in the period before 2001; several social entities came together, each bringing its particular set of concerns, contributing to a political amalgam that exerted a distinctive influence on Afghan society. This amalgam would be disrupted, of course, in 2001, when the Taliban were attacked by the Americans because of their alliance with Osama bin Laden and al-Qaeda. The success of the attack and the subsequent establishment of a new Afghan state with the support of the international community forced the Taliban offstage. Many of them were killed, the rest scattered. The leaders who survived fled into Pakistan—as did hundreds of the Pakistani military and intelligence officers who had supported them against the Americans. Even though Osama bin Laden and Mullah Muhammad Omar had not been apprehended, observers supposed they would soon be captured or killed. But since that crushing defeat their fortunes have turned. In this section I outline the conditions under which the new Taliban organization took form, from the period when they were scattered and defeated up to 2007 when they were resurgent.[46]

Scarcely more than a year after their defeat, the situation had changed. Many of the best American military assets had been removed from Afghanistan, in preparation for the invasion of Iraq; the Bush administration and the rest of the world were preoccupied elsewhere. Mainly, things were not going well in Afghanistan. A new state was being established, a governmental system to replace the one that had dissipated in the course of many years of war. Prominent among the leadership of the new state were some of the commanders—now being called "warlords" by the expatriate community—whom the original Taliban had risen up against in 1994. Former adversaries were allied to the Americans, and some of them were flush with funds from the international community intended for the development of the country. And sometimes they labeled their enemies "Taliban" and "al-Qaeda" in order to win Americans' help in doing away with them.

In the meantime the economy languished. There was little employment. Electric power was scarce, even in the capital. Despite much talk of aid from the capitalist world and much bluster among the Kabul diplomatic corps and the influx of foreign nongovernmental organizations, few gains were reaching the ordinary people. The police were being accused of corruption. Businessmen were kidnapped for ransom. The only part of the economy doing well was the poppy crop. Farmers had at first welcomed the arrival of the Afghan government because it rescued them from the Taliban, who had outlawed poppy, but the new administration quickly dispatched agents to destroy their crops. The continued presence of American troops, later NATO, in Afghanistan may also have galled some former Taliban; at least the zeal with which they would turn against them expressed the same deep antipathy that the mujahedin had felt for the Soviets.

Besides, the new government in Kabul was no longer essentially Pashtun. Even though Karzai was Pashtun, most of his cabinet were not; the tradition of Pashtun dominance was again compromised. At the same time the moral vision that had animated the mujahedin and the Taliban was still alive in the tribal areas, objectified in the tapes and discs being sold in the markets. Videos displayed heroic exploits against the Soviets, and also the destruction of Afghan homes by American bombs; by implication the Americans were like the Soviets. Narratives celebrating jihad against alien *kafirs* (unbelievers) declared that the holy struggle against unbelievers was not over—but now the enemy were Americans.

In this setting the Taliban began to stir. Mullah Omar had instructed his warriors to keep in touch after they returned home, and to "wait for the call." By 2004, Taliban commanders were assessing the condition of their men: those killed, those alive, those able to fight. They excavated caches of weapons and raised funds. Indeed, funds poured in: from businessmen in Karachi, goldsmiths in Peshawar, wealthy Saudis and Kuwaitis, even sympathetic officers in the Pakistan army and intelligence corps. Mullah Omar reconstituted the leadership council and commissioned the infamous Mullah Dadullah, notorious for his massacre of Hazaras in Bamyan, to visit the madrasas of Pakistan to collect dispersed former Taliban and seek new recruits, many of whom were attracted by the videotapes of Dadullah's brutal acts. Pashtuns disaffected by the rough treatment of civilians by the foreign forces—Americans and later NATO troops—and new recruits ready to join the struggle were gathering in the tribal areas of the North West Frontier Province. The Taliban command center was situated in Quetta, supported, according to news reports (but denied officially), by the ISI. Taliban bases in the tribal areas, mainly North Waziristan and South Waziristan, were busy.[47]

Historically the Pashtun tribesmen have resisted outside encroachments, not only by the British in the nineteenth century but also by the Pakistani military in the twentieth. At the same time Pashtun hospitality is legendary. The arrival of Arab-Afghans and Taliban seeking refuge from American attacks in Afghanistan, no doubt stretched their resources. But these Pashtuns already shared many social conventions with the Taliban; as we have said, some joined the Taliban early on. Despite the strain on their hospitality, many tribal

Pashtuns identified with the militant Islamist cause. Pamela Constable described the situation in 2004.

> The [militant] visitors [in the tribal zone] were said to include Naik [Nek] Mohammed, a Waziri tribesman who was one of two men leading the fierce resistance to Pakistani troops in March. Now officially a fugitive, Mohammed is described as a brash young fighter who once commanded guerrillas supporting Taliban forces in Afghanistan . . . The council members [in this tribal community] negotiated directly with Mohammed and other militant leaders and found them to be "very religious people" who declared they had "taken up arms to support oppressed Muslims in Palestine, Iraq, Kashmir, Chechnya and Afghanistan." . . . "These are refugees who share our culture; they carry guns and wear beards, so no one can distinguish them. We consider them not foreigners but friends," said Mohammed Kabarkhel, a landowner in Wana. "The wanted men are few, but the resistance is high, because people are angry. The tribes were used by the government to fight in Afghanistan, and now people feel they are being sold out to the United States in the name of al Qaeda." . . . Despite the council's promise to curb extremist activities among tribal ranks, several analysts said that . . . the militants had gained prestige among tribal people, and would probably receive more protection, especially in Waziristan, where conservative Islamic parties enjoy strong support . . . "People are upset, because these men are holy warriors and we respect them," said Asad Khan, a beardless shopkeeper. He said the Islamic parties are popular because they fought for the Taliban and have promised to bring religious law to Pakistan. "Everyone wants sharia to be implemented here. We have no problem

with this so-called al Qaeda," he added. "We know America is against Islam, and we need someone to defend us."

On July 19, Nek Muhammad was killed in a Pakistan army raid.[48]

As the Taliban and al-Qaeda in the Federally Administered Tribal Areas of Pakistan grew stronger, they began to raid police and military forces inside Afghanistan. The cross-border attacks induced the Pakistani army, under American pressure, to undertake, for the first time in the history of the country, a military incursion into the tribal areas in search of al-Qaeda fugitives. The invasion by eighty thousand troops in March 2004 outraged the local populations. Resistance, organized by Taliban commanders, was intense and effective: 250 Pakistani soldiers were killed. The Taliban negotiated the truce, an indication that power had shifted from the tribal elders to the Taliban. The army mounted eight more raids over the next two years, first into South Waziristan, then North Waziristan. The Taliban punished them severely. After one very costly encounter, the Taliban, not the elders or the military, paid compensation to the families of the dead. Because of their heavy losses (seven hundred dead, fifteen hundred wounded) the army negotiated two peace accords, in South Waziristan (2004) and North Waziristan (2006). Under these agreements the tribesmen promised to stop attacking Pakistani troops and crossing the border to fight in Afghanistan, while the Pakistani military agreed to halt major ground and air operations, free prisoners, retreat to barracks, compensate for losses, and allow tribesmen to carry small arms. So the Taliban became, in the tribal areas, "a parallel administration with all the functions of the state": they appointed "*emirs* to perform duties with mutual consultation," established sharia courts, police forces, tax collectors, and public offices.[49]

Intended to end violence between tribal militants and Pakistani troops, the deals in fact only opened the way for militants to attack

Afghanistan with impunity. Within days cross-border attacks resumed. The U.S. military says militant attacks in Afghanistan near
the Pakistan border tripled in some areas following the North Waziristan deal. NATO registered two hundred cross-border "actions"
in November 2006. In the meantime, more foreign militants arrived,
mainly (it was said) from Uzbekistan and Iraq.[50]

By 2006 the influence of the Taliban in the tribal areas and intermittently in many communities of southern and eastern Afghanistan
was secure and pervasive. Afghan news sources reported on the existence of several training camps.[51] Militants from elsewhere—Arabs
from Saudi Arabia, Iraq, and Palestine—were training recruits in the
tribal areas about improvised explosive devices and suicide bombing.
Afghanistan officials claimed that a system of large-scale indoctrina-
tion of suicide bombers was operative in the tribal areas. They had
captured a suicide bomber wearing a vest filled with explosives who
claimed to have been sent by the head of a religious school in Bajaur
where as many as five hundred to six hundred students were being prepared for suicide attacks, financed by a former head of Pakistani intelligence.[52] By the fall of 2006, insurgents in Iraq were shifting their attention to Afghanistan. According to Rotella Sebastian,
"Muslim extremists aspiring to battle the West [are turning] their attention back to the symbolically important and increasingly violent
turf of Afghanistan . . . An accelerating Afghan offensive by the resurgent Taliban offers a clearer battleground and a wealth of targets"
for suicide bombers.[53]

The influence of the Taliban has grown inside Afghanistan, placing many residents in untenable positions. Afghan journalists in
April 2007 described a community in southern Afghanistan that was
seriously riven by internal conflicts: some residents supported the
Taliban, others who opposed them fled, feeling unsafe in the village.[54] Elizabeth Rubin described the experience of a person who had

worked with the Taliban. Beaten by the Afghanistan police, he was advised by the tribal elders to flee to Pakistan. There he joined the Taliban. But after a year, tired of the fighting, he accepted an offer of reconciliation by an Afghanistan general. For that he was imprisoned by the Pakistani government until he agreed to rejoin the struggle against the Americans.[55]

The Taliban, at first consisting of a few religious students and their teachers, gathered force for local reasons, but the infusion of other interest groups transformed the movement, broadening its horizons and connecting it into a network of like-minded insurgent groups elsewhere. By 2007 the Taliban consisted of a loose alliance of several kinds of people: former anti-Soviet mujahedin, Pashtun clerics, Pashtun tribesmen, Arab and Pakistani Islamists, even some officials of the Pakistan government—all of them now linked into an international network of anti-Western militants. From a homogeneous Pashtun group in 1994 the Taliban had become an assemblage of diverse social and ethnic types engaged in a larger cause. They now have links to other insurgent groups. The videos being seen in Pakistan include images of the Palestinian struggle, creating the sense that the losses to the Americans in Afghanistan and the embarrassments of the Palestinians under Israel demand a fresh urgency for holy war on behalf of oppressed and occupied Muslims everywhere.[56]

Their involvement with the Arab-Afghans and the Pakistani military transformed the Taliban's rhetoric to reflect the universal visions of Islamists elsewhere. Taliban leaders are as likely as any Arab Muslim organization to voice the concerns of insurgent groups in Iraq, Palestine, Chechnya, Kashmir, or Uzbekistan—places about which the peoples of Afghanistan formerly had no knowledge or interest. Like other Islamist organizations struggling against regimes that dominate them, the Taliban perceive their ultimate struggle to be against the West, especially the United States, which they hold responsible for the injustices they see. "We are defending the country from the infidels," Elizabeth Rubin was told.[57] Islamism, for some frustrated people in the Middle East and Central Asia, has provided the explanation for their common predicament. We hear it in various forms. According to Loretta Napoleoni, militant Islamists in the Middle East were saying, "The victory over communism was won with weapons under the leadership of God . . . Democracy, modernization à l'Americaine, had nothing to do with it."[58] A Shia militiaman favorable to Muqtada al-Sadr put it this way to John Burns of the *New York Times* in the spring of 2004: "It was God who finished Saddam, not the Americans. The Americans broke all their promises to us, and they have brought their infidel beliefs to Iraq. We hate them, and they are worse than Saddam."[59]

Especially since the American invasion of Iraq in 2003, localized insurgent groups in Afghanistan have taken up the rhetoric of militant Islamism, which in Afghanistan is manifest in the broadening interest of religious leaders in Middle Eastern affairs. In Herat, Islamic authorities heading the Koran Memorization School, for instance, claimed solidarity with the global cause when they condemned the murders of Hamas leaders Shaykh Ahmad Yasin and Dr. Abd al-Aziz al-Rantisi on April 18, 2004. What was unusual about this announcement was that, given in Dari, it expressed a concern for Middle Eastern affairs to which the Afghans had hitherto been indifferent: "We urge all countries and international foundations to . . . fight against terrorism and to portray the racist regime of Israel as a symbol of government terrorism in the world."[60] Even so, such rhetoric conceals local concerns. Gulbuddin Hekmatyar, head of the Hizb-e Islami mujahedin party, expressed his sympathy for the global Islamic struggle on April 11, 2004—that is, at a time when in Iraq supporters of the Shiite cleric Muqtada al-Sadr were clashing with American forces: he called for Afghans to rise up against the U.S.-led coalition in Afghanistan. But his speech was made in Pashto: he was appealing to a local audience.[61]

In suggesting that in the late High Middle Ages the demise of old "certainties" would lead to a "search" for "a new way of linking fraternity, power and time," Benedict Anderson implies that human beings crave a grand moral frame of reference within which to imaginatively situate themselves. His wording indicates a conjunction of cultural features by which individual experience—human suffering—is given significance: by a sense of community ("fraternity"); by a recognition of authority through which dominance may be exercised ("power"); and by a cosmology situating one's past, present, and future in a meaningful frame ("time").[62]

The concept of the "nation," as it took form in Europe in the seventeenth and eighteen centuries, satisfied this need in a period when a new class, a bourgeoisie, was learning to define its collective interest. A similar "search" for such "certainties" seems to be taking form as a new social body in Greater Central Asia becomes conscious of its commonality of interests—an assemblage of frustrated, unemployed, culturally unfit, socially alienated young men. True, there have always been such in this area and elsewhere. But its scale is new: approximately half of the population in Greater Central Asia are under the age of 25 and the proportion is growing. And their predicament is ever more urgent; their demands will likely become more strident. The rising interest in Islam in recent times, especially among the young people of the Muslim world, reflects the failure of other moral idioms to provide hope, a way to respond; Islamism is, for them, a creative way to link fraternity, power, and time.

There was a time when I thought the search for a firm way to link fraternity, power, and time was still on, still alive among Muslims of the Middle East and Central Asia. In fact, for many young Pashtuns in southern Afghanistan and Pakistan's tribal areas the search may be over. Political Islam—political and military action justified in Islamic terms and aimed toward Islamic ends—has filled the void. The Islamist reaction, they suppose, is the answer. It provides the moral critique that enables many to share a common conception of the problem and to envision a solution. It is now, for them, the articulate voice by which to escape their constraints and to oppose the ultimate source of their problems, the West, especially the one great power. So the cause is international.[63]

These Islamists share a sense of *fraternity* as Muslims, in fact, in this case as Sunni Muslims, who desire a more just world in which Muslims have more leverage, more dignity, more hope. They share a common conception of *power* in that they grant leadership to individuals who speak in the name of God and can muster a force by which to actively confront the cultural juggernaut of the West, some of them even supposing that their martyrdom for this cause would be honorable and spiritually rewarded. They share a common sense of *time* in the sense of a cosmology and an eschatology that situates their present dilemmas in a trajectory of history. I speculate that many of them, like many Christians, suppose that this world is in its last throes—it is a notion that appeals as more people lose hope. Pierre Bourdieu, writing about the Algerian war of the 1950s, said, "To express the present state of affairs the old Algerians often say: 'We are now in the fourteenth century.' To them the fourteenth century is the century of the end of the world, at which time everything that was the rule will become the exception, when all that was forbidden will be now permitted."[64] It is now several decades after the Algerian war, but the sense that this conflicted world is advancing toward a cataclysmic demise resonates with some.

That sense was alive in the summer of 2004 in Iraq, for instance, where Muqtada al-Sadr, leading an insurgency of Shiites against the

United States in Iraq, announced that the Mahdi (who, many Muslims believe, will appear at the end of the age) "would arrive any day now." In fact, according to al-Sadr, the reason the Americans attacked Iraq was because they knew that the Mahdi's arrival was imminent and they wanted to capture and kill him.[65] It was alive in Afghanistan in the 1990s. When Zoya, a young woman trapped in Kabul as the mujahedin occupied the city in 1992, told her grandmother about the terrifying acts of the mujahedin, the old woman's "eyes filled with tears, and she started praying aloud . . . She told me [says Zoya] 'It means that we are close to the Day of Judgment.'"[66] I don't know how broadly this view of the times is among the rising tide of Islamists in Greater Central Asia, but I hope that, for some of them at least, the search is still "on" for another way to link fraternity, power, and time meaningfully together.

CHAPTER SEVEN

Moderate Taliban?

Robert D. Crews

> *Our jihad has two targets. One is America and the other is the For-*
> *eign Ministry of the Taliban.*
>
> OSAMA BIN LADEN (AS QUOTED
>
> BY WAHID MUZHDA)

Do "moderate Taliban" exist? Knowledgeable Afghans like Hamid Karzai and Zalmay Khalilzad (U.S. ambassador to Afghanistan, Iraq, and the United Nations) have responded in the affirmative on key occasions. They have maintained that the movement included a substantial number of representatives with whom foreign diplomats, humanitarian aid workers, international energy company executives, and even domestic foes could come to some agreement. Despite outsiders' early attention to the theatricality and violence of their Islamizing project, the notion that the Taliban encompassed moderates is as old as the movement itself.[1]

Following the collapse of the Taliban regime and the dispersal of the movement in November and December 2001, the Bonn process that led to the formation of an interim government under Karzai excluded representatives of the Taliban, but the search for moderates among them nonetheless continued. From the autumn of 2001, Pakistan's leader, General Pervez Musharraf, lobbied for the inclusion of such Taliban in the new Afghan government. In Kabul, Karzai's administration announced a series of amnesties and, from April 2003, overtures aimed at integrating Taliban fighters who agreed to give up their arms and pledge loyalty to the government. In late 2003, U.S. military officials began to offer their formal approval for the scheme. While making an official visit in April 2004 to Kandahar, the movement's birthplace, Karzai made an emotional appeal. He invited members of the Taliban to participate in upcoming elections and take part in reconstruction efforts. Echoing similar remarks by Ambassador Khalilzad, Karzai distinguished between those Taliban "who want to work and farm here," who would be welcomed, and "the top Taliban—who may number no more than 150 people—who had links with Al-Qaeda." As "the enemies of Afghanistan," only the latter would be blocked from reintegration efforts.[2] In January and again in March 2007, as Taliban spokesmen threatened to broaden their struggle against the government in a spring offensive, Karzai reiterated his calls for reconciliation.

Others have vociferously rejected the possibility of applying the label *moderate* to any Taliban. From the appearance of the movement in 1994 to the present, its opponents have depicted both leaders and followers as equally "extremist."[3] In mid-April 2004, some two hundred protesters gathered in Kabul to voice opposition to negotiations with elements of the old regime. They accused top administration officials, ethnic Pashtuns, of seeking Taliban cooperation as part of a wider plot to push non-Pashtuns from positions of power throughout the country. Calling for the resignation of Karzai, the minister of finance, the minister of the interior, and the head of the Central Bank, the demonstrators shouted, "Death to Taliban and their supporters in the government."[4]

Since its establishment in the spring of 2005, the Afghan Independent Human Rights Commission has called for closer scrutiny of the amnesty process. Its demands for accountability reflected the views of 75 percent of Afghans polled by the commission, together with the United Nations, who insisted on accountability for war crimes committed since the communist revolution.[5] But in an environment marked by instability and insecurity, and without judicial institutions to investigate and prosecute crimes against humanity like those established for the former Yugoslavia, Rwanda, or South Africa, Afghans appeared unlikely to arrive at a consensus regarding the reintegration of Taliban elements or even of their communist or mujahedin predecessors.

As of the spring of 2007, the Karzai government had prosecuted only one figure, Assadullah Sarwari, head of intelligence under the communist regime. Although Sarwari received the death penalty in February 2006 in a trial condemned as unfair by international human rights groups, mujahedin commanders retained key posts in government ministries and the parliament in Kabul as well as in the provinces; and the government continued its program of recruiting figures it labeled moderates, including former Taliban who had stood in the parliamentary elections of fall 2005.

On March 10, 2007, Karzai signed a broader amnesty plan, the National Stability and Reconciliation bill proposed by the Afghan National Assembly. Despite criticism from groups ranging from human rights activists to the highest-ranking Islamic authorities, the bill exempted from prosecution all combatants and parties involved in the jihad era and civil war—including the Taliban. It also declared them immune "from any criticism," a sentiment voiced loudly by crowds estimated at 25,000 to 30,000 who marched in Kabul in a rally for the bill. At the Ghazi stadium, the former site of Taliban executions and other punishments, the former Islamist commander and current parliamentarian Abdul Rabb al-Rasul Sayyaf declared, "Whoever is against mujahideen is against Islam and they are the enemies of this country."[6]

Between 2001 and 2007, no clear legal or political guidelines distinguished "moderates" from "extremists." The Karzai government never published a list of the 100 to 150 Taliban who were to be ineligible for the amnesty. The head of the amnesty program once offered to pardon Mullah Muhammad Omar but subsequently reversed himself. At the same time, the United States military continued to hold hundreds of figures suspected of Taliban ties. According to the charges presented to military tribunals in the first four months of 2005, the Guantanamo Bay prison camp held Taliban commanders, foot soldiers, and cooks (plus at least two assistant cooks).[7] In 2005 and 2006, a few of these suspects—including a former Taliban ambassador to Pakistan—were released from the camp. While some senior former Taliban officials ran for parliament, others remained in custody at Bagram airbase and in secret prisons within Afghanistan and perhaps in other countries. Another prompted international attention and controversy by enrolling at Yale University.[8] What kept the cooks in Guantanamo out of the Ivy League remains to be explained.

The term *moderate* is so difficult to define, after all, because it belongs to a vocabulary of polemics. For centuries, Muslim scholars have used this elastic concept in debates about wide-ranging theological, legal, and ethical issues. In European languages, its use in religious disputes dates at least to the Reformation. Valued by Enlightenment thinkers, moderation in religion became a central pillar of many conceptions of modernity in Europe and, with colonial expansion, other parts of the world. Moderation was an attribute of civility.

During both the Cold War and its aftermath, this vocabulary served as a means to create bridges between revolutionary movements like the Taliban and the international actors whose resources they needed to project power and build legitimacy. In the 1980s, for example, the Reagan administration asserted that it was reaching out to "moderate elements" in the Islamic Republic of Iran when it traded "arms for hostages." In American political discourse, the terms *moderate* and *radical* signal political affiliations: the former are "good" because they assent to Washington's policies, while the latter are "bad" because they do not. Since September 11, this polemical language has been used to categorize Muslim loyalties throughout the globe.[9]

In the case of the Taliban movement, its members were varied enough—and included enough English speakers and expatriate advocates—to permit outsiders to identify useful interlocutors, particularly when so many foreign oil companies, security agencies, and other organizations sought some foothold in Afghanistan after the tumult of the jihad era. The language of moderation facilitated the transformation of a movement, what the anthropologist Bernt Glatzer has likened to a "caravan, to which different people attached themselves for various reasons," into a formalized state structure.[10] The category "moderate Taliban" gave an identity to the constituencies within the Taliban who were devoted to constructing a state. This aspiration depended in key respects on the assistance of outsiders who did not share the ideology of the Taliban.

Claims to represent moderation became a calling card for aspiring intermediaries. They became a framework for negotiation with foreigners who might confer international legitimacy on the Taliban regime—one of the constant aspirations of much of the Taliban elite, even after the destruction of the Bamyan Buddhas in March 2001. The term *moderate* makes up part of the symbolic repertoire of state-building elites who have struggled to solicit, but also manage, the foreign intervention and patronage that have sustained the Afghan state in modern times.

For the Taliban, the rhetoric of moderation had another crucial audience. The Taliban leadership was not particularly responsive to the public will, but it did crave legitimacy in the eyes of foreigners and Afghans alike. Much of the Taliban elite recognized that its Pashtun identity was both a benefit and a burden. To a domestic public, the regime presented itself as a guardian of supraethnic Afghan nationalism, and a foe of extremism, especially after a series of military setbacks and popular resistance from 1997 onward. It articulated this image most frequently in locales where its position was fragile, and where local populations challenged Taliban supremacy. Using radio and print media, the Taliban regime turned a "moderate," nationalist face not only to the diplomatic corps of Washington and New York, but also to the often hostile peoples of Afghanistan. Dependent upon foreign support, Taliban state-building efforts relied, too, on recruiting—and retaining—Afghans to serve in the state apparatus. Similarly, many Taliban recognized the need to persuade local elites to acquiesce to Taliban dominance. While a millenarian vision inspired many Taliban mullahs and foot soldiers, a concern with guarding national boundaries and projecting sovereignty over all of Afghanistan betrayed the fact that some key Taliban elites had more conventional political interests, which they shared in common with other modern state builders in a world defined by nation-states.

The Karzai administration was not the first Afghan government to face the challenge of creating legitimacy in a fractured society. The

Taliban themselves had confronted a similar dilemma. From the outset, the Taliban state-building project brought to the fore many tensions, rivalries, and limitations within the movement. Several of the architects of the institutions of the Taliban regime attempted to present themselves as moderate voices within a wider movement of mullahs, madrasa students, and Pashtun mujahedin commanders. Through negotiations with local elites and military conquest, the movement swept across the southwest of the country beginning in 1994 and ultimately seized Herat in September 1995 and Kabul in September 1996. They freely resorted to violence, of course, and terrorized enemy populations who resisted their rule. Yet a number of Taliban officials also devoted serious attention to the possibility of creating legitimacy in other ways. Throughout this period and indeed until their demise in the fall of 2001, they sought to convince Afghans and international actors alike that they represented the rightful heirs of an Afghan state tradition.

These state-building efforts merit closer scrutiny, both for a more complex understanding of the movement, and for the lessons such an analysis might produce for Afghanistan's present crisis. Taliban elites set for themselves a daunting task. They attempted to resurrect a ruined state apparatus and project its sovereignty in the international community while simultaneously implementing their vision of an Islamic order built on resort to exemplary violence against their mujahedin rivals and, in the urban centers, against the ostensible enemies of the new order.

The polity constructed by the Taliban is often remembered as "a short-lived Islamic regime that left no written records, rarely explained its actions and shunned contact with outsiders."[11] Mullah Muhammad Omar's aversion to being photographed, meeting with foreigners, or even leaving his compound in Kandahar would seem to affirm this image. Indeed, senior Taliban figures like Mullah Hassan

Akhund railed against the printed word. In one fit of rage, this mullah reportedly tore newspapers to bits and had them baked into a cake. Yet the same Mullah Hassan advocated the use of radio.[12] Despite Taliban hostility toward televisions, video players, and stereos, they quickly transformed Radio Kabul into Radio Voice of Sharia. Radio played a critical, if underappreciated, role in Taliban efforts to control the circulation of information in the country (and into neighboring Pakistani provinces).[13] They used radio broadcasts to incite violence against Shias and to announce repressive decrees.

Yet the government also used it to communicate propaganda in support of its policies. In fact, Radio Voice of Sharia became *the* medium through which the regime attempted to persuade the peoples of Afghanistan of its legitimacy. More striking still, the Taliban utilized a number of newspapers and journals to communicate their views about international politics, Islamic law, and the new regime. Speaking in Quetta, the Afghan minister of information boasted that Taliban attention to restoring Afghan media had demonstrated the superiority of Taliban governance to that of their rivals.

Which steps for the betterment of the people have the Taliban not taken[?] In the Rabbani era one single newspaper was published from Kabul in fifteen or twenty [copies] and with difficulty at that. Rabbani used to extort millions of rupees from the people on that pretext. Now the Taliban have started from scratch work on the ministries of information and broadcasting. They have restarted the seventy-year-old newspaper "Tuloo-e-Afghanistan" from [Kandahar]. Newspapers are now being published from Neemrowz [Nimroz] and Ghazni; radio stations have been set up in Ghazni, Neemrowz, [Kandahar], Herat and [Farah]. The main radio station in Kabul was reconstructed and renovated on modern lines. Now its services can be heard in Delhi. So whose is the better government, the Taliban's or that of Rabbani?[14]

Like other modern revolutionaries before them, Taliban officials were obsessed with talking about themselves—and about their right to rule—though not in media that were always readily accessible to foreigners.

Similarly, observers of the Taliban have commented repeatedly on the Taliban's inattention to government institutions. Fourteen months after Taliban forces seized Kabul, a journalist for *The Guardian* reported that the minister of health, Mullah Abbas, "hasn't been seen for a month." After closing hospital wards for women throughout the capital, he had vanished, possibly to the northern front. At the minister's office, the journalist found "four faded pink files stacked in an empty wall unit" as the "only signs of administration of a health service for a population of 19 million people." "The country's administrators," she observed, "seem to be on a permanent bank holiday."[15]

Though the Taliban did not make the hospitals of Kabul a major concern, a number of their most influential representatives did make the construction of a functioning administrative apparatus a central priority. With the capture of the capital, the armed formations of the movement began to assume control of the institutions of the Afghan state. Symbols and protocol formed an essential part of the projection of Taliban power over the capital—and over Afghanistan. Within two days of their entry into the city, Mullah Rabbani and Mullah Ghaus received their first foreign diplomat. The mullahs greeted the head of the United Nations peace mission in the royal reception hall of the former president's place, identifying themselves as "acting Prime Minister" and "acting Foreign Minister" of Afghanistan.[16]

Taliban leaders continually spoke of the early community of Islam as the model of their own realization of the "Islamic state." But like their revolutionary neighbors in Iran, they adopted the basic structural features of the modern nation-state, complete with a ministerial system of government and an extensive bureaucracy.[17] The old regime continued to exert a magnetic force on the imagination of Taliban notables. As in revolutionary France, bureaucratic institutions were "hunted for among the wreckage of the old order and duly salvaged."[18]

Yet the enduring effects of the Cold War limited the range of options available to those who would revive the Afghan state. Taliban foraging in the rubble of Kabul, Herat, Jalalabad, and other towns yielded only anemic administrative bodies. Less than a few decades old and largely limited to urban centers, their infrastructure and personnel had poorly served the developmentalist ambitions of the pre-revolutionary Afghan state. By the mid-1970s, the government employed about a hundred thousand employees in various offices and development projects, though fully one-half of them were concentrated in the capital. Following the communist coup in 1978, the ministries expanded, but resistance in the countryside blunted the aspirations of the communists and limited their impact on rural Afghanistan. Soviet subsidies sustained the state budget during the jihad, but Moscow's own fiscal crisis not only brought about the withdrawal of the Red Army but also contributed to the collapse of the Afghan state and its infrastructure.[19] War among the mujahedin militias further hastened their disintegration. Throughout this period, vast numbers of Afghan professionals, bureaucrats, and technical specialists abandoned their official posts and emigrated.

Despite this deficit, Taliban state-building efforts began in earnest following the capture of Kabul. Though still concerned with conquering the rest of the country, the autumn of 1996 represented a moment of consolidation. Amid the improvisation that marked the first days after the murder of Najibullah, the former communist head of state, international actors assumed a pivotal role. Some NGO workers reported finding cooperative Taliban officials who permitted their work to continue, while others found the administration chaotic and capricious.[20]

Like the administrative apparatus of previous Afghan regimes, this one grew out of contact with international organizations and foreign military powers. The Pakistani ISI and army supplied officers, logistical support, intelligence, arms, and troops, while various Arab states subsidized the growth of the Taliban state.[21] Aid organizations, too, contributed to the solidification of Taliban control over Kabul and other provinces. With aid representing the second largest sector of the economy after agriculture, their input was essential to the relative stabilization of areas that the Taliban claimed to administer. Indeed, half of the population of the capital would continue to depend on international assistance for food.[22]

The United Nations made an immediate imprint on the young Taliban state, on its prospects for establishing legitimacy, and on its ambitions in the international arena. With Najibullah's body still swinging from a lamppost in Kabul, the UN general secretary ordered Norbert Heinrich Holl, the head of the special peace mission, to visit the new rulers of Kabul as soon as possible, despite his objections that this visit may confer undue credibility on a group that had just violated the sanctity of a UN compound and brutally murdered people in its charge.[23] In this and other visits with Taliban officials (which they did not balance with similar meetings with Northern Alliance counterparts), the United Nations appeared to be backing Taliban claims to authority over the domestic as well as international institutions of the Afghan state. In Holl's very first meeting with Mullah Ghaus, the new foreign minister, he received a handwritten note demanding Afghanistan's seat at the General Assembly in New York.

But the UN was not alone in rushing to engage the new regime in Kabul. On Holl's way to the airport for departure, he caught a glimpse on Kabul's otherwise empty streets of a convoy speeding a delegation from the Pakistani Foreign Ministry to the presidential palace. When Holl met some of these same Taliban statesmen again in 1997, they presented him with freshly printed English-language business cards, complete with their new titles, in preparation for an appearance at a meeting of the international Organization of the Islamic Conference.[24]

The Americans, too, hastened to shape the emergence of the new regime. A declassified internal State Department cable of September 27, 1996, instructed ambassadors in the region to "demonstrate USG [U.S. government] willingness to deal with them as the new authorities in Kabul." It authorized staff in Islamabad to travel to Kabul "to make initial contact with the Taliban interim government." Instructed to express concern about "stability, human rights, narcotics, and terrorism," the envoys were also to seek the reopening of the U.S. embassy in Kabul and to ask the Taliban to "propose soon an envoy to represent your government in Washington," adding that the State Department would not renew the visas of the current (anti-Taliban) Afghan diplomats.[25]

The symbolism of international support for the Talibanization of the national capital was not lost on opponents of the Taliban. Any suggestion that the loss of the symbol of national unity would be permanent, and backed by international recognition, provoked consternation. In 1997 a proposal by Dr. Abdullah Abdullah of the Northern Alliance to make Mazar-e Sharif a "provisional capital," until the "historical" one, Kabul, could be recaptured prompted controversy among opposition parties. Hizb-e Islami opposed the idea. But a spokesman for Hizb-e Wahdat argued that, although Kabul was "undoubtedly the official and legal capital of Afghanistan," it was now occupied "by the enemies of the state." Given the fact that the "state of Aqa Ostad Rabbani is the legal and official state of Afghanistan under the protection of the United Nations and other societies and countries of the jihad," the Hizb-e Wahdat would support the use of Mazar-e Sharif as "the provisional capital of the country for the enemies of the Taliban."[26] By this stage, however, the most powerful actors of the international community had largely chosen the side that they wanted to inherit the Afghan state.

In 1997, in turn, several delegations of Taliban officials visited Washington, New York, Omaha, Nebraska, and Sugarland, Texas. While pursuing pipeline negotiations with Unocal and the State Department, they protested the absence of an international outcry following the recent massacre of some three thousand Taliban POWs at the hands of Northern Alliance militias and demanded international recognition from the United States and the UN.[27] In New York, Taliban representatives lobbied foreign diplomats. In appeals such as one entitled "Time to Recognize Afghanistan's Legitimate Government," Abdul Hakim Mujahed challenged foreigners' accounts of events in Afghanistan and criticized their seemingly selective attention to human rights. Pledging his government's respect for "international norms and principles of human rights," the restoration of "individual rights, according to Sharia," and even the Geneva Conventions, Mujahed objected that foreign critics of the Taliban

> were silent while Afghans suffered the cruel reign of factional chaos [before Taliban rule] because it served their needs. They ignored the ethnically motivated genocide and rapes. They said nothing. There were no human rights monitors, no re-

porting, and no protests. The Feminist Majority did not know Afghanistan existed much less condemn the restrictions on women in the pre-Taleban era. The state[-]mandated hijab all women had to wear, as they do in Iran, went unnoticed. The women who refused the party line were chased out or killed. They had no international advocates. Rampant looting, warlords, drug-lords and lawlessness were willfully ignored because it suited a purpose . . . In the Summer of 1996, the last of Afghanistan's Moscow[-]backed regimes fled the capital and the IEA [Islamic Emirate of Afghanistan] took over the seat of government. They brought a war-torn fabric together. Their society withstood twenty years of onslaught from friend and foe and achieved the improbable. Most of the country is now peaceful, disarmed, together and surviving more austere conditions than widely appreciated.

Joined by the "Taliban Support Council" in London and other expatriate groups, Mujahed presented the Taliban, not as an "extremist" movement that engaged in terror and the abuse of human rights, but as a government committed to "a traditional style of Afghan self-rule" that "honors and protects all Afghan women," who enjoy a position of "dignity and honor" and represent "the crucible of our culture."[28]

Such Taliban spokesmen devoted considerable effort to refute the image of the Taliban as extremists and pariahs in the international community. They spoke not only to an audience in Europe and North America but also to a regional one. Taliban emissaries appeared frequently in Pakistan. In 1998, Minister of Information Mullah Amir Khan Mottaqi sought to reassure an audience in Quetta that the Taliban were victims of a campaign of disinformation. "Today the enemies of Islam are spreading the propagation [*sic*] against the Taliban, that they are violating human rights. My assertion is that from Kabul is emanating the scent of Sharee'ah [sharia], contrary to the days of yore when the foul smell of blood and gunpowder used to come from Kabul. The news from Kabul used to be that a Muslim girl had jumped from the sixth floor to put an end to her miserable life. Today from the same city news of the blessing of Islam, of the sanctity of human life are being broadcast." He reiterated the claim that Taliban rule had restored security and prosperity, so that "today . . . a tiny letter of the Ameer-ul-M'umineen [Mullah Omar], an inch long only, if sent from [Kandahar] is respected and revered by every person from Turkham to Ghowrband, from Ghowrband to Turghandi." "Under Taliban rule there is peace and security everywhere," Mottaqi noted, "whereas in the Rabbani era women and children were afraid to venture out of their homes even in broad daylight."[29] The Taliban press in Pakistan further countered international criticism of their gender policies by asserting that women actively contributed to the Taliban cause. "Crowds upon crowds of 'Burqa'-clad women," one such account claimed, could be seen forming lines to Mullah Omar's offices in Kandahar, where "they donated their jewelry, their money to the Ameer-ul-M'umineen. They gave him the authority to spend their money wherever and however he chose. Our correspondent says that it was a strangely moving scene when women with tears running down their cheeks surpassed themselves in giving away their wealth for the holy cause of [jihad]. Their tears were tears of joy and gratitude they said. They were thankful on getting an opportunity to give something in the way of Allah."[30] Rejecting accounts of oppression, Taliban spokesmen crafted a narrative that would demonstrate to Afghans and the entire world that they were Afghanistan's sole saviors—the only authentic political organization that, because it enjoyed broad popular support, could put an end to the civil war, revive the economy, and preserve the honor and dignity of women.

Despite this Taliban media campaign, relations with the United States nonetheless worsened in 1997 and deteriorated sharply in 1998 in the wake of the African embassy bombings and Taliban refusal to extradite Osama bin Laden. Still, in secret phone conversations two days after an American missile attack on bin Laden's camps in Khost in August 1998, Mullah Omar "indicated a willingness for dialogue," in the words of a State Department report. Omar followed up with a fax in September 1998, calling for a change in American policies focused on capturing bin Laden and citing a passage of the Quran identifying Christians as allies (and Jews as enemies). But the negotiations did not develop further.[31] Public outcry over Taliban atrocities against women and the lingering dispute over bin Laden gradually undermined American hopes for energy pipelines and the isolation of Iran and Russia from south Asian energy markets. In March 2001 the Taliban shelling of the Bamyan Buddhas further isolated the regime and suggested a greater role for bin Laden and al-Qaeda in charting a more confrontational approach to outsiders.

Following the destruction of the Buddhas, however, Rahmatullah Hashemi, a young Taliban envoy, toured the United States (as well as Europe and the Middle East) visiting college campuses and other venues to explain the Taliban cause. Seeking to account for the severity of Taliban rule as well as for its gender policies, he highlighted the enduring consequences of the anti-Soviet war and its chaotic aftermath and drew attention to more recent obstacles, drought and famine. Hashemi, like other Taliban spokesmen of the period, sought to use the humanitarian rhetoric of their critics against them, charging that they cared more about statues than women and children suffering from hunger.[32] Such efforts helped keep lines of communication with the outside world open. Moreover, in April 1999, Mullah Omar issued a ban on the cultivation of hashish (*bang*) and in August ordered producers to scale back opium cultivation, which he finally banned in July 2000. The opium ban may have been in response to the overproduction of poppies, which the Taliban had always taxed, and may have been intended to raise prices (along with traffickers' profits and state revenues); however, these anti-drug measures simultaneously established channels of negotiation with the international community.[33] In May 2001 the State Department, in turn, announced a $43 million grant, in part to curb poppy production in Taliban-controlled Afghanistan.

Enabled by this vocabulary of moderation, engagement with international organizations and foreign states confronted the Taliban with a critical opportunity. Like Afghan leaders before them, the Taliban saw external aid as the essential linchpin of state building. Their challenge was then to resurrect formal institutions that had acted as intermediaries to the outside world—and its resources—in the past. Councils, or shuras, formed the institutional locus of Taliban policy-making under the authoritarian leadership of Mullah Omar. But alongside them, the Taliban soon began to revive ministries and their bureaucracies. Within a year, some twenty-seven ministries were functioning in Kabul.

The Taliban inherited yet another dilemma from the past: how could the regime hire and retain professional personnel? How they attempted to solve this problem suggests a key to understanding both the relative stability and the underlying vulnerabilities of the regime. The movement grew out of a small core of Kandahari mullahs and mujahedin who later formed the bulk of a Supreme Shura, composed of thirty to forty members, who convened periodically in Kandahar. Their armed forces drew from wider circles of Pashtun students, orphans, and commanders, though apparently with a strong reliance on figures claiming Durrani descent. Former communists of Khalq, the military, and the security services, KHAD, assumed more technical posts in the armed forces (for example, piloting MiG fighter jets). But the new regime broke from modern Afghan state traditions when it assigned leading roles in the state apparatus to mullahs (and clerics with similar ranks). Madrasa and kinship networks seem to have determined the staffing of the ministerial and other upper-level positions.[34]

Yet continuities with the past remained. According to many sources, the Taliban were forced to rely on holdovers from previous regimes to staff the ministries.[35] In the provinces, government depended to an even greater extent on the cooperation of such figures. This policy of accommodation, even if only of necessity, drew non-Taliban policemen, bureaucrats, technical specialists, professionals, and others into the regime. The prospect of Pashtun rule brought former communists, including schoolteachers and petty officials, into the regime. The need for a salary and some sense of normalcy after some two decades of civil war attracted non-Pashtuns as well. To run the local radio and television station and edit a newsletter entitled *Justice* in Nimroz, for example, the Taliban recruited the Baluch intellectual (and memoirist) Abdul Rahman Pahwal, who briefly ran the station under the supervision of a minor Taliban official, an illiterate herder who nonetheless treated Pahwal "respectfully."[36]

Another memoirist, a purported insider and midlevel official in the regime, has produced an account that offers a clearer picture of the appeal of the regime for those closer to the center of power, but not formally part of the madrasa network of the Pashtun belt, and of the momentum the Taliban seemed to create through their state-building efforts. A native of Baghlan Province and a former student of Kabul University in his late forties, Wahid Muzhda claimed to have served a number of years in the Foreign Ministry, though without formally enlisting in the ranks of the Taliban. A former Hizb-e Islami editor of the journal *Shahadat* in Peshawar, Muzhda ultimately broke with the movement and published his account in Iran. Muzhda's work displays a studied ambivalence, however. It demonstrates sympathy with Taliban efforts to resurrect the Afghan state and to make use of it for the creation of an "Islamic order" *(nizam-e Islami)*. But his portrayal is also designed to distance the author and like-minded Islamists from the "calamity" visited upon both "religion and society" by the "fanaticism" and excesses of the rural mullahs whose worldview was shaped, he maintained, by only a handful of books, occasional news from radio broadcasts, and familiarity with only one or two of the country's provinces.[37]

Mullah Muhammad Omar figures as one of the chief villains of this narrative. Known as a "hard-headed" character and a "tyrant," Mullah Omar intimidated followers. At a shura of some fifteen hundred ulama in April 1996, the mullah assumed the title "Commander of the Faithful" *(Amir al-Muminin)*. Emboldened by this new title, Muzhda asserts, the amir treated any disagreement with him as a violation of the sharia, a view not shared, Muzhda adds, by many of the ulama who had voiced support for Mullah Omar and anathematized President Burhanuddin Rabbani at the gathering. By this account, power corrupted an otherwise noble vision, alienating Muzhda and other fellow travelers "working within the system" *(andarkaran)*, who, however, could not protest publicly.[38]

Muzhda identified another "deviation" under the new regime in its reliance on the Ministry for the Promotion of Virtue and the Prevention of Vice. Alongside the Ministry of War, it was the most active of the Taliban ministries. A few of its policies had already been introduced under President Rabbani's government; but it rapidly expanded the number of rules regarding "virtue" and "vice" and devised new strategies of implementation. With its own funding from sources in the Persian Gulf, this ministry employed militias to terrorize men and women in the streets of Herat, Kabul, and other urban areas. The ministry's choice of recruits—and the extraordinary latitude they enjoyed to humiliate, arrest, injure, and kill—gave the ministry and its militias a particular dynamism. The recruitment of rural teenagers and young men, often orphans raised within the walls of madrasa compounds in Baluchistan and the North West Frontier Province of Pakistan and neighboring Pashtun areas in Afghanistan, gave it an anti-urban cast. The male youths the ministry empowered viewed cities as dens of depravity that had rejected all regard for Islamic morality and decency. These youths compelled men to attend mosques and unescorted women to remain at home. Armed with whips, radio antennas, and other weapons, they arrested men who shaved and women who revealed ankles, and they waged war on television, music, kite flying, and other activities that might distract the faithful from prayer and corrupt the chaste purity of women.

Littering the trees with cassettes and smashed equipment, they injected new norms of violence into the everyday life of the cities in the name of "commanding good and forbidding evil." In July 1998 an official Taliban newspaper, *Anis,* justified this violence with the observation, "You don't build a truly Islamic state with preaching and propaganda alone, and in the struggle with evil and immorality one must resort to force."[39] But disagreements persisted among the Taliban about the conduct of the ministry. When critics appealed to the exemplary practice of the early community of Islam on behalf of privacy rights, the minister warned, "Do not compare the people in the early period of Islam with those of this age. These people are more corrupt, and for the most part this depravity [*fasad*] takes place in the homes . . . [where] people listen to music and have television and video."[40]

Though these actions seemed incomprehensible to aid workers and other foreign observers in Afghanistan's cities, Taliban media celebrated such policing as the ultimate and long-overdue fulfillment of the historical calling of the Afghan ulama. On July 17, 1997, *Anis* advised its readers that they "should pray to the Almighty that under the leadership of the ulama in our country, peace, security, and calm will always be established in our country."[41] In a similar vein, the minister for pilgrimage and endowments, Mawlawi Abdul Shukur Haqqani, asserted the power of the prayer leaders and other ulama of the 250 mosques in the capital. In an article in *Shariat* in January 1997, he observed that "in the absence of the commander of the faithful [amir ul-muminin], they represent his caliphs." Other essays highlighted the complementary, though subordinate, role of the ulama. Their role, though central to the "Islamic revolution" under way, remained distinct from that of the Taliban, "the loyal sons of the ulama."[42] Though clerical titles proliferated, the broader political aims of the Taliban circumscribed the power of the ulama: in October 1997 the leadership renamed the country the Islamic Emirate of Afghanistan, but the basic structure of the old ministerial system persisted.[43]

Atrocities committed by the ministry in charge of Islamic morality seem to have given some fellow travelers pause; but the inability to pay salaries and to transmit central authority into the outlying provinces may have played a more influential part in undermining the loyalties of local representatives of state power. Despite substantial income from overland transit, foreign subsidies, opium production, and the smuggling of drugs, minerals, and timber, the government could not afford to pay salaries for several months at a time. In the field of provincial administration, the Taliban regime displayed more modest objectives than it did in major urban areas and retained local commanders, who enjoyed some autonomy in many locales. In

Nuristan, for example, the Taliban assigned nine mullahs of local origin to staff district centers but apparently did not even appoint a governor.[44]

A weak state apparatus meant fragile control of Taliban subordinates. The inability to function as a "normal" state—that is, to administer effectively and gain the loyalty of local populations—amplified the insecurities of Taliban elites. Signs of official anxiety had emerged already in 1997. In February their hold on the recently seized eastern provinces of Laghman, Kunar, and Nangarhar appeared precarious when tribal rebels, apparently crossing over from Pakistan and in protest against disarmament efforts, attacked Taliban positions in the district of Asmar in Kunar Province.[45] Between May and July 1997, the Taliban suffered setbacks throughout the north, including the loss of Mazar and many prisoners to the Northern Alliance. That autumn, the government renewed its efforts to discipline and consolidate control over Taliban military units and to deepen ties to the provinces. In October, members of the Ministry of Defense and the Ministry for the Promotion of Virtue and the Prevention of Vice, as well as of the military court, announced a plan to "jointly visit military units and companies in order to draw the attention of the personnel to their duties and responsibilities, in light of the sacred religion of Islam," adding that they would press the soldiers "to work harder on this path, facilitating the implementation of the Islamic Emirate of Afghanistan's programs in the country."[46] The regime also announced personnel changes in the intelligence services and appointed new heads of their branches in Paktya and Khost.[47]

The regime relied heavily on radio to project the appearance of close administrative control over its subalterns in the provinces and to display official concern for the common folk. On November 8, Radio Voice of Sharia broadcast a report on meetings between Mawlawi Abdul Kabir, the deputy chairman of the Supervisory Council

(Shura-ye Sarparast) and various commanders of the "Islamic Army." After pledging their "readiness to defend the values of the Islamic Emirate and its territorial integrity," the mullahs in command of these "mujahedin units" received "the necessary instructions" from Abdul Kabir, who also "clarified the current duties of the party in Laghman Province." The same broadcast announced that Abdul Kabir had received delegations of provincial "ulama and officials" who gave an account of "the work and activities of the peasants of Andar District in Ghazni Province and the state of the Taliban's duties in Logar Province." As with the military commanders, Radio Voice of Sharia announced, "the esteemed Maulavi Abdul Kabir clarified the details of the work of the peasants in Andar District and the Taliban from Karwar District in Logar Province, and gave the necessary instructions."[48]

At the same time, the Taliban began to make more overt appeals to represent not just Pashtuns but the entire Afghan nation. Amid fighting in the north, anti-Taliban militias (composed primarily of Uzbek fighters) killed some two thousand Taliban prisoners of war. Like was done in Rwanda in 1994, the regime utilized radio to warn listeners of the violent "treachery" of the enemy. Northern Alliance atrocities committed against Taliban POWs in the north transformed Taliban soldiers into symbols of victimhood and national authenticity. Following the discovery of mass graves in Jawzjan Province in November 1997, Radio Voice of Sharia announced the staging of Quranic recitations throughout the country to remember the fallen "innocent seekers of knowledge." It instructed "all officials and compatriots" to participate in the recitations. The broadcast thus presented the massacre not simply as a blow to the Taliban movement or as an affront to religion. Rather, the regime insisted that the event be remembered as a national tragedy: "This mass killing is such an act of treachery by the enemy that it will always live on in the memory. And *the sons of this country* will register their self-sacrifice with golden words in the history of the country in order to keep the jihadi memories [of the martyrs] alive and to continue their struggle and the acts of martyrdom for the preservation of the *territorial integrity* of the Islamic society."[49]

Taliban propaganda highlighted the regime's care for justice and efficient administration, what one would in other developmentalist contexts term "good government." Just as the Taliban leadership struggled to direct the "work of the peasants" and the religious obligations of its soldiers, however, it faced difficulties in disciplining its own officials. In November 1997, the central government sent a delegation under the minister of justice, Mullah Nuruddin Turabi, to inspect local government offices. Radio Voice of Sharia reported that the delegation uncovered local officials who had accepted bribes. The head of a local appellate court and a cashier were both found guilty "on the basis of *sharia* law." Upon the orders of a sharia court, the police painted their faces black, and "they were paraded around the town of Maydanshar as a lesson to others." Mullah Muhammad Omar issued a decree, distributed nationwide and printed in the official press, threatening to impose a five-year prison sentence on any government officials who betrayed the principles of an "Islamic order" (*nezam-e Islami*) by taking bribes.[50]

The regime had announced the firing of smaller numbers of officials in the past for violating rules mandating that civil servants grow beards and wear turbans, but in Jalalabad, the delegation purged the local government of some four hundred officials. Turabi targeted holdovers from the pre-Taliban government, including various professionals and university lecturers, and may have also sought to diminish the power base of a senior Taliban official, Mullah Rabbani, thought to be a potential challenger to Mullah Omar. Moreover, the delegation seems to have arrived in a locale experiencing rapid turnover and low morale among state employees. According to sources across the border in Peshawar, the regime had not paid its officials in the eastern provinces in half a year, forcing many of them to abandon their posts for Pakistan.[51] It is in this wider context of vulnerability in November that the acting minister of information and culture, Amir Khan Mottaqi, invited Burhanuddin Rabbani and Abdul Rabb al-Rasul Sayyaf to take posts in the Taliban government in Kabul.[52]

Vulnerable in the north and parts of the east, the Taliban hold on Pashtun communities became shakier as well. Despite the periodic influx of busloads of madrasa students from Pakistan, the high rate of Taliban casualties in 1997 meant that the regime had to resort to wider-scale conscription. Taliban disarmament campaigns had already provoked some disturbances, but conscription efforts in early 1998 apparently triggered significant uprisings in Helmand Province and, especially, Kandahar Province. They may have also spread to Wardak and Paktya provinces. Though short-lived, the clashes between local communities and Taliban troops apparently cost dozens of lives.

In March, communities in Kandahar rose up against conscription again. Flooding in Kandahar and Helmand and the forced removal of local populations may have also stoked unrest. In Jalalabad, the Taliban claimed to uncover a coup attempt in October and confronted student protests in December. Behind each of these events, observers discerned a split between Mullah Omar and more internationally oriented, "moderate" members of his circle, particularly Mullah Rabbani, who had a following in Jalalabad, and Mullah Ghaus, who met in Kabul with an American envoy, Bill Richardson, in April. "Taliban leaders in the Kabul and Jalalabad shuras [councils]," Ahmed

Rashid writes, "were feeling the growing public discontent at rising prices, lack of food and the cut-back in humanitarian aid."[53]

Such disturbances highlighted the challenges of establishing a functioning state apparatus and ultimately undermined the legitimacy of a regime that increasingly aspired to function as a conventional nation-state but struggled to find a symbolic language to order a more prosaic form of politics. In June 1998, for example, the Taliban convened ulama from throughout the country at a kind of constitutional assembly at the royal palace in Kabul. They were to draft a "Fundamental Law"—an institution, its architects contended, of great importance for "*every* country and government"—but with the proviso that all laws be scrutinized by the ulama for conformity with the sharia. Its first article declared Afghanistan an "Islamic emirate," but then reproduced much of the language from the same article of previous Afghan constitutions, declaring the country "free, independent, one, and indivisible."[54]

Such nationalist appeals did not entirely deflect charges of corruption, military setbacks, and growing international isolation; and the regime seems to have increasingly resorted to purges of its government officials. Some of the inspectors who had led investigations in 1997 and 1998 themselves fell victim to later purges. In January 2000, a paper affiliated with the Northern Alliance reported that the chairman of the Taliban military court, Sayyed Abdurrahman Agha, had been convicted of bribery. According to this report, the feared prosecutor who meted out lashings and amputations was jailed for accepting a bribe worth some $7,400 from a suspected murderer.[55] Undermining its own capacity to administer increasingly restive populations, the regime continued to rotate the same officials among various posts.[56]

The evolution of the language of Taliban propaganda reflected the growing insecurity and isolation felt by many Taliban officials. In early 2000, Taliban authorities initiated a public campaign to rebut charges that their officials were acting in their own self-interest. They even felt obliged to address fellow Pashtuns in places like Herat through the local Pashto-language press. Conceding that the country faced numerous problems, an article in *Etefaq-e Islam* of January 13, 2000, nonetheless insisted that "it has never been the case for officials of the Islamic Emirate of Afghanistan to be indifferent to national pride, honorable history and valuable customs of the people in order to protect their [official] positions and achieve some vulgar political goals." Rather, the Taliban, "the true sons of the country," had "risen to protect the dignity of the Islamic system and of the Afghan culture." The article called on the people to join the struggle on behalf of "the nation and the system." The success of the emirate depended now on "the people's support for and cooperation and solidarity with the system." The time had grown all the more urgent for "the full cooperation of all compatriots," *Etefaq-i Islam* warned its readers, because "there is a war between Islam and infidels across the world." The ultimate success of the Islamic Emirate of Afghanistan hinged, the article concluded, on the "support and solidarity of the nation."[57]

Framed in nationalist language, this search in early 2000 for a broader base of support may have also informed overtures to the regime's opponents. The Taliban leadership had begun to pursue its mujahedin rivals—Masud, Dostum, Sayyaf, and Rabbani—while seeking to elevate the status of its state institutions by filing murder charges against them before the Supreme Court. On the holiday of Id al-Fitr, however, Mullah Omar apparently declared a general amnesty for the enemies of the Taliban. A Pakistani newspaper, *Ausaf,* reported that Mullah Omar now sought the cooperation of his rivals "in view of the new conspiracies and campaigns of anti-Islam forces in Chechnya, Bosnia, and Kashmir."[58]

This sense of insecurity about the linkage between the regime and the "nation" was confirmed within days. On January 23, 2000, an Iranian news agency reported that an uprising had begun in the town of Khost in Paktya Province. The practice of appointing Kandaharis to local administrative positions now seems to have met with resistance.[59] Tensions had been building between the Taliban and the varied Pashtun tribes of the province for at least one year. Violence had already erupted in January 1999 when Taliban officials ordered children to stop playing a traditional game of egg fighting, condemning it as "un-Islamic." The Voice of the Islamic Republic of Iran claimed that locals had seized the administration. The rebels demanded that the Taliban abandon the area or agree to a set of conditions guaranteeing greater local control, including the dismissal of officials who had been appointed from Kandahar.[60] They may also have opposed Taliban efforts to supplant local customary law (Pashtunwali) with their understanding of the sharia. According to a correspondent for Agence France-Presse, locals protested Taliban appropriation of land, the shifting of local financial resources to other regions, and forced conscription. The Taliban quickly relented on one of the demands and replaced the unpopular governor with another official.[61]

The regime's Radio Voice of Sharia nonetheless issued indignant denials. Characterizing the reports of unrest in Khost as "part of a propaganda war being waged by enemies of the Islamic Emirate of Afghanistan," a broadcast on January 27 maintained that "with every passing day the religious Muslim people of Afghanistan are more prepared than ever to support their Islamic Emirate of Afghanistan, which is legitimately the allegory of desires and initiatives of *the entire mujahid Afghan nation,* pursuing continuous efforts to realize the aims and humanely benevolent programs of the leadership of the Emirate." Radio Voice of Sharia pledged that "the realities will be made clear to the international community and the face of the fabricators and opponents will then be disclosed."[62]

In the same broadcast, a correspondent of the Bakhtar Information Agency described how the facts on the ground in Khost contradicted "negative propaganda." Denying any uprising, the report focused instead on a special meeting held at the grand mosque of Khost at which "scholars, tribal leaders, and peoples' representatives of Khost, Paktya and Paktika Provinces have emphasized the unity and Islamic brotherhood between the people and various tribes of the provinces under the leadership of the Islamic Emirate of Afghanistan." The report noted the attendance of a number of ministers of the central government, though it stopped short of explaining why they found themselves assembled in Khost at that moment.

In addition to the powerful minister of justice, Mullah Nuruddin Turabi, and the general director of management and administration, Mullah Amir Khan Mottaqi, the deputy minister of higher education, the president of the Academy of Sciences, as well as the present and former governors of Khost Province had taken part in the gathering. Following the recitation of Quranic verses, local elites, including the leaders of the Gorbuz, Kochi, Zadran, and other tribes, joined the visiting representatives of the regime in voicing support for the emirate. According to this report, the speakers reaffirmed, "We had accepted all the sacrifices and long periods of emigration in order to set up the Qur'anic order in our beloved country; thanks to our great God we have achieved this great aspiration by establishing Islamic order, an order under which in conformity with Qur'anic guidance the rights and interests of all people are protected." "It is a necessity," the broadcast continued, "for men and women, rich and poor, children and adults to cherish and protect this legitimate order:

they should not be deceived by the propaganda of hypocrites and strangers."

Repeating claims about the Taliban's defeat of "decay and corruption and misfortune inside the country" and restoration of "national unity and wide-ranging peace," the report maintained that the speakers "emphasized once again the indestructible unity of all the tribes and nationalities" of the country. Before placing flowers "on the heads of the Taliban" and crying "God is the greatest," the "religious people of Khost" agreed to a seven-point communiqué, ostensibly authored by "the tribes of the southern provinces." It proclaimed that there never had been any "difficulties with the Islamic Emirate of Afghanistan" and that "we are living here alongside one another like brothers." The communiqué also expressed opposition to the interference of the former king, Muhammad Zaher, while reaffirming their commitment to the rule of the sharia: "The people of Khost Province are confident of the confirmation of the Islamic Sharia and resolving of its problems in the light of Islamic Sharia under the flag of the Islamic Emirate of Afghanistan and do not hesitate to make every sacrifice to consolidate the Islamic Emirate." Despite such avowals about a national consensus supporting the supremacy of Islamic law over Pashtunwali, the regime may have been forced to make further concessions. Faced with opposition to house searches—an explosive issue that would later fuel opposition to U.S.-led forces in Afghanistan, Mullah Muhammad Omar issued a decree in February 2001 that aimed to placate local communities by imposing greater transparency and discipline on the process and to deter abuses (ostensibly committed by miscreants disguised in "Taliban clothes").[63]

Dissent among Pashtun tribesmen in eastern Afghanistan seems to have paralleled deepening fissures within the government. By Muzhda's account, Osama bin Laden consistently undermined figures like Wakil Ahmad Mutawakkil, who served as foreign minister from mid-1997. Indeed, from 2000 or so, the movement was at war with itself, Muzhda asserts, with bin Laden supposedly naming Mutawakkil as the second target, after the United States, of his jihad. Exacerbated by a growing humanitarian crisis caused by a serious drought, the stalled advance on the northern front played a role as well, along with international economic sanctions and criticism. The regime may have reached the height of desperation in its recognition of Chechnya. But when a Chechen delegation arrived for a visit in Kabul, it apparently heard scolding lectures from officials of the Ministry for the Promotion of Virtue and the Prevention of Vice about the "un-Islamic character" of its recent elections.[64]

It was no doubt in this same moment that figures like Muzhda and Mutawakkil gave serious thought to alternative paths toward the creation of a just Islamic order. The crisis of September and October 2001 seems to have only hastened efforts already under way to remake reputations. These early steps toward defection may help explain the speed and relative ease with which the Taliban movement was disbanded, though not entirely defeated, and the alacrity with which its officials have recast themselves.

Within weeks of the collapse of the regime, a number of "moderates" regrouped in Islamabad. In December 2001 they announced the formation of the "Servants of the Quran" (Khaddam al-Furqan) with an eye to returning to Afghan politics. Foreign observers noted that the group included the likes of the minister of foreign affairs, Wakil Ahmad Mutawakkil, the minister of education, Mawlawi Arsala Rahmani, and the UN envoy, Abdul Hakim Mujahed.[65] In late 2001 the group apparently sought representation at the Loya Jirga and made overtures to Hamid Karzai. The interim president reciprocated interest in the group as a means to bolster his fragile standing among Pashtuns. Apparently supported by Pakistani security forces, its representatives sought to distance themselves from Mullah Omar, the shelling of the statues of Bamyan, and the regime's sheltering of bin Laden.[66]

Other Taliban remained in the open in Afghanistan. After some eighteen months in U.S. custody, Mutawakkil, who has since claimed that he warned the Americans about al-Qaeda's September 11 plot in advance, became a free man. Coalition forces sought his assistance in coaxing other Taliban down from the hills and out of hiding. In January 2002 a reporter from the *Christian Science Monitor* interviewed the former deputy minister of the interior, Mullah Abdul Samad Khaksar, in Kabul.[67] Once responsible for the police forces of the Taliban, he still occupied a desk with an "official-looking nameplate," though now with a framed portrait of Ahmad Shah Masud behind him. The correspondent claimed to find "dozens of mid-level officials" looking for positions in the interim government. Like Sayyed Marajuddin Nazari, an official in the Department of Transportation, many had abandoned their turbans for the *pokhol,* the wool hat associated with the Northern Alliance. With a new headdress and "a slight trim of the beard," former Taliban officials returned to their old posts. In remaking themselves, they insisted that they had tried "to fight the system from within, that they had no choice but to work for the previous government—and that they never really liked the Taliban anyway." Mullah Khaksar pointed to his personal quarrels with both Mullah Omar and bin Laden, adding that he had even attempted to persuade Omar to share power with regional elites, including non-Pashtuns.[68]

Functionaries like Wahid Muzhda, the former Foreign Ministry employee who penned the insider's account of the regime, also returned to work in Kabul. By February 2004 Muzhda had donned a coat and tie and found a new job as a senior aide at the Supreme Court of Afghanistan.[69] An English speaker, Muzhda became a spokesman for Karzai's policy of reconciliation with Taliban moderates and served as an expert on the Taliban for international media outlets such as the *New York Times*, the *Washington Post*, National Public Radio, and the BBC.[70] "All Taliban [were] not very extremist people," he explained. Like Mutawakkil, Muzhda also appears to have assumed the role of mediating on behalf of the Taliban. Stressing Karzai's dependence on the Taliban "in several provinces" but avoiding direct invocation of the Pashtun issue, Muzhda noted that the Taliban had conditions for giving up their struggle and joining the new order: "They won't join the government unless Karzai cracks down more on moral corruption and becomes more rigorous in promoting Islamic values."[71] In August 2005 he vouched for four senior leaders (two of whom were connected to the Foreign Ministry) who had recently accepted Karzai's offer of amnesty.

To facilitate such negotiations with Taliban defectors, in 2005 the Karzai government established the National Independent Commission for Peace and Reconciliation, headed by Sebghatullah Mojaddedi, a pivotal figure in the anti-Soviet jihad and a descendant of one of the country's most revered clerical families. In early 2005 a senior U.S. military official projected that the recruitment of moderates under the amnesty program, together with significant financial incentives on offer, would allow American forces to withdraw substantially by summer.[72] In the autumn of 2005, a number of senior Taliban officials ran in the parliamentary elections. The electoral commission excluded roughly two dozen candidates, citing ties to "warlords," but former Taliban were not among them. Mutawakkil joined two commanders, Abdul Salam "Roketi" from Zabul, and Abdul Wahid Baghrani from Helmand, in standing for parliament. Mawlawi Kalamuddin, former chief of the Ministry for the Promotion of Virtue and the Prevention of Vice, who boasted in 1997 that the public stoning of two accused adulterers in 1996 had "ended adultery in Kandahar forever," also ran. Arrested in April 2003, he appears to have gained his freedom as part of Karzai's amnesty.[73] Their campaigns looked back, not to the reign of the mujahedin or the Taliban, but to the anti-Soviet jihad.

As of the summer of 2007, the two most famous senior Taliban who had signed on to the commission's work remained Mutawakkil, an advocate of talks with senior Taliban commanders, and Mullah Abdul Salam Zaif, the Taliban ambassador to Pakistan, who returned to the country in 2005 after nearly four years at Guantanamo.[74] Along with parliamentarian "Roketi," these figures likely played a role in March 2007 in negotiations between the Italian and Afghan governments that arranged for the exchange of five captured Taliban fighters for the *La Repubblica* journalist Daniele Mastrogiacomo (but not his Afghan driver, Sayed Agha, whom the Taliban beheaded, or his interpreter, Ajmal Naqshbandi, whom they also killed). By early 2007, more than 3,500 lower-ranking Taliban, along with members of Hizb-e Islami and other groups fighting against the government, took part in ceremonies arranged by Mojaddedi's reconciliation commission and swore allegiance to Karzai.[75]

As Amin Tarzi shows in Chapter 8 of this book, these overtures to moderates did not dampen the heterogeneous "neo-Taliban" insurgencies and centrifugal forces that plagued the central government. Instead it caused new cleavages. Defectors were marked for assassination. Mutawakkil's brother was shot to death in Quetta. Mawlawi Abdullah Fayaz, the head of the council of ulama who formally offered religious backing for Karzai and annulled Mullah Omar's status as emir, was also assassinated in May 2005. His funeral opened up a new stage in the neo-Taliban movement when a suicide bomber attacked mourners inside a Kandahar mosque.[76] Neo-Taliban assassins killed a number of other clerics as well.

Primarily aimed at reintegrating Pashtuns, the amnesty program continued to divide Afghans as well as the NATO countries, who in 2006 and 2007 disagreed more sharply among themselves about military tactics and prospects for negotiations with the Taliban. Whereas the Italian government bargained for the release of a hostage and Dutch forces sought dialogue with militias on the ground, the United States remained skeptical about such approaches. At the same time, continued American and NATO military operations, including house-to-house searches and lethal aerial bombardment, hardened a number of Pashtun communities against Karzai, a figure whom they regarded as a puppet of foreigners.[77] For Hazaras and other groups targeted by the Taliban regime, the policy of reconciling with former Taliban members threatened to alienate them further from Kabul.[78] It is in this context that the 2007 amnesty bill, like the flawed trial of the former communist intelligence head, Sarwari, represented to many Afghans a symbol of the failure of the post-Taliban order to overcome the crimes of the past.

In the period following the collapse of formal Taliban rule, the categories of moderation and extremism have been deployed by the Karzai administration against a variety of groups that question its right to govern. In this setting, the meanings of these terms have shifted. Since 2001 the label *moderate Taliban* has operated as a code word in the effort to integrate Pashtuns without resorting to a vocabulary of ethnicization and giving support to the accusation that Karzai and those around him are hostile to non-Pashtuns. At the same time, the March 2007 amnesty bill retreated from these labels, opting instead for a far more inclusive vision of reconciliation.

For their part, key Taliban leaders such as Mullah Omar continued in 2007 to speak on behalf of an Afghan nation, despite mounting evidence that the post-2001 insurgencies waged by Taliban fighters were limited to Pashtun communities.[79] Against the backdrop of intense fighting and mounting civilian casualties in the southern provinces in 2006 and 2007, the search for moderates had not yielded significant reconciliation with Pashtun communities. For many Pashtuns, the insurgencies straddling the Afghan-Pakistan border and sweeping across southern Afghanistan had become far more effective means to shape Afghan politics. The strategic appeal to moderate Taliban entailed other costs as well. Originating as a way to bolster the legitimacy of actors within a fragmented state-building movement and hostile international climate, it now threatened to deepen the divide between Pashtuns and non-Pashtuns and keep alive the vivid memories of the unhealed wounds of Afghanistan's thirty-year war.

CHAPTER EIGHT

The Neo-Taliban

Amin Tarzi

The Taliban [don't] exist anymore, they're defeated. They are gone.

—HAMID KARZAI, FEBRUARY

2004

The Taliban and other terrorists continue to seek to destabilize Afghanistan.

—ZALMAY KHALILZAD, APRIL

2004

The surrender of the Taliban in December 2001 signaled the official end of the regime headed by the *Da Afghanistan da Talibano Islami Tahrik* (Afghanistan's Taliban Islamic Movement)— the Taliban. Taliban leaders had already fled Kabul and had lost control of most of Afghanistan. With the order to surrender Kandahar, the last stronghold and the birthplace of the Taliban regime, Taliban leader Mullah Muhammad Omar Mujahed relinquished his remaining political power. The leaders scattered, fleeing Afghanistan for the safe havens nearby, and the regime fell.

Afghanistan and the world seemed to close this chapter in Afghanistan's history and sought to move forward with rebuilding the country. However, after a few months of silence, reports surfaced of Taliban activities attempting to disrupt this process, forcing the world to reopen the Taliban chapter and take notice. Questions arose about the authenticity of the Taliban's claims: Was this the same Taliban emerging from defeat to reassert their hold on power, or were other groups attempting to capitalize on the Taliban name and legacy to appeal to certain pockets of the Afghan population? Was this a resurgence of Taliban might, or had a new political opponent been born? There was no consensus even at the top levels of the Afghan and U.S. governments, as evidenced by the opening quotations by Afghan President Hamid Karzai and former American ambassador to Kabul, Zalmay Khalilzad, about how to characterize this challenge to the state-building process.[1]

This chapter examines the events following the fall of the Taliban regime and charts the emergence of this political resistance and terror movement. It shows that this is not solely the reemergence of the old regime. The labels *Taliban* and *neo-Taliban* have both been used to define the movement that emerged in 2002 to counter the state-building efforts of the new Afghan government and challenge its authority. Nomenclature is a powerful tool. How people define themselves in groups is often captured in the names they choose. The question whether this was the same outfit, "the Taliban," or a new manifestation of resistance with a similar mission, a kind of "neo-Taliban," is embodied in the terminology used to describe this movement. The fact that both terms are used interchangeably conveys the confusion over the identity and makeup of this group. To further confuse the terminology, the armed opposition that has been active in Afghanistan since 2002 has begun to identify itself as not only the Taliban, but also the "mujahedin." *Mujahedin* is a term that, in the course of Islamic history, has been used by many groups to identify their struggles to defend Islam or Islamdom. The term gained global currency in Afghanistan during the 1979–1989 Soviet occupation.[2] The original Taliban, who emerged from the ranks of the mujahedin in the mid-1990s, differentiated themselves as talibs—seekers or students of Islamic sciences—and sought to remove the mujahedin from power. The reintroduction of this title, which has surfaced primarily in Internet postings, raises more questions regarding the identity and mission of the armed resistance.[3]

The use of the label *Taliban* elicits certain images and promotes particular political, cultural, and religious ideologies. It is a powerful name that instills fear and anger in some while uniting others. Its use can be a political tool to rally supporters, polarize the population, or demonize the opposition. The term *neo-Taliban* first surfaced in a 2003 article in *The Economist* and has been gaining currency among Afghanistan observers.[4] What it conveys is that the opposition maintains certain characteristics of, and links to, the old regime but also points to important differences. Whereas use of the word *Taliban* may limit understanding of the motivations and makeup of the varied actors that have surfaced since 2002 to oppose the post-Taliban order, the category "neo-Taliban" better characterizes an opposition that has evolved beyond the old regime to encompass new groups with new agendas.

The U.S.-led military campaign against the Taliban regime and the al-Qaeda terrorist network it was sheltering began on October 7, 2001. The campaign, dubbed Operation Enduring Freedom, initially relied on aerial bombardments and missile attacks from U.S. and British surface ships and submarines. On November 9, Mazar-e Sharif, the largest city in northern Afghanistan, fell to forces that were ostensibly part of the National Islamic United Front for the Salvation of Afghanistan *(Jabha-ye Mottahed-e Islami-ye Melli Baraye Nejat-e Afghanistan)*, popularly referred to as the Northern Alliance.[5] This signaled the beginning of the end of the Taliban regime's rule over Afghanistan. On November 13, the Taliban evacuated Kabul without a fight as the Afghan capital was being overrun by the Tajik elements within the United Front.

According to a book by Wahid Muzhda, a member of the Afghan foreign ministry during the Taliban regime, Taliban leader Mullah Omar recognized the impending danger a few days after the commencement of aerial attacks on Afghanistan and sent his family and close relatives to safety across the border to Pakistan.[6] According to Mullah Omar's personal driver, the Taliban leader rejected the pleas of his advisors to leave as well.[7] During the initial phases of the military campaign, Mullah Omar allegedly believed that his forces, along with the Pakistani volunteers sent to reinforce the Taliban troops, would hold their ground. With the fall of Mazar-e Sharif and the bombardments of Kandahar, he began to understand that his hold on power was tenuous. In an unexplained move, but perhaps for fear of being detected through electronic signals, he terminated all direct contact with his field commanders, who only communicated with him when needing tactical direction to minimize potential for compromise.[8] The absence of commands from Mullah Omar reportedly led to countless casualties among the Taliban forces in northern Afghanistan.

Sometime in late November, Mullah Omar realized that to prevent his regime's last stronghold, Kandahar, from being forcefully conquered, the city would have to be surrendered to the opposition forces that had surrounded it. Based on Muzhda's account, Mullah Omar made the decision to abandon Kandahar upon learning of the annihilation of his forces that he had dispatched to retake the neighboring Uruzgan Province from anti-Taliban leader Hamid Karzai.[9]

In early December, Mullah Omar issued the order to surrender Kandahar, effectively relinquishing all political power in Afghanistan. On December 6, the Taliban cabinet met in Kandahar under the leadership of Defense Minister Mullah Obaidullah Akhund and decided that the Taliban would transfer power to the tribal council headed by Hamid Karzai. They also declared that their forces would surrender their weapons to the same council.[10] On the following day, December 7, the birthplace of the Taliban movement, and the last major city in its control, was in the hands of a tribal council—thus ending the Taliban movement's seven-year quest to establish an exemplary Islamic emirate in Afghanistan.

Prior to assuming control of the Interim Authority of Afghanistan on December 22, as stipulated by the Bonn Agreement, Karzai declared from his base in Uruzgan Province a general amnesty for all of the Taliban forces.[11] The details of the amnesty declared by Karzai and apparently supported by Gul Agha Shayrzai and Mullah Naqibullah Alakozai, two principal power brokers in the immediate aftermath of the Taliban capitulation, are not clear.[12] After assuming his position as leader, Karzai clarified that only "criminal" elements within the Taliban movement would be pursued and possibly prosecuted.[13] However, he did not elaborate on who these criminal elements were or what specific steps were planned to apprehend them or prevent their escape. Therefore the amnesty was liberally applied.

The general amnesty led to what a Western intelligence officer called "the great escape." But it may have been facilitated by what might be called "the great release." As described by figures such as Khaled Pashtun, a spokesman for Kandahar Province, and Governor Gul Agha Shayrzai, leaders of the former Taliban regime who had been jailed in Kandahar were released as part of the general amnesty. Individuals who were purportedly freed by authorities in Kandahar included Mullah Obaidullah Akhund and Mullah Nuruddin Turabi, the former ministers of defense and justice. Jalal Khan, an associate of Shayrzai, went further to say, "Those men who have surrendered are our brothers, and we have allowed them to live in a peaceful manner." According to Jalal Khan, the people who were freed after the handover of Kandahar in late 2001 promised that they would not participate in politics. By the end of 2001, reports suggested that most of the important leaders of the Taliban had either managed to escape to Pakistan or were hiding inside Afghanistan. Mullah Abdul Samad Khaksar, who served as the deputy minister of the interior during the Taliban period, but who was allegedly an agent of the United Front, named several top members of the Taliban administration who had moved to Pakistan and were "living in luxury in fine houses."[14]

Such news did not, however, prompt a reversal of Karzai's attempts at reconciliation. In an unheralded speech before an audience of religious scholars in Kabul in April 2003, Karzai officially announced his policy to make a distinction between two categories of the Taliban. A "clear line" had to be drawn between "the ordinary Taliban who are real and honest sons of this country" and those "who still use the Taliban cover to disturb peace and security in the country," Karzai told the gathering of the Islamic scholars. No one had "the right to harass/persecute any one under the name of Talib/Taliban anymore." John Heller, a freelance journalist who frequented Afghanistan soon after the establishment of the Interim Authority, reported that while in Pakistan earlier that month, Karzai had demanded that Islamabad arrest key Taliban leaders to prevent cross-border terrorist activities but had offered amnesty to "thousands of ordinary Taliban" and asked them to return to Afghanistan. At the time Karzai's reconciliation policy was backed by the special representative of the United Nations secretary general for Afghanistan, Lakhdar Brahimi, who, without uttering the "T-word," told the UN Security Council in May that "those who did not oppose the peace process and who were committed to non-violent means must be provided with political space and equal opportunities, regardless of their political or ethnic affiliation, to help the peace process along."[15] The United States also supported this process, though its initial approval was unofficial.

In the former mujahedin camp, however, this offer of reconciliation caused furious reactions. The United Front, whose members were the most important elements within the Afghan administration at the time, was fiercely against this olive branch to the Taliban. They had fought against the Taliban regime and had successfully removed them from power. The assimilation of former Taliban, predominantly Pashtuns, into the political sphere challenged the United Front's nascent political authority and appeared to present Pashtuns with an opportunity to reassert their dominance in Afghan politics. One of the United Front's newspapers, *Payam-e Mojahed* (the mouthpiece of the Jamiat-e Islami party's chief ideologue, Hafizullah Mansur), called Karzai's proposal "a betrayal of Islam, betrayal of the nation, betrayal of humanity." Students demanded that Karzai step down. According to diplomats in Kabul, the Jamiat-e Islami–dominated National Security Department had a hand in the organization of these student protests.[16]

In October 2003, rumors circulated that the United States had released the highest-ranking member of the Taliban regime in its custody, former foreign minister Mullah Wakil Ahmad Mutawakkil. Mutawakkil had been considered a moderate voice within the Taliban structure and, during his tenure as the Taliban's foreign minister, had attempted to improve the relations between the Taliban regime and the United States, according to Wahid Muzhda's account. The presence of al-Qaeda in Afghanistan, however, had thwarted his plans. Because of Mutawakkil's efforts while foreign minister, Osama bin Laden repeatedly stated that "two entities were opposed to his jihad: the United States and the Foreign Ministry of the Taliban."[17] At the outset, Karzai categorically denied reports of Mutawakkil's release.[18] Afghan Foreign Ministry spokesman Muhammad Omar Samad, who belonged to the United Front, went a step further by ruling out the possibility that any negotiation between his government and former members of the Taliban regime had occurred, citing that regime's inhumane policies. However, the country's chief justice, Mawlawi Fazl Hadi Shinwari, a conservative Pashtun, while admitting he had no specific information concerning Mutawakkil's release, added that "no matter who is pleased and who is not . . . talks with the Taliban . . . have begun."[19]

While recognizing the controversy sparked by his reconciliation efforts, Karzai pressed ahead with promoting inclusion of former Taliban in the political process. In February 2004, Karzai said that he was considering meeting the former Taliban foreign minister.[20] In April, while visiting his native Kandahar, he called on former Taliban members to participate in Afghanistan's presidential and parliamentary elections. "If the rest of the people—Taliban or non-Taliban, especially those in the Taliban—want to come and live in this country, if they want to work and farm here, they are most welcome. This is their country, their home. Our dispute is only with those who destroy Afghanistan, who blow up bombs and who, with the support of foreigners, bring destruction here," Karzai said. He added that only a few hard-core members of the Taliban were unworthy of rehabilitation. "Our problem is mainly with the top Taliban—who may number no more than 150 people—who had links with al-Qaeda," Karzai stressed, referring to this small group as "enemies of Afghanistan."[21] Around the same period, through its ambassador to Kabul and special presidential envoy, Zalmay Khalilzad, the United States began to place its support openly behind Karzai's call for the reintegration of former members of the hard-line group into Afghan society.

Karzai's motivation for the general amnesty seemed odd at the time, given U.S. support in the fight against the Taliban. Karzai's strategy of strengthening his political position among the various competing political factions by publicly extending an offer of reconciliation to most members of the Taliban regime gave further currency to the charge that the Karzai administration viewed the Taliban's past as neither reprehensible nor reproachable. Karzai did not call to account those who committed atrocities through some form of a reconciliation process; instead, he welcomed them to the political discussion. It seems that Karzai used this amnesty to reach out to the former opposition to bridge the differences and bring into the fold those opposed to this new government. Also as a man with a minimal personal support base among Afghans in general, and his own Pashtuns in particular, Karzai may have wished to foster the backing of southern Pashtuns as a counterweight against the forces of the United Front, who were clearly on the ascendance. What is clear is that this amnesty afforded members of the fallen regime the opportunity to either regroup or recalibrate their political, cultural, and religious ideologies.

In its initial months in office, the Afghan Interim Authority could do no wrong in the eyes of its foreign backers. In March 2002, the U.S.-led Operation Enduring Freedom finished its last major conventional battle, Operation Anaconda. The main targets of this operation had been Osama bin Laden and other senior leaders of al-Qaeda, many of whom remained uncaptured. While announcing the completion of the operation, U.S. Air Force General John W. Rosa Jr. announced that as part of Operation Enduring Freedom, the coalition was "still actively" pursing al-Qaeda and Taliban personnel "throughout" Afghanistan.[22] By November the United States had already declared a shift to the reconstruction phase of engagement, in "at least three-quarters" of the country.[23] As part of the policy to provide security for reconstruction projects, initial deployments of U.S.-led coalition forces entered into southeastern Afghanistan, mainly Paktya Province, to quell the budding anti-Karzai activities. A December 2002 United Nations report indicated that al-Qaeda was regrouping and forming some training bases in the eastern region of Afghanistan, close to the border with Pakistan.[24]

In a November 2002 speech in New York, Hamid Karzai paid tribute to his people's efforts in rebuilding the country during Afghanistan's first year of independence following the fall of the Taliban. He appealed to other countries in the region to desist from interfering in Afghan affairs and give the country a chance to prosper. "I hope our neighbors will leave us alone. And I hope Osama [bin Laden] will leave us alone."[25] Both of Karzai's hopes were to be dashed in the following year.

In December a suicide bomber attacked the main base of the International Security Assistance Force (ISAF) on the outskirts of Kabul, killing two Afghan interpreters and wounding two French soldiers. Afghan Deputy Minister of the Interior Helaluddin Helal blamed al-Qaeda and claimed that two Pakistanis had been arrested in connection with the attack and had confessed that they had been sent to Afghanistan along with a group of Arabs, Chechens, and other Pakistanis to carry out such attacks.[26] However, ISAF's spokesman, Turkish colonel Samet Oz, said the bombing did not appear to be the "carefully planned and executed work of a professional terrorist organization."[27]

In 2003, sporadic attacks against aid workers, Afghan officials, and U.S.-led coalition forces became more customary. Aid agencies in particular began worrying about their presence in the country, especially in southern and southeastern Afghanistan. In January a clandestine radio station calling itself Voice of Afghan Resistance began random broadcasts in Paktya airing fatwas against Karzai's authority.[28] The security situation throughout the country, especially along Afghanistan's border with Pakistan, began to deteriorate as the year progressed. By midyear, firefights, explosions, and car bombings had increased in frequency without much apparent coordination or claims of responsibility.

In June a suicide attacker crashed his car into a bus carrying German troops attached to ISAF in Kabul, killing four and injuring more than twenty. This attack, for which no one claimed responsibility, highlighted the reach of the resistance and its chameleon-like operations and further heightened outsiders' confusion regarding its identity. Karzai initially argued that the suicide-killer was likely not an Afghan and that the planners of the attack were probably foreigners. However, Afghan interior minister Ali Ahmad Jalali identified the suicide bomber as an Afghan man named Abdul Rashid from the Khogiani district of Nangarhar Province. German defense minister Peter Struck blamed the attack on al-Qaeda and said that it was likely that financial and logistical backing came from elements loyal to the ousted Taliban regime as well as Gulbuddin Hekmatyar, the former prime minister during the mujahedin period and radical leader of the political party Hizb-e Islami.[29]

Afghan authorities blamed the majority of these disruptive campaigns on former Taliban members, al-Qaeda, and Hekmatyar, while increasingly pointing the finger of accusation toward Pakistan. In reality, the situation proved far more complicated. Both local and foreign elements were finding reasons to reignite the Afghan conflict. Some of the battles were the result of warlords settling old accounts, fighting to reclaim or gain new turf or control over the poppy fields.[30] In some cases, initial allies of Karzai resorted to violence to demonstrate their displeasure with the new government. Elements within the former Taliban regime, al-Qaeda, and Hekmatyar's party contributed to the rising violence and insecurity. Other players also began to surface and claim responsibility for attacks. New styles of violence with new rallying cries emerged. Something new and very violent had arrived on the scene.

Questions began to arise as the opposition became more vocal and violent and began aligning itself with the former regime. How was this possible? Was this the dreaded Taliban regime? Who would want its return? The story of the Karzai amnesty suggested an answer. The willingness of the authorities in Kandahar to participate in the general amnesty, and the fact that they allowed the former leaders of the Taliban regime to return to their homes and villages or cross over to neighboring Pakistan with impunity, demonstrated that not all Afghans regarded the Taliban as unfavorably as did the international press or community. Key clues to their behavior can be found in Afghanistan's history.

The vast number of Pashtuns did not hold the same opinion as the international community about the Taliban. While the Pashtuns may not have supported all the platforms and ideologies of the Taliban, they appreciated the position of power the Pashtun-dominated Taliban held over the population. With the arrival of Karzai and the Interim Authority, the Pashtuns lost the political influence to which they were accustomed.

In the wake of the political vacuum created by the downfall of the Taliban in December 2001, the Pashtuns realized that the new system being established in Afghanistan, despite being led by a Pashtun, did not direct governing power to the Pashtuns as a group, but rather sought to set up an interim governing system that was not based solely on ethnicity. The new government had a strong sponsor in the United States and garnered much international support, as the majority of the international community had not approved of the Taliban rulers, who defined their rule by very conservative Pashtun traditions. The Pashtuns' sense of entitlement was not placated by the fact that the president of the Interim Authority, Hamid Karzai, was one of their own. Not only was Karzai viewed as an impotent figurehead surrounded by foreigners and non-Pashtuns, but many Pashtuns also blamed him for facilitating the ultimate ascent of non-Pashtuns to power in Afghanistan. Karzai came to be seen as the front man, or the legitimizing factor, for other individuals within the United Front.

To his critics, this facade was clear, and people from all sides began openly criticizing and even threatening Karzai. Non-Pashtuns accused him of being soft on the Taliban and of lacking legitimacy to rule the country, whereas Pashtuns were unhappy because they felt he was pandering to the powerful Tajiks of the United Front's "Supervisory Council" (Shura-ye Nezar), a loose group formed around the former Afghan defense minister and celebrated commander Ahmad Shah Masud. Karzai's authority and ability to centralize power were challenged by the presence in Kabul of forces loyal to the Shura-ye Nezar. The subsequent refusal by that group's military leader, Marshal Muhammad Qasim Fahim, to withdraw his forces from the capital blatantly flouted Karzai's governing authority. Barnett R. Rubin remarked that this was the "first major violation" of the Bonn Agreement, which stipulated that Kabul should be free of factional Afghan military forces.[31] It was also the first major threat to Karzai's efforts to unify Afghanistan as a nation-state.

For the Pashtuns, already skeptical of the Bonn process, it symbolized their marginalization in the power process. The Shura-ye Nezar's insistence on maintaining its military units in Kabul, as well as the U.S. policy of using various militia forces in its operations against the remnants of the Taliban and al-Qaeda, deprived the Pashtuns of their historical sense of entitlement as the main source for Afghan military forces. What came to be known as the Afghan Militia Forces (also referred to as the Afghan Military Forces) was composed primarily of non-Pashtuns. These forces were engaged in battles with the remnants of the Taliban and their Pashtun sympathizers. These forces were eventually absorbed into the Afghan National Army (ANA). Between the initiation of ANA recruitment in mid-2002 and 2004, there arose a disparity in ethnic representation within the leadership of the ANA, which further entrenched the idea of marginalization in the minds of the Pashtuns. Although Pashtuns made up 40 percent of the population of Afghanistan and accounted for more than 52 percent of ANA troops, only about 36 percent of the noncommissioned officers (NCOs) and 32 percent of officers were Pashtun. In comparison, the Tajiks, who constituted roughly 25 percent of the Afghan population and 37 percent of ANA troops, made up 53 percent of NCOs and almost 56 percent of officers.[32] According to Antonio Giustozzi, the "superiority of the Tajik militias certainly helped them to retain more officers [within the ANA], but the discrepancy is so great that allegations of deliberate ethnic cleansing of the recruits acquire some credibility."[33]

The Pashtuns felt further sidelined by the Shura-ye Nezar's capture of key positions in the interim government. Throughout the modern history of Afghanistan, whoever has controlled Kabul has been viewed as the ruler of the country. The fact that Marshal Muhammad Qasim Fahim became the defense minister and his colleagues Abdullah Abdullah and Muhammad Yunos Qanuni took the foreign and interior ministries, respectively, demonstrated that this new governing system did not perpetuate the Pashtun dominance within the political system. While the Tajik-dominated Shura-ye Nezar and other factions within the United Front were basking in their achievements and expanding their zones of power, the collapse of the Taliban and the rise of the Interim Authority under the Bonn process "left most Pashtuns without a stake in the political process."[34]

Pashtuns' feeling of political impotence was coupled with their sense of helplessness in the face of attacks against Pashtuns in the northern parts of Afghanistan and frustration from their perception of being unjustly targeted by coalition forces in counterinsurgency attacks. Some Pashtuns were being classified as Taliban sympathizers, regardless of whether they supported the ousted regime, and thus were subjected to attacks. In a 2002 report on abuses against Pashtuns in northern Afghanistan, Human Rights Watch documented "widespread looting and extortion of Pashtun communities" as well as "killings, rapes and abductions." One of the report's findings is crucial to understanding the nature of the anti-Pashtun activities in areas where Pashtuns were a minority. The report points out that atrocities against Pashtuns "[took] place against the background of a legacy of Taliban atrocities."[35] While the graver retribution crimes have since subsided, Pashtuns in northern and western Afghanistan continue to live with the stigma of the Taliban and remain politically excluded.

Especially during the early stages of the U.S.-led military campaign in Afghanistan, the Pashtuns felt that the coalition forces sought them out specifically, unjustly targeting them as threats to the new governing process based solely on their ethnicity. Some of these attacks appeared to have resulted from an overall lack of cultural and historical awareness about Afghanistan, false information, and carelessness. For example, at the beginning of the war the U.S. special forces group Task Force 121, which was assigned to find high-valued targets, was "using 19th-century British anthropology to prepare for Afghanistan."[36] The U.S. military gradually has become more culturally adept and has paid more attention to cultural aspects of the Afghan war, but the initial engagement left its mark. Allegations have also circulated that some attacks against Pashtuns resulted from malicious intent on the part of the United Front or even rival Pashtuns providing false intelligence to the coalition. Additionally, the

United States, which carried out the bulk of aerial campaigns in Afghanistan, has acknowledged past mistakes. On one occasion, angry members of a tribe who had lost members during an erroneous U.S. bombing raid reportedly killed a U.S. soldier, the first to die in Operation Enduring Freedom.[37] In 2003, Colonel Roger King, a spokesman for the U.S. forces in Afghanistan, conceded making mistakes and assured the Afghan authorities that the U.S. was no longer launching "attacks on a single source of intelligence because people have their own reasons for telling us things."[38] These attacks and actions nonetheless reinforced the view within the Pashtun community that this new government was not favorable to Pashtuns and would not afford Pashtuns the political power they deserved. The sentiment of Pashtun disillusionment was captured by Sayyed Ishaq Gailani, a Pashtun religious and political leader, when he told the Brussels-based International Crisis Group (ICG) in 2003, "Bonn had created the false hope that some form of political power will be transferred to the majority Pashtuns. That didn't happen."[39]

There was another opportunity to ease some of the Pashtuns' sense of marginalization with the advent of the Loya Jirga (Grand Assembly). A sense began to emerge early in 2002 among many Pashtuns, including members of Karzai's administration and even Karzai himself, that without the support of a majority of the Pashtuns, governing Afghanistan could only be done by reliance on foreign force. Moreover, such a government, lacking legitimacy among 40 percent or so of the Afghan population, would be at best fragile and at worst unsustainable in the long run. Karzai's first opportunity to put this thinking into action came during the June 2002 Emergency Loya Jirga. The Loya Jirga was to transfer power from the Interim Authority to the Transitional Administration. The Loya Jirga selected Karzai, a Pashtun, as head; however, it failed to repair the ethnic imbalance in the cabinet. The only significant change made to the cabinet was the selection of Taj Muhammad Wardak, a Pashtun, to replace Interior Minister Qanuni, who remained in the cabinet as minister of education and special advisor to Karzai on security matters. One key aspiration of the ordinary Pashtuns was calculated to have been the appointment of the former Afghan monarch Muhammad Zaher to a prominent role within the Transitional Administration. Prior to the Loya Jirga the ICG wrote, "There will be deep Pashtun discontent if Muhammad Zaher is excluded from playing an important role."[40] After the Loya Jirga, Pashtun military commanders interviewed by the ICG said that they had pinned their hopes for "reclaiming lost ground in Kabul on the former King's candidacy to head the Transitional Administration." An unidentified delegate to the Loya Jirga stated, "The unceremonious manner in which . . . [the former King] was shown the exit . . . created the impression that the Loya Jirga was a rubber-stamp for the Panjshiri-dominated Interim Authority." Rasul Amin, who served as the education minister during the Interim Authority, told the ICG, "The perception that Karzai had betrayed his ethnic Pashtuns is now firmly in the minds of the Pashtuns."[41]

The sense of alienation and failure to secure an amicable result during the Loya Jirga further underscored the Pashtuns' impotence in the new governing process. This, combined with being the target of repeated attacks on property and person, could explain how resistance to the new government could swell. While there is no solid evidence that the Pashtuns in this current mindset looked upon the former Taliban regime with a sense of nostalgia, one could understand how this community might reflect on the days when their community was in power and seek to reassert their control. The fact that, due to the general amnesty, there were those who held to the Taliban ideologies freely in their midst, it is not so far-fetched to suppose that some of the more extreme Pashtuns began to align themselves with

these individuals to fight against a government they felt had excluded
them. The environment was ripe for the resurgence of the former regime or factions within it.

Unlike the arrival of the Taliban, this resistance to the new government did not emerge as a cohesive group with a uniform mission.
Instead, a series of disparate events gave rise to the concept of resistance. As the events unfolded, Afghan authorities, various warlords working under official auspices, and the Western supporters of
the post-Bonn administrations attempted to identify or characterize
those involved in the opposition. The Taliban, as the ousted regime,
was the mostly likely candidate; however, it became apparent that the
resistance went beyond the confines of the former regime's agenda
and organization. There did not appear to be an umbrella organization or a centralized body directing activities, but instead several independent groups loosely linked by their drive to oust the foreign
forces in order to establish their own strongholds of power.

Much confusion surrounds the identity of the opposition. Its organization can be described as, at best, haphazard.[42] But it appears
questionable whether these opposition groups in general obey or
have respect for Mullah Omar as a leader. During the early days of
the Taliban movement, Mullah Omar's simplicity of lifestyle and
participation in the military activities of the group afforded the leader
of the Taliban almost legendary qualities. Initially the Taliban declared that their goal was to rid the country of factionalism and the
rule of warlords. Ruling the country was not the objective. However,
in 1996 Mullah Omar proclaimed himself *Amir al-Muminin* (Commander of the Faithful), thereby declaring himself the ruler of Afghanistan. This assumption of power changed the internal structure
of the Taliban movement from loose pockets of fighters led by a consultative council, in which Mullah Omar was *primus inter pares,* into

a theocratic regime increasingly ruled with secrecy and terror. No longer was their leader accessible to the people. As Mullah Omar became more radical and detached from his people, his image began to erode.[43]

There are a few reports from within the opposition claiming the existence of a central council under the leadership of Mullah Omar; however, the reality, as gauged from the movement's activities and statements, is most likely that there are small bands of people led by local leaders who may at times coordinate their activities with other bands. They unite only in mission, to rid Afghanistan of foreign forces and to establish an Islamic state based on sharia. They believe that those who support the policies of the United States in Afghanistan are guilty and are offending Islam. The difference lies in both their goals and their methods.

Absent a single, unifying voice, many figures have announced their underground presence as spokesmen for those opposing the new government and its foreign backers. Some who speak on behalf of the opposition claim to be Taliban but, in fact, maintain ideas foreign to them. Such groups reveal much about the character of the opposition. Their words demonstrate the lack of a single entity spearheading a cohesive guerrilla operation and expose the factional nature of their efforts.

In their proclamations these spokesmen reveal the nature of the individual groups fighting under the common mission. Their declarations suggest a division between, on the one hand, those who concentrate their energies on Afghanistan and limit their activities to those that might result in their coming to power in Afghanistan, and, on the other hand, those who, under the influence of foreign governments or the international Islamist movement, identify their struggle as a global plan with little regard to Afghanistan or its people. One of the many figures identifying themselves as the official spokesman for the Taliban, Hamid Agha, announced in an April 2004 statement faxed to a Pakistani daily that if Karzai is serious about bringing peace and stability to Afghanistan, he should ask the United States to withdraw its troops from Afghanistan, stop bombing Afghan villages, and end victimizing those Afghans who support the Taliban. Karzai "should initiate release of those Afghans, whose ages are beyond 80 years and are languishing in [Guantanamo prison in] Cuba," the statement added.[44] What is of interest here are the goals outlined in this communication. Hamid Agha's requests were based on Afghan concerns and confined to the Afghan theater. His tone and the list of demands could have very well been made by a legitimate Afghan political organization, or even privately by Karzai himself.

In contrast, in March 2004 the Center for Islamic Studies and Research, a Web-based organization with al-Qaeda connections, posted on its website a taped message from an unidentified Afghan opposition member, purportedly representing the Taliban. The speaker initially recounted the aims of the Islamic Emirate of Afghanistan. The Islamic Emirate was created by Mullah Omar to establish a government based on sharia and to remove "all aspects and symbols of polytheism and superstition from the Afghan society." The Taliban aspired to "[revive] the spirit of jihad in the [Afghan] people against the U.S., the Crusaders and their agents."[45] The list goes on to include the defense of al-Aqsa Mosque in Jerusalem; support for Muslims in Chechnya, Kashmir, and Myanmar; and the sheltering of "immigrants and mujahedin" such as bin Laden and his group. The speaker added that Mullah Omar sacrificed his power and army, but refused to hand over al-Qaeda leaders to the United States. The speaker concluded that Mullah Omar instructed Mullah Obaidullah, the former Taliban defense minister, and Mullah Baradar to rearrange the organization of mujahedin groups against Karzai's administration and his foreign backers, namely, the United States.[46] They reportedly formed part of a ten-member leadership council established by Mullah Omar.[47] This opposition position goes beyond the Afghan theater and represents an ideology similar to universalist Islamist organizations such as al-Qaeda.

The varied opposition groups' tactics also reflect ideological differences. A look at three distinct reactions to the murder of Bettina Goislard, a French national working for the United Nations High Commissioner for Refugees in Ghazni in November 2003, illustrates the distinct motivations of the different groups. On November 19, following Goislard's murder, Abdul Samad, purporting to speak on behalf of the Taliban, said that his organization killed the French woman because she was spying on members of the Taliban.[48] On the same day, Akbar Agha claimed to speak in the name of the "Taliban Movement's Army of Muslims." He told an Arabic-language daily, without any reference to Goislard's case, that his organization was attacking foreign aid organizations because they were "an extension of the foreign occupation and are carrying out a dangerous proselytizing role."[49] However a day later, Hamid Agha, the self-identified official Taliban spokesman discussed above, rejected the claim made by Abdul Samad. He asserted via fax that statements regarding the killing of Goislard attributed to a Taliban spokesman—himself—were baseless.[50] He added that the Taliban had never targeted, nor ever would target, the employees of relief organizations who were there to help reconstruct the country and serve the people of Afghanistan.

Almost three years later, internal contradictions among the neo-Taliban remained, most likely because of miscommunication among various members of the movement and the lack of a central ideology and policy governing the neo-Taliban. On September 10, 2006, a suicide bomber killed Paktya governor Hakim Taniwal and three other people. Soon after the attack, Muhammad Hanif, speaking in the name of the Taliban, claimed responsibility for the attack, adding that the suicide attack was "carried out by a resident of Paktya, namely Gholam Gol."[51] On the same day, the website purporting to represent the Islamic Emirate of Afghanistan posted a report confirming Muhammad Hanif's claim and identifying the suicide attacker as a "heroic mujahed, seeker of knowledge [*talib al-ilm*] of the Islamic Emirate"—using the term *talib* in its traditional linguistic, not political, meaning.[52] The next day, another suicide bomber targeted a number of Afghan security officials attending Taniwal's funeral in Khost province, killing six people. Again the purported website of the Islamic Emirate of Afghanistan immediately claimed responsibility for carrying out the attack. However, at the same time, in a different venue, Muhammad Hanif expressed his "strong condemnation," adding that the Taliban movement did not carry out the attack on the funeral.[53] A number of the neo-Taliban militants and sympathizers might well have viewed the assassination of Taniwal as legitimate. He was a close confidant of Karzai. These militants, having been indoctrinated by the global jihadists, view any opportunity to strike at an enemy not only as legitimate, but also as their duty. However, others within their ranks held to their Pashtun tribal norms, which would generally prohibit an attack on the attendees of any funeral service. Thus, differences and internal contradictions continued.

As different spokesmen continued to emerge, the obvious lack of coordination, uniformity of activities and goals, and organization exposed the power struggles and the absence of a strong, centralized movement. In June 2003, Muhammad Mokhtar Mujahed, claiming to be the spokesman for the Taliban, announced the formation of a ten-member Leadership Council. According to Mujahed, eight of the ten people in the council were from Kandahar, and one each from Paktya and Paktika provinces.[54] He asserted that everyone in the movement accepted the leadership of Mullah Omar. Three months later, claiming to be speaking as the spokesman of the Taliban, Hamid Agha also reported the establishment of a ten-member Leadership Council under the chairmanship of Mullah Omar.[55]

Besides Mujahed and Hamid Agha, others have claimed to speak for the movement, often in contradictory terms. Mullah Abdul Samad, Muhammad Amin, Saif al-Adl, Ustad Muhammad Yaser, Mufti Latifullah Hakimi, Muhammad Hanif, Muhammad Yusof Ahmadi, and Zabiullah Mujahed have also identified themselves as Taliban spokesmen, while a number of other individuals have claimed to speak on behalf of the Taliban in capacities as commanders or other functionaries. In February 2004, refuting comments by Saif al-Adl, the Taliban faxed a statement to several news organizations naming Hamid Agha as the movement's only authorized spokesman.[56] Yet, later in 2004, Hakimi emerged as the primary voice of the Taliban and, unlike Hamid Agha, who usually contacted sources by fax, Hakimi began giving telephone interviews, initially with Pakistan-based news organizations and then to other outlets, including Western and Kabul-based media. In December 2004 the Peshawar-based Afghan Islamic Press quoted Hakimi as saying that Muhammad Yaser "has replaced Hamed Agha as the head of the Taliban cultural council." According to *Islam*, a jihadist daily published in Karachi, Muhammad Yaser was appointed in January 2005 as the chief spokesman for the Taliban and Hakimi was made his assistant. Whereas Muhammad Yaser has occasionally appeared on an Arabic television network, Hakimi acted as the main voice of the Taliban from the latter half of 2004 until his arrest by Pakistani authorities in October 2005.[57] Since Hakimi's arrest, Muhammad Hanif and Muhammad Yusof Ahmadi became the most visible voices for the Taliban, until Muhammad Hanif was arrested in January 2007.[58]

It would be erroneous to claim that the former Taliban rulers who took advantage of the general amnesty did not individually plan some sort of political activity. Many who formerly aligned themselves with the Taliban remained outside of the political process. However, those who chose to enter did not do so as a single front. As early as December 2001, rumors of activities attributed to the leaders of the fallen regime began circulating, and many began discussing the future of the movement despite the fact that most former members were on the run.

Two streams of thought held by those close to the Taliban regime began to materialize: one focused on gradually gaining political influence, the other on jihad. Those on the first path, such as Mullah Agha Jan Motasem, who served as the finance minister under the Taliban, wanted to work within the nascent system to influence the unfolding political process. Motasem apparently stated from an undisclosed hideout inside Afghanistan that if the Bonn Agreement led to the establishment of a "strong Islamic government" in Afghanistan, the Taliban would not "resort to any kind of activities against" it. He even offered advice to the United States, that "if the Americans have really come to Afghanistan to help the Afghans, then it is necessary for their troops to leave" the country and for Washington to allow the Afghans to form their own government without interference.[59] Motasem's views could be regarded as comments from a man with no influence, but they can also be seen as the beginning of the reemergence of the Taliban's political platform calling for the establishment of an "Islamic Republic."

Those former Taliban opposing the new government and calling for jihad allegedly issued a fatwa, dated February 17, 2003, and signed "Amir al-Muminin, the Servant of Islam, Mullah Muhammad Omar Mujahed." It proclaimed that some sixteen hundred "prominent scholars from around Afghanistan" had agreed that it was every Muslim's duty to wage jihad "at a time when America has invaded Islam's limits and the Muslim and oppressed nation of Afghanistan." The fatwa warned that anyone who "helps the aggressive infidels and joins their ranks under any name or task" deserved death. It further specified that after the issuance of the fatwa, people working with the coalition or the Afghan administration would "be considered as Christians by God and the Muslims," and that they would face punishment "in accordance with human society and by the mujahed[in?] of Islam and the scholars." The statement appealed to "the Muslim people of Afghanistan" to either wage jihad against the U.S. forces or, if they were unable to join in the struggle, to separate themselves from the Americans, "their allies and their puppet government . . . so that Muslims are differentiated from Christians."[60] According to information provided by the Pakistani Islamist group Jama'atul Dawa, Mullah Omar had by January 2003 already regrouped the ranks of his movement by assigning people to head operations in thirteen provinces to increase attacks on the United States and its allies in Afghanistan.[61]

A second fatwa from Mullah Omar and his supporters arrived on April 1, 2003. Repeating the call to jihad against the United States following the invasion of Iraq, the new fatwa reportedly had the signatures of the former Taliban head and six hundred Afghan clerics. Mullah Omar wrote that the U.S. attacked Afghanistan because the Taliban regime sheltered Osama bin Laden, whom the Americans "alleged" to be a terrorist, but asked, "What crime did Iraq commit?" The leader of the Taliban regime added, "[in my] capacity as leader of Muslims, I rule [Arabic: *ufti*] that jihad against the U.S. troops is a duty. I also issue a fatwa ordering the murder of anyone who cooperates with the Americans." The fatwa concluded by arguing, "There are two poles in the world at present: Islam, which is symbol of peace, and Bush, who is the symbol of terror and hatred."[62]

In a statement congratulating the Afghans on the end of Ramadan in 2004, Mullah Omar promised to continue jihad against the United States and its "agents" in Afghanistan. He pointed in particular to the arrest of religious leaders, tribal elders, and mujahedin. "In addition to other crimes," he criticized "this atheism led by the American dictatorship [which] is trying to lead the Afghan people astray by different methods and different plans such as the Loya Jirga, the constitution, and the election process. Under these pretexts it wants to implement the moral corruption program of 'fake democracy.' The puppet administration and agents are installed to destroy the courage and belief of the Afghans, their faith and their morally clean society."[63] He went on to identify the high level of crime, the existence of adultery, consumption of alcoholic beverages, and other issues offensive to the common views of conservative Afghan men as vices of the Karzai regime.

At the same time, other calls for jihad surfaced outside the Taliban ranks. Just prior to Mullah Omar's Ramadan message, a hitherto unknown group calling itself Tazim al-Fatah Afghanistan (Afghanistan Victory Organization) issued a call for jihad against the U.S. forces in Afghanistan. On February 10, the group left their message in the form of a pamphlet at the Press Club in the Pakistani city of Chaman, near the Afghan border. Written in Pashto, this fatwa stated that because the U.S. forces had killed "thousands of Taliban and Arab mujadedin," it was the duty of Muslims to wage jihad against the United States. The Chaman fatwa also stipulated that those Muslims assisting the United States and its allies, naming only the United Kingdom, "in killing thousands of Taliban and Arab mujahedin, do not remain Muslims anymore and their murder is allowed in this great jihad." The Chaman fatwa did not carry any signatures but did end with the slogan "Long Live Gulbuddin Hekmatyar."[64] Was this a new group coalescing around the image of Hekmatyar, the former Afghan prime minister and head of his own branch of Hizb-e Islami? Or had the Tazim al-Fatah Afghanistan allied itself with Hekmatyar, who himself may have formed a coalition of sorts with the Taliban?

Hekmatyar and the Taliban leadership did not see eye to eye when the Taliban were in power. Hekmatyar was forced into exile following the Taliban victory in 1996. Pakistan's favorite Afghan client among the mujahedin leaders, Hekmatyar fell from grace in the mid-1990s when Islamabad found a more efficient ally in the Taliban. With little power remaining, he fled to Iran. However, soon after the collapse of the Taliban regime in December 2001, Hekmatyar said that he would call on not only the Taliban forces, but also "all the national and jihadi forces that resisted the Russian [Soviet] invasion and rejected any foreign interference" in Afghanistan's domestic affairs to oppose the presence of U.S. forces in the country.[65] In late 2002, reports emerged that despite their previous differences Mullah Omar and Hekmatyar had agreed to form a united front. Later that year, Hekmatyar declared a jihad to liberate Afghanistan from foreign domination and claimed he had formed an alliance with the Taliban and al-Qaeda.[66] Beginning in spring 2002, U.S. officials acknowledged a possible alliance between the former Taliban, al-Qaeda, and Gulbuddin Hekmatyar. The idea of a "triangle of terror" gradually gained more currency as Hekmatyar became more vocal about his anti-Western coalition sentiments. In February 2003 the United States designated Hekmatyar a terrorist for supporting "terrorist acts committed by al-Qaeda and the Taliban" but refrained from assigning the same label to his political party.[67]

Yet the degree of coordination between the former Taliban and Hizb-e Islami remained vague. Both the Taliban and Hekmatyar made contradictory claims about their alliance. In early 2003 Hekmatyar distanced himself from his statements of late 2002 and denied any coordination or partnership. Soon after the reports surfaced about the formation of an alliance between the former Taliban, al-Qaeda, and Hekmatyar, Hekmatyar denied the existence of such a front and stated that he wanted to make it clear that "neither in the past nor at present" had he or his party "reached any accord with the

Taliban."[68] He did express his desire to form a union with the two groups but stated that "unfortunately" such a front did not exist for reasons that he did not elucidate. However, in March 2007, when Hekmatyar offered to enter into discussions with the Karzai administration to bring about peace, Hekmatyar revealed that his party had had ties since 2003 with the Taliban but that it had severed them because "certain elements among the Taliban rejected the idea of a joint struggle against the aggressor"—the United States and its allies. "It was not a good move by the Taliban to disassociate themselves from the joint struggle," Hekmatyar added.[69]

While Hekmatyar may have been the best-known figure to flirt with joining the neo-Taliban, other individuals began to splinter off and create their own organizations. In August 2004, Saber Momen, who had served as a deputy operations commander for the opposition in southern Afghanistan, claimed that a breakaway faction called Taliban Jamiat Jaish-e Moslemin (Muslim Army of the Taliban Society) had split ranks with the rest of the movement. According to Momen, the new faction, led by Mullah Sayyed Muhammad Akbar Agha, was formed as a result of internal differences within the opposition and criticism of its poor leadership, which had resulted in serious losses to the group. The breakaway faction did not follow the leadership of Mullah Omar. Claiming to speak for the Taliban, Hamid Agha challenged the legitimacy of Jaish-e Moslemin, indicating that the new organization was "basically not the Taliban," since all "Taliban commanders are united under the leadership" of Mullah Omar.[70]

This new faction gained more prominence two months later when, in October 2004, unidentified gunmen in Kabul abducted three foreign nationals working for the UN-Afghan Joint Electoral Management Body in charge of monitoring Afghanistan's first post-Taliban presidential elections. The abductees included two women, from North-

ern Ireland and Kosovo, and a man from the Philippines. At the outset Muhammad Akbar Agha, calling himself the leader of Jaish-e
Moslemin, claimed responsibility for the kidnapping but did not set
any demands for the release of the captives.[71] The group's spokesman,
Mullah Muhammad Ishaq, called on the hostages' home countries to
withdraw their forces in exchange for the hostages. When informed
that neither Serbia and Montenegro nor the Philippines had any
troops in Afghanistan, he said that those "countries should condemn
the invasion [of Afghanistan] by other countries." On the same day,
Al-Jazeera television aired a video clip of the three UN employees,
adding that their kidnappers were demanding the release of all Afghan detainees held in U.S. custody at Guantanamo Bay and request-
ing that the United Nations declare "Britain and America's meddling
in Afghanistan illegal."[72]

Commenting on the kidnapping, the Taliban spokesperson Hakimi
claimed they had no information regarding the incident. Though
Hakimi expressed admiration for the kidnapping of the foreign election workers, he doubted that Jaish-e Moslemin was responsible for
it "because they are a very limited number of people and they don't
have access to Kabul to carry out operations." When asked what the
Taliban would have demanded for the release of the hostages, had
they been in their custody, Hakimi responded that the Taliban would
have demanded the release of the organization's "supporters" from
the U.S. detention center in Guantanamo Bay.[73]

The fact that Jaish-e Moslemin eventually included the release of
the Taliban prisoners in its list of demands possibly indicated that a
link existed between Jaish-e Moslemin and some members of the
Taliban. Another possibility, which became clearer after the hostages
were released, was that Jaish-e Moslemin was more interested in
gaining financially from the kidnapping. Their inability to articulate
their demands coherently in their public statements possibly led to

their taking inspiration from Hakimi's comments. Abdullah Lagh-mani, the Afghan government intelligence chief in Kandahar, said that Jaish-e Moslemin represented a split in the ranks of the Taliban. One group remained loyal to Mullah Omar, while another faction followed Muhammad Akbar. According to Laghmani, Muhammad Akbar's men have been operating in southern Afghanistan in cells of two or three individuals, a statement that corresponded to Hakimi's views regarding the Jaish-e Moslemin composition and areas of op-erations.[74]

Yet another splinter group of former Taliban members arrived on the Afghan political landscape shortly after the demise of the regime. According to John Heller, a group of former Taliban members es-pousing nonviolence emerged under the name Khaddam al-Furqan (Servants of the Koran).[75] In its early stages, the Khaddam al-Furqan was led by an Islamic cleric, Amin Mojaddedi. Later the leaders of the Khaddam al-Furqan were former Taliban education minister Arsala Rahmani and former deputy minister for information and cul-ture Abdul Rahman Hotak.[76] Just before the fall of the Taliban re-gime, Mojaddedi had issued a fatwa that referred to the enemies of the Taliban—the United Front—as "infidels" who could be slain with impunity. In a complete ideological turnaround, in 2002 Mo-jaddedi encouraged nonviolent political struggle. The stated policy of Khaddam al-Furqan was based on the rejection of the jihadist poli-cies of the Taliban and integration of the group into the political pro-cess in Afghanistan. As time passed, it became clearer that Khaddam al-Furqan was part of a larger reconciliation policy initially spear-headed in secret by Karzai.

Beyond negotiations with Mutawakkil and individual members of the ousted Taliban regime, the earlier rumors about the existence of Khaddam al-Furqan gave way to reality in early 2005 when four former members of the Taliban regime entered into talks with the

Karzai government. During the talks, one of the four people in-volved, the former unofficial representative of the Taliban regime to the United Nations, Abdul Hakim Mujahed, said that their group was not part of the Taliban but was representing Khaddam al-Furqan. Mujahed emphasized that the group no longer recognized Mullah Omar as their leader.[77]

Comparing the ideology of the neo-Taliban to that of the original Taliban movement, one similarity and several differences can be ob-served. Like their predecessors, the neo-Taliban base the legitimacy of their cause on divine law, as understood by them. They believe that it is divinely sanctioned that the sharia be implemented in the lands of Islam.

Originally the Taliban regime sought to establish power and create a strong Islamic country with viable commercial relations with its neighbors and the international community. The original Taliban ideology, at least among its leaders, grew out of experiences in the war against the Soviets and in refugee camps in Pakistan and from the teachings of foreign Islamists and interactions with individuals within the Pakistani government. Initially they gained a large degree of popular support in the Pashtun heartlands by bringing law and or-der. The Taliban consistently tried to convince the United States to recognize it as Afghanistan's legitimate government and to acknowl-edge the regime's peaceful intentions. The Taliban sought support from the United States during the well-known negotiations to con-struct a pipeline through Afghanistan.[78] In a letter sent to missions of a number of member states of the United Nations in New York in 1998, Abdul Hakim Mujahed stated that "[the] only position that any government of Afghanistan can take in order to maintain a long and lasting peace is one of mutual respect and noninterference with its neighbors." Terrorism was not only against Islam, Mujahed continued, but it was also "completely against the proud character and values of the Afghan people."[79] However, as the Taliban cemented their relationship with the pan-Islamist al-Qaeda leadership, the nature of the regime shifted to theocratic autocracy based on terror with a more pan-Islamist than Pashtun focus.[80] In retrospect, it is clear that al-Qaeda was not interested in Afghanistan as an end, but needed the country as a base for its global jihadist plans. Therefore it can be argued that al-Qaeda's main policy would have required keeping Afghanistan—that is, the Taliban regime—from ever becoming palatable internationally. It would not have served al-Qaeda's aims to have a self-sustaining, functional government in Afghanistan. Worse yet would have been international recognition and legitimatization of the Taliban regime, as this most likely would have translated into the exiting of the Arabs and their allies. An unproven theory suggests that some of the actions of al-Qaeda, specifically the terrorist attacks against U.S. embassies in Nairobi and Dar es Salaam in 1998 and the destruction of the Buddha statues in Bamyan in 2001, were in part an attempt to create a larger gap between the Taliban regime and the rest of the world, especially the West. In 1998 a consortium led by the U.S.-based company Unocal signed an agreement with the Taliban regime to build a gas pipeline from Turkmenistan to Pakistan, through Afghanistan, despite mounting opposition by international women's rights groups and other activists. This would have brought Afghanistan into the licit international hydrocarbons market and would have brought foreign investment to the country. Al-Qaeda could have seen this as a threat to their position within the Afghan power structure. The African embassy bombings prompted the United States to launch missiles into Afghanistan, the location from which al-Qaeda operated, and Unocal withdrew its support for the pipeline project—Afghanistan was now seen as a pariah. However, that gain for al-Qaeda was short-lived, as the United States continued to seek rapprochement with the moderates in the Taliban regime. The issue of poppy eradication in 1999–2000 brought the two parties together. To thwart the moderates and undermine the nascent and strained relationship between the two parties, al-Qaeda orchestrated a symbolic attack in March 2001 on cultural and religious symbols in Afghanistan—the two Buddha statues in Bamyan. The Taliban carried out the destruction; however, their actions were reportedly in response to Arab pressure. It is important to note that the Taliban had been in control of Bamyan since 1999 and could have destroyed the statues but had decided to let them stand. The fact that the Taliban changed their position provides a degree of currency to this unproven theory. The public outcry against the destruction of the statues certainly had the intended effect—if, indeed, al-Qaeda wanted to use the event to make the Taliban unapproachable. The Taliban received their worst press after this event, and not after their numerous atrocities against humans.

The neo-Taliban, by contrast, can be divided into two principal ideological groups. The first are those who align themselves with the al-Qaedaists and the views eventually adopted by Mulla Omar and the more radical Taliban toward the end of the Taliban regime. The other group of neo-Taliban seems to have gone back to their more traditional Pashtun roots and is trying to become a voice, not only for the Pashtuns, but also for traditionalist Muslims in Afghanistan. The latter category of the neo-Taliban draw their adherents from—and appeal to—a great number of alienated Pashtuns, a community that one CIA station chief has dubbed the "pissed-off Pashtuns."[81]

Which ideological front would prevail? By the latter part of 2004, it appeared that the more traditionalist Pashtun camp would predominate. According to rumors, Osama bin Laden planned to cut in half his aid to the resistance effort in order to channel more funds to the insurgents in Iraq. As bin Laden appeared to be shifting his attention away from Afghanistan to concentrate on Iraq, the more traditionalist camp within the neo-Taliban seemed to become more dominant. From the latter part of 2004, neo-Taliban statements generally suggested that a more traditionalist viewpoint was gaining ground.

While bin Laden's influence may have waned, the role of foreigners continued to play a central role in the evolution of the neo-Taliban. Contrary to what Karzai had hoped, foreigners have not afforded Afghanistan the time it has needed to develop into a functioning state. Both state and nonstate actors have found in Afghanistan a fertile ground for their activities. Foreign entities played a key role in the success of the Taliban movement and continue to play a significant role in the rise of the neo-Taliban.

While the original Taliban were backed financially and politically by Pakistan almost from the outset, the scope of the neo-Taliban's reliance on foreign patrons, both state and nonstate actors, is not totally transparent. Their influence cannot be underestimated, however. The neo-Taliban have acknowledged that there are foreign fighters in their ranks. Yet their identity remains shadowy. Most likely al-Qaeda has infiltrated the various neo-Taliban groups. While al-Qaeda had a prominent role in the Taliban regime, there is no evidence of concerted cooperation between al-Qaeda and the neo-Taliban in southern Afghanistan. But in eastern and northeastern Afghanistan, some neo-Taliban factions have resurrected old ties with al-Qaeda in search of funds, recruits, and technical support. Also, al-Qaeda's Iraqi branches have used the media to inspire the neo-Taliban and have provided support and training. In March 2006, speaking for the Taliban, Muhammad Hanif told an Italian newspaper that his movement had no "operational ties" to al-Qaeda, but added that the two organizations have "tactical alliances based on given circumstances and territorial situations." In his interview, Muhammad Hanif said that the

Taliban had no "specific strategy" but rather "adopted different tactics according to circumstances."[82]

At the same time, most of the state-sponsored support for the resistance emanates from Pakistan. The ousting of the Taliban left Pakistan's security vulnerable. Pakistan's strategic depth created by having a client regime in Kabul was reversed, and the new government did not assuage Pakistan's fears of being left exposed to threats from India. Islamabad has on a number of occasions since 2003 alleged that India is using Afghanistan as a base from which to interfere in Pakistan's internal affairs.[83] Islamabad is reluctant to allow Afghanistan to become a strong state with nationalistic agendas toward Pashtuns in Pakistan and strong ties with India. While Islamabad is fighting al-Qaeda as part of the global war on terror, it does not consider the neo-Taliban to be terrorists.[84] It sees the neo-Taliban as potential new allies who can further Pakistan's regional policies. What needs clarification is the extent to which various branches of the Pakistani government are actively involved in supporting neo-Taliban efforts. According to Seth G. Jones, by 2007 there was "virtual unanimity" among officials from the United States, NATO, the United Nations, and Afghanistan that Pakistan's Inter-Services Intelligence Directorate (ISI) "has continued to provide assistance to Afghan insurgent groups."[85]

The Afghan government has launched its own accusations against Pakistan and its apparent support for the destabilizing violence. It accused Pakistan of providing a safe haven to those whom Afghanistan considers terrorists and of serving as a base for the insurgency. In a speech in July 2003, Karzai said that the seeds of plans to radicalize the Afghan opposition and extremist foreign fighters still present in the region are "emerging within Pakistan."[86] According to Karzai, the reason for the continued assistance provided by Pakistan to the Afghan insurgency is to continue the "hidden invasion" of Afghani-

stan.[87] Meanwhile, as the two pivotal allies of the United States refuse to recognize each other as legitimate states and continue to point
fingers at each other in a ceremonial volley of accusations, the neo-
Taliban phenomenon is thriving—despite the efforts by NATO, and
despite their own disorganization and seeming lack of unified command and purpose.

Beyond Pakistan, Iran is also attempting to influence Afghanistan
both strategically and tactically. Although the official stance of the
Karzai administration is that Iran is not meddling in Afghanistan's
affairs, beginning in 2007 Afghan officials in the western provinces
began alleging that Iran was conducting incursions into Afghanistan,
violating Afghan airspace, and supporting terrorists in Iranian-oper-
ated camps. Unlike its reported involvement in Iraq, Tehran has not
created much noticeable trouble for foreign forces operating in Afghanistan; however, lack of action has not meant lack of resources.
Tehran has continued to cultivate political allies among diverse Afghan political groupings.[88] In the myriad groups forming the neo-
Taliban, Iran is also playing its own cards, further complicating the
nature of the Afghan opposition, the neo-Taliban.

Examining the current Afghan reality through the Taliban looking-
glass fails to capture the complexity of the emerging resistance. Unlike the Taliban regime, actors participating in this insurgency are not
a cohesive group under a single banner. Thus, the term *neo-Taliban*
has been coined to recognize that this new phenomenon encompasses both the past and new agendas, players, and engagement strategies. As the Afghan government and its supporters seek to curb the
violence, they must recognize that they are facing a complicated,
multifaceted enemy. It appears that any counterinsurgency strategy
that ignores the foreign influences and the domestic criminality rampant in Afghanistan will fail, because these finance and support the

resistance. As long as these latter realities remain within Afghanistan, there will always be disenfranchised, frustrated, or power-hungry populations who can be influenced to fight against stability.

There are those within the neo-Taliban who are more moderate and are seeking to become a voice in the political dialogue. As of 2004 they were gaining ground, but more recently the more violent contingent has regained prominence. By 2007, Afghanistan found itself again facing a fierce armed struggle throughout most of its territory, especially in the south and the east. Unlike in the initial stages of the resistance, the international community and the Afghan government have come to appreciate the complexity of the insurgent groups and their networks of support. No longer is it just a resurrection of the Taliban regime. They recognize it as multidimensional and an uncoordinated or quasi-coordinated alliance of forces. It is not only "Taliban" or those struggling to reinstate the Islamic Emirate of Afghanistan, but also those using the Taliban name to further their causes, such as disenchanted political personalities and groupings, centuries-old tribal rivals, and the foreign players—not limited to Pakistan—and their finance and support networks of druglords and warlords. These insurgents, or the neo-Taliban, continue to attempt to undermine the authority of the central government. Through daily acts of violence, the neo-Taliban are spreading fear and instability. This could breed hopelessness in the general population, who have supported the state-building process for the last six years. If Karzai and his foreign backers cannot incorporate some of the more moderate elements into the political system, and at the same time eradicate the domestic criminal networks, cut off the foreign lifelines, and isolate and defeat the remaining pockets of insurgency and terrorist elements, the Afghan government may lose the general population's support, as it seeks alternatives to improve its daily life. That is what the neo-Taliban are counting on.

Epilogue

Afghanistan and the Pax Americana

Atiq Sarwari and Robert D. Crews

The year 2001 has been remembered in the United States as a water-shed year. It recalls both 1941 and 1945, telescoping Pearl Harbor and victory in Europe and the Pacific into just three short months between the attacks of September 11 and the Taliban flight from their last refuge in Kandahar on December 7. From Washington's point of view, victory over al-Qaeda and the Taliban regime was un-expectedly swift and inexpensive. "In all," Bob Woodward writes in his insider's account, *Bush at War*, "the U.S. commitment to over-throw the Taliban had been about 110 CIA officers and 316 Special Forces personnel, plus massive airpower." The CIA spent only $70 million to reward Afghan militia leaders for fighting on the ground on behalf of the United States against the Taliban. The American commander in chief called it "one of the biggest 'bargains' of all time."[1]

The collapse of the Taliban regime generated dramatic symbols of liberation. Women raised their burqas to reveal their faces to journalists and photographers eager to tell their tale of suffering under the clerical regime. Music returned to enliven the bustling streets of Kabul and other urban centers. Boys and girls dreamed of reentering the classroom. Bollywood movies and televisions resurfaced from their hiding places. Afghans were now free to pursue traditional pastimes such as kite flying, bird keeping, and dog fighting without fear of the whip of the Taliban censor. The international community pledged several billion dollars in aid and launched Afghanistan on a path of reconstruction and democratization. Roads were paved, schools constructed, wells dug, and clinics opened. Refugees returned from abroad, the population of Kabul swelled, and newly bought cars and goods choked the streets of the capital. In 2004, Afghan men and women elected a president; in 2005 they chose representatives to serve in parliament and provincial councils.

With "Operation Enduring Freedom" the United States pledged to liberate the population of Afghanistan from the yoke of the Taliban. Having put an end to the Taliban regime, the United States also assumed primary responsibility for the rebuilding of a country ravaged by twenty-three years of nearly continuous war. In late 2001 and early 2002, Washington began to improvise the construction of a democratic and market-oriented state out of the rubble of a former haven for Osama bin Laden. Together with the amnesties proclaimed by Hamid Karzai, choices made by American elites would have a profound impact on Afghan politics for years to come. As a recent International Crisis Group report has concluded, the United States and its partners "opted for a quick, cheap war followed by a quick, cheap peace."[2]

Despite early White House pronouncements about a "Marshall Plan for Afghanistan," the American commitment to democratization and reconstruction ultimately followed a minimalist design that privileged military power over diplomatic and other strategies. Concerned with leaving a "light footprint," the Pentagon resorted to the use of small elite units. More important, it relied extensively on indigenous militia groups. The decision to engage these groups in both northern and southern Afghanistan—despite amply documented records of human rights abuses, drug and weapons trafficking, as well as ideological affinities with central aspects of Taliban rule—cast a deep shadow over subsequent state-building efforts.

The Americans claimed to be engaged in a "new kind of war." It was to be simultaneously a humanitarian intervention against the despotic Taliban and a precedent-setting action against the harboring of terrorists. Gradually the United States described the engagement as "nation-building" and "democratization" in the Muslim world. A wider view of American involvement reveals instead that Afghanistan's inclusion in the Pax Americana was marked less by a break from the past than by a deep continuity with older patterns of interaction between Afghanistan and the great powers. What haunted the Americans in Afghanistan was not simply the specter of the elusive neo-Taliban examined in this book by Amin Tarzi. Nor were vestiges of this lingering past solely the underlying social, ethnic, and political cleavages that both preceded and outlived the Taliban.

The inheritance of the Cold War determined the basic parameters—and limits—of the American project in Afghanistan. The lingering ghosts of the struggle against the Soviets included the American-backed mujahedin who turned against their former sponsors on September 11. The infrastructure of the Afghan civil war constructed by the superpowers also persisted. Land mines, unexploded ordinance, poisoned wells, destroyed roads, refugees, displaced persons, orphans, widows, and the maimed still disfigured the Afghan landscape. The personal networks forged with the support of the security forces of the superpowers survived as well. Besides al-Qaeda, more than a

dozen jihadist parties, all of whom at various times had received support from the governments of Pakistan, the United States, Saudi
Arabia, and other states, continued to link militants on both sides of
the Afghanistan-Pakistan border. Regional militias maintained their
political autonomy in the provinces. First formed in the 1980s, their
smuggling networks continued to flourish, moving opium and people,
including fighters, across mostly unguarded borders that stretch some
5,500 kilometers and adjoin six neighboring states.

The American vision for Afghanistan extended beyond the destruction of al-Qaeda and the Taliban. The ambitious campaign to
control, but also to improve, Afghanistan owed much to a deep-
rooted history. As the historian Odd Arne Westad has argued, for
countries of the "Third World" such as Afghanistan, "the continuum
in which the Cold War forms a part did not start in 1945, or even
1917, but in 1878—with the Conference of Berlin that divided Africa between European imperial powers—or perhaps in 1415, when
the Portuguese conquered their first African colony."[3] Washington
prescribed a formula for post-Taliban Afghanistan that resembled
American models for other countries where the United States had
intervened in the twentieth century. Viewed from Washington—as
well as from the social science departments of many American universities, Afghanistan needed modernization. Markets, elections, and
technological know-how would be introduced to transform Afghanistan and make it safe for America and the world. No longer aimed
against the Soviet foe, a policy of containment targeted a new enemy,
Islamist terror. But Afghanistan's role remained much the same as
in the late nineteenth and early twentieth centuries, the era of the
"Great Game" between the Russian and British empires for mastery
of Central Asia and the Middle East. No longer a buffer state between these empires, or later between the Soviets and the Americans,

a remade Afghanistan would now serve to protect the United States against terrorism.

For Afghans, too, this modernist agenda of developmental transformation was not entirely new. Beginning in the 1920s, Afghan monarchs built up the country's infrastructure and introduced a wide range of political and social reforms. Intellectuals proposed state-directed measures to improve the status of women, spread literacy, and improve agricultural production. In the 1950s, Kabul introduced economic planning, borrowing the Soviet model of the "five-year plan." Between 1957 and 1978, the Afghan government received over $750 million in aid from the Soviet Union, some $346 million from the United States, and 764 million Deutsche Marks from West Germany. The Soviets constructed roads, irrigation networks, mines, electricity stations, and airports, including those at Kabul and Bagram; the Americans built roads, schools, a university in Kabul, a dam on the Helmand River, and an airport at Kandahar; and the Germans initiated a development project in the eastern province of Paktya to modernize the local economy and integrate this border region more closely into the Afghan state.[4]

Following the coup of April 1978, the Afghan communists pledged, in the words of one of their Soviet counterparts, "to effect social, economic and cultural transformations . . . that would lead to the creation of a new and just democratic society in Afghanistan, where the exploitation of man by man, hunger, poverty, unemployment and illiteracy would be wiped out forever." The liberation of women was central to the communists' revolution. Their famous "Decree No. 7" of October 1978 promised to guarantee "equal rights of women with men" and to abolish "the unjust patriarchal feudalistic relations between husband and wife."[5] Thus within a twenty-five-year period Afghan women became the object of emancipation at the hands of four separate regimes: the communists, the mujahedin, the Taliban, and the American-led coalition all presented the amelioration of the plight of women as an obligation that made their rule legitimate.[6]

Like other Cold War–era superpower interventions and their colonial antecedents in the Third World, the American involvement in Afghanistan has yielded, in Westad's formulation, "a state of semi-permanent civil war."[7] One could tell this story through the history of the Red Army and its atrocities or, as Neamatollah Nojumi has shown in this book, through the mujahedin backed by the United States, Pakistan, Iran, Saudi Arabia, and other Muslim countries. A focus on the millions of land mines and poppy seeds laid in the wake of the Soviet invasion would also be revealing.

But the United States did not simply inherit what it found on the ground in Afghanistan in the fall and winter of 2001. It fostered conditions that reanimated the civil war and gave it a new direction in the post-Taliban era. If Latin America was a laboratory for the grand projection of American power on the global stage during the Cold War, post-Taliban Afghanistan served as a workshop for a new model of hegemony, one defined, above all, by its extreme minimalism.[8] Like American secretary of defense Donald Rumsfeld's vision of a compact, mobile army, this scheme sought to do much with little. In 2003, before the implications of this design became fully apparent, Washington exported many of its features to Iraq.

Actively undermining the resuscitation of the Afghan state, one of the hallmarks of this approach was the remilitarization of postwar politics. Rather than build up the capacity of civilian state institutions to provide security and social services, Karzai's American backers relied on proxy warriors and their own military forces to pursue a wide range of political aims. From the rearming of militias and the use of private security firms to the disbursement of aid through military personnel, the United States preferred militarized solutions to Afghan problems. Of these choices, arguably the most consequential was the continuous resort to air power—a strategy that facilitated the rapid projection of coalition power against insurgents but yielded numerous civilian casualties. Along with house-to-house searches, air strikes that failed to distinguish friend from foe turned many Afghan communities against foreign troops and the Afghan leader they backed in Kabul.

Another was the creation of an Afghan government whose sovereignty was circumscribed by numerous international actors, and by the Americans in particular. Americans, Italians, Germans, Canadians, Britons, Japanese, and other foreigners trained the army and police, provided reconstruction and humanitarian aid, and worked to reform government institutions. Agencies in Washington, rather than the Afghan Ministry of Finance, largely controlled how public expenditures were channeled in the country. Afghanistan emerged from the shadow of the Taliban as an American protectorate. The closest parallel may be found in those parts of colonial Africa where European states conjured up chieftainships to whom they assigned nearly autocratic authority over local subjects but whose power was never great enough to interfere with the political aims of their foreign patrons.

Beginning in 2001, Washington issued numerous promises about remaking Afghanistan. Yet, six years on, these vows have yielded few concrete changes in the lives of most Afghans. They are significant insofar as such pledges raised expectations that the United States, the international community, and the Karzai government proved unable to meet. As of mid-2007, electricity supplies to Kabul remained sporadic, despite the capital's status as the power base of Hamid Karzai and the hub of essential international aid organizations. Opium dominated the economy, and armed militias, including many recently backed by the United States, governed most of the country. And, as in 1994, the Taliban claimed to offer a solution to lawlessness, the corruption of officials and soldiers sent from the center, and the disillusionment with what many Afghans referred to as the "foreign occupation." "We have done much for the people," asserted Mullah Mansur Dadullah, a commander in southern Afghanistan in an interview in June 2007. "During our rule Afghans enjoyed what occupation troops from 42 countries have not been able to offer: security . . . [and] the dignity of Muslims was protected."[9]

Driven primarily by the desire to guard American security, Washington's design for stabilizing and transforming Afghanistan entailed the least expensive investments its policy makers could devise. Sporadic and punitive displays of lethal military force became their primary instruments, though these, too, yielded neither stability nor control. The Pax Americana had mobilized numerous and varied opponents but won over few supporters, creating conditions for the reanimation of the neo-Taliban and other oppositional groups.

Many of the basic structural features of the Afghan crisis were consolidated, and still others were created, during the first twenty or so months of the American intervention. Most of these, in turn, flowed from the initial military campaign. U.S. dependence on northern anti-Taliban militias, which seized Kabul on November 13, to do the limited fighting that occurred on the ground dictated the shape of the new government. These included some of the same Islamist figures, with backgrounds in drugs and arms trafficking, that the United States had backed against the Soviets. Despite this interdependence, relations were often strained. Many of the Americans involved in negotiations with them viewed their partners with disdain, calling Afghans (together with their Persian "cousins") "all carpet salesmen at heart."[10] Like proxy warriors elsewhere, these militias did not always do as they were told, as when they ignored orders not to take the capital. The Americans imposed Karzai, but the critical ministries (defense, interior, and foreign affairs) were already in the hands of a small number of figures from the Panjsher Valley who dominated the Supervisory Council of the Northern Alliance. The Americans and the Karzai administration would subsequently depict political instability in the country as a function of the struggle between the central government, dominated by enlightened and democratic technocrats, against nefarious "warlords" left over from the mujahedin period. Yet the ministries in Kabul were intensely factionalized from the outset, paralyzing government at key moments in the post-Taliban transition period.

A second component of the initial anti-Taliban offensive with long-term implications took shape in the south. In Kandahar and other southern and eastern provinces, U.S. Special Forces distributed arms and weapons to local elites, who, in exchange, agreed to remain neutral or fight against the Taliban. That some of these militia fighters nonetheless maintained neutrality at critical junctures may have contributed to the escape of high-level Taliban and al-Qaeda figures at Tora Bora and other locales. Equally important for the post-Taliban era, this initial move created serious obstacles to the disarmament plans introduced later. The influx of cash and weapons may have also seeded the opium boom that began in these southern provinces in late 2001, ultimately transforming Afghanistan into the world's number one producer, with some 40 percent of its GDP derived from poppy cultivation and trade by 2004. All of these factors facilitated a re-regionalization of Afghanistan after 2001. Karzai was demoted to the status of "mayor of Kabul" in folk humor, in significant part because regional elites had larger armies, more cash, and their own access to international trade networks.

For its part, the United States blocked early calls from Karzai and the United Nations for an international security force beyond Kabul. Confined to the capital, the International Security Assistance Force (ISAF) consisted in 2002 of only 4,500 troops.[11] Some twenty thousand American forces patrolled the south and east. Together, beginning in 2003, they manned roughly twenty "Provincial Reconstruction Teams" combining humanitarian and security activities. In 2004, ISAF (under NATO command from August 2003) finally extended its purview beyond Kabul. But it largely limited its presence to the north, with the creation of Provincial Reconstruction Teams.

The impact of this resort to proxy warfare involved much more than increasing the amount of weapons and money in the hands of former mujahedin fighters and opium entrepreneurs in north and south. Under American air cover, the Northern Alliance offensive that swept from Mazar-e Sharif and other northern centers brought with it a wave of extrajudicial violence distinct from combat against the Taliban. In November 2001, militias coordinated by American Special Forces took several thousand Taliban POWs. Northern Alliance fighters packed many of them into unventilated metal containers and either shot into the containers or left the POWs to die in the scorching desert heat. Many witnesses charged American forces with complicity in a war crime that gained very little attention outside of Afghanistan (and Europe). The bombing campaign itself likely claimed at least a thousand civilian victims by the end of 2001. Afghan militia commanders denounced their rivals to U.S. troops, soliciting arrests and, more dramatically, air strikes such as the one on December 20 that hit a convoy in Paktya Province. The U.S. military asserted that the victims were Taliban leaders, but locals insisted they were elders on the way to Karzai's inauguration. Anthony Shadid reported that several hours of continuous bombing also destroyed nearby houses—and a village six miles away.[12]

The fate of the Pashtun communities of the north is better documented. Mass expulsions, murder, rape, and mayhem accompanied the Northern Alliance advance and the American-led bombing campaign. Thousands of Pashtuns fled and were forced from their homes. Tension and violence between Pashtuns and non-Pashtuns in the northern provinces date to the settlement policies of Amir Abdul Rahman in the late nineteenth century, as Nazif Shahrani notes in his essay. But the revenge killings and opportunistic crimes of fall and winter 2001–2002 took place as the north fell into a state of anarchy. The murder of POWs and crimes against civilians contributed to a climate of impunity and further ethnicized politics throughout the country. The lawlessness and bloodshed of the immediate post-Taliban aftermath created grievances that would be directed against perpetrators who gained seats in the central government and shored up their hold over provincial fiefdoms—as well as against their foreign sponsors.

At the same time, the civilian casualties of the American bombing campaign of autumn 2001, and the subsequent detention of Afghans in secret prisons, left deep resentment. In Khost and elsewhere, locals erected shrines to the foreign Arab fighters and Taliban killed by American air strikes. In 2005 and 2006, reporters witnessed local people visiting the graves of these "martyrs" in hopes of receiving spiritual blessings and cures.[13]

Though the United States depended heavily on intermediaries on the ground, it enjoyed more autonomy in selecting and mobilizing the expatriates (including a number of figures who initially supported the Taliban) who would make up the technocratic elite of the new government. Monarchists exerted pressure on the discussions of Afghanistan's future at Bonn, but the Pentagon, State Department, and CIA succeeded in turning other expatriates against them. This strategy hinged on the selection of a trusted figure to lead a post-Taliban government, in effect a shadow government in the American embassy.

In December 2001 the United States chose Hamid Karzai to be the first post-Taliban leader of the country. The international conference at Bonn ratified the decision. Indeed, the first draft of the Bonn resolution had a curious but meaningful omission reflecting Washington's priorities. The American representative at the talks, James Dobbins, recalled, "It was the Iranian delegate who first suggested that the Bonn Agreement really ought to contain some mention of democracy, which the first draft had neglected to include." Significantly, Dobbins had "no instructions [from Washington] on the subject, but," he added, "it seemed a reasonable proposal to me and I supported it."[14]

The mechanism for legitimizing these decisions in Afghanistan itself was the Loya Jirga convened in June 2002. Presented to foreign audiences as a quasi-democratic institution that had traditional, tribal roots, this staging of a grand assembly—under a tent brought from Germany—became a model for the management of consensus. Like previous loya jirgas, these assemblies did not derive their legitimacy from free and fair elections. They revolved instead around bargaining conducted by a small number of elites.[15] Their aim was to confer legitimacy upon the American vision of executive authority. In the meantime, a retired British diplomat stationed in Kabul in 2002 writes, "While I was running around encouraging and cajoling politicians to engage in the *loya jirga* process, the purpose of which was in part to take power back from the warlords, others [among the foreign diplomats] were running around doling out bribes to buy loyalty amongst those very same warlords" and to retain them "to track down the terrorists, Al-Qaeda and the remnant Taliban or 'AQT' as they were known."[16]

In 2004 the American imprint on Afghan democracy would be felt again when presidential elections were held in advance of the U.S. presidential election of November. Karzai enjoyed exclusive access to U.S. security and transportation. American military helicopters shuttled Karzai from town to town, making him the only candidate who campaigned in person throughout the country. Until November 2005, American agents or contractors provided for his personal security. The American ambassador, Zalmay Khalilzad, whom diplomats and other observers referred to as the "viceroy," acted as a co-ruler of sorts, wielding the authority of the U.S. military and treasury.

The central government nonetheless struggled to extend its authority beyond the capital. The United States strongly opposed calls from Germany and other allies to contemplate the creation of a federal system. Washington insisted instead on a strongly centralized system, including the appointment of governors by the executive.[17] It demanded a handful of senior positions for women, but human rights groups concluded that women remained marginalized in the new order.[18] In 2005, Afghans elected provincial councils, but their powers remained very limited.

The American-backed preference for a centralized structure deepened the mistrust of regional, especially non-Pashtun, elites who since the 1980s had enjoyed broad administrative autonomy and, under communist rule, a reversal of previous regimes' pro-Pashtun cultural policies.[19] Thus to non-Pashtuns, calls from the minister of finance, Ashraf Ghani, and other Western-educated technocrats for increased power for technical experts in the government heightened suspicion of a Pashtun restoration. Minorities feared the return of Pashtun domination. Kabul's removal of local officials and their replacement with Pashtuns intensified opposition to the central government; for example, in Balkh province, in October 2003, the government appointed a Pashtun from Kandahar as local chief of police, despite opposition from Uzbeks and Tajiks who form a majority of the population of the province.[20]

Beginning in 2002, numerous observers echoed the Karzai administration in castigating regional "warlords" as the primary source of corruption, violence, and instability. But as Antonio Giustozzi has shown, if the term *warlord* is to have any meaning, then it would also apply to numerous ministers (and those under them); warlord politics would also characterize many of the strategies of the Kabul government. In many cases, the center—not the periphery—injected violence into localized contests for authority. It sought to undermine regional power brokers both by denying them international funding and by supporting rival militia commanders. Against Ismail Khan in Herat, the government backed a former Taliban supporter and local district head, Amanullah Khan, in 2002. In Herat and elsewhere, the policy led to fighting between competing militias.[21] In 2004, Kabul dispatched the national army to Herat to quell violence. Yet as Giustozzi has pointed out, this policy of "buying off middle level warlords and turning them against their old patron" meant official support for characters whose record of drug smuggling and human rights abuses scarcely differed from figures such as Ismail Khan whom the modernizers targeted. At the same time, he notes, the inclusion of such figures in the administrative apparatus has undermined its effectiveness.[22]

Despite the aim of centralization, the Americans and other international donors acted haltingly in seeking to increase the influence of the Kabul government. This was most visible in provisions for post-Taliban security. Under the umbrella of air power supplied by bases in surrounding countries and the Indian Ocean, the Pentagon rarely deployed more than 20,000 troops for a country of some 31 million; in 2007, NATO and U.S. forces grew to some 40,000.[23] (Following the U.S.-led invasion of Iraq, with some 26 million inhabitants, American troop levels in Iraq reached a high point of roughly 160,000 in the summer of 2007.) Peacekeeping operations in Somalia, Haiti, Kosovo, Bosnia, Northern Ireland, Iraq, and elsewhere had higher ratios of peacekeepers per inhabitant. In comparative terms, for every 1,000 Afghans, there was less than 1 American or coalition soldier (0.5) to provide security in 2002 (versus 23.7 per 1,000 in Kosovo in 1999, 6.1 per 1,000 in Iraq in 2003, and 3.5 per 1,000 in Haiti in 1994).[24] Even before American attention shifted to Iraq in the winter and spring of 2002–2003, per capita aid levels—$57 per Afghan—remained well below those of other conflict environments such as East Timor ($233), Kosovo ($526), or Bosnia ($679).

In 2002 roughly 1 of every 7 Afghan men of military age was potentially attached to a militia, including the 75,000 to 250,000 employed principally as fighters. To counterbalance these forces, Kabul planned the building of an Afghan National Army (ANA) of some 80,000 men and a police force of some 70,000. Yet U.S. military policies also undermined this long-term goal. In 2002 the Americans paid militia fighters $150 to $200 a month to fight (and their commanders up to $2,000), but recruits in the ANA received only one-third the salary of a militia member. Even independently of the United States, militias typically paid more than the ANA. As a result, desertion to locally based militias has periodically drained the ANA by as much as 50 percent.[25] Despite early promises to address the goals of disarmament and suppression of the opium economy, it was not until 2003 that the British, Japanese, and other governments began to establish rudimentary programs.

The legitimacy of the Karzai government also suffered from its inability to sustain a police force to maintain security in the provinces. In the absence of police, local commanders and militias secured major roads and levied their own "Islamic" taxes. Roadblocks and checkpoints run by nonstate authorities proliferated, as they had on the eve of the Taliban's arrival in 1994. And, as in the early 1990s, locals chafed under the capricious rule of armed men and faulted the central government for not fulfilling its duties. Where police were present, many of them also collected their own "fines" and "taxes" from local residents and travelers. In some locales, police forces, like many army units, did double duty in the service of local commanders. The American military pressured Kabul to appoint some of its allies in the militias to head up police forces in places like Helmand, for example.[26] In the volatile Panjwayi District of Kandahar Province, where fighting raged through much of summer 2006, a correspondent for *The Economist* found policemen whose salaries were $70 a month. For 110 policemen in the district, there were only 20 guns. "The police force is one reason why," the journalist concluded, "five years this week since the austere and brutal regime of the Taliban was overthrown, so many people in Kandahar cannot decide whom they hate more: the new government or the Taliban revivalists fighting it."[27]

While popular distrust of the police and the army was partly a legacy inherited from previous governments, the international sponsors of the Karzai government created new impediments to its functioning. For much of the twentieth century, Afghan states had received nearly half of their budget from abroad and had worked to build their legitimacy by redistributing much of this aid among elites. But after 2001, international donors sought greater control. Foreign organizations, rather than the government, now dispersed most of the donated funds. Not only did this strategy bypass the Afghan government, it deprived Kabul of one of its only mechanisms to exert influence in the provinces. In 2004–2005, donors permitted the Afghan government to spend only $1.4 billion out of a total of $4.9 billion of this aid.[28] A World Bank report concluded that the bypassing of the central government undermined its power to "stay 'in charge' of the development agenda," while creating a "'second civil service' consisting of NGOs, consultants, advisers, and employees of UN and other international agencies, including expatriate consultants and Afghans attracted by relatively high salaries."[29] In 2005, the Afghan government dispersed only 30 percent of this public spending through its budget. As Barnett Rubin has pointed out, the army and police depended entirely on foreign funding, and the central government scarcely had authority over its own budget, despite much fanfare abroad surrounding elections.[30]

Moreover, the policy of contracting private corporations to assume state functions—a practice that would attract critical attention in Iraq in 2003—had already become widespread in Afghanistan in 2002. The Center for Public Integrity reports, for example, that Chemonics, based in Washington, D.C., received U.S. government contracts worth some $600 million to conduct "socio-economic assessments" and "food market analysis" to improve food security in Afghanistan.[31] Significant amounts of development funding offered by the United States simply recirculated into the hands of American contractors such as the Louis Berger Group, which paid Afghan construction workers $5 to $10 a day for twelve-hour shifts and built schools and clinics for a price tag of $226,000 per building.[32]

At the same time, a dense network of American-run secret prisons and military bases within Afghanistan further circumscribed the reach of the Afghan state and its judicial authority over Afghan territory and its own citizens. In 2002, Afghanistan became the hub for a secret U.S. prison system. American-controlled military facilities in Bagram and Kandahar housed Afghans suspected of being Taliban and al-Qaeda militants. Families of inmates directed protests against both the Americans and the Karzai government. While most were captured on the battlefield or ransomed by anti-Taliban militias in Afghanistan, prisoners included Europeans and other non-Afghans whom the Americans brought from Pakistan and elsewhere in transit to the facility at Guantanamo; former captives there later alleged that the prisons in Afghanistan were also centers of torture and murder.[33]

Although the Americans supplied most of the Afghan budget and specified how most of the international aid was to be spent on behalf of Afghans, some branches of the central government exercised a notable degree of autonomy. In the first months of 2002, the Supreme Court emerged as a kind of brake on various foreign-sponsored transformations in the post-Taliban era. Not only its ideas, but its personnel, represented a direct inheritance of the jihad and Taliban eras. The Islamist commander and founder of the Ettehad-e Islami, Abdul Rabb al-Rasul Sayyaf, succeeded in placing his clients in top court positions, while former members of the Taliban bureaucracy such as Wahid Muzhda moved seamlessly to occupy lower-level positions at the court. The court's head, septuagenarian religious scholar Mawlawi Fazl Hadi Shinwari, was also the senior figure in Afghanistan's Council of Islamic Scholars. As Supreme Court judge, he acted as moral guardian, censor, and defender of broad jurisdiction for the sharia. One of his first targets was cable television. Outraged by the influx of Bollywood films and other entertainments brought by returning Afghans and the international staffs of NGOS, he also called for women to wear head coverings (the *hejab*) and protested female presenters on television.

The judge reaffirmed opposition to coeducation, a position that has gained widespread sympathy in provinces where local activists, many associated with the neo-Taliban, burned coeducational schools. Shinwari deviated from the Taliban legacy in approving urban female work outside the home, though his permission included the proviso that such women must wear head scarves. Beyond his intervention on such cultural and social issues, Shinwari's court oversaw the staffing, funding, and direction of courts from the capital to the remotest district.[34] Shinwari failed, however, to check the cultural changes under way in Kabul, as the capital flourished with the arrival of myriad NGOs and foreign experts.

The transformation of Kabul in the post-Taliban era created new tensions. Electricity remained scarce, and traffic snarled. The influx of NGOs, journalists, the internally displaced, expatriates, and refugees returning from Pakistan, Iran, and other neighboring countries created intense competition for real estate. New building projects sponsored by foreign aid workers—as well as by Afghan notables flush with cash from the opium economy—forced prices and rents skyward. Kabulis grumbled about property speculation by government officials.

The new international presence left its mark on the physical structure of the city, prompting criticism from residents. More than the new commercial activity and construction, American fortification of areas such as Shar-e Naw alienated Kabulis and revealed the political weakness of the Karzai government and its lack of control even over the capital. City residents protested against the closing of roads, the erection of concrete barriers, and arbitrary searches by foreign security personnel, but the Afghan government proved powerless to resist foreigners' security demands for their embassy compounds and other buildings. For foreign embassy staffs, these security measures further isolated them from what was happening in the country. Carne Ross, a British diplomat posted there in 2002, recalled that his "dream of sitting in tea-houses in Kabul with 'ordinary' Afghans remained a fantasy. It was easier for me to meet them in New York."[35] For the Afghans who encountered these barricades and security personnel, the public face of the Americans was represented by the same private security contractors who served as bodyguards for Hamid Karzai. Hired by the United States, armed employees of Virginia-based DynCorp conducted searches and interviews at checkpoints in the city and in homes adjoining sites they were charged with securing.

DynCorp was only one of many foreign security contractors operating in the capital, but it appears to have gained the most attention. On August 29, 2004, the DynCorp headquarters was bombed. The attack killed three Americans and seven Afghans. Resentment was not confined to the unknown militants behind this bombing, however. The sight of machine-gun-wielding foreigners in fatigues and sunglasses in Kabul neighborhoods frequently evoked comparisons between the Americans and the Soviets. One eighty-one-year-old resident of a neighborhood in the shadow of the DynCorp contractors complained to a journalist, "We are scared of the Americans." "The Russians," he observed, "were here for 10 years and their military stations were out of the city, not among families. I passed the difficulties of the Russian occupation. But as difficult as that was, it wasn't as hard as this."[36] These tensions set the stage for rioting in Kabul on May 29, 2006, after an American military vehicle killed five civilians in a collision that ignited a day of anti-U.S. and antigovernment rioting and U.S. reprisals that left some twenty people dead.

These hostilities were indirectly related to another aspect of the U.S.-led military intervention: a shift in the way humanitarian aid has been provided in Afghanistan. Besides the U.S. military and its Provincial Reconstruction Teams, aid organizations, private contractors, and development agencies proceeded in 2002, as Antonio Donini has pointed out, as if the war with the Taliban had concluded. Like the coalition forces, the United Nations Mission in Afghanistan (UNAMA) announced a policy of supporting the Karzai government. This created a dilemma for other aid organizations. "By aligning themselves with the new government and UNAMA," Donini notes, "they were also aligning themselves de facto with the military intervention and its objectives, which were and are closer to the 'global war on terror' than peacebuilding. By implication, humanitarian agencies were forsaking neutrality and independence because they chose to engage in 'controversies' of a fundamentally political nature." Surveys conducted in 2006 revealed a dramatic shift in public perceptions of aid organizations. Once widely respected, NGOs had become the focus of widespread disappointment in foreign aid projects that largely circumvented the government. Numerous Afghans expressed mistrust of their work and complained that such groups did not do more to improve the country through large-scale public infrastructure projects and greater attention to security. It was not only the neo-Taliban who saw their work as politicized. An editorial in a paper affiliated with the Jamiat-e Islami lamented that Afghans had "jumped from a simple life to modernization and [a] free market economy" and "subordinated the Afghan government to foreign advisors . . . We made a mistake. Technocrats were not better than the mojahedin. Their literacy, English dialect, suit, necktie and stylish shoes did not bring relief to us . . . Coca Cola does not rescue people from hunger, does not reconstruct any ruin, and does not industrialize our country."[37] Alexander Cooley's observations about popular frustration aimed at reconstruction schemes in Iraq, Kosovo, and Bosnia also applied to Afghans: "Perceptions that reconstruction efforts were primarily geared to funding Western companies and NGOs, as opposed to dealing with the needs of local people, are widespread and the contracting process has been severely criticized for its rigidity, cronyism, and waste."[38]

Outside of Kabul, increased attention to disarmament and the opium economy sharpened conflicts between international actors and Afghans beginning in 2003. Plans to disarm militias and eradicate poppies met with diverse forms of resistance. In the Panjsher Valley, the transfer of heavy weapons, including tanks, rockets, and armored vehicles, from local villagers to the Afghan National Army in late 2003 and early 2004 prompted cries of betrayal. "We rescued the country from Taliban and Soviet invasion," one villager protested, "now they are taking the weapons we had saved by blood and give us nothing instead. We have no roads, no schools and no clinics." Another called the cache "the property of thousands of martyrs" and wondered why disarmament had to begin there, and not elsewhere in the country. Select allies of the Americans remained immune from disarmament.[39]

While numerous commentators have focused on the nexus of opium revenues and insurgent violence, the proliferation of inexpensive weapons, especially small arms and mines, played a less visible role in undercutting disarmament efforts. Apart from the bequest of arms left over from the superpower struggle played out in Afghanistan in the 1980s, new weapons have reached the country from international markets. In 2001 the United States military famously injected even more arms into an environment already awash with automatic weapons when it supplied Afghan militias who it enlisted to fight against the Taliban and al-Qaeda. Pakistan and other neighboring countries, including Uzbekistan and Tajikistan, became major purchasers of U.S. arms, and some of these weapons may have crossed these country's porous borders with Afghanistan. In 2005 alone, the United States and other arms exporters delivered half a billion dollars' worth of weapons to Afghanistan and another half a billion to Pakistan.[40] Earmarked for the Afghan National Army and police, many of these weapons have entered the domestic market or become the private property of the high percentage of Afghan soldiers who desert within a few months of enrollment.

Closely related to the proliferation of arms, opium cultivation emerged as another pivotal area of conflict. Afghanistan has produced opium from time immemorial. But change came with the arrival of Western tourists in the 1970s and, more importantly, the anti-Soviet jihad. Linked to international smuggling networks and intelligence agencies in Pakistan and the United States, the mujahedin and local communities began to produce enormous quantities for a global market. The Taliban raised revenue by taxing production, and opium cultivation flourished between 1995 and 1999, when the area under cultivation increased from 54,000 hectares to 91,000 hectares. Seeking favor in the international community (and likely the fruits of market manipulation as well), the Taliban successfully banned opium production in 2001.[41]

The Pax Americana created conditions for an opium boom. Though a number of Afghans regard the cultivation of opium as contrary to Islam, cultivation spread in 2002 to regions where it had not been prevalent before. Some 63 percent of the Afghan farmers who grew opium chose to begin in that year. In 2003 the area of land devoted to opium poppy cultivation surpassed the areas of poppy growth during the Soviet occupation and civil war. Under the Taliban, poppy cultivation peaked at 91,000 hectares in 1999; however, it reached 131,000 in 2004. In 2006 the spike continued, increasing to 165,0000. According to a United Nations estimate, the opium harvest rose to 6,100 tons and was worth over $3 billion. Afghanistan, with a GDP of $6.9 billion, produced 92 percent of the world's supply. And 2.9 million people (roughly 12.6 percent of the country's population) were involved in cultivation. An Afghan farmer who chose to plant opium could expect to make five times the per capita income.[42]

As with disarmament, the narcotics issue evoked no coordinated policy from Kabul and its international sponsors, though all actors agreed that the opium economy in some way enriched regional militias and terrorist organizations. Nigel Allan points to a number of the unintended consequences of policies that worked at cross purposes. Paradoxically, the arrival of humanitarian aid early in the post-

Taliban period may have freed up food-producing land for opium cultivation. Wary of direct military confrontation with growers, American authorities have experimented with paying farmers not to grow opium poppy. In 2002 the United States paid farmers $1,750 per hectare in the eastern province of Nangarhar not to cultivate the crop. When farmers in the northern province of Badakhshan learned of the program, they began planting poppy plants in hopes of receiving the same compensation. But the Americans never carried out this scheme in Badakhshan, Allan notes, and the new opium growers there were left with no option but to market their precious harvest.[43] Other efforts to combat opium production fell victim to broader political concerns. One campaign was abandoned on the eve of the presidential elections of 2004, and despite a $150 million contract to DynCorp, one of its programs was suspended when it faced resistance. In April 2005 residents of Maywand District in Kandahar Province demonstrated against the government's poppy eradication program. Fighting the next day between protestors and the police led to the suspension of the program.[44] Where the anti-narcotics campaign achieved success, Kabul had to depend on local strongmen to coerce local farmers. As a result, according to a study of the drug economy in Laghman and Nangarhar provinces, "arbitrary rule by force and by patronage was strengthened."[45]

While the opium economy kept the Afghan economy afloat, the glut of opium and refined heroin, combined with a host of other social ills, increased local consumption, addiction, and HIV infections in Afghanistan and neighboring states. Trafficking threatened to destabilize governments throughout the region.[46] In the meantime, as during the 1990s, extraordinarily high external demand for heroin from users in Europe and North America linked Afghan farmers to a highly integrated world market.

Despite challenges posed by the opium economy and insecurity in various regions of the country, many in the Kabul government and in international development agencies remained committed to the transformation of Afghan society, even if this was always, in reality, a much lower priority for Washington than the military struggle against al-Qaeda and the Taliban. For many Afghan government officials and their foreign advisers, this project entailed not only freeing Afghanistan of the Taliban but remaking the country. Like Afghan modernizers under the monarchy and the socialist regime before them, reform advocates took aim at traditional society. The need to reeducate Afghans, as Conrad Schetter has noted, was an underlying theme of reform. "It has to be recognized that a large proportion of the country has little or no direct experience or understanding of how a free market economy functions," complained one Afghan minister and presidential adviser, adding that "many continue to look to the government to control the economy, set prices, and provide employment for large numbers of people. There is much that needs to be done to educate the public on the way a market economy works and what it requires of them."[47]

The most ambitious program to draw rural communities into this enterprise called for the radical remaking of local community governance based on "participatory and inclusive decision-making processes," "gender equity," "transparency and accountability," and "sustainability." Launched in 2002, this "National Solidarity Program" envisioned "Community Development Councils" (CDCs) as the building blocks of a transformed countryside in which tribal or ethnic solidarities and gender inequality would be swept aside. Working through CDCs chosen through free and fair elections and with strict gender equality, local communities were to be involved in making their own choices about development projects and brought into contact with government institutions and donors. At the same time, the procedures established by the National Solidarity Program aimed to level

the heterogeneous political, social, ethnic, religious, and gender relations that obtained in different locales. Thus, separate CDCs on the
basis of "political, ethnic, or family groups" were not permitted. Like
previous reform projects that have politicized gender and ethnicity
in modern Afghanistan, this one has relied on an extensive publicity campaign. By April 2007, according to official statistics, 17,340
communities had been "mobilized," and 16,753 councils had been
elected.[48] In May 2005 the Public Communications Department of
the National Solidarity Program launched a radio soap opera, *Let's
Build Our Village*, to publicize the CDCs.

In 2004 and especially 2005, a wide range of grievances against the
Kabul government and its international backers mobilized a growing
number of Afghans in the provinces. The American press tended to
speak of a single "insurgency," but heterogeneous actors lay behind a
broad spectrum of actions, some part of wider coordinated movements, others spontaneous and localized.[49] In 2005 alone, fighting
claimed some fifteen hundred Afghan lives. For American troops,
Afghanistan was more dangerous than Iraq. The casualty rate in Iraq
was 0.9 per 1,000 soldiers in Iraq, while in Afghanistan it was 1.6 per
1,000. For aid workers and other civilians, Afghanistan was more
hazardous than comparable postwar environments in Liberia, Angola,
and elsewhere.[50] After twenty-four years in the country—throughout
the Soviet occupation, the civil war, and the reign of the Taliban—
Doctors without Borders/Médecins sans Frontières left the country
in August 2004, and smaller groups joined them in abandoning or
scaling back their operations. In 2006, Mercy Corps withdrew its international staff from the south.[51] Excluding road construction workers, who have been targeted at a higher rate, twenty-four aid workers
were killed in 2004 and thirty in 2005.[52] In the first half of 2006, militants launched some two hundred attacks on schools in twenty-

seven provinces, killing forty-one people—including students—attached to them.[53] Reports of the burning of girls' schools—and even of the stoning of alleged adulterers—have also emerged from territories never under Taliban rule.[54] Violence did not necessarily follow party or ethnic lines and was not limited to militants under the Taliban banner. Although the neo-Taliban insurgencies attracted the most attention, fighting spread beyond the southern and eastern provinces.

A look at northern Afghanistan is instructive. Military commanders who cooperated with the United States after September 11, 2001, and later allied themselves with Karzai's government continued to battle. In February 2004, for example, rival commanders of the Jamiat-e Islami clashed in the northeastern province of Badakshan. The fighting, which may have killed some thirty people and wounded another fifty, appears to have been over the imposition of a tax on land used to grow poppies.[55] In early August 2006, fighting between some three hundred militia members under commanders loyal to General Abdul Rashid Dostum and General Abdul Malik dragged on for a week and claimed over a dozen lives in Faryab Province. Although the Afghan Interior Ministry responded by seeking to outlaw the political parties under these two figures, commanders such as Dostum retained posts in the presidential cabinet and parliament, and NATO officers continued to treat them as linchpins of local security. Local populations, in turn, took to the streets to protest attempts at dissolving these parties.[56] While these provinces were generally more secure than the south, foreign journalists and aid workers still fell victim to violence there.

In Nuristan, northeast of the capital, the Taliban had never sunk deep roots, but the region was so violent in the post-Taliban era that, after a few foreign security firm employees and aid workers were murdered, foreigners largely abandoned the area. The violence had diverse causes, some of them stretching back decades. The commu-

nist coup and anti-Soviet struggle had divided local elites among the
Peshawar parties, as elsewhere, but the war also had distinctive consequences in the region. Long-standing conflicts between the northern and southern halves of the Bashgal Valley over access to water
and land intensified; in the north, a mullah declared himself the
"amir" of an independent Islamist-oriented state, backed by the Saudis, while Hizb-e Islami held sway in the south. Mawlawi Afzal, a
local head of the anti-Soviet jihad, retained control of the Saudi-
inspired fiefdom established in the 1980s. This "Islamic Revolutionary State of Afghanistan" had its own consulates in Saudi Arabia and
Pakistan. It was during this period, Max Klimburg has argued, that
Muslim missionaries from Pakistan and Arab countries who have
been active in the area since the 1970s made an enormous impact on
religiosity in communities that the government of Abdul Rahman
Khan forcibly converted only in the late nineteenth century. Mostly
gone are the singing, dancing, feasting, and mixing of the sexes that
had distinguished this area, still conscious of its identity as "Kafiri-
stan" or "land of the unbelievers," before its conversion, and the adoption of its new name, "land of light," Nuristan.[57]

When the Taliban arrived in 1996, they scarcely challenged Nuristani autonomy. They made a concession to local sentiment by recognizing the region as a separate province and did not disarm the
population. Local politics persisted: villages pursued old rivalries over
water and land with small arms, rockets, and land mines.

Aggravated by the drought of 2000–2001, violence flared again in
Nuristan, and local communities began to battle not over opium but
over the cedars of the local Himalayan forests. Timber harvested
from the dense, high-elevation forests attracted smugglers and local
peasants, who stood to earn a living from exports to Pakistan. In
the meantime, post-Taliban Nuristani elites have managed to maintain a ban on girls' education, and the region is said to be a base of

operations for Gulbuddin Hekmatyar, the Pakistani militant group Lashkare Taiba, and possibly al-Qaeda.[58]

The integration of reconstruction, humanitarian aid, and military operations frequently positioned American forces in the middle of such disputes among Afghans, making them actors in political struggles for which they were rarely prepared. Many of these dynamics can be seen in a single locale, the eastern province of Kunar, which has been a focus of the American anti-insurgency campaign. According to interviews with local residents, militants successfully evaded the U.S. forces that periodically swept through the area and returned to their homes upon the departure of the Americans. Heavily forested and at high altitude, the Korengal Valley in Kunar became what an American soldier told BBC reporters was "enemy central." On June 28, 2005, insurgents shot down a Chinook helicopter, killing sixteen Special Forces and the crew. The valley was also said to be home to followers of Hekmatyar's Hizb-e Islami and an al-Qaeda leader who had settled there during the anti-Soviet jihad.[59]

Reports from Kunar revealed that one of the American tactics involved threats of collective punishment for the population of the Korengal Valley if they did not take up arms against the militants. U.S. Army forces blockaded the only road into the valley to punish communities whom they accused of assisting the Taliban. As an incentive to cooperate with the Americans, they also built a bridge over the Pech River to facilitate trade in the valley. An American officer explained that the goal of this policy was to divide pro-Taliban elders from their opponents, to create "a fracture between two groups." According to a transcript of a radio broadcast obtained by the BBC, a text issued in the name of the local government, but apparently composed by the U.S. military, warned that if the people of Korengal "are not going to comply with the demands of expelling the enemy from their villages then we will be forced to continue to pursue the enemy relentlessly until the elders either force them to leave or the hand of our national security troops force them out. The people of Korengal are either with the people of Kunar or against them." Though a U.S. military spokesman denied that the Americans had written the text, Afghan officials pointed out that this was "how the foreigners speak," adding, "It will make things worse." A Human Rights Watch researcher called the threat "a violation of the Geneva Conventions and other laws of war."[60]

Meanwhile the central government pursued a more conciliatory policy. Karzai appointed as governor of this restive province Muhammad Didar Shalizi, a veteran of the jihad whose supposed links to the Taliban disqualified him from running for parliament in 2004. Elders of Kunar nevertheless complained of government corruption and violence against civilians and their livestock. In Korengal, locals denied support for the Taliban and criticized the blockade.[61]

As at Bagram, Guantanamo, and Abu Ghraib, American forces invented what they thought to be culturally specific forms of humiliation in confrontations with the residents of the Korengal Valley and other locales where they suspected the presence of militants. In Kandahar Province on October 1, 2005, American troops burned and desecrated the bodies of two dead Taliban fighters near a village north of Kandahar. A "psychological operations" team, composed of army reservists from an Arkansas unit attached to the 173rd Airborne Brigade, then turned loudspeakers toward the village to taunt its inhabitants, hoping to draw militants into a fight. Calling the suspected Taliban in the village "cowardly dogs," the soldiers goaded the villagers. "You allowed your fighters to be laid down facing west [away from Mecca] and burned. You are too scared to retrieve their bodies. This just proves you are the lady boys we always believed you to be."[62] Hamid Karzai denounced the act, and the Afghan Independent Human Rights Commission condemned the desecration, calling it "against the Islamic beliefs and traditions of Afghanistan and a violation of the Geneva Conventions and of international humanitarian law."[63] Despite the international outcry and the criticism of the Afghan government, the Pentagon labeled the incident "an act of poor judgment, but not a violation of the laws of war." The four soldiers received "administrative punishment."[64]

The American practice of raiding homes in search of militants, weapons, and, in some cases, drugs appears to have broadened the base of the diverse groups opposed to the Karzai regime and its foreign sponsors. In Pashtun areas, villagers regarded such raids as assaults on their honor. The detention of women was especially controversial. In the spring of 2005, Afghans demonstrated against reports of abuses at Guantanamo, Bagram, and elsewhere. In April 2005, hundreds protested in Jalalabad against home searches. The protests against opium eradication described above shook Kandahar in the same month. In May, three female aid workers were hanged in Pul-e Khumri in Baghlan Province. Notes attached to their bodies warned other women against working for foreign aid organizations.[65]

Critics of American military actions evoked the legacy of the anti-Soviet jihad and likened the foreign presence to an "occupation." Gulbuddin Hekmatyar, the former favorite of Pakistani intelligence and American patronage during the jihad years, cast American measures as part of a general war on Pashtuns. His rhetoric labeled such military activities an American-led "genocide of Pashtuns" and depicted the resistance as "the national uprising." "The Americans are fighting Pashtuns in the provinces of Paktia, Paktika, Khost, Nangarhar, Kunar, Kandahar, Helmand and Urozgan—because they realize Pashtuns hold on to their faith, defend religious sanctities and national interests and reject foreign oppression. It is no coincidence that 85 per cent of US military operations have been in Pashtun areas, where US troops shelled villages, pounded mosques, searched homes for weapons and ammunition, erected checkpoints on public roads, and detained Pashtun leaders and chiefs in its Bagram base or in Guantanamo Bay." Another of his pamphlets called for resistance against the Americans, "who have no consideration for our honor and the chastity of our women . . . They want to weaken our precious Islam."[66] In an interview conducted from a secret location, Mullah Omar echoed such views in early 2007, though he avoided explicit mention of a Pashtun cause. "Nobody can tolerate this kind of subjugation and sacrilege of their culture and religion," Omar argued, adding, "No nation can accept the dictates of a handful of dollar-greedy and treacherous people."[67]

This rhetoric of anti-imperialism, national liberation, and honor was not limited to Hekmatyar or Mullah Omar. Accusing the United States of supporting both the Taliban and bin Laden in the 1990s, some Afghan intellectuals expressed skepticism that the "occupying forces" were committed to democracy and noted their lack of trust in Afghan democratic forces.[68] Others criticized American authorities for imprisoning Afghans for three or four years in a prison at the Soviet-built Bagram airbase without charging them with crimes. Their families, lawyers, and human rights activists contended that many of those held at Bagram, Guantanamo, and other secret prisons were ransomed by bounty hunters seeking compensation or by personal foes who, pursuing vendettas unrelated to real crimes, denounced them to the Americans as "al-Qaeda" and "Taliban."[69]

In an even more dramatic departure from previous patterns of Afghan politics, more and more Afghans saw themselves as part of a global Muslim community, as Robert L. Canfield has shown in this book, and events in distant countries began to animate how Afghans perceived foreign forces. In February 2006, Afghans protested for several days in Kabul, Herat, Jalalabad, and other towns against the publication in Denmark of cartoons satirizing the Prophet Muhammad. Several hundred rioters attacked the compound of a Norwegian-led Provincial Reconstruction Team in Maymana. In Kabul, demonstrators denounced Karzai and George W. Bush and threw stones at ISAF headquarters and the U.S. embassy. Security forces killed two rioters near the Bagram base, three in Laghman, and three in Maymana.[70] The Kabul market riots of late May following the involvement of a U.S. military vehicle in a traffic accident grew out of this atmosphere of distrust.

The conflict between Israel and Hizbullah in the summer of 2006 may have been a critical turning point for Afghan public opinion and its newfound concern with global politics. Oppositional figures in parliament criticized American backing for Israel and called on the Afghan government to express solidarity with the Lebanese against Israel. At a rally in Kabul on July 31, protestors chanted, "Israeli crime, American support." One parliamentarian, a former mujahedin commander Ahmad Shah Ahmadzai, complained that "America is acting contrary to its stated principles—it proclaims slogans about human rights, yet it violates human rights. America calls for democracy, yet takes away the freedom of nations." Salma, a female civil servant in Kabul, offered a similar critique of American views of human rights: "It means that if the Americans kill innocent people, women and children, it doesn't matter . . . Democracy means that Americans can freely attack other's beliefs, insult them and do whatever they like." A deserter from the Afghan National Army told an Afghan reporter that locals in Kandahar had opted to join the Taliban and fight against the army only when they heard news of events in Lebanon, which led them to conclude that the "Americans are the enemies of Muslims."[71]

This internationalization of the antigovernment mobilization brought with it new fighting tactics. The introduction of suicide

bombing reflected both a break from more conventional forms of violence in Afghanistan and the neo-Taliban's access to the expertise
and personnel of militants far beyond the Afghan-Pakistan frontier.
The Iraqi insurgency had become a model for emulation: DVDs produced in Pakistan and distributed along the border drew analogies
between the two conflicts.[72] The formerly iconophobic Taliban resorted to emotional visual images of carnage elsewhere to inspire new
recruits. In contrast to the handful of suicide attacks between 2001
and 2004, there were 20 or more in 2005. In the first three months
of 2006, there had already been a dozen such bombings; by late
October, there had been 106 such attacks.[73] In January 2006, one of
the deadliest of these attacks killed twenty-seven people and injured
forty in Spin Boldak in Kandahar Province.

Militants also launched a wave of assassinations and kidnappings. Assassins traveling by motorbike terrorized Ghazni, two hours
south of Kabul by car. In late 2005 and early 2006, insurgents killed
twenty-eight officials in Andar, a mostly Pashtun district in southern
Ghazni. Beheadings, kidnappings, and the use of "improvised explosive devices" targeted not just government officials, but also aid workers, teachers, and other civilians, as well as mullahs and former Taliban who had broken with the cause. When authorities in Ghazni
banned motorbikes in mid-April 2006, the Taliban countered by
threatening to strike all automobile traffic. Cars disappeared from local roads. "The real authority in the countryside," complained a local
bus driver, "is in hands of the Taliban who are patrolling in the area
freely, without any fear, day and night." He added, "It looks like 100
years ago. Everyone travels by bicycle or donkey. They do not dare to
bring their vehicles on roads."[74] Nor were American bases or even the
capital immune: in late February 2007 a suicide bomber detonated a
bomb at Bagram airbase when the U.S. vice president Dick Cheney
was inside, and in early May a roadside bomb targeted an Afghan

National Army bus in Kabul, wounding twenty-two soldiers. Suicide bombers repeatedly struck Kabul. Their attacks spread throughout the country and, as tensions between Pakistani president Pervez Musharraf and militants in the North West Frontier Province and Federally Administered Tribal Areas worsened after the storming of the Red Mosque in Islamabad in July, an arc of suicide bombings stretched across the Afghanistan-Pakistan frontier.

Like the elusive Taliban of the 1990s, the neo-Taliban insurgents defy simple categorization. Building on cross-border ties between Pashtun communities and religious leaders in Pakistan and Afghanistan, numerous fighters infiltrate Afghanistan from Pakistan. But many more appear to have emerged from Pashtun communities in the southern and eastern interior of Afghanistan. A number of such domestic militants appear to have signed up for fighting to earn a livelihood. According to a United Nations survey, the Taliban were said to offer daily wages twice what a sharecropper cultivating opium might earn.[75] One Afghan NGO head estimated that only 10 percent of the Taliban fighters were motivated by a strong desire to restore the Taliban to power, while 60 to 70 percent had joined the movement for a wage. In February 2006 in Zabul Province, a twenty-eight-year-old member of the Taliban described fighting a week or so out of the month in exchange for "a salary, new clothes, shoes, a motorbike and a Kalashnikov rifle." Although he had fled conscription when the Taliban came to power and emigrated to Pakistan, he enlisted recently to receive a $300 signing bonus and $150 a month in salary. In a province without international aid organizations, the funds allowed him to take care of his family (including his brother, whom he helped marry) and rebuild his home. According to this same Afghan NGO source, the remaining 20 or 30 percent have joined the cause to avenge abuses committed by Afghan officials or the coalition forces. Human rights groups have accused local authorities of falsely imprisoning and torturing civilians. Speaking with foreign journalists, some locals in the Pashtun belt expressed growing nostalgia for the security that some continued to associate with the Taliban.[76]

In some areas, militants fighting under the Taliban banner have acted more as a conventional mafia operation or, like militant groups in Colombia, as foot soldiers guaranteeing the functioning of the international drug trade. In exchange for securing roads and poppy fields, merchants and landowners have retained fighters with a regular salary. Elsewhere, they have extorted money from local communities. In places like the Andar District of Ghazni Province, just southwest of Kabul, villagers reportedly turned over aid money from a local U.S. Provincial Reconstruction Team to the Taliban who permeated the area. While some residents complained of extortion, others expressed support for the cause.[77] Similarly, when Taliban fighters took the district center of Musa Qala in Helmand Province on February 1, 2007, many residents fled, while local poppy harvesters welcomed them as a guarantee that neither the Kabul government nor NATO forces would eradicate their crops.[78]

The activation of neo-Taliban forces throughout much of Afghanistan in 2006 caught U.S. and NATO officials by surprise and defied simple explanations about the identities and motivations of the militants who managed to seize—but not always hold—growing numbers of districts. Some twenty-eight thousand American and international troops continued to provide security in Kabul and a few other major urban centers. In July, NATO expanded into the south to relieve some twenty-five hundred American troops.[79] These forces were caught off guard by the strength of the insurgency, which proved capable of waging major standing battles involving assaults by hundreds of militants. Comparing the intensity of the fighting to that of the Korean War, a British officer confessed that the "effectiveness of the enemy was much greater than we anticipated." In September, for example, NATO forces asserted that their "Operation Medusa" had killed a thousand Taliban fighters outside Kandahar. In fighting that raged for some ten days in September 2006 in a village west of Kandahar, American, Afghan, and Canadian forces killed some five hundred Taliban fighters. But according to Afghan government authorities, the battle also claimed the lives of some fifty civilians.[80]

In 2006, a surge of U.S. Air Force bombings (totaling some 987 bombs between June and November) outstripped the total number (of 884 bombs) dropped between 2001 and 2004, and the mounting civilian casualties that resulted provoked intense criticism of both American forces and the Karzai government in the nascent Afghan media. The killing of civilians in aerial attacks by coalition forces and raids on homes became central themes in criticism and propaganda mounted against the Karzai by diverse actors ranging from the neo-Taliban and the members of parliament to human rights groups. The president's inability to secure the release of detainees or protect civilians from American bombings and searches further weakened his authority in the eyes of many Afghans.[81]

While mounting violence in 2006 and 2007 sharpened disagreements between Karzai and his international sponsors, fighting also deepened divisions among NATO members about how to coordinate counterinsurgency tactics. A British deployment to Helmand in the summer of 2006 was among the most controversial developments. In the words of Leo Docherty, a veteran of the campaign, the British strategy was to create "within an inkspot haven of security the comprehensive approach" that would "nurture civil development and governance." Instead, Docherty charges:

The troops, deployed in isolation, had no real means of win-
ning hearts and minds; they could offer no practical developmental improvements and were unable to even state the British policy on opium production. Their presence soon became
antagonistic; like honeypot targets, they attracted anyone fan-
cying a crack at the invading infidel, seemingly no better than
the Russians before them.[82]

British and Canadian forces suffered serious casualties. While military activities were conducted in tandem with American air power,
British resort to negotiations with local tribal elders prompted disagreements with U.S. commanders. In September, British forces turned
the district center of Musa Qala over to elders in exchange for leaving the immediate area. Criticized by the Americans as a surrender
to de facto Taliban control, the protocol came to a violent end on
January 31 when U.S. air strikes killed a Taliban commander in
the area—a development, Thomas Ruttig observes, that had scuttled
similar "peace treaties" in October 2006 between Pakistani Taliban
and the Musharraf government in the tribal areas bordering Afghanistan.[83] In the meantime, Dutch and German troops developed their
own approaches, seeking to distance themselves from the Americans.
German troops admitted that they avoided mixing with Americans
out of fear that Afghans would fail to distinguish between them or
that they would lose their "good reputation" among Afghans.[84] In
October 2006 the Bundeswehr faced its own scandal, however, when
macabre photographs appeared in the press showing German soldiers in Afghanistan posing with skulls. In December, German authorities concluded that no crimes had been committed—because
the skulls had not involved the desecration of a cemetery. In a policy
that the Canadians would soon emulate, the Dutch sought to employ
alternatives to fighting in areas suspected of Taliban sympathies. As

Docherty recalled, NATO and ISAF troops were confronted with an extraordinarily complex situation. "The British face a broad spectrum of opposition in Helmand. The enemy cannot simply be described as 'Taliban.' A Helmand poppy-farmer can hang up his hoe over lunch-time, pick up his Kalashnikov, shoot at the British and be back in the fields for the rest of the afternoon. The farmer has nothing ideologically in common with the Taliban but they may share a common aim, for example the absence of foreign troops, for different motives."[85] Confronted with such challenges, reports of the killing or wounding of more than forty Afghan civilians near Jalalabad in March suggested that U.S. Marines had fired on Afghans for a distance of some ten miles after fleeing the scene of a suicide bombing.[86] Launched on March 6, 2007, "Operation Achilles," a NATO offensive focusing on northern Helmand, brought more political controversy. On May 2, 2007, following air strikes that killed fifty or more civilians in Herat Province and a raid in Nangarhar Province that prompted several days of protests by more than a thousand students, Karzai protested to NATO commanders that "civilian deaths and arbitrary decisions to search people's houses have reached an unacceptable level."[87]

Perhaps no other issue divided NATO states like the American use of airpower. Already in early 2002, British commanders had developed a critical view of the U.S. strategy. One British officer recounted to a diplomat an episode that encapsulated the limits of aerial reconnaissance and foreigners' knowledge of local communities: A British patrol was sent to investigate what appeared to be an al-Qaeda or Taliban camp with suspicious-looking fortifications and weapons on the border with Pakistan. Upon descending from a hilltop into the village, however, the patrol discovered that "the 'gun pits' were circles made in the grass by goats tied to stakes. The 'trenches' were drainage ditches and the 'camouflaged trucks' were ragged old tents." The site turned out to be an encampment of Afghan nomads.

The point of the officer's story was that, had the Americans received the same intelligence, "they would have bombed it flat."[88]

Together with troop casualties among British and Canadian soldiers who have seen fierce fighting in the volatile Helmand and Kandahar provinces, the civilian deaths caused by air strikes in 2006 and 2007 mobilized opposition in many NATO countries against further participation in ISAF and Operation Enduring Freedom. Canadian opposition parties opposed extending beyond early 2009 the mission of Canadian forces (whose ISAF contingent numbered roughly 2,500). Politicians in the Netherlands, with some 2,200 troops facing occasional fighting and suicide bombings in Uruzgan Province, expressed skepticism about staying beyond 2008. Among countries whose forces have not been involved in the same kind of active combat, like Italy and Germany (with 2,000 and 3,000 troops, respectively), public support for military involvement also declined. In June 2007, for example, Caritas International, a German aid group, called for a "stricter division between military and civilian tasks." It sharply criticized "the instrumentalization of humanitarian aid for military purposes" and recommended the transfer of all military operations to the command of the United Nations to offset the impression that "the country is under occupation by Western states."[89]

Meanwhile, insecurity infected more and more districts. Between January and August 2006, the insurgency claimed more than two thousand Afghan lives—a threefold increase from the previous year. As of February 2006, the United Nations warned, half of all Afghan children were malnourished, and more than half of the population lived in poverty.[90] Disarmament programs had stalled almost completely.[91]

The regional context remained critical to the destabilization of Afghanistan and the ascent of the neo-Taliban. Despite American pressure, Iran contributed substantially to reconstruction and the consolidation of relative stability in western Afghanistan.[92] But tensions persisted as officials in the Afghan government continued to accuse Pakistan of active complicity in the Taliban resurgence. For its part, Pakistan faced its own serious challenges. Following September 11 and formal declarations of support for U.S. operations in Afghanistan, domestic critics called into question Musharraf's Islamic credentials. In addition to numerous assassination attempts, a host of nationalist and tribalist insurgencies pushed back at the expanding power of the central government. The Pakistani army confronted an open revolt in the resource-rich province of Baluchistan. In the North West Frontier Province and the Federally Administered Tribal Areas, Islamist political parties tried to introduce a Taliban-inspired campaign to enforce sharia norms in local government, while Pashtun tribes fighting under the name of the Taliban resisted central authority. Facing American pressure, Musharraf made intermittent efforts to project the authority of the central government into the provinces neighboring Afghanistan. The regime used a combination of violence and negotiation to expand its authority.

Despite targeted assassinations of nationalist and other opponents, Pakistan nonetheless remained a refuge for militants of various kinds, with areas such as North Waziristan in a state of civil war. In Quetta, the capital of Baluchistan Province, reports circulated in early 2006 that commanders such as Mullah Dadullah and Mullah Abdul Ali Deobandi were in the city. Bookstores sold Taliban publications and religious songs. An Afghan journalist found a twenty-five-year-old madrasa student from Afghanistan, Saadullah, who explained that he had been recruited by a friend who told him "terrible things about the Afghan government" and about the Americans, who "were always abusing people, killing them, going into their homes and insulting their religion." Though he was enlisted to conduct a suicide attack on an Afghan army base in Kandahar, he turned back when his friend left him at the border, wished him luck, gave him $30, and returned to Quetta. A Taliban spokesman, Qari Yusof Ahmadi, denied Pakistani support. He claimed that "Pakistan is an ally of America, not of the Taliban." "The Taliban are sons of Afghanistan," he added, who "are in Afghanistan and . . . will fight in Afghanistan."[93]

Pakistan's madrasas continued to produce some 250,000 students a year, and many of these young men were potential recruits for cross-border military action.[94] The Dar al-'Ulum Haqqaniyya madrasa in Akora Khattak, perhaps the true spiritual center of the movement, remained open. The madrasa's bakery produced eight thousand loaves of bread a day for its thousands of students. Its head, Samiul Haq, a member of the Pakistani parliament, continued to voice support for the Taliban and "our struggle for freedom." Declaring America "our opponent," Haq insisted that "it is not only the Taliban, but all Afghans who do not want to live under foreign rule . . . The Afghans do not accept slavery."[95]

Where some saw a broad-based insurgency fueled by opium profits and widespread disillusionment with the government in Kabul due to corruption and insecurity, others saw a well-coordinated strategy to undermine American-led forces in Afghanistan by Taliban and al-Qaeda commanders. According to Syed Saleem Shahzad, a Pakistani journalist, the Taliban leadership had planned the offensive of 2006 for a year or more from their bases in the tribal areas of Pakistani North and South Waziristan.[96] There madrasa students joined other fighters in training sessions led by veterans of the Iraqi insurgency, who taught them how to construct improvised explosive devices and trained them to carry out suicide bombings.

By Shahzad's account, the Taliban offensive assumed such breadth because it had been well prepared. Its foundations had been laid by the sort of diplomatic negotiations analyzed by Abdulkader Sinno in this book, which were the key to the Taliban's mobilization of Pashtuns in the mid-1990s. Mullah Dadullah, a one-legged commander of the Taliban's northern front in the 1990s and a key actor in the central command of the movement after 2001, appears to have coordinated these militias in Waziristan and convinced them to heed a call from Mullah Omar to cease hostilities against the Pakistani government and focus exclusively on Afghanistan. At the same time, Dadullah claimed to have dispatched a host of emissaries throughout Afghanistan to patch together a coalition of militia leaders to wage a campaign against the Karzai government and its foreign backers. According to Shahzad, a delegation sent by the former head of al-Qaeda in Iraq, Abu Musab al-Zarqawi, visited Afghanistan, where they supposedly met with Mullah Omar, Osama bin Laden, and Ayman Zawahiri and shared expertise about the use of suicide attacks in Iraq.[97]

In early September tribal elites sympathetic to the Pakistan-based Taliban struck a truce with the Pakistani government. For Islamabad, the accord with tribal elites in North Waziristan was aimed at reducing friction with the local population, who had resisted Pakistani military operations against tribal forces and their allies among foreign militants and local Taliban militias. The government pledged to end major military activities and withdraw most of the forces who had frequently fought with local militias in the previous five years. In exchange, the council (jirga) of tribal elders promised to end incursions into Afghanistan and to refuse sanctuary to foreign militants. Following on efforts to recruit "moderate Taliban," the Karzai government then raised this Pakistani model of negotiation as a means to gain the assistance of Pashtun communities in excluding Taliban militants from their midst. But, as in Pakistan, the policy met with criticism from numerous quarters, and radical elements—including

Mullah Omar—openly refused to participate in these councils. Pakistani proposals to fence and mine the border only exacerbated the Karzai government's mistrust of Islamabad.

In 2007 a Taliban spring offensive within Afghanistan coincided with the further destabilization of Waziristan due to fighting among militant groups—and the spread of pro-Taliban militancy to Islamabad itself in the form of a campaign led by clerics and students of the Red Mosque who attempted to impose Taliban-style strictures on the capital. In the first half of the year, some 2,800 Afghans had lost their lives to neo-Taliban attacks and fighting between insurgents and coalition forces.[98] In May a coalition strike killed Mullah Dadullah, who had played an instrumental role in coordinating cross-border attacks and suicide bombings. In June, however, his brother Mullah Mansur Dadullah, who had been released from prison by the Afghan government in exchange for the Italian journalist Daniele Mastrogiacomo, announced that he had assumed his brother's command. Declaring that the Taliban struggle was a "global" one, he threatened more suicide bombings carried out by attackers, who, he charged, had been recruited by "our enemies: the crusaders. The terror of the infidels like that at Abu Ghraib, Guantanamo as well as at Afghan prisons at Bagram and Kandahar is the motivating force for young Muslims." While figures like Mullah Mansur Dadullah adopted an internationalist rhetoric, other commanders fighting under the Taliban banner focused on more localized concerns. In July a Taliban spokesman claimed that they had hanged three highway robbers before a crowd in Badghis Province in the northwest.[99] The event was notable not only because it reflected the geographic expansion of neo-Taliban activity. Such acts aimed to rekindle the movement's original self-image as a pious force for order, morality, and justice in the face of corruption and insecurity. Since 2001, in addition to the political marginalization of Pashtuns, the presence of foreigners and the vulnerability of poppy farmers have served as new symbolic resources that neo-Taliban actors have adapted to present themselves to disgruntled and insecure communities as the saviors of Afghanistan—and perhaps of Pakistan as well.

Even despite these regional conflicts, the reanimation of the Taliban movement was far from a foregone conclusion. As with the initial appearance of this movement of "knowledge seekers" from the madrasas and orphanages of the Afghanistan-Pakistan border, international actors played a central role in creating the conditions for their reemergence. Yet here it was the policies of the United States, the guardian of the central Afghan state, that contributed to the instability that the neo-Taliban rhetoric of a religiously inspired law and order sought to combat.

Having insisted on a tightly centralized state to the exclusion of other models that might have shared power more evenly among Afghanistan's diverse regions, the Americans then failed to back Kabul's authority. Rather than construct a viable state that would gain legitimacy among a wide variety of Afghan social groups, Karzai's backers undermined his authority by depriving him of a proper treasury and by continuing to wield military power through punitive expeditions that turned communities against the post-Taliban government but failed to provide security. As in 1994, Afghans sought not only order, but justice. Like the rulers of Afghanistan before them, the masters of Kabul had not resolved the crisis of the Afghan state and its dislocation from the diverse communities that make up that country. The Pax Americana promised development but only expanded the wide fissures cutting through Afghan society and, in mobilizing diverse foes against the center, rekindled memories of grievances feeding thirty years of war.

NOTES

CONTRIBUTORS

ACKNOWLEDGMENTS

INDEX

NOTES

Introduction

1. See "Living under the Taleban," *Institute for War and Peace Reporting: Afghan Recovery Report,* no. 249 (April 4, 2007), www.iwpr.net; "Taliban Hang Three Afghans in Captured Town," Agence France-Presse, April 1, 2007. For further evidence of increasing support among poppy farmers for the Taliban, see Conrad Schetter, Rainer Glassner, and Masood Karokhail, "Beyond Warlordism: The Local Security Architecture in Afghanistan," *Internationale Politik und Gesellschaft* 2 (2007): 136–152.

2. For an early assessment of the military campaign, see Anthony H. Cordesman, *The Lessons of Afghanistan: War Fighting, Intelligence, and Force Transformation* (Washington, DC: Center for Strategic and International Studies, 2002), 8.

3. The International Crisis Group observes that from January to August 2006, twenty-three nongovernmental organization workers were killed: "one was in the south, eight in the north, ten in the west and four in the central regions" ("Countering Afghanistan's Insurgency: No Quick Fixes," *Asia Report,* no. 123 [November 2, 2006]: 1). On the adaptation of former militants and others to the post-Taliban political order, see Thomas Ruttig, "Islamists, Leftists—and a Void in the Center: Afghanistan's Political Parties and Where They Came From (1902–2006)," Konrad-Adenauer-Stiftung (November 26, 2006), www.KAS.de.

4. Sami Yousafzai and Urs Gehringer, "Der Kodex der Taliban," *Die Weltwoche,* no. 46 (2006); "Unser Kampf ist global," *Die Weltwoche,* no. 26 (2007); Gilles Dorronsoro, "L'impasse afghane," *Les Nouvelles d'Afghanistan,* no. 116 (February 2007): 3–4; Schetter, Glassner, and Karokhail, "Beyond Warlordism"; and "Trouble on All Fronts in Helmand," *Institute for War and Peace Reporting: Afghan Recovery Report,* no. 259 (July 6, 2007).

5. Thomas Ruttig, "Die Taliban—Bewegung 'aus dem Nichts'?" *Inamo* no. 17 (Spring 1999): 12–16. See also William Maley, "Interpreting the

Taliban," in *Fundamentalism Reborn? Afghanistan and the Taliban,* ed. William Maley (New York: New York University Press, 1998), 18–19.

6. Paul Richards coined this term. In Richards's view, academics and journalists have treated the small wars following the end of the Cold War in Yugoslavia, Africa, and elsewhere as a "new barbarism"—as a novel form of violence resulting from essential cultural differences and brutal competition for resources and "driven by environmental and cultural imperatives which the West has had no hand in shaping, and now has no responsibility to try to contain." The purveyors of this "new barbarism" thesis cautioned policy makers that such violence was "politically meaningless and beyond the scope of conventional diplomacy or conciliation." See Paul Richards, *Fighting for the Rainforest: War, Youth, and Resources in Sierra Leone* (Portsmouth, NH: Heinemann, 1996), xiii–xxix.

7. Ahmed Rashid, *Taliban: Militant Islam, Oil and Fundamentalism in Central Asia* (New Haven: Yale University Press, 2000); and Richard Mackenzie, "The United States and the Taliban," in Maley, *Fundamentalism Reborn,* 90–103. See, too, the essays by Anthony Hyman, Anwar-ul-Haq Ahady, Ahmed Rashid, William Maley, Michael Keating, and Anthony Davis in Maley's *Fundamentalism Reborn.* For journalistic coverage attributing post-2001 Taliban activities to Pakistani government support, see, for example, Sarah Chayes, *The Punishment of Virtue: Inside Afghanistan after the Taliban* (New York: Penguin, 2006).

8. For an insightful critique of this interpretation, see Charles Hirschkind and Saba Mahmood, "Feminism, the Taliban, and Politics of Counter-Insurgency," *Anthropological Quarterly* 75, no. 2 (2002): 339–354.

9. Most of these studies trace the story of the Taliban through the late 1990s and offer valuable analyses of Taliban expansion and rule during this period. See Rashid, *Taliban;* Maley, *Fundamentalism Reborn;* Peter Marsden, *The Taliban: War, Religion and the New Order in Afghanistan* (1998; London: Zed Books, 2002); Larry P. Goodson, *Afghanistan's Endless War: State Failure, Regional Politics, and the Rise of the Taliban* (Seattle: University of Washington Press, 2001); Neamatollah Nojumi, *The Rise of the Taliban in Afghanistan: Mass Mobilization, Civil War, and the Future of the Region* (New York: Palgrave, 2002); and R. R. Sikoev, *Taliby (religiozno-politicheskii portret)* (Moscow: Institut vostokovedeniia RAN, 2002).

10. On the structural features of insurgency, see James D. Fearon and David D. Laitin, "Ethnicity, Insurgency, and Civil War," *American Political Science Review* 97, no. 1 (February 2003): 75–90; and George M. Derluguian, *Bourdieu's Secret Admirer in the Caucasus: A World-System Biography* (Chicago: University of Chicago Press, 2005), 32–33. For a snapshot

of Afghan demographics, see Stefan Schütte, "Searching for Security: Urban Livelihoods in Kabul," *Afghanistan Research and Evaluation Unit Report* (April 2006): 10.

11. Erwin Grötzbach, *Afghanistan: Eine geographische Landeskunde* (Darmstadt: Wissenschaftliche Buchgesellschaft, 1990), 17–55; Louis Dupree, *Afghanistan,* rev. ed. (Princeton: Princeton University Press, 1980), 1–54; Lutz Rzehak, ed. and trans., *Die Taliban im Land der Mittagssonne: Geschichten aus der afghanischen Provinz* (Wiesbaden: Reichert Verlag, 2004), xiii.

12. Conrad Schetter, *Kleine Geschichte Afghanistans* (Munich: Verlag C. H. Beck, 2004), 23.

13. On the Taliban and the Durand Line, see Zahid Hussain, *Frontline Pakistan: The Struggle with Militant Islam* (New York: Columbia University Press, 2007), 30.

14. See Grötzbach, *Afghanistan,* 56–89; these specific figures from a study of 1988 are analyzed on p. 57.

15. Ibid., 138–141.

16. Estimates in A. D. Davydov, V. G. Korgun, and R. R. Sikoev, eds., *Afganistan: Spravochnik* (Moscow: "Vostochnaia literatura" RAN, 2000), 29; and Grötzbach, *Afghanistan,* 60.

17. Grötzbach, *Afghanistan,* 186–190. Emigration during the anti-Soviet jihad also had a strongly pronounced regional character. Over 50 percent of the population of the provinces of Kandahar, Paktika, Ghazni, Paktya, Logar, Laghman, and Kunar may have fled to Pakistan; a similar proportion of inhabitants on the Iranian border (from Herat, Farah, and Nimroz provinces) may have fled to Iran. At the same time, refugees clustered around Kabul and Mazar-e Sharif as well as in the central highlands of the Hazarajat. See ibid., 65, on the war dead.

18. Academic writing, too, tends to depict regional Afghan commanders as uniformly "self-interested actors" motivated by "parochial interests" who should be displaced by a centralizing state. Critical of American support for many of these figures in Afghanistan, Kimberly Marten, in "Warlordism in Comparative Perspective," *International Security* 31, no. 3 (Winter 2006/2007): 41–73, argues for international promotion of a program of state formation and cultural transformation, including a literacy campaign, to combat these local elites. For an informed answer to this celebratory view of state centralization and technocratic vision in post-Taliban Afghanistan, see Antonio Giustozzi, "'Good' States vs. 'Bad' Warlords? A Critique of State-Building Strategies in Afghanistan," Crisis States Programme Working Papers Series No. 1 (2004).

19. For a critique of this view, see M. Nazif Shahrani, "Introduction: Marx-

ist 'Revolution' and Islamic Resistance in Afghanistan," in *Revolutions and Rebellions in Afghanistan: Anthropological Perspectives,* ed. M. Nazif Shahrani and Robert L. Canfield (Berkeley: Institute of International Studies, University of California at Berkeley, 1984), 3–10.

20. Landmark studies of ethnicity in Afghanistan include Shahrani and Canfield, *Revolutions and Rebellions;* Erwin Orywal, ed., *Die ethnischen Gruppen Afghanistans: Fallstudien zu Gruppenidentität* (Wiesbaden: Reichert Verlag, 1986); Jean-Pierre Digard, ed., *Le fait ethnique en Iran et en Afghanistan* (Paris: Centre National de la Recherche Scientifique, 1988); Olivier Roy, *Afghanistan: From Holy War to Civil War* (Princeton, NJ: Darwin Press, 1995); and Conrad Schetter, *Ethnizität und ethnische Konflikte in Afghanistan* (Berlin: Dietrich Reimer Verlag, 2003). See also, Christine Nölle-Karimi, "Die paschtunische Stammesversammlung im Spiegel der Geschichte," in *Rechtspluralismus in der Islamischen Welt,* ed. Michael Kemper and Maurus Reinkowski (Berlin: Walter de Gruyter, 2005), 177–194.

21. See "Language Groups," in *Historical Dictionary of Afghanistan,* by Ludwig W. Adamec (Metuchen, NJ: Scarecrow Press, 1991), 148.

22. Antonio Giustozzi, *War, Politics and Society in Afghanistan, 1978–1992* (London: Hurst and Co., 2000).

23. Giustozzi dates the intersection of interethnic violence and the struggle between the mujahedin and government forces to the summer of 1982, when Uzbek troops clashed with Pashtun nomads in the northern province of Faryab in a series of reprisal killings (ibid., 117–118).

24. Pashtuns are also referred to as "Pushtuns," "Pukhtuns," or, in the Pakistani context, "Pathans." See James W. Spain, *The Way of the Pathans,* 2nd ed. (Karachi: Oxford University Press, 1972), 22–26.

25. Bernt Glatzer, *Afghanistan: Im Auftrag der Friedrich-Ebert-Stiftung und der Gesellschaft für Technische Zusammenarbeit* (Bonn: Friedrich-Ebert-Stiftung, 2003), 19; Schetter, Glassner, and Karokhail, "Beyond Warlordism."

26. In 2004, Panjsher, previously a district in Parwan Province, was made into a separate province.

27. Glatzer, *Afghanistan.*

28. Robert L. Canfield, "New Trends among the Hazaras: From 'The Amity of Wolves' to 'The Practice of Brotherhood,'" *Iranian Studies* 37, no. 2 (June 2004): 241–262.

29. Glatzer, *Afghanistan,* 19.

30. For the CIA estimate as of December 3, 2006, see www.cia.gov/cia/publications/factbook/geos/af.html#People. It lists the rest of the population as "Tajik 27 per cent, Hazara 9 per cent, Uzbek 9 per cent, Aimak 4 per cent, Turkmen 3 per cent, Baluch 2 per cent, other 4 per cent."

31. Schetter, *Kleine Geschichte Afghanistans,* 23–24. American studies of the 1960s and 1970s tended to estimate the proportion of Pashtuns at 50 percent to 55 percent. See, for example, Vartan Gregorian, *The Emergence of Modern Afghanistan: Politics of Reform and Modernization, 1880–1946* (Stanford: Stanford University Press, 1969), 25; Richard S. Newell, *The Politics of Afghanistan* (Ithaca: Cornell University Press, 1972), 14. A recent Russian reference guide estimates the Pashtun population at 51–53 percent of the prewar and 47–49 percent of the postwar Afghan population. See *Afganistan: Spravochnik,* 31.

32. See, for example, "Taliban Support Council Issuances, 1993–1997," Hoover Archive on War, Revolution, and Peace, Stanford University.

33. The seven parties were the Harakat-e Inqelab-e Islami-ye Afghanistan (Islamic Revolution Movement of Afghanistan), led by Mawlawi Muhammad Nabi Muhammadi; Harakat-e Islami-ye Afghanistan (Islamic Movement of Afghanistan); Hizb-e Islami–Hekmatyar faction (Party of Islam), led by Gulbuddin Hekmatyar; Hizb-e Islami–Khales faction (Party of Islam), led by Mawlawi M. Yunos Khales; Ettehad-e Islami (Islamic Unity), headed by Abdul Rabb al-Rasul Sayyaf; Jabha-ye Nejat-e Melli-ye Afghanistan (National Liberation Front of Afghanistan), led by Sebghatullah Mojadeddi; Jamiat-e Islami-ye Afghanistan (Islamic Society of Afghanistan), headed by Burhanuddin Rabbani; and Mahaz-e Melli-ye Islami-ye Afghanistan (National Islamic Front of Afghanistan), led by Sayyed Ahmad Gailani.

34. This party was the Hizb-e Wahdat-e Islami-ye Afghanistan (Party of Islamic Unity of Afghanistan). The Persian title of this constitution was *Qanun-e asasi-ye jomhuri-ye federal-e Islami-ye Afghanistan* (Sarwar Danish, ed., *Matn-e kamil-e qawanin-e asasi-ye Afghanistan [as 1301 ta 1372 sh]* [Qom: Markaz-e Farhangi-ye Nawisendagan-e Afghanistan, 1995], 282–310).

35. General Dostum expressed his opinion about the creation of a federal state in Afghanistan to one of the authors (A. T.) in 1996, during a meeting in Tashkent, Uzbekistan.

36. See the insightful treatment by Schetter, *Ethnizität und ethnische Konflikte,* 438–439.

37. Some accounts identify Omar instead with the Hizb-e Islami led by Mawlawi M. Yonus Khales. See the excellent accounts in Ruttig, "Die Taliban"; and Schetter, *Ethnizität und ethnische Konflikte,* 524–525. Schetter notes that, as of January 1998, forty-three of the sixty-eight top Taliban leaders (including provincial governors) had belonged to the Harakat-e Inqelab-e Islami.

38. Quoted in Schetter, *Ethnizität und ethnische Konflikte,* 524.

39. On these groups, see Muhammad Amir Rana, *A to Z of Jehadi Organiza-*

tions in Pakistan, trans. Saba Ansari (Lahore: Mashal, 2004), 203–206; and Hussain, *Frontline Pakistan* (57, 82–83, on these foreigners).

40. Ruttig, "Die Taliban." See also, Maley, "Interpreting the Taliban," which adds another Pashtun element: "At least some of the Kandahari *Pai luch* brotherhood, a secret society with a distinctive uniform whose members could be seen in company of the Taliban in Kabul in mid-1997, and which had been involved in anti-modernist disturbances at the instigation of conservative clerics in Kandahar in 1959" (15).

41. Alex Klaits and Gulchin Gulmamadova-Klaits, eds., *Love and War in Afghanistan* (New York: Seven Stories Press, 2005), 60.

42. Ibid.

43. Rzehak, *Die Taliban im Land der Mittagssonne*, 22.

44. Hafizullah Emadi, "The End of *Taqiyya*: Reaffirming the Religious Identity of Ismailis in Shugnan, Badakhshan—Political Implications for Afghanistan," *Middle Eastern Studies* 34, no. 3 (July 1998): 117. For an account of an Uzbek mullah's confrontation with Tajik Taliban mullahs in northern Afghanistan, see Klaits and Gulmamadova-Klaits, *Love and War in Afghanistan*, 276–278.

45. See the report by Amnesty International, web.amnesty.org/library/Index/ENGASA110071998?open&of=ENG-AFG.

46. Emadi, "The End of *Taqiyya*," 118. Rashid notes that the original ten-member Supreme Council of the Taliban included only one non-Pashtun, Mawlawi Sayyed Ghiasuddin, a Tajik from Badakhshan (*Taliban*, 98). On Omar's rejection of the Pashtun label, see Ismail Khan, "Omar Threatens to Intensify War: Talks with Karzai Govt Ruled Out," *Dawn*, January 4, 2007.

47. For Nimroz, see Rzehak, *Die Taliban im Land der Mittagssonne*, 30–31.

48. Omid Marzban, "Mullah Dadullah: The Military Mastermind of the Taliban Insurgency," *Terrorism Focus* 3, no. 11 (March 21, 2006): 3–4.

49. See the fascinating study by Mohammad Suleman and Sue Williams, "Strategies and Structures in Preventing Conflict and Resisting Pressure: A Study of Jaghori District, Afghanistan, under Taliban Control," March 2003, www.cdainc.com/publications.

50. See Rzehak, *Die Taliban im Land der Mittagssonne*.

51. In a September 1996 interview posted on the Taliban website, Mullah Omar referred to the movement as a grouping of "reformers." See A. A. Kniazev, *Afganskii konflikt i radikal'nyi islam v Tsentral'noi Azii: Sbornik dokumentov i materialov* (Bishkek: "Ilim," 2001), 70. On Pashtunwali in the 1970s, see Willi Steul, *Paschtunwali: Ein Ehrenkodex und seine Rechtliche Relevanz* (Wiesbaden: Franz Steiner Verlag, 1981); and Alef-Shah Zadran, "Socioeconomic and Legal-Political Processes in a Pash-

tun Village, Southeastern Afghanistan" (Ph.D. diss., State University of New York at Buffalo, 1977).

52. Vali Nasr, "The Iranian Revolution and Changes in Islamism in Pakistan, India, and Afghanistan," in *Iran and the Surrounding World: Interactions in Culture and Cultural Politics*, ed. Nikkie R. Keddie and Rudie Matthee (Seattle: University of Washington Press, 2002), 327–352.

53. On the variety of Afghan and Pakistani religious experiences, see, for example, David B. Edwards, *Heroes of the Age: Moral Fault Lines on the Afghan Frontier* (Berkeley: University of California Press, 1996); Barbara D. Metcalf, *'Traditionalist' Islamic Activism: Deoband, Tablighis, and Talibs* (Leiden: ISIM, 2002); Thomas Barfield, "An Islamic State Is a State Run by Good Muslims: Religion as a Way of Life and Not an Ideology in Afghanistan," in *Remaking Muslim Politics: Pluralism, Contestation, Democratization*, ed. Robert W. Hefner (Princeton: Princeton University Press, 2005), 213–239; Mukulika Banerjee, *The Pathan Unarmed: Opposition and Memory in the North West Frontier* (Karachi: Oxford University Press, 2000); Oskar Verkaaik, *Migrants and Militants: Fun and Urban Violence in Pakistan* (Princeton: Princeton University Press, 2004); and Magnus Marsden, *Living Islam: Muslim Religious Experience in Pakistan's North-West Frontier* (Cambridge: Cambridge University Press, 2005).

54. See Robert W. Hefner, "Introduction: Modernity and the Remaking of Muslim Politics," in Hefner, *Remaking Muslim Politics*, 1–36; Metcalf, *'Traditionalist' Islamic Activism;* and, more generally, Dale F. Eickelman and James Piscatori, *Muslim Politics* (Princeton: Princeton University Press, 1996).

55. Gilles Dorronsoro, *Revolution Unending: Afghanistan, 1979 to the Present*, trans. John King (New York: Columbia University Press, 2005), 21.

56. See, for example, the language of Nizamuddin Shamzai at a seminar in Pakistan in October 1996 in *Afganskii konflikt*, 78–79.

57. Senzil K. Nawid, *Religious Response to Social Change in Afghanistan, 1919–29: King Aman-Allah and the Afghan Ulama* (Costa Mesa, CA: Mazda, 1999), on opposition to girls' schools, 96–97; and see also the valuable introduction to *Kabul under Siege: Fayz Muhammad's Account of the 1929 Uprising*, trans. and ed. Robert D. McChesney (Princeton: Markus Wiener, 1999), 1–29.

58. See Helena Malikyar and Amin Tarzi, "The Jîlânî Family in Afghanistan," *Journal of the History of Sufism* 1–2 (2000): 93–102.

59. See Edwards, *Heroes of the Age*; Asta Olesen, *Islam and Politics in Afghanistan* (Richmond, UK: Curzon Press, 1995); and Dorronsoro, *Revolution Unending.*

60. Maliha Zulfacar, "The Pendulum of Gender Politics in Afghanistan," *Central Asian Survey* 25, nos. 1–2 (March–June 2006): 27–59, here 39.

61. Amin Tarzi, "The Judicial State: Evolution and Centralization of the Courts in Afghanistan, 1883–1896" (Ph.D. diss., New York University, 2003).

62. Gregorian, *Emergence of Modern Afghanistan,* 248–252.

63. Without ignoring the severity of Taliban rule, Maliha Zulfacar highlights continuity between the policies of the mujahedin and the Taliban and treats the period from 1992 to 2001 as a distinctive moment in the history of Afghan women. See Zulfacar, "The Pendulum of Gender Politics." There were also cases of stonings of women by mujahedin. See, for example, a case in the northern province of Konduz in Klaits and Gulmamadova-Klaits, *Love and War in Afghanistan,* 201.

64. On these parties, see the excellent account by David B. Edwards, *Before Taliban: Genealogies of the Afghan Jihad* (Berkeley: University of California Press, 2002), 225–278, quote at 270.

65. See Diego Cordovez and Selig S. Harrison, *Out of Afghanistan: The Inside Story of the Soviet Withdrawal* (New York: Oxford University Press, 1995).

66. Barnett R. Rubin, *The Fragmentation of Afghanistan: State Formation and Collapse in the International System* (New Haven: Yale University Press, 1995).

67. On Casey, see Steve Coll, *Ghost Wars: The Secret History of the CIA, Afghanistan, and Bin Laden, from the Soviet Invasion to September 10, 2001* (New York: Penguin Press, 2004), 92–98; Cordovez and Harrison, *Out of Afghanistan;* and on American anticommunist efforts in Afghanistan, see also Odd Arne Westad, *The Global Cold War: Third World Interventions and the Making of Our Times* (Cambridge: Cambridge University Press, 2005), 328; Rubin, *The Fragmentation of Afghanistan,* 182–183.

68. "Statement by Abdul Hakim Mujahed," May 1, 1997, 3. This document was distributed to UN member states and obtained by Amin Tarzi.

69. Ibid.

70. Maley, "Interpreting the Taliban," 20, emphasis in the original.

71. P. W. Singer, *Children at War* (New York: Pantheon, 2005), 26. While Muslim clerics had never ruled Afghanistan before the Taliban, the fighting bands of young men under their control had on occasion appeared in other Muslim societies in the past. In nineteenth-century Iranian cities, for example, madrasa students as well as male toughs (known as *lutis*) had sometimes acted as the enforcers of Muslim clerics. See

Willem M. Floor, "The Political Role of the Lutis in Iran," in *Modern Iran: The Dialectics of Continuity and Change,* ed. Michael E. Bonine and Nikki R. Keddie (Albany: State University of New York Press, 1981), 83–95.

72. On executions of mullahs, see Wahid Muzhda, "Chera Taliban beh mulla koshi roy awarda and?" BBC Persian.com, June 15, 2005; and on the execution video, see Farangis Najibullah, "Afghanistan: Boy-Executioner Video Outrages Afghans, World," Radio Free Europe/ Radio Liberty, April 24, 2007.

73. Muhammad Qasim Zaman, "Pluralism, Democracy, and the Ulama," in Hefner, *Remaking Muslim Politics,* 37–59, here, 63.

74. See Christine Noelle, "The Anti-Wahhabi Reaction in Nineteenth Century Afghanistan," *Muslim World* 85 (1995): 23–48.

75. Ibid., 67.

76. Rashid, *Taliban;* and Nazif Shahrani, "The Taliban Enigma: Person-Centered Politics and Extremism in Afghanistan," *ISIM Newsletter,* no. 6 (2000): 20–21.

77. Sikoev, *Taliby,* 67–68.

78. Ibid., 67.

79. Ibid., 69–70. On his use of titulature, see Muhammad Riza Hajj Babai, ed., *Qawanin-e Mulla Omar: Majmua-ye qawanin va ayin namahha-ye Taleban dar Afghanistan* (Tehran: Nigah-e emruz, 1382 [2003]). In an interview with the newspaper *Al-Sharq al-Awsat* in May 1998, Mullah Omar responded to a question about whether or not his use of the title *amir* applied beyond the borders of Afghanistan by demurring, "If two individuals accept me to be their amir, I accept; and if 100,000 people accept me as their amir, I accept. It is up to the Muslims in the other Muslim countries. If they want me to be their amir, I have no objection." See "Taleban Leader Explains Policy," BBC Summary of World Broadcasts, May 21, 1998.

80. See the Radio Voice of Sharia report, "Taleban Execute Murderer," BBC Summary of World Broadcasts, June 30, 1998. On the ministries, see Sikoev, *Taliby,* 71–73.

81. See Pierre Centlivres and Micheline Centlivres-Demont, "Les martyrs afghans par le texte et l'image (1978–1992)," in *Saints et Héros du Moyen-Orient contemporain,* ed. Catherine Mayeur-Jaouen (Paris: Maisonneuve et Larose, 2002), 319–333.

82. See Michael Cook, *Commanding Right and Forbidding Wrong in Islamic Thought* (Cambridge: Cambridge University Press, 2002), 522.

83. Babai, *Qawanin-e Mulla Omar,* 9.

84. They were issued primarily as *firmans* and *ahkam*s in the name of "the [highest] office of the Islamic Emirate of Afghanistan" *(Maqam-e Amirat-e Islami-ye Afghanistan).* See ibid.

85. Klaits and Gulmamadova-Klaits, *Love and War in Afghanistan,* 61.

86. For examples of popular resentment against Kabul among residents of a nearby valley, see Nigel Allan, "The Modernization of Rural Afghanistan: A Case Study," in *Afghanistan in the 1970s,* ed. Louis Dupree and Linette Albert (New York: Praeger, 1974), 124.

87. Sikoev, *Taliby,* 108–109. The Shiite rite of Ashura was not banned outright, but confined to Shiite mosques.

88. Bruce Lawrence, ed., *Messages to the World: The Statements of Osama bin Laden,* trans. James Howarth (London: Verso, 2005), 98–99.

89. See Engseng Ho, "Empire through Diasporic Eyes: A View from the Other Boat," *Comparative Studies in Society and History* 46, no. 2 (April 2004): 210–246.

90. See Wahid Muzhda, *Afghanistan wa panj sal sulta-ye Taleban* (Tehran: Nashr-e ney, 1382 [2003].)

91. Zalmay Khalilzad, "Afghanistan: Time to Reengage," *Washington Post,* October 7, 1996. See also Nancy DeWolf Smith, "These Rebels Aren't So Scary," *Wall Street Journal,* February 22, 1995, which warned, "If the policy makers get too hung up on those black turbans, they're going to miss some white hats underneath." The author, an editor at the *Wall Street Journal,* described their campaign in 1995 against "anti-Western" mujahedin and "long-haired" drug dealers approvingly: "For a few chaotic days, the air in Kandahar was thick with smoke, as Taleban systematically attacked and disarmed every commander, and every long-haired gang of heroin traders for miles around. Some terrified bad guys tried to escape by hiding under long women's burqas. To the delight of cheering townspeople, the Taleban deputized small boys to peek under these tents and de-veil the former big shots trembling underneath. Caravans of cars left Kandahar in a hurry, their occupants tossing incriminating knives and guns out the windows onto a highway already dotted with abandoned television sets." From a very different perspective, Timothy Mitchell has identified a pattern that explains relations between the United States and Middle Eastern states—with the exception of Iran (and Israel): "As a rule, the most secular regimes . . . have been those most independent of the United States. The more closely a government is allied with Washington, the more Islamic its politics." See his "McJihad: Islam in the U.S. Global Order," *Social Text* 20, no. 4 (Winter 2002): 1–18.

92. Indeed, the burqa remained ubiquitous in the northeastern corner of the

country, which was never occupied by the Taliban. "Why," the anthropologists Charles Hirschkind and Saba Mahmood ask, "were conditions of war, militarization, and starvation [under the mujahedin] considered to be less injurious to women than the lack of education, employment, and, most notably, in the media campaign, Western dress styles [under the Taliban]?" See their "Feminism, the Taliban, and Politics of Counter-Insurgency," 345. While politicians, journalists, and scholars frequently treat the Taliban and Chechen militants as part of a single front against the West, each movement's trajectory has proved, in fact, quite distinctive. On the peculiarly Soviet—and global—specifics of the Chechen case, see Georgi M. Derluguian, "Che Guevaras in Turbans," *New Left Review*, September–October 1999, 3–27.

93. We are grateful to Nigel Allan for suggesting this possibility.

94. "During the Taliban rule," recalled the Taliban foot soldier Gulbuddin, "increasing numbers of people suffered from poor harvests and cruel punishments. I grew convinced that Allah was on the side of the Americans and the Northern Alliance. For this reason, shortly before the Taliban were expelled from northern Afghanistan, I defected to the other side." See Klaits and Gulmamadova-Klaits, *Love and War in Afghanistan*, 68.

1. Explaining the Taliban's Ability to Mobilize the Pashtuns

Portions of this chapter were previously published in Abdulkader Sinno, *Organizations at War* (Ithaca: Cornell University Press, 2008).

1. Gilles Dorronsoro traces the origins of the Taliban to a client group of Muhammad Nabi Muhammadi's Harakat-e Inqilab-e Islami created around 1990 called Jamia-e Taliban. While the name and constituency of the 1990 and 1994 groups are similar, I believe there is little reason to think that this was the same organization. See Dorronsoro, *La révolution afghane: Des communistes aux tâlebân* (Paris: Karthala, 2000), 269.

2. Those who argue that the Taliban were supported by Pakistan from the outset point to some evidence to make the case that the Spin Boldak depot was depleted before its seizure by the Taliban. The Pakistanis and Taliban, they say, only pretended it contained enough weapons to equip the organization for years, in order to explain its access to an obviously large supply of weapons.

3. Interestingly, the same structural factors that led to the disintegration of Afghan political parties were so extreme in and around Kandahar that even the shura that was formed there after the collapse of the Kabul regime eventually disintegrated.

4. See, for example, *The Economist,* October 28, 1995, 38.

5. For more on these events, see Hafizullah Emadi, "The Hazaras and Their Role in the Process of Political Transformation in Afghanistan," *Central Asian Survey* 16, no. 3 (1997): 383–385.

6. Ralph H. Magnus, "Afghanistan in 1997: The War Moves North," *Asian Survey* 28, no. 2 (February 1998): 109–116.

7. For example, P. Stobdan, *The Afghan Conflict and India* (New Delhi: Institute for Defense Studies and Analyses, 1998), 9–18.

8. Anthony Davis, "How the Taliban Became a Military Force," in *Fundamentalism Reborn? Afghanistan and the Taliban,* ed. William Maley (Lahore: Vanguard, 1998), 69.

9. Barnett Rubin, "The Political Economy of War and Peace in Afghanistan," *World Development* 28, no. 10 (2000): 1794.

10. For a detailed study of outside aid to the Taliban and its rivals, consult "Afghanistan: The Role of Pakistan, Russia, and Iran in Fueling the Civil War," *Human Rights Watch Report* 13, no. 3 (July 2001).

11. Ahmed Rashid, "Pakistan and the Taliban," in Maley, *Fundamentalism Reborn,* 76; and Rashid, *Taliban: Militant Islam, Oil and Fundamentalism in Central Asia* (New Haven: Yale University Press, 2000), 139, 201.

12. Anwar-ul-Haq Ahady, "Saudi Arabia, Iran and the Conflict in Afghanistan," in Maley, *Fundamentalism Reborn,* 125.

13. Rashid, *Taliban,* chaps. 3 and 14.

14. Rashid, "Pakistan and the Taliban."

15. Anthony Davis, "Afghanistan's Taliban," *Jane's Intelligence Review* 7, no. 7 (July 1995): 315.

16. Larry Goodson, *Afghanistan's Endless War: State Failure, Regional Politics, and the Rise of the Taliban* (Seattle: University of Washington Press, 2001), 109–111.

17. Barnett Rubin, *The Fragmentation of Afghanistan: State Formation and Collapse in the International System* (New Haven: Yale University Press, 1995), 262.

18. "Revenge of the Pathans," *The Economist,* February 25, 1995, 26. See also David Edwards, *Before Taliban: Genealogies of the Afghan Jihad* (Berkeley: University of California Press, 2002), 293, 295.

19. Antonio Giustozzi, *War, Politics and Society in Afghanistan, 1978–1992* (London: Hurst, 2000), 242.

20. A list compiled by Rashid reveals that there were more Ghilzai than Durranis among top-tier Taliban leaders. See *Taliban,* appendix 2.

21. Edwards, *Before Taliban,* 294.

22. Dorronsoro, *La révolution afghane,* 271.

23. Rashid, *Taliban*, 33; and Davis, "How the Taliban Became a Military Force," 51.

24. *Asiaweek*, September 22, 1995, 35; and Kamal Matinuddin, *The Taliban Phenomenon* (Karachi: Oxford University Press, 1999), 88.

25. Davis, "Afghanistan's Taliban," 321; Matinuddin, *The Taliban Phenomenon*, 77; and Rameen Moshref, *The Taliban* (East Hampton, NY: Afghanistan Forum, 1997), 5 and n. 21.

26. Peter Marsden, *The Taliban: War, Religion and the New Order in Afghanistan* (Karachi: Oxford University Press, 1998), 55; and Matinuddin, *The Taliban Phenomenon*, 264.

27. Matinuddin, *The Taliban Phenomenon*, 103–104.

28. Dorronsoro, *La révolution afghane*, 280.

29. Emily MacFarquhar, "A New Force of Muslim Fighters Is Determined to Rule Afghanistan," *US News and World Report*, March 6, 1995, 64–66. See also Nasreen Ghufran, "The Taliban and the Civil War Entanglement in Afghanistan," *Asian Survey* 41 (2001): 468.

30. Ahmad Mansur, *Mustaqbal Afghanistan* (Beirut: Dar Ibn Hazm, 1995), 54.

31. For a detailed account of the political economy of Afghanistan under the Taliban, see Rubin, "Political Economy of War and Peace."

2. The Rise and Fall of the Taliban

1. See Hafizullah Emadi, *State, Revolution, and Superpowers in Afghanistan* (New York: Praeger, 1990); and Amin Saikal and William Maley, *Regime Change in Afghanistan* (San Francisco: Westview Press, 1991).

2. John K. Cooley, *Unholy Wars: Afghanistan, America and International Terrorism* (London: Pluto Press, 1999), 9–45; and Charles C. Cogan, "Partners in Time: The CIA and Afghanistan," *World Policy Journal* 10, no. 2 (Summer 1993): 373–374.

3. Cooley, *Unholy Wars*, 47–64.

4. Ayesha Jalal, *Democracy and Authoritarianism in South Asia* (Cambridge: Cambridge University Press, 1995), 80–110.

5. Cooley, *Unholy Wars*, 61. Hekmatyar's friendship with General Zia and close connection with ISI generals such as Hamid Gul were formed through Hekmatyar's ideological partnership with Qazi Ahmed Hussein, the leader of the Jama'at-e-Islami. Qazi Hussein was a close and strong supporter of General Zia, and he had many followers within the military as well as in the ISI.

6. Olivier Roy, *Islam and Resistance in Afghanistan* (New York: Cambridge University Press, 1990), 73.

7. Neamatollah Nojumi, *The Rise of the Taliban in Afghanistan: Mass Mobilization, Civil War, and the Future of the Region* (New York: Palgrave, 2002), 86.

8. Except for the Revolutionary Islamic Council of Afghanistan (also known as Shura-e Hazarajat), Harkat-e Islami (led by Muhammad Asef Mohseni), and the People's Mujahedin, an underground group of progressive educated individuals who followed a political ideology similar to that of the People's Mujahedin of Iran (and whose leadership was anonymous), all other Afghan Shiite groups received funding from Iran. The most extreme group was Sazman-e Nasr-e Islami; it had a style of leadership and ideology similar to that of Hekmatyar's group. It was thought of as the Shiite Muslim Brothers, and, just like Hekmatyar's group warred against other Sunni groups, it waged internal war against the Revolutionary Islamic Council of Afghanistan, which caused the deaths of thousands of Shiite mujahedin in the Hazarajat throughout the early 1980s.

9. Author's interview with Sayyed Murtaza Husseini, who was injured on the side of Iranian forces against Iraq, spring 1985, Mashhad, Iran.

10. For more on the Afghan response to the Soviet invasion, see M. Hassan Kakar, *Afghanistan: The Soviet Invasion and the Afghan Response* (Berkeley: University of California Press, 1995).

11. See Nojumi, *Rise of the Taliban.*

12. Ibid.

13. Author's interview with S. Bahauddin Majruh, Baluchistan, Pakistan, 1984.

14. See Fredrik Barth, "The Cultural Wellspring of Resistance in Afghanistan," in *The Great Game Revisited,* ed. Rosanne Klass (New York: Freedom House, 1987).

15. In the 1980s, pro-democracy forces in Afghanistan also suffered at the hands of the PDPA regime. The communist regime jailed and executed thousands of moderate and nationalist politicians, including prominent clergy, Sufi leaders, college and university students and professors, and former civil and military officers.

16. Author's interview with Gh. M. M., Jamiat-e Islami-ye Afghanistan, led by Burhanuddin Rabbani, Afghanistan and Iranian border, 1984.

17. Author's interview with a group of Afghan businessmen based in Mashhad, Iran, fall 1985.

18. Author's interview with Hizbullah commanders in western Afghanistan, fall 1985.

19. Author's interview with families of victims and two survivors of kidnapping by Islamist covert networks in Mashhad, Iran, fall 1984.

20. Ibid.

21. Author's interview with teachers during a visit to religious seminaries, Peshawar, Pakistan, winter 1984.

22. Author's interview with members of the executive committee of the Hizb-e Islami, led by Hekmatyar, Peshawar, Pakistan, 1984.

23. See Ahmed Rashid, *Taliban: Militant Islam, Oil and Fundamentalism in Central Asia* (New Haven: Yale University Press, 2000), 106.

24. Author's interview with Mullah Abdul Jalil, a unit commander of the Jamiat-e Islami-ye Afghanistan, Peshawar, 1984.

25. Author's interview with Hojat al-Islam Musawi, member of the executive committee of Nasr-e Islami, Qom, Iran, 1985.

26. Author's interview with Karim, representative of the Afghan Shura-ye Etifaq-e Islami in Iran, who was arrested by the Iranian Revolutionary Guard and deported from Mashhad, Iran, in the spring of 1985.

27. Author's personal notes, visiting a school established and controlled by Jamiat-e Islami, Hizb-e Islami, and Harkat-e Islami Afghanistan, Peshawar, Pakistan, 1984.

28. Rashid, *Taliban*, 106.

29. See *Shahadat*, publication of the Hizb-e-Islami (Hekmatyar), Peshawar, Pakistan, fall 1986.

30. Author's interview with Daud Matin, a freelance Afghan journalist, Pakistan, summer 1995.

31. Diego Cordovez and Selig S. Harrison, *Out of Afghanistan: The Inside Story of the Soviet Withdrawal* (New York: Oxford University Press, 1995), 135.

32. Stephen Tanner, *Afghanistan: A Military History from Alexander the Great to the Fall of the Taliban* (New York: Da Capo Press, 2002), 236.

33. For detailed information, see Nojumi, *Rise of the Taliban.*

34. For more information on the Central Asian oil and gas resources, see the U.S. Energy Information Administration at www.eia.doe.gov/emeu/cabs/turkmen.html. See also Jan H. Kalicki, "Caspian Energy at the Crossroad," *Foreign Affairs* 80, no. 5 (September–October 2001): 120–134.

35. Neamat Nojumi, "Afghanistan: A Regional Economic Highway," *Effort Journal* 1 (October 1998).

36. Barnett R. Rubin, "Women and Pipelines: Afghanistan's Proxy Wars," *International Affairs* 73, no. 2 (1997): 283–286.

37. These mobile military convoys changed the balance against Ismail Khan's forces and subsequently captured Herat in September 1995 (author's interview with Commander Salahuddin, Herat, summer 1995).

38. Quoted by Alexander Cockburn, "This Is Victory?" *The Nation,* January 27, 1997.

39. Nojumi, *Rise of the Taliban,* 171.

40. Lawrence Lifschultz, "Bush, Drugs and Pakistan: Inside the Kingdom of Heroin," *The Nation,* November 14, 1988.

41. Author's note, number of Afghan moderates, including Majruh and Dr. Yosuf, accusing the Afghan Islamist leaders based in Peshawar of accepting Pakistan's in-depth policy toward Afghanistan. They were suggesting that these leaders, especially Hekmatyar, had agreed with General Zia to form an Islamic federation of Afghanistan and Pakistan,

42. Nojumi, *Rise of the Taliban,* 117–122.

43. Ibid.

44. Ibid.

45. See Rashid, *Taliban;* and Rashid, *Jihad: The Rise of Militant Islam in Central Asia* (New Haven: Yale University Press, 2002).

46. A religious Islamic center established 150 years ago in the town of Deoband, India, made a sharp distinction between "revealed" (sacred) knowledge, and "human" (secular) knowledge. The school excluded all learning that was not obviously Islamic by firmly rejecting other religious traditions (the Hinduism of India and the Christianity of the British missionaries) and forbidding Western-style education and the study of any subjects not directly related to the study of the Quran.

47. See Louis Dupree, *Afghanistan* (Princeton: Princeton University Press, 1980).

48. Ibid.

49. Rashid, *Taliban,* 106.

50. Muhammad Musa, "Junbesh-e Taliban wa ahdaf-e shan," quoted in Nojumi, *Rise of the Taliban,* 154.

51. Maududi was a significant contributor to "democratic theocracy," which has recognized modern democratic measures such as parliamentary elections.

52. See Nojumi, *Rise of the Taliban.*

53. See Amin Tarzi, "The Judicial State: Evolution and Centralization of the Courts in Afghanistan, 1883–1896" (Ph.D., diss., New York University, 2003).

54. See Vartan Gregorian, *The Emergence of Modern Afghanistan* (Stanford: Stanford University Press, 1969).

55. Amnesty International, *In the Firing Line: War and Children's Rights* (London: Amnesty International U.K., 1999).

56. Rashid, *Taliban,* 112.

57. Ibid.

58. Robert A. Scalapino, "The Transition in Chinese Party Leadership: A Comparison of the Eighth and Ninth Central Committees," in *Elites in the People's Republic of China*, ed. Robert A. Scalapino (Seattle: University of Washington Press, 1972), 67–148.

59. Hannah Arendt, *The Origins of Totalitarianism* (New York: World, 1958), chaps. 11 and 12.

60. Author's interview with Sayyed Murtaza Husseini; and www.pakistanlink.com/sah/04202001.htm.

61. *The Guardian*, October 11, 2001.

62. Nojumi, *Rise of the Taliban*.

63. Anthony Downs, *Inside Bureaucracy* (Boston: Little, Brown, 1967), chap. 6.

64. Ahmad Shah Masud, "A Message to the People of the United States of America," U.S. Senate Committee on Foreign Relations, Committee Hearing on Afghanistan, October 8, 1998.

65. Author's interview with Dr. Abdullah and Harun Amin, Boston, February 1999.

66. Nojumi, *Rise of the Taliban*.

67. Yossef Bodansky, *Bin Laden: The Man Who Declared War on America* (Roseville, CA: Prima, 2001), 91–115.

68. Ibid., 226.

69. See Larry Goodson, "Afghanistan's Long Road to Reconstruction," *Journal of Democracy* 14 (January 2003): 82–99.

70. Kamal Matinuddin, "Reconstruction of Afghanistan," *The News: Jang* (Pakistan), January 13, 2003.

3. The Taliban, Women, and the Hegelian Private Sphere

An earlier version of this essay was published in
Social Research 70, no. 3 (Fall 2003): 771–808.

1. Jürgen Habermas, *The Structural Transformation of the Public Sphere*, trans. Thomas Burger with Frederick Lawrence (Cambridge, MA: MIT Press, 1993), 7, 11.

2. Joan B. Landes, "The Public and the Private Sphere: A Feminist Reconsideration," in *Feminism: The Public and the Private*, ed. Joan B. Landes (Oxford: Oxford University Press, 1998), 138.

3. Seyla Benhabib, "Models of Public Space: Hannah Arendt, the Liberal Tradition, and Jürgen Habermas," in Landes, *Feminism*, 86.

4. Georg Wilhelm Friedrich Hegel, *Hegel's Philosophy of Right*, trans. T. M. Knox (Oxford: Clarendon Press, 1942), 118–119, para. 172.

5. Ibid., 114, para. 168.

6. Dorothy Rogers, "Hegel and His 'Victims': On Women and the Private Sphere," in *Topics in Feminism, History, and Philosophy*, ed. Dorothy Rogers et al. (Vienna: IWM, 2000), www.iwm.at/publ-jvc/jc-06–01.pdf.

7. Husni Jindi, *Damanat hurmat al-hayah al-khususah fi al-Islam* (Cairo: Dar al-Nahdah al-Arabiyah, 1993).

8. For Afghanistan's recent history, see Shah Mahmoud Hanifi, "Interregional Trade and Colonial State Formation in Afghanistan" (Ph.D. diss., University of Michigan, 2001); Vartan Gregorian, *The Emergence of Modern Afghanistan* (Stanford: Stanford University Press, 1969): Louis Dupree, *Afghanistan* (Princeton: Princeton University Press, 1973); Ashraf Ghani, "Production and Domination in Afghanistan, 1747–1901" (Ph.D. diss., Columbia University, 1982); David B. Edwards, *Heroes of the Age: Moral Fault Lines on the Afghan Frontier* (Berkeley: University of California Press, 1996); and Barnett R. Rubin, *The Fragmentation of Afghanistan: State Formation and Collapse in the International System*, 2nd ed. (New Haven: Yale University Press, 2002).

9. Valentine M. Moghadam, *Modernizing Women: Gender and Social Change in the Middle East* (Boulder, CO: Lynne Rienner, 1993), 218–220.

10. For the condition of women in refugee camps around Peshawar, see Ana Tortajada, *El Grito Silenciado* (Barcelona: Mondadori, 2001).

11. See Juan Cole, "Modernity of Theocracy," in *Sacred Space and Holy War: The Politics, Culture, and History of Shi'ite Islam* (London: Tauris, 2002).

12. On the Taliban, *inter alia*, see Larry P. Goodson, *Afghanistan's Endless War* (Seattle: University of Washington Press, 2001); Ahmed Rashid, *Taliban: Militant Islam, Oil, and Fundamentalism in Central Asia* (New Haven: Yale University Press, 2000); Changiz Pahlavan, *Afghanistan: 'Asr-e Mujahedin va baramadan-e Taleban* (Tehran: Nashr-e Qatra, 1999); and Fahmi Huwaydi, *Taliban: Jund Allah fi al-Ma'rikah al-Ghalat!* (Cairo: Dar al-Shuruq, 2001).

13. Cole, "Modernity of Theocracy."

14. Robert L. Canfield, "The Ecology of Rural Ethnic Groups and the Spatial Dimensions of Power," *American Anthropologist* 75, no. 5 (October 1973): 1511–28.

15. Goodson, *Afghanistan's Endless War*, 79

16. Norimitsu Onishi, "A Tale of the Mullah and Muhammad's Amazing Cloak," *New York Times*, December 19, 2001. For the founding of the shrine to the Prophet's cloak, see Ghani, "Production and Domination."

17. "Architect Who Built Omar's Complex Says Omar Did Not Marry Bin Laden's Daughter," PRNewswire, January 13, 2002.

18. Pahlavan, *Afghanistan*, 218.

19. Michel Foucault, *Discipline and Punish* (New York: Vintage Books, 1979).

20. Jan Goodwin, "Buried Alive: Afghan Women under the Taliban," *On the Issues* 7, no. 3 (Summer 1998).

21. Zoya, with John Follain and Rita Cristofari, *Zoya's Story* (New York: William Morrow, 2002), 150.

22. Latifa, *Visage Vole: Avoir vingt ans a Kaboul* (Paris: Anne Carrièrre, 2001), 65.

23. Goodwin, "Buried Alive."

24. "Taliban Repeat Warning of Punishment for Prayer Shirkers," Agence France-Presse, October 31, 1996.

25. Huwaydi, *Taliban*, 68.

26. Latifa, *Visage Vole*, 55.

27. Ibid., 204–205.

28. Zoya, *Zoya's Story*, 161–162.

29. Imtiaz Gul, "From Chaani," *The Friday Times* (Lahore), September 22, 2000.

30. Latifa, *Visage Vole*, 56.

31. Jamil Hanifi, private communication, December 24, 2002.

32. Wahhabism is a sect of Islam that predominates in Saudi Arabia. Unusually puritanical and iconoclastic, it was begun in the eighteenth century. It has tended to condemn non-Wahhabi Muslims as infidels.

33. Huwaydi, *Taliban*, 81. Huwaydi calls him Kamal al-Din, but this appears to be a simple transposition, since Qalamuddin, or the "pen of the religion," is a name unknown in Egypt, and we know that Qalamuddin was the head of this ministry in 1998.

34. Latifa, *Visage Vole*, 62.

35. Huwaydi, *Taliban*, 66–68.

36. Michel Foucault, *The Order of Things: An Archaeology of the Human Sciences* (New York: Vintage Books, 1973).

37. Hanifi, private communication.

38. Hanifi, private communication.

39. Latifa, *Visage Vole*, 203.

40. Ibid., 70–71.

41. Zoya, *Zoya's Story*, 148.

42. Ibid.

43. Goodwin, "Buried Alive."

44. Abdul Hamid Muharez, *Haqayiq wa tahlil wa waqayi'-e siyasi-ye Afghanistan, 1973–1997: Az soqut-e saltanat ta zuhur-e Taliban* (Peshawar: Hamid Nur, A.H. 1376 [1997]).

45. Moghadam, *Modernizing Women*, 223–225, 232–233, 240–247.

46. Huwaydi, *Taliban,* 69

47. Ibid., 72–75.

48. Ibid., 72.

49. Ibid., 73.

50. Ibid., 70–71.

51. Rosemarie Skaine, *The Women of Afghanistan under the Taliban* (Jefferson, NC: McFarland, 2002), 13–14.

52. Huwaydi, *Taliban,* 71.

53. Pahlavan, *Taliban,* 218; Skaine, *Women of Afghanistan.*

54. Rashid, *Taliban,* 108.

55. Pahlavan, *Taliban,* 219–220.

56. Zoya, *Zoya's Story,* 128.

57. Pahlavan, *Taliban,* 226.

58. Zoya, *Zoya's Story,* 144–145.

59. Ibid., 150.

60. Trudy Rubin, "Visit with Afghan Women Reveals a Picture That Isn't Quite So Hopeless," *Philadelphia Inquirer,* December 19, 1999.

61. Latifa, *Visage Vole,* 60, 87–88, 57.

62. Jami'at-e Inqelabi-e Zanan-e Afghanistan, "Qayd wa bandha-ye Talibi-ye Zanan ra bah khudkushi mikashanad," *Guzareshha-ye Sarzamin-e faji'ihha,* April 2000, rawa.fancymarketing.net/lyda.htm.

63. Physicians for Human Rights, "1999 Report: The Taliban's War on Women—A Health and Human Rights Crisis in Afghanistan," www.phrusa.org/research/health_effects/exec.html.

64. Huwaydi, *Taliban,* 68.

65. Zoya, *Zoya's Story,* 142–143.

66. Ibid., 146.

67. Tortajada, *El Grito Silenciado,* 152–153.

4. Taliban and Talibanism in Historical Perspective

1. Zalmay Khalilzad and Daniel Byman, "Afghanistan: The Consolidation of a Rogue State," *Washington Quarterly* 23, no. 1 (Winter 2000): 67. See also Ahmed Rashid, *Taliban: Militant Islam, Oil and Fundamentalism in Central Asia* (New Haven: Yale University Press 2000); and various authors in William Maley, ed., *Fundamentalism Reborn? Afghanistan and the Taliban* (London: C. Hurst, 1998).

2. Important exceptions include Olivier Roy, *Afghanistan: From Holy War to Civil War* (Princeton, NJ: Darwin Press, 1995). Roy examines the evolving relationship between the notions of *qawm* (language, kinship, sectarian and locality-based solidarity groups) and ideologically organized Islamist political groupings during the jihad and its immediate af-

termath. See also David B. Edwards, *Heroes of the Age: Moral Fault Lines on the Afghan Frontier* (Berkeley: University of California Press, 1996). Edwards blames the coexistence of three sets of contradictory and incompatible moral codes—honor-based ultra-individualism *(nang)*, the universalist moral principles of Islam, and the rules of state and kingship—that undergird Afghan society. See, too, Peter Marsden, *The Taliban: War and Religion in Afghanistan* (London: Zed Books, 2002), which emphasizes differences between the rural Taliban and urban Kabuli religious outlooks, as well as the Taliban's anti-Shia attitude and practices.

3. See Zalmay Khalilzad, Daniel Byman, Elie D. Krakowski, and Don Ritter, *U.S. Policy in Afghanistan: Challenges and Solutions*, Afghanistan Foundation White Paper (Washington D.C., 1999), 7.

4. See Marsden, *The Taliban*. Some of these questions have been addressed in Nazif Shahrani, "War, Factionalism, and the State in Afghanistan," *American Anthropologist* 104, no. 3 (September 2002): 715–722; Shahrani, "The Taliban Enigma: Person-Centered Politics and Extremism in Afghanistan," *ISIM Newsletter*, no. 6 (2000): 20–21; Shahrani, "Resisting the Taliban and Talibanism in Afghanistan: Legacies of a Century of Internal Colonialism and Cold War Politics in a Buffer State," *Perceptions: Journal of International Affairs* 5, no. 4 (December 2000–February 2001): 121–140; and Shahrani, "The Future of the State and the Structure of Community Governance in Afghanistan," in Maley, *Fundamentalism Reborn*, 212–242.

5. Marsden, *The Taliban*, 44.

6. Following the U.S. military intervention that ousted the Taliban and installed Hamid Karzai's government, security in Kandahar remains a major concern for the people of the city. On March 8, 2005, Dari/Persian broadcasting services from both the BBC and VOA reported violent demonstrations by the people of Kandahar against their Kabul-appointed former "warlord" governor because of the deteriorating security situation in their city, as witnessed in the increasing abduction of children. See Amin Tarzi, "Analysis: Afghan Demonstrations Test Warlords-Turned-Administrators," *Radio Free Europe/Radio Liberty Afghanistan Report*, March 9, 2005, www.rferl.org/reports. During the years 2005–2007, frequent suicide attacks against international forces and government installations, as well as assassination of officials or sympathizers, added to security concerns in the city of Kandahar and beyond.

7. See Marsden, *The Taliban*, 61–65.

8. Quoted in ibid., 65. Initially captured by U.S. forces and jailed, Mutawakkil was latter dubbed a "moderate" Taliban leader by the Karzai

regime and released from jail. He then lived in Kabul and reportedly headed up a Taliban negotiation team with the Karzai regime. For an account by Satar Saidi of the BBC radio Dari program, "Hamkari Wakil Ahmad Mutawakkil dar Muzakera-ye Dowlat-e Afghanistan ba Taliban," see www.bbc.co.uk/persian/iran/story/2005/03/050302_a _afgh_negotiation.shtml.

9. Their patrons included the al-Qaeda terrorist organization as well as the governments of Pakistan and Saudi Arabia. The Taliban also enjoyed the vociferous support of many highly educated Pashtuns living in Europe and the United States who served in the "interim" and "transitional" Karzai governments and who have retained key positions since the elections of October 2004.

10. For a description and analysis of this phenomenon, see the classic ethnography of Fredrik Barth, *Political Leadership among Swat Pathans* (London: Athlone Press, 1959).

11. Eric Wolf, *Europe and the People without History* (Berkeley: University of California Press, 1982), 94, emphasis added. For further development of this idea, see M. Nazif Shahrani, "State Building and Social Fragmentation in Afghanistan: A Historical Perspective," in *The State, Religion and Ethnic Politics: Afghanistan, Iran and Pakistan,* ed. Ali Banuazizi and Myron Weiner (Syracuse, NY: Syracuse University Press, 1986), 23–74.

12. For more detailed discussion of this issue, see Shahrani, "State Building."

13. For a valuable discussion of this issue during the 1920s, see Senzil K. Nawid, *Religious Response to Social Change in Afghanistan, 1919–29: King Aman-Allah and the Afghan Ulama* (Costa Mesa, CA: Mazda, 1999).

14. Sultan Mahomed Khan, *The Life of Amir Abdur Rahman Khan, Amir of Afghanistan* (1900; Oxford: Oxford University Press, 1980). It appeared in Persian as *Taj al-tawarikh* (The Crown of Histories).

15. Ibid., 2:176–177.

16. Ibid., 2:216–217.

17. What is noteworthy about these remarks is that he was, by his own admission, not fond of reading and writing and was barely literate. See ibid., 1:37–39. However, he was miraculously able to read a love note sent to him by his fiancée from Kabul! The Iron Amir's greatest political education came from his experience of ten years of exile in Tashkent under tsarist Russian colonial rule (ibid., 2:178–190).

18. Ibid., 2:242.

19. Ibid., 2:177.

20. Donald Wilber, "Constitution of Afghanistan, with Commentary," *Middle East Journal* 19, no. 2 (Spring 1965): 215–216.

21. Ibid.

22. See Sayed Askar Mousavi, *The Hazaras of Afghanistan: An Historical, Cultural, Economic and Political Study* (New York: St. Martin's Press, 1997); Hassan Poladi, *Hazaras* (Stockton, CA: Mughal, 1989); and M. Hasan Kawun Kakar, *Government and Society in Afghanistan: The Reign of Amir 'Abd al-Rahman Khan* (Austin: University of Texas Press, 1979).

23. Such exceptions include Nancy Tapper, "The Advent of Pushtun Maldars in Northwestern Afghanistan," *Bulletin of the School of Oriental and African Studies* 36, no. 1 (1973): 55–79; and Jon Anderson and Richard F. Strand, eds., *Ethnic Processes and Intergroup Relations in Contemporary Afghanistan*, Occasional Paper No. 15, Asia Society, Afghanistan Council (New York, 1978). For a preliminary examination of the topic, see Shahrani, "Resisting the Taliban."

24. See Sayyid Abdulebari Azmi, *Amir-e Bukhara* (Gaziantep, Turkey, 1367 [1997]), 49.

25. For a detailed discussion of these questions, see M. Nazif Shahrani, "Pining for Bukhara in Afghanistan: Poetics and Politics of Exilic Identity and Emotions," in *Reform Movements and Revolutions in Turkistan, 1900–1924: Studies in Honour of Osman Khoja*, ed. Timur Kocaoglu (Haarlem, Netherlands: SOTA, 2001), 369–391.

26. For the "official" Afghan accounts, see Nawid, *Religious Response to Social Change*, 70.

27. See Muhammad Ibrahim Afifi, "Mukhtasaraki Khaterat, bakhsh duwum," *Omaid Weekly*, no. 244 (1996): 4. See also Muhammad Ismail Mushfiq, "Hatam Beg (Atam Beg) Cheguna ba Shahadat Rasid," *Andisha* 7 (1372 [1993]): 18–23. Hatam Beg was one of Ibrahim Beg's well-known commanders. *Andisha* (Reflection/Warning) was a short-lived journal published by the Junbesh-e Milli-ye Islami-ye Afghanistan (National Islamic Movement of Afghanistan), in Mazar-e Sharif during General Abdul Rashid Dostum's semi-independent rule (1992–1998) in parts of Afghan Turkestan.

28. See Kamoloudin Najmudinovich Abdoullaev, "Central Asian Refugees: A Historical Retrospective," *Central Asian Monitor*, no. 5 (1994): 26.

29. Gulbuddin Hekmatyar and Zalmay Khalilzad are among the more prominent figures of the *Naqelin* from Baghlan and Mazar-e Sharif, respectively.

30. See "Wazir Muhammad Gul Khan Muhmand wa Karnamaha-i Fashisti Au," *Andisha,* no. 6 (1372 [1993]): 16–43, and no. 7, 24–28.

31. For a detailed ethnographic study of one such community in the northern city of Konduz and later in exile in Pakistan, see Audrey Shalinsky,

Long Years of Exile: Central Asian Refugees in Afghanistan and Pakistan (Lanham, MD: University Press of America, 1994).

32. For a brief discussion of these literary productions, see Shahrani, "Pining for Bukhara."

33. Two things are striking about the nature of this textual production, especially the materials produced in Afghanistan or by Central Asian authors concerning their experiences of exile in Afghanistan: first, the sheer volume of what is being produced in a wide variety of genres and media; second, the obvious political nature and deeply emotional quality of these writings in which poetry seems to remain the dominant form and style of expression. These phenomena, though novel at this juncture in the history of Central Asian exile literature, are nevertheless not unusual, because politically the peoples of Afghan Turkestan (including post-Bolshevik exiles) had long been prevented from any form of self-expression. That is, for well over six decades their heart-rending stories of human suffering were kept untold and even untellable; their personal and collective efforts to make sense of the historic events that brought them so much grief under the yoke of an internal colonial occupation were publicly banned. However, as the recent outpouring of literary production demonstrates, the muffled voices of those who have lost their *watan* (homeland), and with it significant aspects of their personal and collective identities, including, potentially, their self-respect, were not totally erased, and their search for meaning continues.

34. The formation in April 2007 of a new political bloc, the United Front of Afghanistan (Jabha-ye Mutahed-e Afghanistan), is a clear indication of the rising tensions and frustration among those who are increasingly marginalized from the centers of political power over the last six years. Consisting of many former mujahedin leaders now in the government or parliamentarians, former communist politicians, and a grandson of the ex-king Muhammad Zaher and led by former president Burhanuddin Rabbani, it has pledged to fight corruption in the government and to demand a constitutional amendment to allow for the election of provincial governors and a shift from the current strong presidential system to parliamentary governance. President Karzai has reacted by accusing them of having foreign supporters and by declaring that the United Front wants a federal system and that a federal system is utterly inappropriate for Afghanistan and will be resisted by his government. See Ron Synovitz, "Afghanistan: New Political Bloc Unites Old Adversaries," in *Radio Free Europe/Radio Liberty Afghanistan Report* 6, no. 7 (April 27, 2007).

35. The government has created large numbers of provinces and district

units in Pashtun-inhabited areas for relatively small numbers of people while creating fewer such electoral units in non-Pashtun areas with larger populations. Hamid Karzai's attempt to appease his Panjsheri partners in the Transitional Government by proclaiming that the Panjsher district will be elevated into a province was another example of this policy.

36. Lahouari Addi, "Religion and Modernity in Algeria," *Journal of Democracy* 3, no. 4 (October 1992): 4.

37. For a discussion of this general tendency in Islamist political movements and the history of Islamic states, see Fatima Mernissi, "Arab Women's Rights and the Muslim State in the Twenty-First Century: Reflections on Islam as Religion and State," in *Faith and Freedom: Women's Human Rights in the Muslim World,* ed. Mahnaz Afkhami (Syracuse: Syracuse University Press, 1995), 36.

38. For earlier manifestations of similar movements in the country, especially during the 1920s in opposition to King Amanullah's reforms, see Nawid, *Religious Response to Social Change.*

39. The Taliban also demonized their opponents' foreign patrons, Muslim and non-Muslim, such as Shiite Iran, Russia, and the Central Asian republics (with the exception of Turkmenistan).

40. When the so-called "Iron Amir," Abdul Rahman, assumed power in 1880 at the end of a long war of succession, and when Nader Shah came to power during the civil war of 1929, both drew on patronage from British India and the discourse of jihad against their real and presumed enemies. For details on the involvement of Pakistan, Saudi Arabia, and others in the region, see Rashid, *Taliban;* and Maley, *Fundamentalism Reborn.*

5. Remembering the Taliban

1. Both travels were sponsored by the Deutsche Forschungsgemeinschaft.

2. Nurzi are Pashtuns by origin. Members of this tribe still regard themselves as Pashtuns in regions with a predominantly Pashtun population. In regions like Nimroz, where the majority is Baluch, however, most Nurzi switched over to the Baluchi language and even adopted a Baluch identity. Here only elderly Nurzi still use Pashto as their primary language and will specify their ethnicity as Pashtun if they are asked.

3. Historical publications about the Taliban offer no information about the events that took place in the remote province of Nimroz. The chronological overview presented here was compiled according to information given by local informants and in a Persian-language memoir about the reign of the Taliban. See Lutz Rzehak, ed. and trans., *Die Taliban*

im Land der Mittagssonne: Erinnerungen und Notizen von Abdurrahman Pahwal (Wiesbaden: Ludwig Reichert Verlag 2004). For information about the historical and socioeconomic development of the province before 1978, see Erwin Orywal, *Die Balūč in Afghanisch-Sīstān: Wirtschaft und sozio-politische Organisation in Nīmrūz, SW-Afghanistan* (Berlin: Reimer, 1982); and Gholam Rahman Amiri, *Taswir-e az zendegani-ye mardom-e Baluch dar Nimroz wa Hilmand-e sufla qabl az inqelab-e saur* (Kabul: Akadimi-ye ulum-e j. d. Afghanistan: 1365 [1986]).

4. The border between these provinces has since been redrawn: Dilaram now belongs to the province of Nimroz. There is no passable road between Dilaram and Zaranj; one has to know the way across the desert.

5. In 2004, Karim Brahui became the minister of tribal and frontier affairs in the government of Hamid Karzai and moved to Kabul.

6. Barbara Johnstone describes such an *aesthetic model of language and persuasion* for Iran, contrasting it with an *instrumental model* in Western societies, where language is seen mainly as a tool. The contrast is not that in countries like Afghanistan or Iran beauty of language works instead of logic, but that aesthetic of oration is an important additional factor of persuasion. See "Arguments with Khomeini: Rhetorical Situation and Persuasive Style in Cross-Cultural Perspective," *Text* 6, no. 1 (1986): 171–187, esp. 181–182.

7. Performance as well as political and rhetorical aspects of traditional storytelling in Afghanistan are described by Margaret Mills, *Oral Narrative in Afghanistan: The Individual in Transition* (New York: Garland, 1990); and Mills, *Rhetorics and Politics in Afghan Traditional Storytelling* (Philadelphia: University of Pennsylvania Press, 1991).

8. See M. Nazif Shahrani, "Local Knowledge of Islam and Social Discourse in Afghanistan and Turkistan in the Modern Period," in *Turko-Persia in Historical Perspective,* ed. Robert L. Canfield (Cambridge: Cambridge University Press, 1991), 167.

9. I heard this story several times when talking to Afghans inside and outside of Afghanistan. It is given here as published in Raushan Rahmani, *Afsanaha-ye dari* (Tehran: Sorush, 1374 [1995]), 394.

10. Such tales seem to be pure fiction. Indeed, similar stories were recorded in Rhineland, Germany, in the 1930s. In these versions, the German king Frederic the Great takes the place of Amir Abdul Rahman Khan, and the woman was ordered to put a sword into a revolving sheath instead of threading a needle. See Heinrich Dittmaier, *Sagen und Schwänke von der unteren Sieg* (Bonn: Ludwig Röhrscheid Verlag, 1950), 150.

11. The word *riwayat* is used here in its popular meaning, denoting a genre

of folklore. See George Morgenstierne, "Volksdichtung in Afghanistan," *Afghanistan Journal* 1, no. 4 (1974): 2–17; Simadad, *Farhang-e estelahat-e adabi: Wazhanama-ye mafhim-wa estilahat-e adabi-ye farsi wa orupayi* (Tehran: Morwarid, 1378 [1999/2000]), 253–254. For Muslim jurists, this word (mostly in the original Arabic form, *riwaya*) is a technical term in the study of the traditions (*hadith*); see G. Schoeler, "Die Frage der schriftlichen und mündlichen Überlieferung der Wissenschaften im Islam," *Der Islam* 62, no. 2 (1985): 201–230. Zoroastrians use the word *riwayat* to denote certain kinds of juristic texts (Jan Rypka, *Iranische Literaturgeschichte* [Leipzig: VEB Otto Harrassowitz, 1959], 43).

12. In Pashto, typical opening formulas of such prose stories are *yawa wradz, yaw wakht, yaw dzal* (once) or *hal da da che* (the matter is that). Baluchi equivalents are *yak maughe, roch-e* (once) or *hal esh int ke* (the matter is that). Fairy tales start with *wu ka na-wu* (literally: "there was or there was not") in Pashto and with *yak-e bud, yakk-e nabud, chap sha khuda chiz-e nabud* (literally: "there was one and there was no one, with the exception of God there was nothing") in Baluchi.

13. The term *cultural memory* is used here according to Jan Assmann, *Das kulturelle Gedächtnis: Schrift, Erinnerung und politische Identität in frühen Hochkulturen* (Munich: Beck, 1992). See also Lutz Niethammer, *Lebenserfahrung und kollektives Gedächtnis: Die Praxis der "Oral History"* (Frankfurt am Main: Syndikat, 1980); and J. Straub, "Geschichten erzählen, Geschichte bilden: Grundzüge einer narrativen Psychologie historischer Sinnbildung," in *Erzählung, Identität und historisches Bewusstsein: Die psychologische Konstruktion von Zeit und Geschichte*, ed. J. Straub (Frankfurt am Main: Suhrkamp 1998), 81–169.

14. In Afghanistan the informers of the intelligence services are usually disdained. In common speech the word *shaytan* (devil) is used to denote these persons. In a given context, *shaytan* means "informer." This is not extended to the officers of the services, who command proper respect, however, at least as long as they are working for only one institution. All the same people believe that the job of an intelligence officer requires some education.

15. In colloquial Persian the consonant *h* of the plural suffix *-ha* may be omitted, and the plural of *talib* may be formed simply as *taliba*.

16. Informant: Gholam Nabi Sherzi, 27 years old, herdsman from Kang, illiterate, Baluch; date and place of the recording: August 23, 2002, Zaranj, province of Nimroz, Afghanistan (recorded during a gathering in the house of Gholam Sakhi Sherzi); language: Baluchi.

17. How people in Afghanistan generate stories in a quite similar way when they are talking about saints and holy places is shown in Lutz Rzehak,

"Narrative Strukturen des Erzählens über Heilige und ihre Gräber in Afghanistan," *Asiatische Studien* 58, no. 1 (2004): 195–229.

18. Informant: Gholam Nabi Sherzi, 27 years old, herdsman from Kang, illiterate, Baluch; date and place of the recording: August 23, 2002, Zaranj, province of Nimroz, Afghanistan (recorded during a gathering in the house of Gholam Sakhi Sherzi); language: Baluchi, Persian.

19. Informant: Ahmad Shah Khan, about 40 years old, head of the intelligence agency of the province of Nimroz, Farsiwan; date and place of the recording: April 16, 2005, Zaranj, province of Nimroz, Afghanistan (recorded during a meeting of male elders of the Nurzi tribe in the house of Gholam Nabi Sherzi); language: Persian (*farsi-ye kaboli*—colloquial standard of Afghanistan).

20. See Rzehak, *Die Taliban im Land der Mittagssonne.*

21. A more detailed analysis of the narrative structure of this 191-page manuscript is given in ibid., xvii–xxv.

22. James Darmesteter, *Chants populaires des Afghans* (Paris: Imprimerie Nationale E. Leroux, 1888–1890), cxcix. The history of Afghanistan to which he refers is John William Kaye's *History of the War in Afghanistan,* 3 vols. (London, 1857).

23. See 'Abdullah Bakhtani, *Turbresh ya melli sanderi* (Kabul, 1347 [1968]), 78–79. A literary analysis of the genre of *charbayta* in Pashto folk literature is given by G. F. Girs, ed. and trans., *Istoricheskie pesni pushtunov* (Moscow: Nauka, 1984), 30.

24. The song is published here as given by Girs, *Istoricheskie pesni pushtunov,* 107.

25. See L. R. Gordon-Polonskaia, "Voina Afganistana za nezavisimost' i uchastie v nei pogranichnykh pushtunskikh plemen (1919–1921 gg.)," in *Nezavisimyi Afganistan: 40 let nezavisimosti* (Moscow: Izdatel'stvo vostochnoi literatury, 1958), 253.

26. See L. W. Adamec, *Historical and Political Who's Who of Afghanistan* (Graz: Akademische Druck- und Verlagsanstalt, 1975), 122–123.

27. For further details, see Girs, *Istoricheskie pesni pushtunov.*

28. See L. A. Stroptsova, ed., *Kratkaia istoriia literatur Irana, Turtsii i Afganistana* (Leningrad: Izdatel'stvo Leningradskogo universiteta, 1971), 75.

29. See [Duktur] Asadullah Habib, *Adabiyat-e dari dar nima-ye nakhustin-e sada-ye bistum,* 2nd ed. (Kabul: Nasir Ahmad Multahib, 1381 [2002]).

30. Very few scholars can prove the transience of such folklore within their own scholarly careers. George Morgenstierne started his linguistic fieldwork in Afghanistan in the early 1920s. When he went to Afghanistan in 1970, he read some historical songs in the Parachi language that he

had recorded in 1924 to the direct descendants of his informants from the 1920s. They knew not one single song and regarded Morgenstierne as the greatest bard of their people. "Volksdichtung in Afghanistan," 7.

31. "One says one thing, the other another."

32. Informant: Gholam Sakhi Sherzi, about 30 years old, trader (author of the song: Zaher Baluch); date and place of recording: August 28, 2002, Zaranj, province of Nimroz, Afghanistan; language: Baluchi.

33. Informant: Zaher Baluch (author), 40 years old, poet and singer, Baluch; date and place of recording: September 12, 2002, Zaranj, province of Nimroz, Afghanistan (concert at a private gathering); language: Baluchi.

34. Zaher Baluch accompanied his songs and these introductions with a stringed instrument, called a *suroz,* played with a bow. Both of his hands were occupied, so he held with his toes the sheet of paper with the names he had to mention.

6. Fraternity, Power, and Time in Central Asia

I am indebted to Sami Siddiq for comments on an earlier draft of this paper. Nothing in the paper, however, is his responsibility.

1. John Kifner, "Through the Serbian Mind's Eye," *New York Times,* April 10, 1994.

2. *Radio Free Europe/Radio Liberty Caucasus Report* 7, no. 29 (July 23, 2004).

3. Vicken Cheterian, "Where Is Juma Namangani?" *Eurasia Insight,* July 17, 2000.

4. Admittedly, in many cases the leaders of these movements were urbanites and essentially secular in their orientation; Franjo Trudman in Croatia and Slobodan Milosevic in Serbia were notable examples. Also, the leaders of the radical Islamist movements in Central Asia were something other than they appeared. Social movements are in fact complex in their moral inspiration.

5. Benedict Anderson, *Imagined Communities* (London: Verso, 1991), 36.

6. Kathryn Verdery, *The Political Lives of Dead Bodies: Reburial and Postsocialist Change* (New York: Columbia University, 1999), 104ff. Each "people" should have a place, a land of their own. It was, for instance, Richard Wagner's vision for the German people of Europe: In his diary he wrote: "the incomparable magic of my works . . . it is German. But what is this German? It must be something wonderful, mustn't it, for it is humanly finer than all else?—Oh heavens! It should have a soil, this German! I should be able to find my people! What glorious people it

ought to become." See Richard Wagner, *The Diary of Richard Wagner, 1865–1882: The Brown Book,* presented and annotated by Joachim Bergfeld, trans. George Byrd. (Cambridge: Cambridge University, 1980), 73.

7. Bruce Kapferer, *Legends of People, Myths of State: Violence, Intolerance, and Political Culture in Sri Lanka and Australia* (Washington DC: Smithsonian, 1988), 1.

8. Anderson, *Imagined Communities,* 9.

9. Loretta Napoleoni, *Modern Jehad: Tracing the Dollars behind the Terror Networks* (London: Pluto, 2003), 98–99.

10. Nazif Shahrani, "Islam and the Political Culture of 'Scientific Atheism' in Post-Soviet Central Asia: Future Predicaments," in *The Politics of Religion in Russia and the New States of Central Asia,* ed. Michael Bourdeaux (Armonk, NY: Sharpe, 1995), 279.

11. Kristian Berg Harpviken, *Political Mobilization among the Hazara of Afghanistan: 1978–1992* (Oslo: Institutt for Sociologi, Universistetet I Oslo, 1996).

12. In 1989 I visited the bookstore of a madrasa in Peshawar. There, prominently displayed in a window facing the street, was a large map, in Persian, of the early Muslim conquests in the first two centuries of Islam. It was a vivid portrayal of the imaginative world in which the students were trained. See also Ahmed Rashid, *Taliban: Militant Islam, Oil and Fundamentalism in Central Asia* (New Haven: Yale University Press, 2000).

13. Rashid, *Taliban,* 184; and Napoleoni, *Modern Jehad,* 92.

14. Napoleoni, *Modern Jehad,* 88–92.

15. Ibid., 147.

16. See Robert Crews's chapter "Modern Taliban?" in this book.

17. Rashid, *Taliban,* 41.

18. I use the term *clergy* deliberately. In Islam there is no clergy in the sense found in the Roman Catholic or Orthodox churches, but the loose affiliation of religious specialists in some Protestant denominations, such as the Baptists, is scarcely different from the associations of religious specialists in Afghanistan: their relationships and the importance of various members of the informal networks are determined by reputation and numbers of followers.

19. Rashid, *Taliban.*

20. Ibid., 133–134.

21. Ibid., 139.

22. In his oral presentation at the conference "A Decade of the Taliban" at Stanford University, May 6–7, 2004, Thomas Barfield noted that the

Taliban who invaded in Mazar-e Sharif the second time included many non-Afghans.

23. See Neamatollah Nojumi's chapter "The Rise and Fall of the Taliban" in this book.

24. Ibid.; and Crews, "Moderate Taliban," in this book.

25. Rashid, *Taliban*, 140.

26. Napoleoni, *Modern Jehad*, 97.

27. Mariam Abou Zahab and Olivier Roy, *Islamist Networks: The Afghan-Pakistan Connection* (New York: Columbia University Press, 2004), 53.

28. Syed Saleem Shahzad, "Cracking Open Pakistani's Jihadi Core," *Asia Times Online*, August 12, 2004.

29. Ibid.; and Zahab and Roy, *Islamist Networks*, 14. See Zahab and Roy for extensive information on the Islamist organizations in Pakistan. Here I have chosen to ignore the topic of another kind of person who has been involved in Islamist organizations, namely, Western-educated aliens. Several scholars have noted that "terrorists" are usually more highly educated that the rest of the population. (See, for example, Ethan Bueno de Mesquita, "Conciliation, Counter-Terrorism, and Patterns of Terrorist Violence: A Comparative Study of Four Cases," paper presented at the meeting of the International Studies Association, February 2003; and Bueno de Mesquita, "The Quality of Terror," paper presented at the meeting of the American Political Science Association, September 2003.) The rank-and-file Taliban are of course essentially educated in the memorization of the Quran. But associated with the broader movement of al-Qaeda are Islamist Muslims educated in Western subjects. The most notorious of them, perhaps, is Sheikh Omar, who was instrumental in the murder of Daniel Pearl. Omar is a British citizen, educated in Britain, a matriculant of LSE, a former student of Anthony Giddens—certainly not the kind of person we would expect to mastermind the entrapment, murder, and dismemberment of a *Wall Street Journal* reporter. See Bernard-Henri Lévy, *Who Killed Daniel Pearl?* (Hoboken, NJ: Melville House, 2003). No doubt there are others like him who, despite a Western education, have embraced the broad ideals of the Islamist movement. It is well known that some of the leaders of the movement are more highly educated—notably, of course, Osama bin Laden and Zawahiri—than most of the rank-and-file al-Qaeda.

30. The funding and perhaps the motive of these operations could have been the narcotics trade the ISI controlled. Napoleoni says that "the narcotics-based economy took over the traditional agrarian economy of Afghanistan [during the Soviet mujahedin war] and, with the help of

ISI, the Mujahedin opened hundreds of heroin laboratories. Within two years the Pakistani-Afghanistan borderland had become the biggest center for the production of heroin in the world [no date but presumably late 1980s] . . . By 1991, yearly production from the tribal area under the control of the Mujahedin had risen to an astonishing 70 metric tons of premium quality heroin, up 35% from the previous year" (Napoleoni, *Modern Jehad*, 83, 87–88).

31. Shahzad, "Cracking Open Pakistani's Jihadi Core"; and Zahab and Roy, *Islamist Networks*, 35.

32. Arnaud de Borchgrave, "Outside View: Focus on Pakistani's Jihads," United Press International, August 9, 2004. Borchgrave cites the 2003 report of the Human Rights Commission of Pakistan for some of these details.

33. Hassan Abbas, *Pakistan's Drift into Extremism: Allah, the Army, and America's War on Terror* (New York: M. E. Sharpe, 2005), 134.

34. Arnaud de Borchgrave, "Pakistan's ISI 'Fully Involved' in 9/11," United Press International, August 3, 2004.

35. Abbas, *Pakistan's Drift into Extremism*, 224.

36. Borchgrave, "Pakistan's ISI."

37. Ibid. At the Deobandi school in Karachi there is a large image of the now-deceased leader of the Islamic Movement of Uzbekistan, Juma Namangi. That this Uzbek Islamic leader is portrayed as a hero reveals, again, that their moral horizon, and the range of Islamic causes and leaders that interests them, is international. See Lévy, *Who Killed Daniel Pearl?*

38. "Waziristan a Taliban Mini State," *News International*, April 27, 2007.

39. Borchgrave, "Outside View."

40. Stephen Philip Cohen, "The Jihadist Threat to Pakistan," *Washington Quarterly* 26, no. 3 (Summer 2003): 7–25.

41. Tariq Ali, "Pakistan on the Brink," *The Nation*, April 17, 2000.

42. Elizabeth Rubin, "In the Land of the Taliban," *New York Times* October 22, 2006.

43. Ali, "Pakistan on the Brink." The duplicitous policy created strange contradictions: when the United States moved to retaliate for the September 11, 2001, attack, the ISI posted several thousand Pakistanis in Afghanistan to fight alongside the Taliban. See Shahzad, "Cracking Open Pakistani's Jihadi Core"; and Seymour Hersh, "The Getaway: Questions Surround a Secret Pakistani Airlift," *New Yorker*, January 28, 2002. And once the Taliban were defeated, Hersh notes: "The United States Central Command . . . set up a special air corridor to help insure the safety of the Pakistani rescue flights from Kunduz." "Pakistanis were . . . flown to

safety, in a series of nighttime airlifts that were approved by the Bush Administration." "Many of the people they spirited away were the Taliban leadership," and "two Pakistani Army generals were on the flights."

44. Cohen, "The Jihadist Threat," 7, 10.

45. Ali, "Pakistan on the Brink."

46. This section relies mainly on the following sources: Sarah Chayes, "The Night Fairies," *Bulletin of the Atomic Scientists* 62 no. 2 (March–April 2006): 17–19; Barnett Rubin, "Saving Afghanistan," *Foreign Affairs* 86, no. 1 (January–February 2007); Rubin, "In the Land of the Taliban"; Graham Usher, "The Pakistan Taliban," *Middle East Report Online,* February 13, 2007. Other sources can be found on the blog "Vital Concerns for the World" (rcanfield.blogspot.com).

47. Rubin, "Saving Afghanistan," 5.

48. Pamela Constable, "Pakistan's Untamed Frontier: Army's Anti-Terror Offensive Finds Little Support in Semi-Autonomous Tribal Areas," *Washington Post,* April 7, 2004; and *Asia Times Online,* July 20, 2004.

49. Usher, "The Pakistan Taliban."

50. The source of this summary of recent affairs is Usher, "The Pakistan Taliban."

51. Aimal Khan Faizi, "Radical Islamism and Talibanism: Tools of Pakistani Politics," kabulpress.org/English_letters25.htm.

52. "Waziristan a Taliban Mini State," *News International,* April 27, 2007.

53. Rotella Sebastian, "War on West Shifts Back to Afghanistan," *Los Angeles Times,* October 26, 2006.

54. "Living Under the Taleban," *Institute for War and Peace Reporting: Afghan Recovery Report,* no. 249 (April 4, 2007).

55. Rubin, "In the Land of the Taliban."

56. Ibid.

57. Ibid.

58. Napoleoni, *Modern Jehad,* 112.

59. John F. Burns, "The Struggle for Iraq: Ordeal, Anxious Moments in Grip of Outlaw Militia," *New York Times,* April 7, 2004.

60. "The Herat Koran Memorization School Has Condemned the Murder of the Hamas leader, Abd-al-Aziz al-Rantisi," Herat TV in Dari, April 18, 2004.

61. Mahmood Mamdani argues that groups like al-Qaeda are generally motivated by legitimate political grievances with U.S. foreign policy. He discusses in detail the failures of United States policy in respect to Afghanistan. See Mamdani, *Good Muslim, Bad Muslim: America, the Cold War, and the Roots of Terror* (New York: Pantheon, 2004).

62. Anderson, *Imagined Communities,* 36.

63. Note Nojumi's description, in his chapter in this book, of a teacher who claims that a nationalist cannot be a Muslim.

64. Pierre Bourdieu, *The Algerians* (Boston: Beacon Press, 1962), 187.

65. Amatzia Bram, "Praying for Sistani's Good Health," *New York Times,* August 22, 2004. Barry Cooper has an extended discussion, based on secondary sources, of the apocalyptic views of Islamist leaders. See his *New Political Religions, or an Analysis of Modern Terrorism* (Columbia: University of Missouri, 2004).

66. Zoya, with John Follian and Rita Cristofari, *Zoya's Story: An Afghan Woman's Struggle for Freedom* (New York: Morrow, 2002), 76.

7. Moderate Taliban?

1. Ahmed Rashid uses the formulation in his classic study, *Taliban: Militant Islam, Oil and Fundamentalism in Central Asia* (New Haven: Yale University Press, 2000), 104. Other observers have also identified "moderates" within the movement; see, for example, Barbara D. Metcalf, *'Traditionalist' Islamic Activism: Deoband, Tablighis, and Talibs* (Leiden: ISIM, 2002); and Thomas H. Johnson, "Afghanistan's Post-Taliban Transition: The State of State-Building after War," *Central Asian Survey* 25, nos. 1–2 (March–June 2006): 1–26. Kathy Gannon has devoted an entire chapter to them in *I is for Infidel: From Holy War to Holy Terror— 18 Years inside Afghanistan* (New York: Public Affairs, 2005), 51–65.

2. John Heller, "Political Space Is Opening for Taliban Moderates, but Just How Moderate Are They?" *Radio Free Europe/Radio Liberty Afghanistan Report* 2, no. 23 (July 3, 2003), www.rferl.org/reports. Golnaz Esfandiari, "Karzai Calls on Taliban to Participate in Elections," *Radio Free Europe/Radio Liberty Afghanistan Report* 3, no. 16 (April 28, 2004). In October 2003, however, the American commander of coalition forces, General David Borno, gave a slightly lower figure—between 100 and 150—for the number of Taliban who would not be welcomed to "become part of the future of Afghanistan." See Victoria Burnett, "US Backs Afghan Proposal to Woo Moderate Taliban," *Financial Times,* December 31, 2003. On Pakistani support for the inclusion of "moderate Taliban," see Luke Harding, "Taliban Moderates Offered Future Role," *The Guardian,* October 17, 2001; and Zahid Hussain, *Frontline Pakistan: The Struggle with Militant Islam* (New York: Columbia University Press, 2007), esp. 48.

3. See, for example, quotes from the women's journal *Payam-e zan* in R. R. Sikoev, *Taliby (religiozno-politicheskii portret)* (Moscow: Institut vostokovedeniia RAN, 2002), 115.

4. Amin Tarzi, "Demonstrators in Kabul Denounce Karzai and His Aides over Handling of Crisis in Faryab," *Radio Free Europe/Radio Liberty Afghanistan Report* 3, no. 16 (April 28, 2004).

5. N. C. Aizenman, "Four Senior Taliban Leaders Accept Amnesty," *Washington Post*, February 18, 2005.

6. "Afghan Warlords in Amnesty Rally," BBC News, February 23, 2007; Sayed Salahuddin, "Afghan Rally Demands Amnesty for War Crimes," Reuters, February 23, 2007. The text is quoted from "Afghan MPs' Reconciliation Plan Calls for Forgiving Past Deeds," Kabul Tolu Television, January 31, 2007. On the bill, see Amin Tarzi, "Amnesty Bill Places Karzai in Dilemma," *Radio Free Europe/Radio Liberty Afghanistan Report* 6, no. 5 (March 16, 2007).

7. See the tribunal documents at www.pentagon.mil/pubs/foi/detainees/ index.html, 22–24. Note that the identity of "cook's assistant" was an accusation leveled by the American investigators and not, it seems, the detainee's alibi.

8. On Rahmatullah's adventures in the Ivy League, see Chip Brown, "The Freshman," *New York Times Magazine*, February 26, 2006, with remarkable photographs by Reuben Cox.

9. See Eric Hooglund, "The Search for Iran's 'Moderates,'" *Middle East Report*, no. 144 (January–February 1987): 4–6; and Mahmood Mamdani, *Good Muslim, Bad Muslim: America, the Cold War, and the Roots of Terror* (New York: Pantheon, 2004), esp. 20–27.

10. Quoted in Conrad Schetter, *Ethnizität und ethnische Konflikte in Afghanistan* (Berlin: Dietrich Reimer Verlag, 2003), 524.

11. See, for example, Pamela Constable, "Tales of the Taleban: Part Tragedy, Part Farce," *Washington Post*, February 28, 2004.

12. Wahid Muzhda, *Afghanistan wa panj sal sulta-ye Taleban* (Tehran: Nashr-e ney, 1382 [2003]), 49–50.

13. Mark Kukis reports that Radio Voice of Sharia reached into the tribal areas of Pakistan where John Walker Lindh briefly studied; see Kukis, *"My Heart Became Attached": The Strange Journey of John Walker Lindh* (Washington: Brassey's, 2003), 58–59.

14. "Editorial: The Dynamic Address of Mulla Ameer Khan Muttaqi," *Dha'rb-i-M'umin* 1, no. 12 (July 1, 1997), 3.

15. Maggie O'Kane, "A Holy Betrayal," *The Guardian*, November 29, 1997. See also Rashid, *Taliban*, for other examples of the seeming absence of Taliban attention to state building.

16. Norbert Heinrich Holl, *Mission Afghanistan: Erfahrungen eines UNO-Diplomaten* (Munich: Herbig, 2002), 115–122.

17. Sami Zubaida, "Is Iran an Islamic State?" in *Political Islam: Essays from Middle East Report*, ed. Joel Beinin and Joe Stork (Berkeley: University of California Press, 1997).

18. Alexis de Tocqueville, *The Old Regime and the French Revolution*, trans. Stuart Gilbert (Garden City, NY: Doubleday, 1955), 209.

19. See Thomas J. Barfield, "Weak Links on a Rusty Chain: Structural Weaknesses in Afghanistan's Provincial Government Administration," in *Revolutions and Rebellions in Afghanistan: Anthropological Perspectives*, ed. M. Nazif Shahrani and Robert L. Canfield (Berkeley: Institute of International Studies, University of California, 1984), 170–183; Jan-Heeren Grevemeyer, *Afghanistan: Sozialer Wandel und Staat im 20. Jahrhundert* (Berlin: Express Edition, 1987); and Antonio Giustozzi, *War, Politics and Society in Afghanistan, 1978–1992* (London: Hurst, 2000).

20. For a sense of the variety of Taliban interactions with foreign aid groups, see Peter Schwittek, "About the School System under the Taliban Government," in *Afghanistan: A Country without a State?* ed. Christine Noelle-Karimi, Conrad Schetter, and Reinhard Schlagintweit (Frankfurt am Main: IKO-Verlag für Interkulturelle Kommunikation, 2002), 89–95.

21. Anthony Davis, "How the Taliban Became a Military Force," in *Fundamentalism Reborn? Afghanistan and the Taliban*, ed. William Maley (New York: New York University Press, 2001), 43–71.

22. Michael Keating, "Dilemmas of Humanitarian Assistance in Afghanistan," in Maley, *Fundamentalism Reborn*, 135–144, here 136; and A. D. Davydov, "Voina i vnutrennyi rynok," *Afganistan: Voina i problemy mira*, ed. A. D. Davydov (Moscow: Institut vostokovedeniia RAN, 1998), 28.

23. Holl, *Mission Afghanistan*, 109–122.

24. Ibid., 156.

25. U.S. Department of State, cable, "Dealing with the Taliban in Kabul," September 28, 1996, National Security Archive, George Washington University, *The Taliban File: National Security Briefing Book*, no. 97, ed. Sajit Gandhi, September 11, 2003, www.gwu.edu/~nsarchiv/NSAEBB /NSAEBB97/. See also Rashid, *Taliban*, 170–182.

26. Changiz Pahlavan, *Afghanistan: 'Asr-e Mujahedin va baramadan-e Taleban* (Tehran: Nashr-e Qatra, 1377 [1999]), 310–312.

27. See U.S. Department of State, cable, "Afghanistan: Meeting with the Taliban," December 11, 1997, National Security Archive, George Washington University, *The Taliban File*, www.gwu.edu/~nsarchiv/ NSAEBB/NSAEBB97/tal24.pdf; Rashid, *Taliban*, 170–182; BBC News, "Taleban in Texas for Talks on Gas Pipeline," December 4, 1997;

and Caroline Lees, "Oil Barons Court Taliban in Texas," *Daily Telegraph*, December 14, 1997.

28. Abdul Hakim Mujahed, "Time to Recognize Afghanistan's Legitimate Government," October 10, 1998, 1–7. Copy courtesy of Amin Tarzi. See also, "Taliban Support Council Issuances, 1993–1997," Hoover Archive on War, Revolution, and Peace, Stanford University.

29. "Editorial: The Dynamic Address of Mulla Ameer Khan Muttaqi."

30. "Thoughts of Those Who Said Labayk," *Dha'rb-i-M'umin* 1, no. 12 (July 1, 1997), 4.

31. U.S. Department of State, cable, "U.S. Engagement with the Taliban on Usama Bin Laden," ca. July 16, 2001, National Security Archive, *The Taliban File*, www.gwu.edu/~nsarchiv/NSAEBB/NSAEBB97/tal40 .pdf. The State Department translation does not contain a specific reference to the Quranic text, but Omar is presumably quoting the Quran, 5:82. See the cable "Message to Mullah Omar" in ibid.

32. Metcalf, *'Traditionalist' Islamic Activism*, 1, 15.

33. Angela María Puentes Marín, *El opio de los talibán y la coca de las Farc: Transformaciones de la relación entre actores armados y narcotráfico en Afghanistán y Colombia* (Bogota: Universidad de los Andes, 2006), 19; and on the ban on hashish, see Muhammad Riza Hajj Babai, ed., *Qawanin-e Mulla Omar: Majmua-ye qawanin va ayin namahha-ye Taleban dar Afghanistan* (Tehran: Nigah-e emruz, 1382 [2003]), 77.

34. Gilles Dorronsoro, *Revolution Unending: Afghanistan, 1979 to the Present*, trans. John King (New York: Columbia University Press, 2005).

35. See, for example, Larry P. Goodson, *Afghanistan's Endless War: State Failure, Regional Politics, and the Rise of the Taliban* (Seattle: University of Washington Press, 2001).

36. Pahwal left a devastating critique of local figures who joined the Taliban administration in Nimroz—see Lutz Rzehak, ed. and trans., *Die Taliban im Land der Mittagssonne: Geschichten aus der afghanischen Provinz* (Wiesbaden: Reichert, 2005), 30–33, and on Pahwal's own work, xvi–xvii and 94–96.

37. Muzhda, *Afghanistan wa panj sal*, 49.

38. Ibid., 51.

39. Quoted in Sikoev, *Taliby*, 74.

40. Muzhda, *Afghanistan wa panj sal*, 54.

41. Cited in Sikoev, *Taliby*, 73.

42. Ibid., 73, 74.

43. Gilles Dorronsoro, "Les oulémas afghans au XXe siècle: Bureaucratisation, contestation et genèse d'un état clérical," *Archives de Sciences Sociales des Religions*, no. 115 (July–September 2001), 72.

44. Max Klimburg, "A Tense Autonomy: The Present Situation in Nuristan," in Noelle-Karimi et al., *Afghanistan: A Country without a State*, 53–64.

45. Agence France-Presse, "Taliban Allege Rebels in Eastern Kunar Operate from Bases in Pakistan," February 15, 1997; and Xinhua News Agency, "Taliban Crush Tribal Revolt in East Afghanistan," February 24, 1997.

46. "Military Court Personnel to Visit Army Units," BBC Summary of World Broadcasts, Radio Voice of Sharia, Kabul, in Pashto, October 30, 1997.

47. "Taleban Leaders Appoint New Officials to Intelligence Service," BBC Summary of World Broadcasts, Radio Voice of Sharia, Kabul, in Pashto, October 30, 1997.

48. "Taleban Official Receives Local Officials," BBC Summary of World Broadcasts, Radio Voice of Sharia, Kabul, in Dari and Pashto, November 8, 1997.

49. "Taleban Leader Orders Meetings in Memory of Fallen Comrades," BBC Summary of World Broadcasts, Radio Voice of Sharia, Kabul, in Pashto, November 26, 1997, emphasis added.

50. "Taleban Punish Court Officials for Taking Bribes," BBC Summary of World Broadcasts, Radio Voice of Sharia, Kabul, in Pashto, November 23, 1997; Babai, *Qawanin-e Mulla Omar*, 76.

51. "Taleban Dismiss 400 Officials in Eastern Province," BBC Summary of World Broadcasts, Voice of the Islamic Republic of Iran External Service, Tehran, in Pashto, November 17, 1997; see also Goodson, *Afghanistan's Endless War;* and Alex Spillius, "Taliban Fires Beard Trimmers," *Daily Telegraph,* March 26, 1997.

52. "Taleban Offer of Posts to Opposition Rejected," BBC Summary of World Broadcasts, Voice of the Islamic Republic of Iran, Mashhad, in Persian, November 11, 1997.

53. Rashid, *Taliban,* 103–104; Thomas Ruttig, "Die Taliban—Bewegung 'aus dem Nichts'?" *Inamo,* no. 17 (Spring 1999): 12–16. Iranian sources are more detailed, though they betray Tehran's hostility toward the Taliban. See, for example, "Uprisings against Taleban Reportedly Continue in Kandahar," BBC Summary of World Broadcasts, Radio Voice of the Islamic Republic of Iran, Mashhad, January 19, 1998; "Taleban Military Call-Up Provokes Afghan Unrest," BBC Summary of World Broadcasts, Radio Voice of the Islamic Republic of Iran, Mashhad, March 30, 1998; "Afghanistan: Taleban Reportedly Pre-Empt Popular Revolt by Moving Flood Victims," BBC Summary of World Broadcasts, Voice of the Islamic Republic of Iran, Tehran, March 1, 1998.

54. Emphasis added. A Persian text of this constitution was posted at the

Taliban website www.alemarah.org. On previous constitutions, see Mo-hammad Hashim Kamali, *Law in Afghanistan: A Study of the Constitu-tions, Matrimonial Law and the Judiciary* (Leiden: Brill, 1985); and, for a text of the first constitution of 1923 (and amendments), see Leon B. Poullada, *Reform and Rebellion in Afghanistan, 1919–1929: King Amanullah's Failure to Modernize a Tribal Society* (Ithaca: Cornell Uni-versity Press), 277–291.

55. "Taleban Military Court Chairman Jailed for Taking Bribe," BBC Sum-mary of World Broadcasts, *Payem-e Mojahed* website, Parwan, in Dari, January 13, 2000.

56. On the eve of the attacks of September 11, Mullah Omar issued orders rearranging personnel at the level of deputy minister. While Qari Abdul Rashid was promoted from head of Helmand Province to deputy minis-ter of mines and industries, the other officials affected by the changes may have made only marginal gains in shifting to new ministries. For example, the deputy minister of finance became the assistant director of the General Department of Administrative Affairs, and the then-assistant director of the General Department of Administrative Affairs became deputy minister of finance. "Afghan Taliban Reshuffle Deputy Ministers," BBC Summary of World Broadcasts, Radio Voice of Sharia, Kabul, in Pashto, September 8, 2001.

57. "Afghanistan—Provincial Paper Urges Support for Taleban," BBC Summary of World Broadcasts, *Etefaq-e Islam*, Herat, in Pashto, Janu-ary 13, 2000.

58. "Taleban Announce General Amnesty for Foes," BBC Summary of World Broadcasts, *Ausaf*, Islamabad, in Urdu, January 9, 2000. Mullah Omar had used holidays to announce smaller-scale amnesties in previ-ous years.

59. See David B. Edwards, *Before Taliban: Genealogies of the Afghan Jihad* (Berkeley: University of California Press, 2002), 287–308, here, 299; "Uprising in Eastern Afghanistan—Iranian Radio," BBC Summary of World Broadcasts, Voice of the Islamic Republic of Iran, Mashhad, in Persian, January 23, 2000; and, more generally, on tensions with Pashtun communities, International Crisis Group, "Afghanistan: The Problem of Pashtun Alienation," *International Crisis Group Asia Report*, no. 62 (Au-gust 5, 2003).

60. "Uprising in Eastern Afghanistan—Iranian Radio," BBC Summary of World Broadcasts, Voice of the Islamic Republic of Iran, Mashhad, in Persian, January 23, 2000.

61. Mohammad Bashir, "Afghan Taliban Replace Unpopular Khost Gover-nor," Agence France-Presse, January 27, 2000.

62. "Taleban Decry 'Rumours' of Unrest as Part of Propaganda War," BBC

Summary of World Broadcasts, Radio Voice of Sharia, Kabul, in Dari, January 27, 2000, emphasis added.

63. "Tribes in Southeastern Afghan Province Loyal to Taleban—Taleban Radio," BBC Summary of World Broadcasts, Radio Voice of Sharia, Kabul, in Dari, January 27, 2000; Babai, *Qawanin-e Mulla Omar*, 101.

64. Muzhda, *Afghanistan wa panj sal*, 55.

65. See Artie McConnel, "Ex-Taliban Officials Form New Political Group," *Eurasia Insight*, December 27, 2001, www.eurasianet.org.

66. Ibid.

67. The following description is based on Ilene R. Prusher, "Ex-Taliban Officials Change Headdress, Resume Duties," *Christian Science Monitor*, January 14, 2002.

68. Mullah Khaksar is also featured as one of the "moderate Taliban" in Gannon, *I is for Infidel*.

69. Constable, "Tales of the Taleban."

70. See, for example, Wahid Muzhda, "Chera Taliban beh mulla koshi roy awarda and?" BBC Persian.com, June 15, 2005; *Radio Free Europe/Radio Liberty Afghanistan Report* 5, no. 6 (February 28, 2006); Elizabeth Rubin, "In the Land of the Taliban," *New York Times Magazine*, October 22, 2006, 90; and National Public Radio, "Analysis: Taliban Members Joining Afghanistan's Government," August 3, 2004.

71. NPR, "Analysis."

72. Victoria Burnett, "You Don't Have to Die, Taliban Told," *Financial Times*, December 17, 2004; Burnett, "US Extends an Olive Branch to Taliban's 'Moderates'," *Boston Globe*, January 2, 2005.

73. See Somini Sengupta, "A Onetime Talib Hopes for Votes," *International Herald Tribune*, September 19, 2005.

74. On Mutawakil, see "Former Taleban Minister Urges Government to Hold Talks with Insurgents," Kabul Ariana TV, February 10, 2007 (translation from Dari by the Open Source Center, www.opensource.gov).

75. See, for example, "More than 170 Taliban, Islamic Militants Surrender in Afghanistan," Agence France-Presse, February 5, 2006; Habib Rahman Ibrahimi, "Over 160 Dissidents Join Peace Process," Pajhwok Afghan News, November 30, 2006; Habib Rahman Ibrahimi, "115 Dissidents Surrender," Pajhwok Afghan News, February 18, 2007.

76. Amin Tarzi, "Is Reconciliation with the Neo-Taliban Working?" *Radio Free Europe/Radio Liberty Afghanistan Report* 4, no. 18 (June 6, 2005).

77. See, for example, Rachel Morarjee, "Air War Costs NATO Afghan Supporters," *Christian Science Monitor*, December 18, 2006. A number of politicians in NATO countries have nonetheless called for the inclusion

of Taliban in the government. See, for example, the comments by U.S. Senator Bill Frist in "Frist: Taliban Should Be Part of Afghan Government," www.foxnews.com/story/0,2933,217198,00.html.

78. See, for example, the editorial by the Herat News Centre, "Afghanistan: Agency Criticizes Policy of Amnesty for Taliban," Foreign Broadcast Information Service, May 13, 2005.

79. See Ismail Khan, "Omar Threatens to Intensify War: Talks with Karzai Govt Ruled Out," *Dawn,* January 4, 2007.

8. The Neo-Taliban

1. Karzai's remark is reported in Liz Sly, "Rumsfeld, Karzai: Taliban Poses No Threat," *Chicago Tribune,* February 27, 2004. Karzai made the remark during a press conference with visiting U.S. Secretary of Defense Donald Rumsfled in Kabul on February 26, 2004. The quotation from Khalilzad, U.S. ambassador to Afghanistan, is from his remarks at the Center for Strategic and International Studies in Washington, D.C., on April 4, 2004 (www.csis.org).

2. See Amin Tarzi, "Contradictions Hint at Division within Neo-Taliban," *Radio Free Europe/Radio Liberty Afghanistan Report* 5, no. 25 (September 22, 2006), www.rferl.org/reports. Also see Amin Tarzi, "Mujahidin," in *Encyclopedia of Islam and the Muslim World* (New York: Macmillan Reference, 2004), 490–491.

3. Tarzi, "Contradictions." A website claiming to represent the "Islamic Emirate of Afghanistan" was established in Peshawar, Pakistan, in June 2005. Initially in Pashto and Arabic, only the site's Pashto-language pages were updated regularly. In 2006, materials in Persian, Urdu, and English were added; however, only the Pashto and Persian pages were updated regularly. In mid-2006 the website was updated daily and often more than once per day. In late 2006 the website was blocked.

4. The term *neo-Taliban* is not my invention. I first encountered its use in Jonathan Ledgard's "Taking on the Warlords . . . ," *The Economist,* May 22, 2003. After consulting with Ledgard, I began using the term in my writings beginning in June 2003. See *Radio Free Europe/Radio Liberty Afghanistan Report* 2, no. 21 (June 19, 2003). The term was also used in an opinion piece published in the Islamabad daily *The Nation* on June 8, 2003. French daily *Le Figaro* has used the term since June 2003. Prior to the total demise of the Taliban regime in Afghanistan, Lutfi Mestan, deputy chairman of Bulgaria's DPS party, described the resignation of his country's ambassadors to Washington and New Delhi as having "neo-Taliban overtones." See "DPS Security Chairman Mestan Views Party's Role in Bulgarian Politics," *Sofia Pari,* December 4, 2001 (DPS

citation obtained from, and translated from Bulgarian by, the Open Source Center, www.opensource.gov).

5. In this chapter I use the term "United Front" for the anti-Taliban opposition groups popularly known as the "Northern Alliance."

6. Wahid Muzhda, *Afghanistan wa panj sal sulta-ye Taleban* (Tehran: Nashr-e ney, 1382 [2003]), 173. Muzhda's work, to date, is the only insider account of the Taliban.

7. Scott Johnson and Evan Thomas, "Mullah Omar Off the Record," *Newsweek*, January 21, 2002. Mullah Omar's personal driver, identified as Qari Saheb, claimed that the Taliban leader vowed that "even if Bush shows up" at his door, he will not leave Kandahar.

8. Muzhda, *Afghanistan wa panj sal*, 174–175.

9. Ibid., 177. Hamid Karzai was a member of the National Liberation Front of Afghanistan, a Pakistan-based mujahedin group, and later served in the mujahedin government in Kabul. He initially supported the Taliban, but later distanced himself from them and joined the group formed around the former King Muhammad Zaher in Rome. For a biography of Karzai, see Amin Tarzi, "Karzai, Hamid (1957–)," in *Encyclopedia of World Terrorism, 1996–2002* (Armonk, NY: M. E. Sharpe, 2003), 184–185. For a critical Afghan biography of Karzai, see Muhammad Akram Andishmand, *Amrika dar Afghanistan* (Kabul: Maywand, 1384 [2005]), 260–268.

10. "Taliban Forced Out of Afghanistan," *Payam-e Mojahed*, December 13, 2001 (obtained from, and translation from Pashto by, the Open Source Center.)

11. Ibid.

12. Shayrzai assumed the administrative duties in Kandahar while Alakozai took charge of the military affairs of the province. Since 2002 Shayrzai has served twice as governor of Kandahar, once as the minister for urban development, and as of July 2005 as the governor of Nangarhar Province. According to some reports, Alakozai was one of the scores of people killed in an apparent suicide attack in Kandahar in June 2005. See Amin Tarzi, "Suicide Attack Kills at Least 17 in Southern Afghanistan," in *Radio Free Europe/Radio Liberty Newsline*, June 1, 2005, www.rferl.org/newsline.

13. Roy Carrol, "Former Minister Says Fugitive Taliban Leaders Living in Pakistan," *The Guardian*, December 24, 2001.

14. Ibid. Khaksar was killed by unidentified assailants in Kandahar in January 2006. He had accepted the reconciliation offer made by the Karzai government and eventually, in September 2005, made an unsuccessful attempt in Kandahar to win a seat in the Afghan National Assembly.

See Amin Tarzi, "Former Taliban Regime Official Killed in Southern Afghanistan," in *Radio Free Europe/Radio Liberty Newsline,* January 18, 2006.

15. John Heller, "Political Space Is Opening for Taliban Moderates, but Just How Moderate Are They?" *Radio Free Europe/Radio Liberty Afghanistan Report* 2, no. 23 (July 3, 2003).

16. Ibid. Also see Hafizullah Mansur, *Karzai nakhwanda imza maykonad* (Kabul: Maywand, n.d. [probably 2003]), 136–139.

17. Muzhda, *Afghanistan wa panj sal,* 158, 159.

18. See *Radio Free Europe/Radio Liberty Afghanistan Report* 2, no. 36 (October 16, 2003).

19. Ibid., no. 35, October 9, 2003.

20. See ibid., 3, no. 9, March 4, 2004.

21. Golnaz Esfandiari, "Karzai Calls on Taliban to Participate in Elections," *Radio Free Europe/Radio Liberty Afghanistan Report* 3, no. 16 (April 24, 2004).

22. United States Central Command, Operation Enduring Freedom Updates, MacDill Air Force Base, March 18, 2002, www.centcom.mil. According to the update, General Rosa made the comments at a U.S. Department of Defense briefing on March 17, 2002.

23. James Dao, "U.S. Shifts Emphasis in Afghanistan to Security and Road Building," *New York Times,* November 11, 2002. The comments were made by U.S. Joint Chiefs of Staff Chairman General Richard Myers in a speech at the Brookings Institution in Washington, D.C., on November 4, 2002.

24. On coalition deployments, see Amin Tarzi, "International Forces in Afghanistan Stationed in Gardayz," *Radio Free Europe/Radio Liberty Afghanistan Report* 1, no. 3 (December 12, 2002); on the UN report, see Kimberly McCloud, "Gauging the Threat of Terrorism in Afghanistan," *Radio Free Europe/Radio Liberty Afghanistan Report* 2, no. 4 (January 22, 2003); and the report itself, "Third Report of the Monitoring Group Established Pursuant to Security Council Resolution 1363 (2001) and Extended by Resolution 1390 (2002)" contained in the UN Security Council document S/200/1338, December 17, 2002.

25. "Afghan President Accepts Freedom Award in New York," *Radio Free Europe/Radio Liberty Newsline,* November 15, 2002.

26. See *Radio Free Europe/Radio Liberty Afghanistan Report* 2, no. 1 (January 2, 2003).

27. "Two Dead after Kabul Attack," *BBC,* December 20, 2002.

28. For example, between September 2002 and September 2003, armed attacks against the assistance community went up from one attack per

month to one attack every two days, on average. See "Good Intentions Will Not Pave the Road to Peace," a joint report prepared by CARE International and the Center for International Cooperation, September 15, 2003, 1; on the radio station, see Amin Tarzi, "Antigovernment Radio Station Debuts in Paktya," *Radio Free Europe/Radio Liberty Afghanistan Report* 2, no. 2 (January 9, 2003).

29. Amin Tarzi, "'Soft' Target Selection Takes Aim at the Bull's-Eye of Normalcy," *Radio Free Europe/Radio Liberty Afghanistan Report* 2, no. 20 (June 12, 2003).

30. According to the estimates of the United Nations Office on Drugs and Crime (UNODC), Afghan farmers produced 3,400 tons of opium in 2002 compared to 185 tons the preceding year. The numbers have continued to climb. In 2003, a year in which three-quarters of the global opium supply originated in Afghanistan, production increased by another 6 percent to 3,600 tons. By 2006, Afghanistan's opium production had reached a record 6,100 tons, accounting for 92 percent of global output. UNODC has estimated that the output of opium production in Afghanistan in 2006 "netted $3.1 billion for the Afghan economy (accruing to farmers, laboratory owners and Afghan traffickers)." It is estimated that 12.6 percent of the Afghan population—2.9 million people—are directly involved in opium production (*Afghanistan Opium Survey 2006* published by UNODC in October 2006, 5–9). For more, see Amin Tarzi, "Drugs: Afghanistan's Neglected Time Bomb," *Radio Free Europe/Radio Liberty Afghanistan Report* 3, no. 6 (February 12, 2004); and Amin Tarzi, "Containing the Drug Menace," *Radio Free Europe/Radio Liberty Afghanistan Report* 5, no. 24 (September 12, 2006).

31. Barnett R. Rubin, "Is America Abandoning Afghanistan?" *New York Times,* April 10, 2002.

32. Ibid. According to *The World Factbook 2007,* published by the Central Intelligence Agency of the United States, Pashtuns account for 42 percent, and Tajiks for 27 percent, of Afghanistan's population.

33. Antonio Giustozzi, "Auxiliary Force or National Army? Afghanistan's 'ANA' and the Counter-Insurgency Effort, 2002–2006," *Small Wars and Insurgencies* 18, no. 1 (March 2007): 45–67. Giustozzi adds, "Tajik commanders of the ANA battalions deployed in Kandahar in early 2005, for example, refused to speak Pashto to the local authorities and entertained bad relations with local police."

34. "Afghanistan: The Problem of Pashtun Alienation," *International Crisis Group Asia Report,* no. 62 (August 5, 2003), 2.

35. "Paying for the Taliban's Crimes: Abuses against Ethnic Pashtuns in Northern Afghanistan," *Human Rights Watch* 14, no. 2(C) (April 2002).

The report does note that "it would be a mistake to view the attacks against Pashtun communities solely as reprisals for past abuses" (10). Also see "Afghanistan: Country Reports on Human Rights Practices—2003," Bureau of Democracy, Human Rights and Labor, U.S. State Department, February 25, 2004, www.state.gov/g/drl/rls/hrrpt/2003/27943.htm.

36. Montgomery McFate, "The Military Utility of Understanding Adversary Culture," *Joint Force Quarterly*, no. 38 (2005): 46.

37. See Scott Johnson and Evan Thomas, "Mullah Omar Off the Record," *Newsweek*, January 21, 2002. The soldier in question, according to the report, was Special Forces Sergeant Nathan Chapman. According to Pentagon spokeswoman Victoria Clark, Chapman died when he was "trying to get some information with some tribal leaders" when a firefight erupted; see "ASD PA Clarke Interview with Jonathan Karl, CNN," January 5, 2002, www.defenselink.mil.

38. Lutz Kleveman, *The New Great Game: Blood and Oil in Central Asia* (New York: Atlantic Monthly Press, 2003), 230.

39. "Afghanistan: The Problem of Pashtun Alienation," 8. Gailani was a candidate for the Afghan presidential election in 2004 and was elected to the Afghan National Assembly in 2005. Since the early twentieth century Gailani's family has represented the Qadiriyyah Sufi order in Afghanistan; see Amin Tarzi and Helena Malikyar, "The Jilânî Family in Afghanistan," *Journal of the History of Sufism* (Paris), nos. 1–2 (2000): 93–102.

40. "The Loya Jirga: One Small Step Forward?" International Crisis Group, Afghanistan Briefing, May 16, 2002, 2.

41. "Afghanistan: The Problem of Pashtun Alienation," 9. Most members of the Shura-ye Nezar are from the Panjsher Valley, which in April 2004 was elevated to province status to honor Ahmad Shah Masud. According to witnesses outside the Loya Jirga tent, when Muhammad Zaher addressed the delegates, his microphones were off, which later was attributed to a malfunction of the system.

42. Until 2006, when the use of the Internet by the opposition became more organized and systematic, most violent activities were carried out under the "Taliban" name. Beginning in 2006, the website purporting to represent the "Islamic Emirate of Afghanistan" began referring to the opposition as "mujahedin." In the course of Islamic history, many groups have used this term to identify their struggles to defend Islam. It gained global currency in Afghanistan during the 1979–1989 Soviet occupation. See Tarzi, "Contradictions"; also see Tarzi, "Mujahidin," 490–491.

43. See Amin Tarzi, "Mollah Mohammed Omar," in *Encyclopedia of World Terrorism: 1996–2002* (Armonk, NY: M. E. Sharpe, 2003), 195–196.

44. "No Peace until U.S. Expelled, Say Taliban," *The News* (Islamabad), April 27, 2004 (obtained from the Open Source Center).

45. The former website for the Center for Islamic Studies and Research, www.pages4free.bix/image333, is no longer functional. The information used here comes from the Open Source Center, "Afghanistan: Taliban Leader Explains Jihad Strategy," March 18, 2004. The tape is reported to be 29 minutes in Arabic; the English versions used in this chapter are based on the Open Source Center translation.

46. Ibid. The group the unidentified Afghan opposition speaker was addressing must have been made up of Arabs, since at the beginning of his speech he apologizes to his audience for his poor command of the Arabic language.

47. "Taliban Leader Mullah Mohammad Omar Has Named a 10-Member Leadership Council to Organize Resistance to the U.S.-Led Foreign Troops in Afghanistan," *The News* (Islamabad), June 24, 2003 (obtained from the Open Source Center).

48. "Taliban Accept Responsibility for Killing of UN Official in Central Afghanistan," Voice of the Islamic Republic of Iran, External Service, Tehran, in Pashto, November 19, 2003(obtained from, and translation from Pashto by, the Open Source Center).

49. "Taliban Armed Group Leader Threatens to Shift Battle to Kabul," *Al-Hayat*, November 19, 2003 (obtained from, and translated from Arabic by, the Open Source Center).

50. "Al-Jazirah at Midday," *Al-Jazeera* (Doha), November 20, 2003 (obtained from, and translated from Arabic by, the Open Source Center).

51. "Taleban Claim Responsibility for the Death of Afghan Governor," Afghan Islamic Press News Agency, September 10, 2006 (obtained from, and translated from Pastho by, the Open Source Center).

52. "Pa Paktya fidaye hamla kay Hakim Taniwal wwazhal shu," September 10, 2006, www.alamarah.com.

53. Tarzi, "Contradictions."

54. "Taliban Leader Mullah Mohammad Omar Has Named a 10-Member Leadership Council to Organize Resistance to the U.S.-Led Foreign Troops in Afghanistan," *The News* (Islamabad), June 24, 2003. According to the report, the Leadership Council included Jalaluddin Haqani, Saif al-Rahman Mansur, Mullah Dadullah, Akhtar Muhammad Osmani, Akhtar Muhammad Mansur, Mullah Obaidullah, Hafez Abdul Majid, Mullah Baradar, Mullah Muhammad Rasul, and Mullah Abdul Razaq Nafez.

55. "Mullah Omar Has Chaired a Meeting of the Taliban," *Hindukosh News Agency* (Kabul), September 23, 2003.

56. Amin Tarzi, "Neo-Taliban Identify Their Spokesman," *Radio Free Europe/Radio Liberty Afghanistan Report* 3, no. 9 (March 4, 2004).

57. Amin Tarzi, "Neo-Taliban Free to Communicate with Media," *Radio Free Europe/Radio Liberty Afghanistan Report* 4, no. 23 (August 15, 2005). Hakimi—whose first names have appeared in various sources as "Latif," "Abdul Latif," and "Latifullah," and who has been given the religious titles "mufti," "mawlawi" and "mullah"—is not an unknown figure. In early 1999, Shariah Zhagh (Voice of Sharia)—the Kabul government radio station during Taliban rule—mentioned Hakimi as the head of the Justice Department in Herat Province. Later in 1999 and in 2000, Taliban-run media referred to Hakimi as the head of the Information and Culture Department in Herat. In all early references available, Hakimi has been identified as Mufti Latifullah.

58. The Taliban gained the release of Muhammad Yaser and Hakimi, along with three other members of their movement, in March 2007 in a controversial exchange involving Daniele Mastrogiacomo, an Italian journalist they had abducted earlier along with his two Afghan aides. The two Afghans were killed. See "Italian Journalist Freed in Afghanistan in Exchange for Taliban Members," *Radio Free Europe/Radio Liberty Newsline,* March 20, 2007. For the arrest of Muhammad Hanif, see Jessica Coakley, "Afghan Intelligence Arrests Purported Taliban Spokesman," *Radio Free Europe/Radio Liberty Newsline,* January 17, 2007.

59. "Taliban Minister Has 'No Information' about Mullah Omar, bin Laden," Afghan Islamic Press News Agency, December 16, 2001 (obtained from, and translated from Pashto by, the Open Source Center).

60. "Taliban Leader Calls for Holy War, Warns against Helping 'Aggressive Infidels,'" Afghan Islamic Press News Agency, February 17, 2003. The source for this information is a Peshawar-based news agency that describes itself as an independent organization with access to the neo-Taliban. It is not clear in which language the statement was sent to the news agency (obtained from, and translated from Pashto by, the Open Source Center).

61. "Taliban Chief Mullah Omar Reorganizes His Group," Jama'atul Dawa website, January 31, 2003, www.jamatuddawa.org (obtained from, and translated from Urdu by, the Open Source Center). This Pakistani Islamist group was formerly known as Markazul Dawa Wal Irshad. The source lists Mullah Muhammad Allah Khan for Helmand Province; Mawlawi Besmellah Jan for Kandahar Province; Taous Hamid for Uruzgan Province; Salam Dad Agha for Ghazni Province; Mawlana

Qudratullah for Zabul Province; Haji Lawangyar for Khost Province; Sameullah for Nangarhar Province; Numan Muhammad Ashraf for Jalan—not a province in Afghanistan; and Rahmatullah, Mawlana Yaqub and Mufti Abdul Rasul for all provinces in Afghanistan.

62. "Mullah Omar Issues Fatwa, Urges Murder of American, Collaborators," *Al-Hayat*, April 1, 2003 (obtained from, and translated from Arabic by, the Open Source Center).

63. Statement of Mullah Omar was faxed by Hamid Agha to Afghan Islamic Press News Agency on November 12, 2004 (obtained from, and translated from Pashto by, the Open Source Center).

64. "Afghan Scholars Said to Have Issued Fatwa against U.S.A., Muslim Collaborators," *The News* (Islamabad), February 11, 2003. On April 27, 2003, another mysterious group calling itself the Devoted Movement of Martyrs' Sons, sent a statement to newspapers in Peshawar, Pakistan, warning that a war led by the United States and the United Kingdom had been launched against Muslims and calling for jihad against the foreign forces in Afghanistan. The statement claimed that the group had no links to the neo-Taliban, al-Qaeda, or Gulbuddin Hekmatyar. See "New Afghan Movement Declares Holy War on Foreign, Afghan Sources," Afghan Islamic Press News Agency, April 28, 2003 (obtained from, and translated from Pashto by, the Open Source Center).

65. Talib Ahmad, "Interview with Gulbuddin Hekmatyar, Leader of Afghan Hizb-e Islami," *Al-Majallah* (London), December 16, 2001 (obtained from, and translated from Arabic by, the Open Source Center).

66. Amin Tarzi, "Afghanistan Guards against Taliban–Hezb-e Islami Alliance," *Radio Free Europe/Radio Liberty Newsline*, November 20, 2002; and Tanya Goudsouzian, "Hizb-e Islami Leader Declares Jihad to Liberate Afghanistan," *Radio Free Europe/Radio Liberty Newsline*, December 27, 2002.

67. Zalmay Khalilzad, the U.S. special envoy, later also ambassador, to Afghanistan, made the linkage among the Taliban, al-Qaeda, and Hekmatyar in an interview with ICG on April 21, 2002; see "The Loya Jirga: One Small Step Forward?" 4; on the U.S. response, see "Designation of Gulbuddin Hekmatyar as a Terrorist," U.S. Department of State, February 19, 2003, www.state.gov/r/pa/prs/ps/2003/17799.htm. For more on Hekmatyar, see Ishtiaq Ahmad, *Gulbuddin Hekmatyar: An Afghan Trail from Jihad to Terrorism* (Islamabad: Society of Tolerance and Education, 2004); and on the idea of an alliance between the Taliban, al-Qaeda, and Hekmatyar, see Ahmad Zaidan, *'Audah al-rayat al-sud: Thalathiyyah Taliban wa al-Qa'idah wa'l Hizb fi Afghanistan* (Beirut: World Book, 2004).

68. The signed message from Hekmatyar in Pashto, dated January 6, 2003, was reported in full by the Peshawar-based Afghan Islamic Press News Agency on the same day.

69. Amin Tarzi, "Fugitive Former Afghan Premier Sets Conditions for Talks with Karzai," *Radio Free Europe/Radio Liberty Newsline*, March 9, 2007.

70. Saeed Ali Achakzai, "Afghan-Taliban-Split," Reuters, August 9, 2004.

71. In the initial report about the formation of this new splinter group, the organization's name, "Taliban Jami'at Jaish-e Moslemin," indicated that it was formulated by someone using Urdu or that the information was provided to the media by an Urdu speaker. During the kidnapping case, the group converted its name to "Jaish al-Moslemin," an Arabic rendition. While no study is publicly available on the subject of the names used by various terrorists and their affiliated organizations in Afghanistan, the usage of three languages, namely Arabic, Pashto, and Urdu, is common, which perhaps is an indication of the political tilt or targeted audience of the groups involved.

72. Mullah Muhammad Ishaq was also identified as "Ishaq Manzur" (Amin Tarzi, "Kidnapping in Kabul: By Whom and for What?" *Radio Free Europe/Radio Liberty Afghanistan Report* 3, no. 40 [November 8, 2004]).

73. Ibid.

74. Ibid. According to a report by Agence France-Presse on October 28, 2004, an unidentified Pakistani cleric claimed that Jaish al-Moslemin was the "new military wing of the Taliban" under Mullah Omar's leadership.

75. Heller, "Political Space Is Opening." An Islamist group of the same name had been active in Kabul in the mid-1960s when it opposed increasing leftist activities on the Kabul University campus. In 1971, Jamiat-e Khuddam al-Furqan was established under the leadership of Hazrat Sahib of Qala-ye Jawad—a leader of the Naqshbandi Sufi order in Afghanistan. The society published a journal in Dari and Pashto entitled *Neda-ye Haq*. After the communist takeover, the society joined the mujahedin "party" of Mawlawi Muhammad Nabi Muhammadi, the Harakat-e Inqelab-e Islami (Islamic Revolution Movement), from which most of the leading Taliban figures emerged in the mid-1990s. See Basir Ahmad Dawlatabadi, *Shenasnamah-ye ahzab wa jaryanat-e siyasi-ye Afghanistan* (Qom: Farwardin, 1992), 179–181.

76. Heller, "Political Space Is Opening."

77. Amin Tarzi, "In Unfolding Saga, Former Members of the Taliban Regime Confirm Talks with Kabul," *Radio Free Europe/Radio Liberty Afghanistan Report* 4, no. 7 (February 25, 2005). The list of four members

of Khaddam al-Furqan, in addition to Mujahed, included other former Taliban government officials, Arsala Rahmani, the deputy minister of higher education; Rahmatullah Watanyar, the deputy minister of refugees and returnees; and Habibullah Fawzi, who worked as a diplomat in the Taliban regime's embassies in Riyadh and Islamabad. In December 2005, Karzai appointed Rahmani as a member of the newly inaugurated Afghan National Assembly's Meshrano Jirga (Council of Elders). According to the Afghan constitution, the president selects one-third of the members of the 102-member upper house.

78. For more on this, see Kleveman, *The New Great Game;* and Paul Sperry, *Crude Politics: How Bush's Oil Cronies Hijacked the War on Terrorism* (Nashville: WND Books, 2003).

79. Abdul Hakim Mujahed, "Time to Recognize Afghanistan's Legitimate Government," October 10, 1998, 3, 8. In his message Mujahed identifies himself as "Islamic Emirate of Afghanistan, Permanent Representative/Designate to the United Nations." A copy of the letter was obtained by the author from a representative of a mission of a UN member state wishing to remain anonymous.

80. See Tarzi, "Mollah Mohammed Omar"; and Amin Tarzi and Kimberly A. McCloud, "Taliban," in *Encyclopedia of Islam*, 676–678.

81. The unidentified CIA station chief is quoted by Kathy Gannon in "The Afghan Road," *New Yorker,* March 15, 2004.

82. Amin Tarzi, "Could Afghan and Iraqi Insurgencies Muster Operational Ties?" *Radio Free Europe/Radio Liberty Afghanistan Report* 5, no. 14 (May 16, 2006).

83. Amin Tarzi, "Islamabad Anxious as Kabul Gets Chummy with New Delhi," *Radio Free Europe/Radio Liberty Afghanistan Report* 5, no. 11 (April 26, 2006).

84. For a brief summary of Pakistan's policies vis-à-vis Afghanistan and the role of Islam in Islamabad's strategic calculations, see Husain Haqqani, *Pakistan between Mosque and Military* (Washington, DC: Carnegie Endowment for International Peace, 2005), 131–198.

85. Seth G. Jones, "Pakistan's Dangerous Game," *Survival* 49, no. 1 (Spring 2007): 15.

86. Amin Tarzi, "Pakistan and Afghanistan: 'Inseparable Twins' in Need of Separation," *Radio Free Europe/Radio Liberty Afghanistan Report* 5, no. 6 (February 28, 2006).

87. Amin Tarzi, "Karzai's 'First Foreign-Policy Speech' Triggers Anti-Pakistan Riot," *Radio Free Europe/Radio Liberty Afghanistan Report* 2, no. 24 (July 10, 2003).

88. Amin Tarzi, "Kabul's Relations with Its Other Neighbor, Iran," *EurasiaNet*, March 18, 2007, www.eurasianet.org.

Epilogue

1. Bob Woodward, *Bush at War* (New York: Simon and Schuster, 2002), 314, 317.

2. International Crisis Group, "Countering Afghanistan's Insurgency: No Quick Fixes," *Asia Report*, no. 123 (November 2, 2006): 2; Gilles Dorronsoro, "Afghanistan: The Delusions of Victory," *Internationale Politik und Gesellschaft* 2 (2003): 112–122.

3. Odd Arne Westad, *The Global Cold War: Third World Interventions and the Making of Our Times* (Cambridge: Cambridge University Press, 2005), 396.

4. Erwin Grötzbach, *Afghanistan: Eine geographische Landeskunde* (Darmstadt: Wissenschaftliche Buchgesellschaft, 1990), 183–190, 228–230.

5. Quoted in M. Nazif Shahrani, "Introduction: Marxist 'Revolution' and Islamic Resistance in Afghanistan," in *Revolutions and Rebellions in Afghanistan: Anthropological Perspectives,* ed. M. Nazif Shahrani and Robert L. Canfield (Berkeley: Institute of International Studies, University of California, 1984), 11; and Nancy Hatch Dupree, "Revolutionary Rhetoric and Afghan Women," in Shahrani and Canfield, *Revolutions and Rebellions,* 322.

6. See Judith Huber, *Risse im Patriarchat: Frauen in Afghanistan* (Zurich: Rotpunktverlag, 2003), 20–21. Huber also notes that Laura Bush's mid-November 2001 radio address highlighting Taliban atrocities against women was followed two days later by a similar speech from Cherie Blair. See also the critique by Conrad Schetter, "Afghanistan: Willkommen in Umerziehungslager," *FriEnt Impulse,* no. 5 (2006): 6–8.

7. Westad, *Global Cold War,* 398. "So far," he continues, "the combination of stable growth and stable democracies that Washington has ostensibly sought may be visible in two half-states (South Korea and Taiwan), but is absent in around thirty other countries in which the United States has intervened, directly or indirectly, since 1945" (404).

8. See Greg Grandin, *Empire's Workshop: Latin America, the United States, and the Rise of the New Imperialism* (New York: Metropolitan Books, 2006).

9. "Unser Kampf ist global," *Die Weltwoche* no. 26 (2007), www.weltwoche.ch.

10. Gary Bersten, *Jawbreaker: The Attack on bin Laden and al Qaeda: A Per-

sonal Account by the CIA's Key Field Commander (New York: Crown, 2005), 92.

11. The International Crisis Group calculated, by contrast, that "25,000 to 30,000 peacekeepers were needed to secure major cities and transport routes" ("Countering Afghanistan's Insurgency," 3).

12. Judith Huber, "Massaker zweiter Klasse," *Die Wochenzeitung,* April 15, 2004. See also the testimony of witnesses in the documentary film by Jamie Doran, *Afghan Massacre: The Convoy of Death* (2002); Anthony Shadid, "Victims of Circumstance," *Middle East Report,* no. 222 (Spring 2002): 12–17.

13. See Anne Nivat, *The Wake of War: Encounters with the People of Iraq and Afghanistan,* trans. Jane Marie Todd (Boston: Beacon Press, 2005), 252; and Bilal Sarwary, "In Pictures: Taleban Shrine," BBC News, March 6, 2006. On the reputation for rape and violence of Northern Alliance soldiers among Afghan women, see Saba Gul Khattak, "Afghan Women: Bombed to Be Liberated?" *Middle East Report,* no. 222 (Spring 2002): 18–23.

14. Gary Thomas, "Assessing the Bonn Accords," Voice of America News Analysis, December 3, 2006; see also Thomas H. Johnson, "Afghanistan's Post-Taliban Transition: The State of State-Building after War," *Central Asian Survey* 25, nos. 1–2 (March–June 2006): 1–26.

15. See M. Jamil Hanifi, "Editing the Past: Colonial Production of Hegemony through the 'Loya Jerga' in Afghanistan," *Iranian Studies* 37, no. 2 (June 2004): 295–322.

16. Carne Ross, *Independent Diplomat: Dispatches from an Unaccountable Elite* (Ithaca: Cornell University Press, 2007), 42.

17. "On paper," the International Crisis Group points out, "Afghanistan has one of the most centralized administrations in the world. Provincial governors and police chiefs are appointed by the center, which is also where all budgets are set in the line ministries, with no fiscal discretion at provincial level. This centralization of power, based on the perception that giving any away is 'losing it,' is partly responsible for the lack of progress in the provinces" (International Crisis Group, "Countering Afghanistan's Insurgency," 4).

18. See Renate Kreile, "Befreiung durch Krieg? Frauenrechte in Afghanistan zwischen Weltordnungspolitik und Identitätspolitik," *Internationale Politik und Gesellschaft,* no. 1 (2005): 102–120; and "Amnesty International Says Afghan Women Still Facing Abuse," *Radio Free Europe/ Radio Liberty Afghanistan Report* 4, no. 18 (June 6, 2005), www.rferl .org/reports.

19. On Kabul, see Bernt Glatzer, *Afghanistan: Im Auftrag der Friedrich-Ebert-Stiftung und der Gesellschaft für Technische Zusammenarbeit* (Bonn: Friedrich-Ebert-Stiftung, 2003), 13. In addition to the essay by Shahrani in this book, see Gabriele Rasuly-Paleczek, "The Struggle for the Afghan State: Centralization, Nationalism and Their Discontents," in *Identity Politics in Central Asia and the Muslim World: Nationalism, Ethnicity and Labour in the Twentieth Century,* ed. Willem Van Schendel and Erik J. Zürcher (London: Tauris, 2001), 149–188. On the broader Soviet Central Asian context of policies designed to advance the consolidation of national identities, see Adrienne Lynn Edgar, *Tribal Nation: The Making of Soviet Turkmenistan* (Princeton: Princeton University Press, 2004).

20. Antonio Giustozzi, "'Good' State vs. 'Bad' Warlords? A Critique of State-Building Strategies in Afghanistan," Crisis States Programme Working Paper No. 51 (October 2004), 7–8.

21. For further examples, see ibid., 8–11.

22. Ibid., 9–12.

23. This population estimate is based on the CIA *World Factbook.*

24. James T. Quinlivan argues that a ratio of twenty security personnel per one thousand inhabitants is the minimum threshold for success in such missions; Quinlivan, "Burden of Victory: The Painful Arithmetic of Stability Operations," *Rand Review* (Summer 2003), www.rand.org/publications/randreview/issues/summer2003/burden.html.

25. Conrad Schetter, "Kriegsfürstentum und Bürgerkriegsökonomien in Afghanistan," *Arbeitspapiere zur Internationalen Politik und Aussenpolitik* (Lehrstuhl für Internationale Politik, Universität zu Köln), no. 3 (2004): 17–21. See also "Brothers in Arms: Afghanistan's Security Dilemma," *The Economist,* August 9, 2002; and International Crisis Group, "Disarmament and Reintegration in Afghanistan," *ICG Asia Report,* no. 65 (September 30, 2003).

26. See, for example, the story of Dad Mohammad Khan told in Elizabeth Rubin, "In the Land of the Taliban," *New York Times Magazine,* October 22, 2006, 88–89. See also the many examples cited in Conrad Schetter, Rainer Glassner, and Masood Karokhail, "Beyond Warlordism: The Local Security Architecture in Afghanistan," *Internationale Politik und Gesellschaft* 2 (2007): 136–152.

27. "Afghanistan's Auxiliary Police: There's Marijuana in Their Socks," *The Economist,* November 18, 2006. See, too, Schetter, "Kriegsfürstentum."

28. Barnett R. Rubin, "Peace Building and State-Building in Afghanistan: Constructing Sovereignty for Whose Security?" *Third World Quarterly*

27, no. 1 (2006): 175–185, here, 179. See also Carl Robichaud, "Remember Afghanistan? A Glass Half Full, on the Titanic," *World Policy Journal* 23, no. 1 (Spring 2006): 17–24.

29. World Bank, *Afghanistan: State Building, Sustaining Growth, and Reducing Poverty* (Washington, DC: World Bank, 2005), 47–48.

30. Rubin, "Peace Building and State-Building," 182–184.

31. On contractors in Afghanistan and Iraq, see the Center for Public Integrity updates at www.publicintegrity.org/wow.

32. Emmanuel Duparcq, "Afghan Aid 'Wastage' under the Spotlight at London Conference," Agence France-Presse, January 28, 2006. See, too, the comprehensive report by Fariba Nawa, "Afghanistan, Inc.," *Corpwatch Investigative Report,* October 6, 2006. For a critical view of the role of Provincial Reconstruction Teams in hindering the expansion of state authority, see also Touko Piiparinen, "A Clash of Mindsets? An Insider's Account of Provincial Reconstruction Teams," *International Peacekeeping* 14, no. 1 (January 2007): 143–157.

33. Murat Kurnaz, *Fünf Jahre Meines Lebens: Ein Bericht aus Guantanamo* (Berlin: Rowohlt, 2007); and Moazzam Begg, with Victoria Brittain, *Enemy Combatant: My Imprisonment at Guantánamo, Bagram, and Kandahar* (New York: New Press, 2006).

34. On the court, see Scott Baldauf, "The West Pushes to Reform Traditionalist Afghan Courts," *Christian Science Monitor,* February 21, 2006; and Huber, *Risse im Patriarchat.*

35. Ross, *Independent Diplomat,* 46.

36. "Afghans Are Fed Up with Security Firm," *Pak Tribune,* September 28, 2004; and Carlotta Gall, "New Afghan Parliament and Karzai Act to Rid Streets of Kabul of Security Barriers," *New York Times,* January 2, 2006. The American practice of searching houses prompted negative comparisons with the Soviets in other locales as well. See Chris Johnson and Jolyon Leslie, *Afghanistan: The Mirage of Peace* (London: Zed Books, 2004), 14. On DynCorp and other security firms' international activities, see Chalmers Johnson, *The Sorrows of Empire: Militarism, Secrecy, and the End of the Republic* (New York: Metropolitan Books, 2004), 131–149.

37. See the editorial from *Payam-e Mojahed* in "Afghan Paper Lists Mistakes Causing Current Crisis in Country," September 26, 2006, text translated from Dari by the Open Source Center.

38. Antonio Donini, "Local Perceptions of Assistance to Afghanistan," *International Peacekeeping* 14, no. 1 (January 2007): 158–172; Alexander Cooley, *Logics of Hierarchy: The Organization of Empires, States, and Military Occupations* (Ithaca: Cornell University Press, 2005), quoted at 156.

For their part, neo-Taliban spokesmen have issued contradictory statements: in the autumn of 2006 Mullah Sabir condemned all NGOs, arguing that they were not really there to assist the Afghan people and that "in reality they are part of the regime" and the Taliban will not tolerate them, "whether they build bridges, clinics, or schools." But in June 2007 Mullah Mansur Dadullah remarked, "We do not regard all NGOs as hostile, only those with contacts with the security services." Sami Yousafzai and Urs Gehringer, "Der Kodex der Taliban," *Die Weltwoche*, no. 46 (2006); and "Unser Kampf ist global," *Die Weltwoche*, no. 26 (2007), www.weltwoche.ch.

39. "Disarmament Drive in Panjshir Valley Angers Villagers," *Dawn*, February 16, 2004; and Johnson and Leslie, *Afghanistan*, 16–18.

40. Richard F. Grimmett, "Conventional Arms Transfers to Developing Nations, 1998–2005," *Congressional Research Report for Congress*, October 23, 2006, 68; see also Leslie Wayne, "Foreign Sales by U.S. Arms Makers Doubled in a Year," *New York Times*, November 11, 2006.

41. United Nations Office on Drugs and Crime, *Afghanistan Opium Survey 2006: Executive Summary* (September 2006), 2. Nigel Allen identifies the emergence of a tourist market in the 1970s as the critical turning point. He also argues that the Taliban were reacting, not to international pressure, but to market mechanisms: a glut of opium on the market motivated the Taliban to remove as much as possible of the product from the market and retain it in storage. See Nigel J. R. Allan, "Opium Production in Afghanistan and Pakistan," in *Dangerous Harvest: Drug Plants and the Transformation of Indigenous Landscapes*, ed. Michael K. Steinberg (Oxford: Oxford University Press, 2004), 134, 141.

42. United Nations Office on Drugs and Crime, *Afghanistan Opium Survey 2006*, iv–2, 5, and, on negative views of opium, 26.

43. Communication between the two regions was quick: opium is a winter crop in Nangarhar but a spring crop in Badakhshan (Allan, "Opium Production," 144–145).

44. Nawa, "Afghanistan, Inc.," 19–20.

45. Jan Koehler and Christoph Zuercher, "Statebuilding, Conflict and Narcotics in Afghanistan: The View from Below," *International Peacekeeping* 14, no. 1 (January 2007): 62–74, here 71.

46. See, for example, Johan Engvall, "The State under Siege: The Drug Trade and Organised Crime in Tajikistan," *Europe-Asia Studies* 58, no. 6 (September 2006): 827–854.

47. Hedayat Amin Arsala, "Revitalizing Afghanistan's Economy: The Government's Plan," in *Building a New Afghanistan*, ed. Robert I. Rothberg (Cambridge, MA: World Peace Foundation, 2007), 136.

48. Ministry of Rural Rehabilitation and Development, *NSP Operations Manual*, 3rd ed., January 15, 2006, www.nspafghanistan.org. For an excellent review of such ventures, see Schetter, "Afghanistan: Willkommen in Umerziehungslager"; on alternatives, including development work through tribal institutions, see Masood Karokhail and Susanne Schmeidl, "Zur Integration traditionellen Strukturen in den Staatsbildungprozess: Lehren aus dem Tribal Liaison Office in Loya Paktia," *Schriften zur Demokratieförderung under Bedingungen fragiler Staatlichkeit*, vol. 1, trans. Annette Bus and Jochen Schimmang (Berlin: Heinrich-Böll-Stiftung, 2006), 63–81.

49. For a much more nuanced account, see Halima Kazem, "Diverse Afghan Groups behind Unrest," *Christian Science Monitor*, June 10, 2005.

50. See "USIP Peace Briefing: Afghan Insurgency Still a Potent Force," February 2006, United States Institute of Peace, www.usip.org.

51. International Crisis Group, "Countering Afghanistan's Insurgency," 7.

52. Andrew North, "Doubts Grow over US Afghan Strategy," BBC News, November 23, 2005.

53. International Crisis Group, "Countering Afghanistan's Insurgency," 6.

54. For example, "Girls' School Set on Fire in Northeastern Afghanistan," Hindokosh News Agency, February 27, 2004, BBC Monitoring South Asia, which hints at an opium link in the Keshem District of Badakshan.

55. "Afghan Ex-President Party Rivals Clash over Poppy Tax in Northeast," Afghan Islamic Press News Agency, February 8, 2004, BBC Monitoring South Asia.

56. Sayed Yaqub Ibrahimi, "Afghan Interior Ministry Takes on Armed Factions," *Institute for War and Peace Reporting: Afghan Recovery Report*, no. 228 (September 1, 2006).

57. Max Klimburg, "A Tense Autonomy: The Present Situation in Nuristan," in *Afghanistan—A Country without a State?* ed. Christine Noelle-Karimi, Conrad Schetter, and Reinhard Schlagintweit (Frankfurt am Main: IKO-Verlag für Interkulturelle Kommukation, 2002), 53–64.

58. See Daan Van Der Schriek, "Nuristan: Insurgent Hideout in Afghanistan," *Terrorism Monitor* 3, no. 10 (May 19, 2005).

59. Andrew North and Bilal Sarwary, "The 'Enemy Central' Province in Afghanistan," BBC News, December 8, 2005.

60. North and Sarwary, "The 'Enemy Central' Province."

61. Pamela Constable, "In Afghanistan, a New Bridge and a New Blockade," *Washington Post*, September 21, 2006.

62. Golnaz Esfandiari, "Afghanistan: U.S. Military Investigates Burning

of Taliban Bodies," Radio Free Europe/Radio Liberty, October 21, 2005. American forces frequently called the masculinity and sexuality of Afghan males—friend and foe alike—into question. "Homosexuality," writes a former interrogator of suspected terrorists at Bagram and Kandahar, "was pervasive among the Afghans, especially the Pashtuns in the south. Even when they weren't overtly engaged in acts of sex, they would cling to each other, hold each other's hand, and generally cavort in ways that would astonish Westerners and repulse soldiers." This celebratory account confirms charges that American forces engaged in sexual humiliation based on the premise that Muslims were particularly susceptible to the practice. "I knew the presence of a woman," writes Mackey, "would be unsettling for Muslim prisoners, especially as they were being strip-searched." He also notes that, in addition to subjecting prisoners to the Prince song "Rasberry Beret" to deprive them of sleep, the interrogators threatened to turn them and "their women" over to Northern Alliance troops. Chris Mackey and Greg Miller, *The Interrogators: Inside the Secret War against Al Qaeda* (New York: Little, Brown, 2004), 186, 259, 268, 272–273. Together with house-to-house searches, this issue, in turn, became a rallying cry for oppositional figures such as Hekmatyar, who called on Afghans and Pashtuns, in particular, to fight the Americans, "who have no consideration for our honor and the chastity of our women." Quoted in Ishtiaq Ahmad, *Gulbuddin Hekmatyar: An Afghan Trail from Jihad to Terrorism* (Islamabad: Society for Tolerance and Education, Pakistan, 2004), 72.

63. Sultan M. Munadi, "Karzai Condemns Burning of Afghan Bodies by U.S. Troops," *New York Times,* October 22, 2005.

64. Kathleen T. Rhem, "Burning Afghan Bodies Resulted from Poor Judgment, not War Crimes," American Forces Press Service, November 29, 2005.

65. Amin Tarzi, "'Hundreds' Demonstrate against U.S. Military Conduct in Eastern Afghanistan," *Radio Free Europe/Radio Liberty Afghanistan Report* 4, no. 15 (May 9, 2005); International Crisis Group, "Countering Afghanistan's Insurgency," 3–4; and "Afghanistan: Year in Brief 2005—Chronology of Key Events," January 11, 2006, IRINnews.org. For more examples of Afghans joining the struggle against the Kabul government because of "mistreatment of civilians by American forces," see Habib Rahman Ibrahimi, "Over 160 Dissidents Join Peace Process," Pajhwok Afghan News, November 30, 2006.

66. Quoted in Ahmad, *Gulbuddin Hekmatyar,* 72.

67. Ismail Khan, "Omar Threatens to Intensify War: Talks with Karzai Govt Ruled Out," *Dawn,* January 4, 2007.

68. See, for example, V. Ayezh, *Afghanistan: Ulgu-ye dimukrasi-e Amreka'i: Az tahmil-e tirurism ta sodur-e dimukrasi* (Kabul: Idara-e Dar al-Nashr-e Afghanistan, 1384 [2005]). Its cover depicts an octopus dressed in an Uncle Sam top hat stretching its tentacles across a map of Afghanistan.

69. See, for example, Ron Synovitz, "Afghanistan: Kabul Seeks Release of More Bagram Detainees," Radio Free Europe/Radio Liberty, October 5, 2006.

70. "UK Troops Rushed to Afghan Riot," BBC News, February 7, 2006.

71. Hafizullah Gardesh, "Lebanese Conflict Reverberates in Afghanistan," *Institute for War and Peace Reporting: Afghan Recovery Report*, no. 225 (August 3, 2006).

72. One image shows an Afghan being beheaded in front of a photo of Abu Musab al-Zarqawi. See Mark Dummett and Bilal Sarwary, "DVD Role in Afghan Insurgency," BBC News, February 21, 2006.

73. "Kabul Bombers Target Senate Chief," BBC News, March 12, 2006. This latter figure includes attempts. See International Crisis Group, "Countering Afghanistan's Insurgency," 6.

74. Borhan Younus, "Taleban Call the Shots in Ghazni," *Institute for War and Peace Reporting: Afghan Recovery Report*, no. 213 (April 25, 2006); and International Crisis Group, "Countering Afghanistan's Insurgency," 5.

75. UNODC, *Afghanistan Opium Survey 2006*, iv.

76. Kate Clark, "Cash Rewards for Taleban Fighters," File on 4, BBC Radio 4, BBC News, February 28, 2006.

77. Mirwais Atal, "US Hearts and Minds Cash Goes to Taleban," *Institute for War and Peace Reporting: Afghan Recovery Report*, no. 236 (November 28, 2006). See also Rubin, "In the Land of the Taliban."

78. See "Living Under the Taleban," *Institute for War and Peace Reporting: Afghan Recovery Report*, no. 249, April 4, 2007; "Taliban Hang Three Afghans in Captured Town," Agence France-Presse, April 1, 2007.

79. Griff Witte, "U.S. Cedes Duties in Rebuilding Afghanistan: NATO, Other Allies Take on New Roles," *Washington Post*, January 3, 2006.

80. Carlotta Gall, "After Afghan Battle, a Harder Fight for Peace," *New York Times*, October 3, 2006.

81. Johnson and Leslie, *Afghanistan*, 14.

82. Leo Docherty, *Desert of Death: A Soldier's Journey from Iraq to Afghanistan* (London: Faber and Faber, 2007), 188.

83. Thomas Ruttig, "Musa-Qala-Protokoll am Ende," *SWP-Aktuell* (2007), www.swp-berlin.org.

84. See Britta Petersen, *Einsatz am Hindukusch: Soldaten der Bundeswehr in Afghanistan* (Freiburg: Herder, 2005), 18. German soldiers also had the

benefit of an outstanding pocket guide to Afghan culture, politics, and history written by leading scholars in Bernhard Chiari, ed., *Afghanistan* (Paderborn: Ferdinand Schöningh, 2006). See also C. J. Chivers, "Dutch Soldiers Stress Restraint in Afghanistan," *New York Times,* April 6, 2007.

85. Docherty, *Desert of Death,* 190.

86. Ann Scott Tyson and Josh White, "Marines Killed Civilians, U.S. Says," *Washington Post,* April 15, 2007.

87. "Karzai Anger over Civilian Deaths," BBC News, May 2, 2007.

88. Ross, *Independent Diplomat,* 44–45.

89. "Caritas international plädiert für Kurswechsel deutscher Afghanistan-Politik," June 13, 2007, www.caritas-international.de; and "NATO in Afghanistan," *The Economist,* July 14, 2007.

90. "Afghanistan: WFP Urgently Needs US $11 Million," February 27, 2006, IRINnews.org.

91. The International Crisis Group estimates that these casualties were "approximately one-third anti-government militants, one-third Afghan security forces and one-third civilians" ("Countering Afghanistan's Insurgency," 5–7).

92. Mohsen M. Milani, "Iran's Policy toward Afghanistan," *Middle East Journal* 60, no. 2 (Spring 2006).

93. Abdullah Shahin, "Where the Taliban Train," *Institute for War and Peace Reporting: Afghan Recovery Report,* March 3, 2006.

94. Dorronsoro, "Afghanistan," 118.

95. Michael Hanfield, "Was in Afghanistan passiert: Besuch bei einem Taliban," *Frankfurter Allgemeine Zeitung,* July 21, 2006.

96. Syed Saleem Shahzad, "Taliban Resurgence in Afghanistan," *Le monde diplomatique* (September 2006): 6–7.

97. Ibid., 6.

98. On these developments, see "Pakistan's Militant Drift," *The Economist,* April 14, 2007; and *British Agencies Afghanistan Group Monthly Afghanistan Review* (June 2007).

99. "Unser Kampf ist global"; and "Taleban Reported Executing Robbers in Northwest Afghanistan," Afghan Islamic Press, July 21, 2007, text translated from Pashto by the Open Source Center.

CONTRIBUTORS

Abdulkader Sinno, Assistant Professor of Political Science and Middle Eastern Studies at Indiana University, is author of the forthcoming *Organizing to Win in Afghanistan and Beyond* and editor of *Muslims in Western Politics.*

Neamatollah Nojumi is a Senior Research Fellow at the Center for World Religions, Diplomacy and Conflict Resolution at George Mason University and the author of *The Rise of the Taliban in Afghanistan: Mass Mobilization, Civil War, and the Future of the Region.*

Juan R. I. Cole is a Professor in the Department of History at the University of Michigan. He has authored or edited numerous books, including *Napoleon's Egypt: Invading the Middle East; Shi'ism and Social Protest; Comparing Muslim Societies;* and *Sacred Space and Holy War: The Politics, Culture and History of Shi'ite Islam.*

M. Nazif Shahrani is a Professor in the Departments of Anthropology and Central Asian and Middle Eastern Studies at Indiana University. He co-edited, with Robert L. Canfield, *Revolutions and Rebellions in Afghanistan: Anthropological Perspectives* and is the author of *The Kirghiz and Wakhi of Afghanistan: Adaptation to Closed Frontiers and War.*

Lutz Rzehak, Professor, Central Asian Seminar, Humboldt University, Berlin, is the author of *From Persian to Tajik* (in German) and translator and editor of an Afghan intellectual's memoir of life under the Taliban, *The Taliban in the Land of the Noontime Sun* (in German).

Robert L. Canfield is Professor in the Department of Anthropology at Washington University in St. Louis. He is the author of *Faction and Conversion in a Plural Society* and has edited numerous books, including *Afghanistan and the Soviet Union; Turko-Persia in Historical Perspective;* and *Revolutions and Rebellions in Afghanistan: Anthropological Perspectives,* with Nazif Shahrani.

Robert D. Crews, Assistant Professor in the Department of History at Stanford University, is author of *For Prophet and Tsar: Islam and Empire in Russia and Central Asia.*

Amin Tarzi holds a Ph.D. from the Department of Middle East Studies at New York University. He is Director of Middle East Studies at the U.S. Marine Corps University.

Atiq Sarwari is an independent scholar in Washington, D.C.

ACKNOWLEDGMENTS

Many of the essays in this book were originally presented in May 2004 at a workshop sponsored by the Center for Russian, East European & Eurasian Studies (CREEES) at Stanford University, with funding from the U.S. Department of Education (Title VI). We are most grateful to CREEES and its director, Nancy Kollmann, for supporting the event. We would also like to express our appreciation to the additional co-sponsors of the workshop, including the Hoover Institution; the Institute for International Studies; the Office of the Dean for Graduate and Undergraduate Studies, School of Humanities and Sciences; the Center on Democracy, Development and Rule of Law; the Department of History; the Department of Cultural and Social Anthropology; and the Sohaib and Sara Abbasi Program in Islamic Studies at Stanford University. The editors are most grateful to the workshop's other participants, Nigel Allan, Thomas Barfield, Joel Beinin, John Dunlop, David Edwards, Gail Lapidus, Abbas Milani, Mohsen Milani, Senzil Nawid, J. Alexander Thier, and Maliha Zulfacar, for sharing their vast expertise. Mary Dakin, with her customary charm and wit, played a critical role in conceptualizing and running the event, which also benefited from the kind assistance of Sue Purdy Pelosi, Jesse Driscoll, and the late Rosemary Schnoor.

For generous contributions that made this a better book, the editors would like to thank John de Boer, Marvin Weinbaum, Keely Fahoum, Robert Gregg, Thomas Ruttig, Kären Wigen, Gordon

Chang, Huseyin Yilmaz, Elena Danielson, Barnett Rubin, Joshua Charap, and Jonathan Ledgard of *The Economist* (for coining the term *neo-Taliban*). In addition to valuable references and insights from the field of African history, Sean Hanretta offered boundless learning and inspiration. We are also grateful to Radio Free Europe/ Radio Liberty and to its staff, especially Donald Jensen, who kindly supported work on this book, and Abubakar Siddique, who obtained books from Pakistan. For informative meetings in Washington and Kabul, the editors would like to thank Tom Koenigs, Ali Ahmad Jalali, M. Ashraf Haidari, Jennifer Noyon, Hikmet Cetin, and Muhammad Yunos Qanuni. We are particularly indebted to Robert D. McChesney, who has inspired and guided us on the path to learn about Afghanistan.

We owe special gratitude to Joyce Seltzer of Harvard University Press, who generously offered her wisdom, enthusiasm, and patience. For her crucial comments during the editing process, we are grateful to Wendy Nelson, and for an expert job of mapping Afghanistan, we thank Don Pirius. The editors are also grateful to the anonymous readers whose suggestions improved the book.

Finally, we would like to thank our friends Scott Levi, Ken Petersen, and Khaled Akram. We are especially thankful to our families, especially Erika Tarzi and Margaret Sena, for adding so much to this book, while putting up with lives filled with rough drafts. We would like to thank Christopher and Clifford Crews for the happiness they bring—as well as our siblings and, not least, our parents, to whom we dedicate this book.

INDEX

Abduh, Muhammad, 133
Abdülhamid II, 127
Abdullah, Abdullah, 249, 287
Abdul Rahman (Amir), 37, 144, 162–166, 188, 338, 383n40, 384n10
Abdul Rahman Khan. *See* Abdul Rahman (Amir)
Abu Ghraib, 340; Taliban criticism of, 354
al-Adl, Saif, 296
Afghan Independent Human Rights Commission, 240, 340
Afghanistan Transit Treaty Agreement (ATTA), 104–106
Afghan National Army, 22, 287, 325, 332, 343
Afghan Turkestan, 159, 168, 173–176, 381n27, 382n33. *See also* Turkestan
Ahmadi, Muhammad Yusof, 296
Air strikes: in fighting against Taliban, 1, 8, 115, 153, 187, 228, 276, 289, 311, 317, 320–321, 324, 347; used by Taliban, 5, 29, 70; used by British, 202, 204; as source of opposition to foreign forces, 272, 276, 293, 317, 319–321, 347–350
Akbar Agha, 294, 302
Akora Khattak, 353
Alakozai, Mullah Naqibullah, 278, 400n12
Ali, Tariq, 226
Alim Khan, Amir Sayyed, 168–171
Amanullah (King), 25, 35, 122, 126, 144, 166, 169–172, 202–204
Amanullah Khan, 324
Amin, Muhammad, 296
Amir al-Muminin. *See* Omar (Mujahed), Mullah Muhammad
Amnesties: of Taliban and other combatants, 57, 239–241, 270–272, 278–279,

282, 285, 290, 296, 312; by Taliban, 397n58
Angola, 336
Ansari, Khwaja Abdullah, 22
Arab-Afghans, 221–223, 229, 233
Atatürk, Mustafa Kemal, 127, 131

Babar, Nasirullah Khan, 63–64, 101, 103, 218, 225
Badakhshan, 31, 175, 334, 364n46, 413n43
Baghdad, 125
Bagram airbase, 315; as detention facility, 241, 327, 340–344, 415n62; Taliban criticism of, 354
Baluch, 17, 23, 30, 33, 55, 183–185, 193–196, 207–211
Baluch, Zaher, 206–211
Baluchi. *See* Languages
Baluchistan, 17, 207, 257, 351
Bamyan: Taliban destruction of Buddha statues at, 6, 49–50, 107, 131, 243, 253, 269, 305–306; Taliban killing of Hazaras at, 32, 68–69, 125, 229
Banking, 133
Barelvis, 226
Basmachis, 171–176
Bhutto, Benazir, 43, 64, 101–102, 218, 224, 225
Bhutto, Zulfiqar Ali, 43
Blair, Cherie, 409n6
Bosnia, 7, 212, 223, 265, 325, 331
Brahimi, Lakhdar, 110, 279
Brahui, Karim, 185, 187, 384n5
Bukhara, 125, 168–174
Bush, George W., 51, 181, 227, 298, 311, 343
Bush, Laura, 409n6

Canada, 92, 347–350

Carter, Jimmy, 91

Casey, William, 39

Center for Islamic Studies and Research, 293

Central Intelligence Agency, 2, 24, 39, 91, 100, 221, 223, 306, 311, 321

Chaman, 133, 158, 299

Chechnya, 7, 50, 212, 218, 223, 230, 233, 265, 268, 283, 293, 369n92

China, 109, 169

Cold War, 7, 52, 54, 112, 117, 156, 215, 242, 247, 313–314, 316; and Islamism in Afghanistan, 34, 39, 43, 222

Community Development Councils (CDCs), 335–336

Conscription, 36, 94, 262, 265, 345

Constitutions, 87, 108, 116, 139, 164–168, 263

Contractors, working for the U.S. in Afghanistan, 323, 327, 329–331, 334

Dar al-'Ulum Haqqaniyya, 353

Darmesteter, James, 201

Denmark, 343

Deobandi, Mullah Abdul Ali, 351

Deobandis, 42–44, 106–107, 110, 142, 218, 226, 374n46, 390n37

DiCaprio, Leonardo, 132–133

Dorronsoro, Gilles, 4, 35

Dostum, Abdul Rashid, 26, 29, 62, 66–68, 71, 82, 176, 264, 337, 363n35, 381n27

Drought, 6, 52, 68, 183, 253, 268, 338

Drugs. See Hashish; Opium

Durand Line, 15–17

Durrani, Ahmad Shah, 126, 160. See also Pashtuns

Dyncorp, 330, 334

Economy: in post-2001 period, 3, 6, 52, 177, 228, 317, 325, 329, 331, 333–335; and the rise and rule of the Taliban, 70, 72, 78, 101, 103–107, 133, 180–181, 248, 253, 389n30

Edwards, David, 38, 76

Egypt, 35, 91, 122, 133, 134, 142, 221, 222, 377n33

Fahim, Muhammad Qasim, 286–287

Fatwas, 30, 141, 284, 297–299, 303

Federalism, 26–27, 363n35, 382n34

Federally Administered Tribal Areas (FATA), 17, 231, 345, 351

Financial resources: from foreign sponsors, 49, 71, 88, 102, 105–106, 158, 257, 306; Taliban taxation of opium and heroin, 49, 87, 254, 333; taxation of trade, 49, 133; export of lumber and other commodities, 49, 338. See also Opium

Foucault, Michel, 129

France, 128, 201, 247, 283, 294

Gailani, Sayyed Ahmad, 126, 363n33, 403n39

Gailani, Sayyed Ishaq, 289

Ghazni, 3–4, 32, 81, 245, 260, 294, 344, 346

Giustozzi, Antonio, 75, 287, 324

Glatzer, Bernt, 22, 24, 28, 242

Goislard, Bettina, 294

Goodwin, Jan, 129–131, 139, 149

Gorbachev, Mikhail, 214

Guantanamo Bay prison camp, 42, 241, 271, 328, 340; Taliban criticism of, 293, 302, 354; demonstrations in Afghanistan against, 341–342

Gul, Hamid, 224–225, 371n5

Gul, Imtiaz, 133

Habibullah (Amir), 18, 165

Habermas, Jürgen, 119–120, 124, 151

Hakimi, Mufti Latifullah, 296, 302–303, 405nn57,58

Hamas, 234

Hamid Agha, 293–294, 296, 301, 406n63

Hanif, Muhammad, 294–296, 307, 405n58

Haq, Abdul, 83

Haq, Mawlana Samiul, 180, 352

Haqqani, Jalaluddin, 80, 83

Haqqani, Mawlawi Abdul Shukur, 258

Harkat-e Islami, 372n8

Harkatul Ansar, 180

Harkatul Mujahideen, 29, 224

Hashish, Taliban ban on, 49, 254

Hazaras, 6, 23, 26, 31–32, 67–69, 87, 125, 156, 159, 168, 215, 219, 229, 272; percentage of population of Afghanistan, 362n30

Hegel, George Wilhelm Friedrich, 121, 123, 134, 152

Hekmatyar, Gulbuddin, 28, 37–38, 48, 60–68, 71–74, 77, 81, 84–86, 92, 98–101, 104, 117, 219, 234, 284, 299–301, 339–342, 363n33, 371n5, 372n8, 374n41, 381n29, 406n64, 415n62

Helmand, 1, 4, 19, 57, 64, 80–81, 184, 194, 208, 262, 270, 315, 326, 341, 346–347, 349–350

Herat: Taliban capture and treatment of, 5, 47–48, 65–67, 82, 101, 115, 158–159, 186, 244–245, 247, 257, 264; as a major urban center, 15, 18, 22–24, 62, 104, 147, 158, 170, 185; post-2001 politics in, 154, 234, 324, 343, 349

Hicks, David, 29

Hindus, 37, 374n46

Hizb-e Islami, 61–63, 70, 92, 96, 234, 250, 271, 284, 299–300, 338–339, 363nn33,37

Hizb-e Wahdat-e Islami-ye Afghanistan (Hizb-e Wahdat), 23, 62, 65, 219, 250

Holl, Norbert Heinrich, 246, 248–249

Hosseini, Khaled, 5

Hotak, Abdul Rahman, 303

Human Rights Watch, 288, 340

Hussein, Qazi Ahmed, 371n5

Huwaydi, Fahmi, 134–135, 137, 140–143, 148

Ibrahimbek Laqay, Mullah Muhammad, 171–175

International Crisis Group, 289–290, 312

International Islamic Front for Jihad against Jews and Crusaders, 222–223

International Security Assistance Force (ISAF), 115, 178, 229, 283–284, 320, 343, 349–350

Internet, Taliban use of, 46, 276, 293, 295, 364n51, 397n54, 399n3, 403n42, 405n61

Inter-Services Intelligence (ISI), 69–70, 74, 91–95, 100–101, 104, 218–219, 223–225, 229, 248, 308

Iran: energy transportation, 5, 253; conflicts with the Taliban, 6, 31, 68–69, 71; border with Afghanistan, 15, 23, 30, 184–187, 207; assistance to anti-Soviet and anti-Taliban parties, 19, 26, 38, 40, 53, 62, 71, 93–99, 108; revolution in, 34–35, 46, 51, 93–94, 108, 118, 124, 156, 242, 247, 251; trade with Afghanistan, 49, 104–106, 184–185; refugees in, 93–94, 96, 122, 174, 329; television broadcasts in Afghanistan, 196; and post-2001 Afghanistan, 309, 322, 329, 350

Iraq: aid for anti-Soviet jihad, 40; linked to Islamist networks in Afghanistan and Pakistan, 50–52, 56, 222–224, 230, 232–237, 298, 306–309, 316, 343–344, 352–353; war with Iran, 93; as modern state, 122; U.S. invasion of, 227, 236–237, 298, 324–325, 327, 331, 336

Ireland, 132

Ishaq, Mullah Muhammad, 302, 407n72

Islamic Emirate of Afghanistan, 34, 45, 68, 105, 110, 251, 258, 263–267, 293–295

Islamic law. See Law courts; Sharia

Islamic Movement of Uzbekistan, 390n37

Islamic Revolutionary Guards Corps (IRGC), 93, 96

Ismail Khan, 22, 65–67, 71, 80, 82, 84, 159, 186, 324, 364, 373n37

Ismailis, 31, 68, 125

Israel, 224, 233–234, 343

Jaish al-Moslemin. See Taliban Jamiat Jaish-e Moslemin

Jaishe Mohammed, 224

Jalalabad, 4, 5, 66, 77, 203, 247, 261–262, 341–342, 349

Jalali, Ali Ahmad, 284

Jama'at-e-Islami 63, 91, 108, 218, 371n5

Jama'atul Dawa, 298, 405n61

Jamiat-e Islami-ye Afghanistan (Jamiat-e Islami), 25–26, 62, 80, 83, 96, 175, 219, 280, 331, 337, 363n33

Jamiat Ulema-e-Islam, 43, 63, 100–102, 105, 108

Japan, 317, 325

Jones, Seth G., 308

Junbesh-e Melli-ye Islami-ye Afghanistan, 62, 176, 219

Kabir, Mawlawi Abdul, 259–260

Kalakani, Habibullah (Amir), 25, 59, 171–172

Kandahar, 2, 4, 8, 18, 21, 28, 44–46, 50, 64–66, 74, 78–79, 101, 104–105, 107, 112, 126, 133, 157–158, 163–164, 179, 185–186, 194, 208, 218, 220–221, 239, 244–245, 252, 254, 262, 265, 271, 274, 277–281, 285, 295, 303, 311, 315, 319, 323, 326–327, 334, 340–344, 347, 350–351, 354

Karachi, 102, 104, 226, 229, 296, 390n37

Karzai, Abdul Ahad Khan, 83

Karzai, Hamid, 3, 12, 19, 21–22, 49, 51–52, 57, 59–60, 71, 83, 87–88, 115–116, 154, 164, 178, 228, 238–241, 243, 268, 270–272, 274–275, 277–290, 293, 295, 299, 301, 303–304, 307–310, 312, 316–317, 319–330, 337, 340, 341, 343, 347, 349, 353–355, 400n9

Kashmir, 17, 29, 217–218, 223, 230, 233, 265, 293

Kashmiri, Hamid, 205

Kazakhs, 174

Khaddam al-Furqan, 268, 303–304, 407n75, 408n77

Khaksar, Mullah Abdul Samad, 269, 279

Khalilzad, Zalmay, 51, 156, 238–239, 274–275, 281, 323, 381n29, 399n1, 404n67

Khomeini, Ayatollah Ruhollah, 46, 93, 97–98, 108, 124

Khost, 33, 50, 253, 259, 265–267, 295, 321, 341

King, Roger, 289

Korengal Valley, 339–340

Kosovo, 302, 325, 331

Kunar, 4, 71, 77, 259, 339–341

Kyrgyz, 174

Laden, Osama bin: in Afghanistan, 2, 44, 50–51, 105, 112–115, 180, 221, 224, 282–283, 342; protected by the Taliban, 6–9, 71, 85–86, 227, 253, 293, 298, 312; influence upon Taliban, 49–50, 112–113, 127, 131, 221–223, 253, 306–307, 353; financing of Taliban, 105–106, 158, 306; opponents within the Taliban, 110, 238, 267–269, 280–281; as commander of Taliban's 55th Brigade, 125

Landes, Joan, 119–120

Land mines, 313, 316, 338

Languages: Persian, 4, 21, 24–25, 33, 123, 140, 156, 174, 183–205; Urdu, 5, 33, 140, 185; of Afghanistan, 20; Pashto, 20–21, 25–26, 28, 33–34, 174, 178, 185–187, 189, 192–193, 202, 235, 264, 299, 383n2; Dari, 21–22, 178, 187, 189, 192, 234; Turkic, 26, 125, 168, 174–176; Baluchi, 33, 183, 185, 189, 192–193, 196, 383n2; Tajik, 168

Lashkar Gah, 194

Lashkar-e Isar, 99

Lashkare Jhangvi, 29

Lashkare Taiba, 29, 223–224, 339

Latifa, 130, 132, 134–135, 138, 140, 145–149, 152

Latin America, 316

Law courts, 37, 45, 79, 97, 189, 231, 259, 261, 263–264, 269, 328–329

Lebanon, 222, 343

Lenin, Vladimir, 120

Lewinsky, Monica, 143, 153

Liberia, 336

Lindh, John Walker, 29, 393n13

Loya jirgas: historical practice of, 94–95, 97, 141, 163, 167, 322; of 2002, 116, 268, 289–290, 322, 403n41; of 2003, 116, 164; Mullah Omar's criticism of, 298–299

Lutis, 125, 366

Madrasas. See Pakistan

Majruh, Shamsuddin, 94–95

Markazul Dawa Wal Irshad. See Jama'atul Dawa

Martyrdom, 23, 46, 99, 145, 210, 236, 261, 321, 332, 406n64

Mass killings: by insurgents' bombings, 1–4, 284, 343–346; by the Taliban, 6, 32, 48, 68–69, 125, 159, 229, 306; by

Gulbuddin Hekmetyar's forces, 48, 99; by Northern Alliance forces, 68, 87, 250, 260; of Pashtuns following September 11, 2001, 288, 321

Mastrogiacomo, Daniele, 271, 354, 405n58

Masud, Ahmad Shah: as national symbol, 23, 208–211, 269, 403n41; as commander, 26, 59–60, 62, 65–71, 83, 85, 112–115, 220, 264, 286

Maududi, Abu'l Ala, 108, 222, 374n51

Mawlawi Afzal, 77

Mawlawi Qalamuddin, 134–135

Mazar-e Sharif, 18, 31, 47, 62, 65, 67–69, 82, 87, 115, 125, 140, 158, 249–250, 259, 276–277, 320

Mazari, Abdul Ali, 62, 65, 87

Mercy Corps, 336

Mexico, 120

Ministry of Foreign Affairs, 49, 159, 238, 246, 248–249, 256, 267–270, 277, 280–281, 319

Ministry for the Promotion of Virtue and the Prevention of Vice, 47, 49, 79, 109, 111, 134–136, 222, 256, 259, 268, 270

Moghadam, Val, 140–141

Mojaddedi, Amin, 303

Mojaddedi, Sebghatullah, 270

Motasem, Mullah Agha Jan, 297

Mottaqi, Mullah Amir Khan, 251–252, 262, 266

Mubarez, Abdul Hamid, 140

Muhajirin, 168, 171

Muhammadi, Mawlawi Muhammad Nabi, 27, 363n33, 369n1, 407n75

Muhmand, Wazir Muhammad Gul Khan, 174

Mujahed, Abdul Hakim, 40, 250–251, 268, 304

Mujahed, Muhammad Mokhtar, 295–296

Mujahed, Zabiullah, 296

Mullah Abbas, 246

Mullah Baradar, 293, 404n54

Mullah Dadullah, 32, 229, 351, 353, 404n54

Mullah Ghaus, 246, 248, 262

Mullah Hassan Akhund, 244–245

Mullah Mansur Dadullah, 4, 318, 354, 412n38

Mullah Obaidullah Akhund, 278, 293, 404n54

Mullah Rabbani, 110, 246, 261

Mullah Sabir, 3, 412n38

Musa Qala, 1–2, 346, 348

Musharraf, Pervez, 69, 88, 116, 224–226, 239, 345, 348, 351

Mutawakkil, Wakil Ahmad, 159, 267–271, 280–281, 303, 379n8

Muzhda, Wahid, 50, 238, 255–256, 267–270, 277, 280, 328

Myanmar (Burma), 223, 293

Najibullah, 61, 63, 71, 158, 167; Taliban murder of, 130–131, 248

Namangani, Juma, 212, 390n37

Nangarhar, 114, 259, 284, 334, 349

Nasr, Vali, 34–35

National Independent Commission for Peace and Reconciliation, 270–272

National Islamic Movement of Afghanistan. See Junbesh-e Melli-ye Islami-ye Afghanistan

Nationalist rhetoric, of Taliban, 31, 260–267

National Solidarity Program, 335–336

NATO, 1, 10, 52, 57, 178, 219, 228–229, 232, 272, 308–309, 320, 324, 337, 346–347, 349–350

Neo-Taliban, uses of term, 10, 275–276, 399n4

Netherlands, 272, 348, 350

NGOs, 68, 95, 177, 228, 248, 327–331, 345, 359n3; Taliban attitudes toward, 248, 331, 413n38

Night letters, 46

Nimroz, 13, 30–33, 55, 183–187, 191–192, 196, 200–201, 210, 245, 255

Northern Alliance, 22, 51, 68, 71, 112, 125, 154, 250, 260, 263, 269, 277, 319–321, 369n94. See also Supervisory Council (Shura-ye Nezar); United Front (National Islamic United Front for the Salvation of Afghanistan)

Northern Ireland, 302, 325

North Waziristan. See Waziristan

North West Frontier Province (NWFP), 17, 43, 116, 172, 181, 229, 257, 345, 351

Omar (Mujahed), Mullah Muhammad: in anti-Soviet jihad, 4, 28, 37–38, 101, 363n37; style of rule, 7–8, 30, 44–45, 104–105, 110, 125–129, 151, 153, 217, 220–224, 244; as head of state, 19, 32, 45, 47–50, 89, 110, 135, 139, 143, 147, 158–160, 252–256, 261–264, 267; relations with ethnic groups of Afghanistan, 31, 33, 76, 84–85, 143, 269; as Commander of the Faithful, 45, 68, 107, 179; activities after September 11, 2001, 57, 229, 241, 271–272, 274, 277–278, 291–306, 342, 353–354; as Ghilzai Pashtun, 76, 84–85; as head of school, 104

Onishi, Norimitsu, 126

Operation Achilles, 349

Operation Anaconda, 282

Operation Enduring Freedom, 276, 282, 289, 312, 350

Opium: Taliban policies toward, 1, 49–50, 57, 64, 87, 228, 254, 258, 306, 333–334, 346, 355; and post-2001 production spike, 3, 11, 52, 178, 228, 284, 316–320, 329–334, 338, 345–346, 348–349, 352, 355; eradication schemes, 3, 59, 89, 306, 325, 334, 341; taxed by mujahedin, 39, 49, 63, 73, 77, 103, 314

Orphans, 5, 28, 41, 43, 56, 144, 146, 257, 313, 355

Oz, Samet, 283

Pahlawan, Abdul Malik, 67–68, 82

Pahlawan, Rasul, 82

Pahwal, Abdul Rahman, 30, 200–201, 255

Pakistan: and Taliban as cross-border movement, 2, 28–30, 33, 41–44, 46, 49–50, 116–117, 133, 160, 181, 185–187, 218–219, 229–233, 235–236, 245, 251–252, 257–259, 262, 273, 277–279, 283–285, 344–345, 348–355; and anti-Soviet jihad, 5, 19, 26, 37–40, 48, 91–99, 156; Afghan refugees in, 5, 37, 54, 91–99, 122, 141, 174, 304, 329; government support for Taliban, 8–10, 28–30, 33, 52–53, 60–66, 69–72, 74, 76–77, 88–89, 91, 101–110, 113, 158, 223, 248–249, 304, 307–310; border with Afghanistan,

15–17, 34–35, 184; Islamization in, 34–35, 114, 116–117, 180, 223–229, 338. See also Inter-Services Intelligence (ISI)

Palestine, 217, 222, 230, 232–233

Paktya, 22, 33, 65, 259, 262, 265–266, 283, 294–295, 315, 320

Panjsher Valley, 22, 67, 69, 83, 115, 208, 319, 331, 362n26, 383n35, 403n41

Pashto. See Languages

Pashtunistan, 15–17

Pashtuns: relations with other ethnic groups, 6, 22–23, 25–31, 54–55, 155–157, 159, 193–196, 207–208, 210, 228, 260, 270–273, 321–323, 341–342; as dominant ethnic group, 8–9, 21–26, 51, 53, 59, 228–230, 235, 239, 280–282, 285–291, 323, 353–354; as cross-border group, 15–17, 29, 35–36, 49, 160, 255, 257, 345–346; and intermarriage, 22–23, 194–196; as core of Taliban, 25–33, 51, 125, 187, 193, 215–216, 219–221, 243, 254–255, 262, 264, 285, 304–306; Taliban political dealings with, 53, 60–61, 64, 72–88, 264–265, 267–269; and internal colonialism, 54–55, 155–158, 160–181; Ghilzai, 65–66, 76, 84, 168, 174, 370n20; Durrani, 75–76, 83–84, 160–162, 166, 168, 176, 255, 370n20; gender segregation among, 140; Barakzai, 162, 165–166; Sadozai, 164. See also Pashtunwali

Pashtunwali, 27, 33–34, 37, 47, 54, 85–86, 144, 265, 267, 295, 341; Taliban rejection of elements of, 143–144

PDPA (People's Democratic Party of Afghanistan), 26–28, 90

Pearl, Daniel, 389n29

Pech River, 339

Persian. See Languages

Peshawar, 26, 62–63, 95, 102, 199, 202–204, 229, 256, 262, 296, 338

Philippines, 223, 302

Physicians for Human Rights, 148

Print media, of Taliban, 243–245, 251–253, 255, 258–259, 264

Prisoners of war: treatment of Taliban captives by Northern Alliance, 31, 68, 250, 259–260, 320–321; by U.S. forces, 320–321, 327–328, 415n62

Private sphere, Taliban views of, 132–140, 149, 267
Provincial Reconstruction Teams, 320, 330, 343, 346
Psychological operations, 339–341, 415n62
Public display of power, 123–131, 149–152
Punishments. *See* Public display of power

al-Qaeda, 9–10, 29, 39, 42, 49–50, 53, 69, 83, 105–106, 112–116, 125, 127, 131, 158, 180–181, 225, 227–228, 230–231, 239, 253, 269, 276, 280–284, 286, 293–294, 300, 305–308, 311, 313–314, 319, 322, 332, 335, 339, 342, 349–353
al-Qaeda in Iraq, 353
Qanuni, Muhammad Yunos, 287, 290
Qataghan, 174

Rabbani, Burhanuddin, 25–27, 31, 37–38, 46–47, 62, 65–66, 71, 77, 102, 141, 245–246, 250, 252, 256, 262, 264, 363n33, 382n34
Radio, 20, 46–47, 49, 54–55, 118, 124, 126, 132, 149, 153, 159, 178, 206–207, 245, 256, 259–261, 265–266, 283, 336, 339
Radio Voice of Sharia. *See* Radio
Rahmani, Mawlawi Arsala, 268, 303, 408n77
Rashid, Ahmed, 8, 71–72, 218, 221, 263
Rasul, Mullah Muhammad, 186–187
RAWA (Revolutionary Association of the Women of Afghanistan), 123, 147–148
Reagan, Ronald, 91, 242
Red Mosque, 345
Rehman, Mawlana Fazlur, 63, 101, 180
Richardson, Bill, 262
Riwayat, 189–190, 194, 197, 200–201, 384n11
Rogers, Dorothy, 121
Roketi, Mullah Abdul Salam, 3, 270–271
Rosa, John W., Jr., 282
Roy, Olivier, 223
Rubin, Barnett, 70, 286, 327
Rubin, Elizabeth, 232, 234

Rumsfeld, Donald, 316
Ruttig, Thomas, 28–29, 348
Rwanda, 7, 240, 260

al-Sadr, Muqtada, 234, 236–237
Samad, Muhammad Omar, 281
Samad, Mullah Abdul, 294, 296
Saudi Arabia: support for jihadist networks, 91, 100, 105, 225, 314, 316, 338; and the Taliban, 102, 113, 134, 142, 158, 180, 218, 221–222, 229, 232; emigrants from Afghanistan in, 174, 176. *See also* Wahhabis
Sayyaf, Abdul Rabb al-Rasul, 38, 71, 84, 219, 241, 262, 264, 328, 363n33
Schetter, Conrad, 24, 335
Shahidkhayl, Mawlawi Said, 141–145
Shahnama, 201, 205
Sharia, 27, 30, 34, 37, 47, 49, 64, 97, 108, 110–111, 124, 129, 131–135, 139–142, 154, 157, 159, 160, 167, 180, 230–231, 250, 252, 256, 258, 261, 263, 265–267, 292–293, 304, 328, 351
Shayrzai, Gul Agha, 278–279, 400n12
Shiites: Taliban antipathy toward, 6, 29–33, 42–44, 108, 125, 179–181, 186, 245, 368n87; in anti-Soviet jihad, 26, 62, 65–68, 93, 96–98, 372n8; in the politics of Afghanistan, 26, 168; and sectarian violence in Pakistan, 29, 34–35, 43–44; in Iraq, 234–236. *See also* Hazaras; Iran
Shinwari, Mawlawi Fazl Hadi, 281, 328–329
Shrines: Deobandi view of, 42; housing cloak of the Prophet Muhammad in Kandahar, 126, 163, 220; to foreign Arab and Taliban fighters, 321
Sipah-e-Sahaba, 180
Somalia, 7, 221, 223, 325
South Waziristan. *See* Waziristan
Soviet Union, 4, 7, 20, 39–40, 43–44, 48, 53, 61–65, 70, 75, 90, 93–96, 98–103, 105–106, 120, 122, 155–157, 168–169, 172–176, 180–181, 210, 212–215, 223, 247, 276, 314–316, 332–333, 336, 338–341
Stalin, Iosif, 109, 172, 174
State administration: Taliban attempts to

State administration *(continued)*
  construct, 243–248; staffing of, 254–
  259, purges within, 261, 263–264
Stewart, Rory, 18
Suicide bombings, 1, 3–4, 115, 153, 225,
  232, 271, 283–284, 294–295, 343–345,
  349–354, 379n6
Supervisory Council (Shura-ye Nezar), 62,
  286–287, 319, 403n41. *See also* Panjsher
  Valley

Tajikistan, 69, 332
Tajiks, 17, 21–24, 31, 59, 125, 156, 168,
  171–173, 209, 215, 219–221, 286–287,
  324; percentage of population, 402n32
Taliban Jamiat Jaish-e Moslemin, 301–
  303, 407nn71,74
Taniwal, Hakim, 294
Tazim al-Fatah Afghanistan, 299
Titanic, 132–133
Tora Bora, 319
Trade, 17, 23, 49, 52, 64, 70, 133, 158,
  183, 214, 319, 339, 346. *See also* Af-
  ghanistan Transit Treaty Agreement
  (ATTA); Opium
Turabi, Mullah Nuruddin, 261, 266, 278
Turkestan, 169, 171, 174
Turkmen, 17, 168, 170, 173; percentage of
  population of Afghanistan, 362n30
Turkmenistan, 102, 104, 158, 305, 383n39

United Front (National Islamic United
  Front for the Salvation of Afghanistan),
  115, 276–277, 279–282, 286–288, 303.
  See also Northern Alliance; Supervisory
  Council (Shura-ye Nezar)
U.S. Drug Enforcement Agency, 6, 50
U.S. Special Forces, 2, 153, 319–320, 339
U.S. State Department, 249, 253, 254,
  321
Unocal, 5, 51, 102, 250, 305
Uprisings, against Taliban rule, 262, 265–
  266
Uruzgan, 4, 64, 277–278, 350
Uzbekistan, 212, 218, 232–233, 332

Uzbeks, 17, 27, 31, 125, 156, 168, 171–
  173, 215, 219, 324

Vietnam, 39

Wahhabis, 38, 72, 134, 137, 142, 221–222;
  definition of term, 377n32
Wardak, 262
Wardak, Taj Muhammad, 290
Waziristan, 17, 229–231, 351–354
Westad, Odd Arne, 314, 316, 409n7
Winslet, Kate, 133, 153
Wolf, Eric, 160
Women: after collapse of the Taliban regime, 2, 5, 153–154, 312, 316, 323, 328,
  341, 343; Taliban policies toward, 3, 7–
  8, 97, 107–109, 128, 145–146, 149, 159,
  246; foreign attention to Taliban gender
  policies, 6, 8–9, 305; education, 32, 108,
  141, 145; mujahedin treatment of, 36–
  37, 46–48, 55, 74, 141, 366n63; Taliban
  defense of policies toward, 101, 103,
  110, 141–145, 250–253, 266; government reforms, 122, 141, 144, 167; communist policies toward, 315–316

Yaser, Ustad Muhammad, 296, 405n58
Yasin, Shaykh Ahmad, 234
Yosuf, Muhammad, 94

Zabul, 64, 270, 345
Zahab, Mariam Abou, 223, 389
Zaher, Muhammad, 94, 126, 166, 267,
  290, 382n34, 400n9, 403n41
Zaher Shah. *See* Zaher, Muhammad
Zaif, Mullah Abdul Salam, 271
Zaman, Muhammad Qasim, 43
al-Zarqawi, Musab, 353, 416
Zawahiri, Ayman, 353
Zia ul-Haq, Muhammad, 91, 94, 226,
  371n5, 374n41
Zoya, 129, 133–134, 138–140, 145–146,
  149, 237